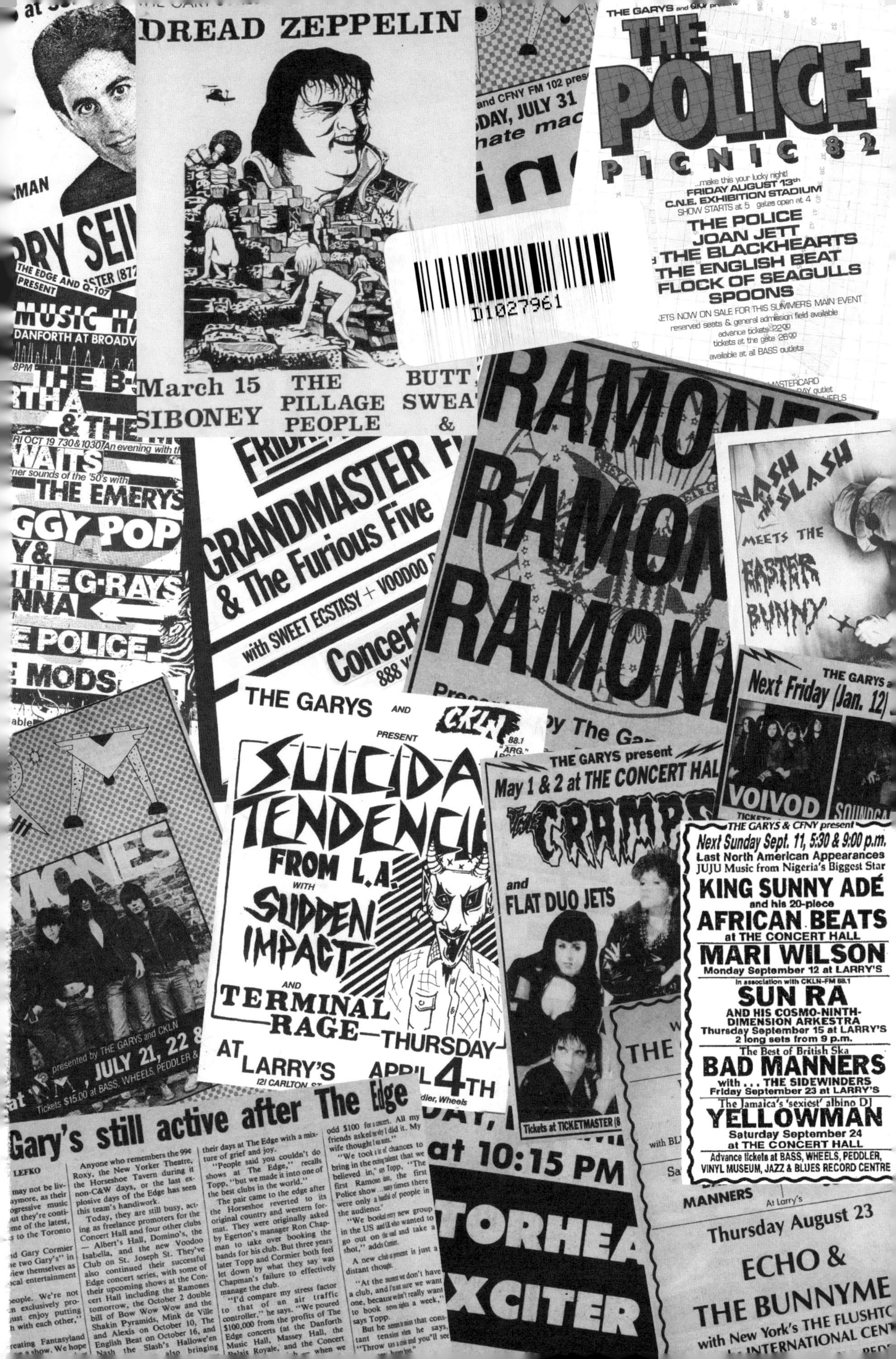
DREAD ZEPPELIN
March 15 SIBONEY
THE PILLAGE PEOPLE
BUTT SWEAT &
THE EDGE AND Q-107 PRESENT
MUSIC HA
DANFORTH AT BROADV
THE EMERYS
GGY POP
THE G-RAYS
E POLICE
E MODS
and CFNY FM 102 present
DAY, JULY 31
THE GARYS and Q107 present
THE POLICE PICNIC 82
...make this your lucky night!
FRIDAY AUGUST 13th
C.N.E. EXHIBITION STADIUM
SHOW STARTS at 5 gates open at 4
THE POLICE
JOAN JETT
THE BLACKHEARTS
THE ENGLISH BEAT
FLOCK OF SEAGULLS
SPOONS
reserved seats & general admission field available
advance tickets 22.00
tickets at the gate 26.00
available at all BASS outlets
GRANDMASTER F
& The Furious Five
with SWEET ECSTASY + VOODOO
Concert
RAMONES
RAMON
RAMON
NASH THE SLASH
MEETS THE
EASTER BUNNY
THE GARYS
Next Friday (Jan. 12)
VOIVOD
THE GARYS AND CKLN 88.1 PRESENT
SUICIDAL TENDENCIES
FROM L.A.
WITH
SUDDEN IMPACT
AND
TERMINAL RAGE
THURSDAY
AT LARRY'S
APRIL 4TH
121 CARLTON ST
THE GARYS present
May 1 & 2 at THE CONCERT HALL
THE CRAMPS
and
FLAT DUO JETS
Tickets at TICKETMASTER
presented by THE GARYS and CKLN
JULY 21, 22
Tickets $15.00 at BASS, WHEELS, PEDDLER
THE GARYS & CFNY present
Next Sunday Sept. 11, 5:30 & 9:00 p.m.
Last North American Appearances
JUJU Music from Nigeria's Biggest Star
KING SUNNY ADÉ
and his 20-piece
AFRICAN BEATS
at THE CONCERT HALL
MARI WILSON
Monday September 12 at LARRY'S
In association with CKLN-FM 88.1
SUN RA
AND HIS COSMO-NINTH-DIMENSION ARKESTRA
Thursday September 15 at LARRY'S
2 long sets from 9 p.m.
The Best of British Ska
BAD MANNERS
with . . . THE SIDEWINDERS
Friday September 23 at LARRY'S
The Jamaica's 'sexiest' albino DJ
YELLOWMAN
Saturday September 24
at THE CONCERT HALL
Advance tickets at BASS, WHEELS, PEDDLER, VINYL MUSEUM, JAZZ & BLUES RECORD CENTRE
at 10:15 PM
TORHEA
XCITER
MANNERS
At Larry's
Thursday August 23
ECHO &
THE BUNNYME
with New York's THE FLUSHTO
Gary's still active after The Edge

Conundrum Press
Wolfville, Nova Scotia, Canada
www.conundrumpress.com

Ephemera contained in this book comes from the archives of Gary Topp and is © respective creators, used by permission. All reasonable attempts have been made to contact creators for permission. www.garytopp.com

Inside Covers: © Daniel Tate, THE FLYER VAULT
Back cover photo was taken in Sudbury on a 1980 drug-fuelled car ride to Vancouver with Larry Hudson
Appendix originally published in *Colliers #1* by Fantagraphics Books, 1991
            © 1991, 2020, David Collier
Quote from Stewart Copeland from video at The New Music, CITY TV
https://www.dailymotion.com/video/xthoy4 (Retrontario, posted 2013)

First Edition
Printed by Gauvin in Gatineau, Quebec, Canada

Library and Archives Canada Cataloguing in Publication

Title: Topp : promoter Gary Topp brought us the world / by David Collier ; with Gary Topp.
Names: Collier, David, 1963- author, artist. | Topp, Gary, author.
Identifiers: Canadiana 20190218975 | ISBN 9781772620320 (softcover)
Subjects: LCSH: Topp, Gary—Comic books, strips, etc. | LCSH: Concert agents—Ontario—Toronto—
   Biography—Comic books, strips, etc. | LCSH: Motion picture theater managers—Canada—Biography—
   Comic books, strips, etc. | LCSH: Collier, David, 1963-—Comic books, strips, etc. | LCGFT:
   Biographical comics. | LCGFT: Autobiographical comics. | LCGFT: Nonfiction comics.
Classification: LCC ML429.T675 C69 2020 | DDC 780.92—dc23

Distributed in Canada by Litdistco
Distributed in US by Consortium
Distributed in UK / International by Ingram

Conundrum Press acknowledges the financial support of the Government of Canada through the Department of Canadian Heritage, The Canada Council for the Arts, and the Province of Nova Scotia through the Creative Industries Fund.

 Canada Council for the Arts **Conseil des Arts du Canada**    NOVA SCOTIA    Canadä

TOPP

"I WOULDN'T HAVE MISSED IT FOR THE WORLD"

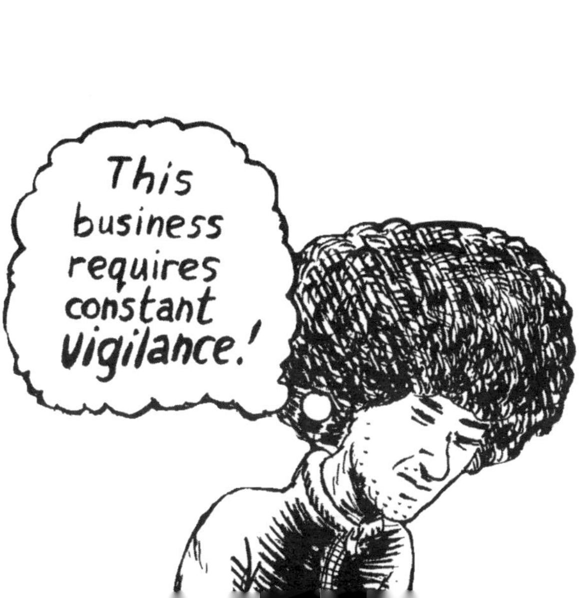
This business requires constant vigilance!

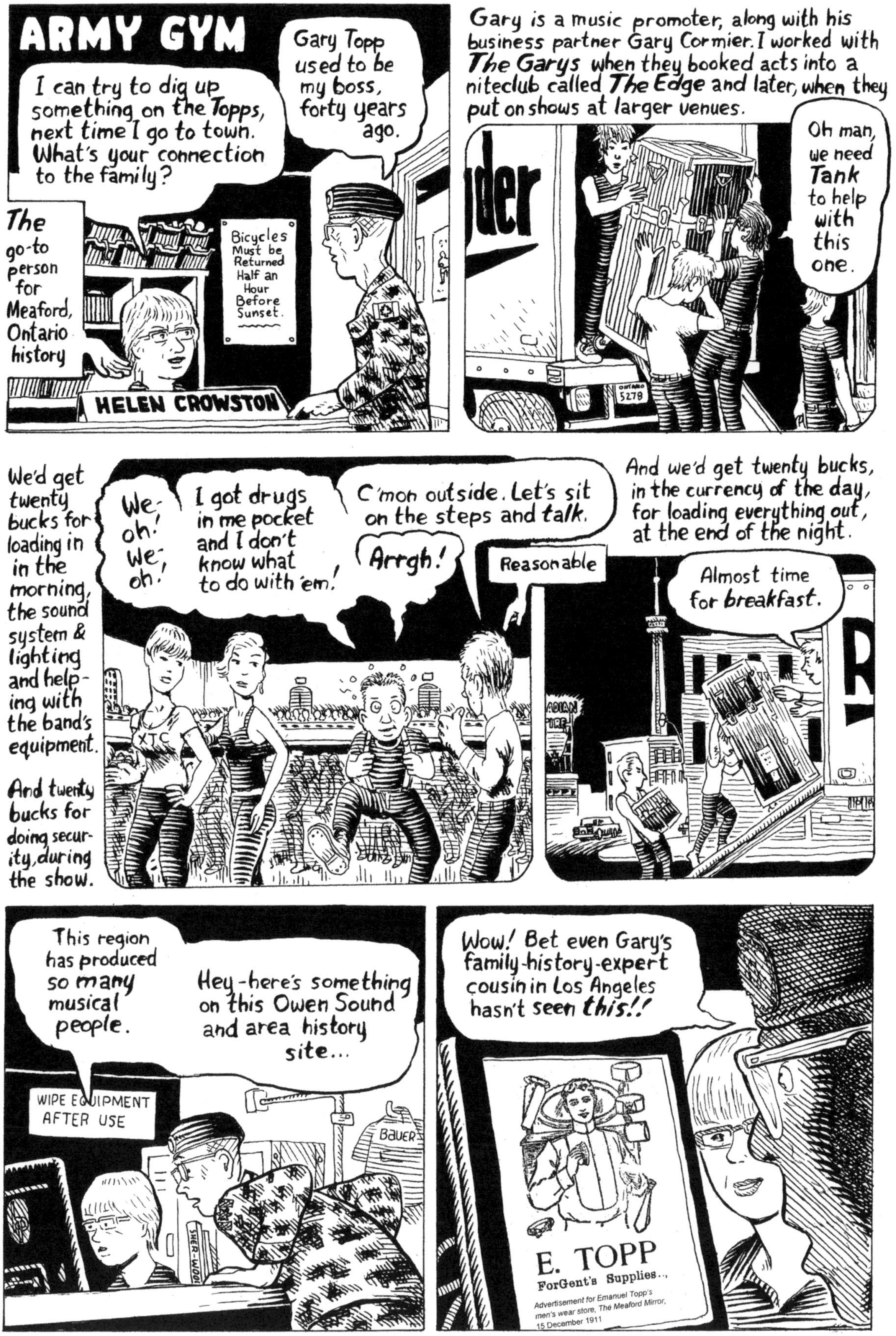
ARMY GYM
I can try to dig up something on the Topps, next time I go to town. What's your connection to the family?
Gary Topp used to be my boss, forty years ago.
The go-to person for Meaford, Ontario history
Bicycles Must be Returned Half an Hour Before Sunset.
HELEN CROWSTON
Gary is a music promoter, along with his business partner Gary Cormier. I worked with The Garys when they booked acts into a niteclub called The Edge and later, when they put on shows at larger venues.
Oh man, we need Tank to help with this one.
ONTARIO 5278
We'd get twenty bucks for loading in in the morning, the sound system & lighting and helping with the band's equipment.
And twenty bucks for doing security, during the show.
We-oh! We-oh!
I got drugs in me pocket and I don't know what to do with 'em!
C'mon outside. Let's sit on the steps and talk.
Arrgh!
Reasonable
XTC
And we'd get twenty bucks, in the currency of the day, for loading everything out, at the end of the night.
Almost time for breakfast.
This region has produced so many musical people.
Hey-here's something on this Owen Sound and area history site...
WIPE EQUIPMENT AFTER USE
BAUER
SHER-WOOD
Wow! Bet even Gary's family-history-expert cousin in Los Angeles hasn't seen this!!
E. TOPP
ForGent's Supplies..,
Advertisement for Emanuel Topp's men's wear store, The Meaford Mirror, 15 December 1911

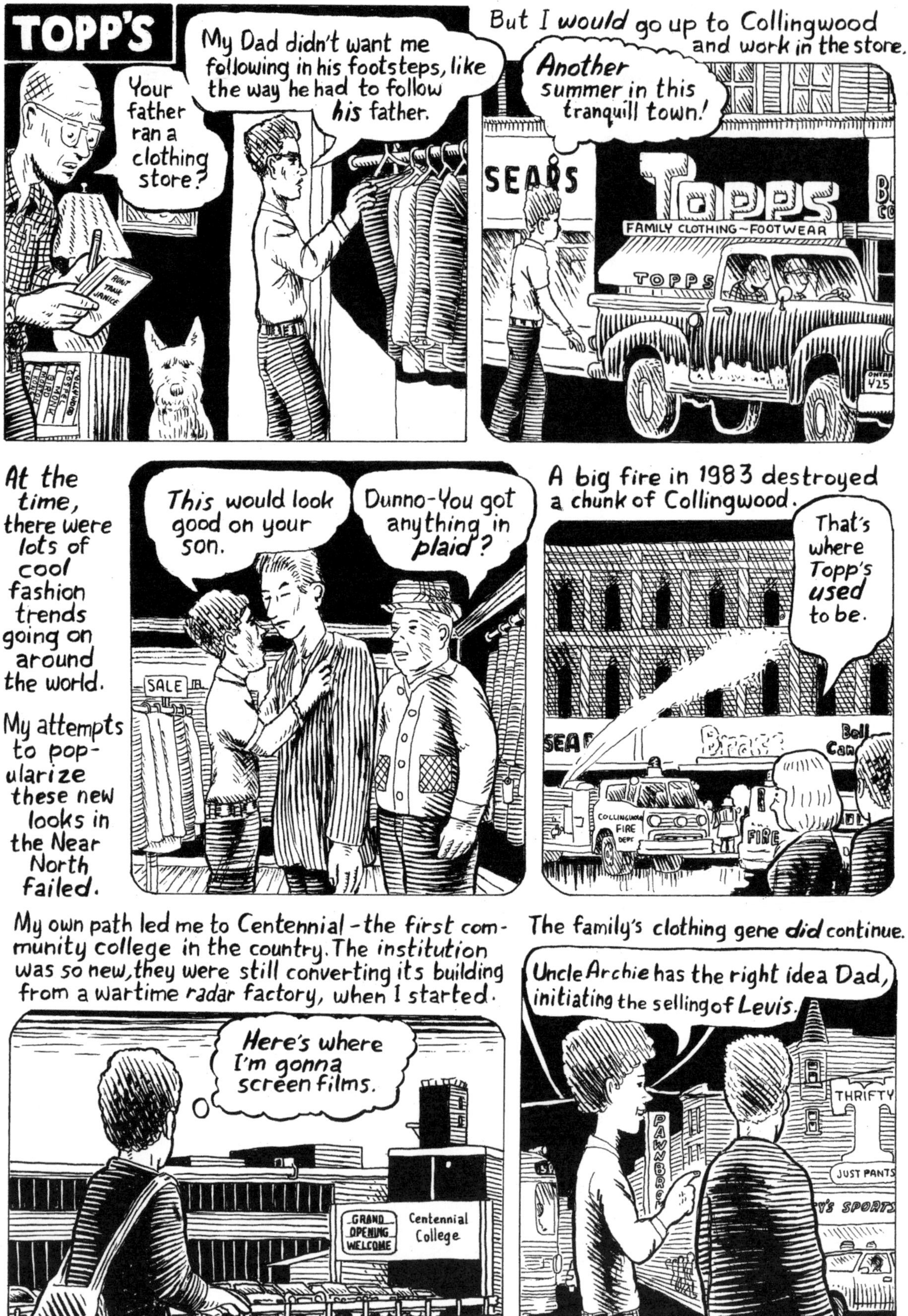
TOPP'S
Your father ran a clothing store?
My Dad didn't want me following in his footsteps, like the way he had to follow his father.
But I would go up to Collingwood and work in the store.
Another summer in this tranquill town!
SEARS
TOPPS
FAMILY CLOTHING ~ FOOTWEAR
TOPPS
At the time, there were lots of cool fashion trends going on around the world.
My attempts to popularize these new looks in the Near North failed.
This would look good on your son.
Dunno- You got anything in plaid?
SALE
A big fire in 1983 destroyed a chunk of Collingwood.
That's where Topp's used to be.
FIRE
My own path led me to Centennial - the first community college in the country. The institution was so new, they were still converting its building from a wartime radar factory, when I started.
Here's where I'm gonna screen films.
GRAND OPENING WELCOME
Centennial College
The family's clothing gene did continue.
Uncle Archie has the right idea Dad, initiating the selling of Levis.
THRIFTY
JUST PANTS

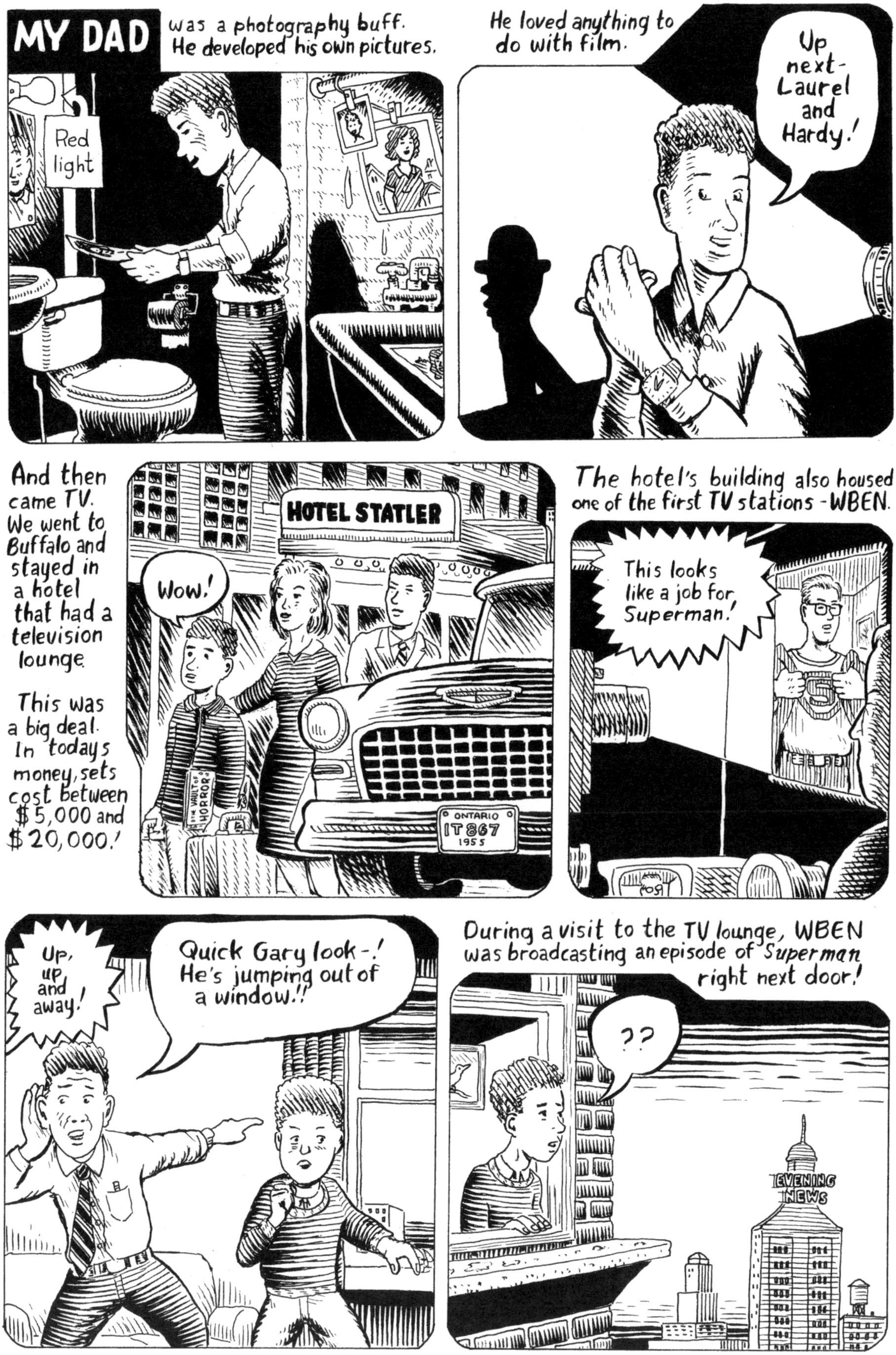
MY DAD was a photography buff. He developed his own pictures.
Red light
He loved anything to do with film.
Up next- Laurel and Hardy!
And then came TV. We went to Buffalo and stayed in a hotel that had a television lounge.
This was a big deal. In todays money, sets cost between $5,000 and $20,000!
HOTEL STATLER
Wow!
THE VAULT OF HORROR
ONTARIO
IT 867
1955
The hotel's building also housed one of the first TV stations -WBEN.
This looks like a job for, Superman!
Up, up, and away!
Quick Gary look-! He's jumping out of a window!!
During a visit to the TV lounge, WBEN was broadcasting an episode of *Superman* right next door!
??
EVENING NEWS

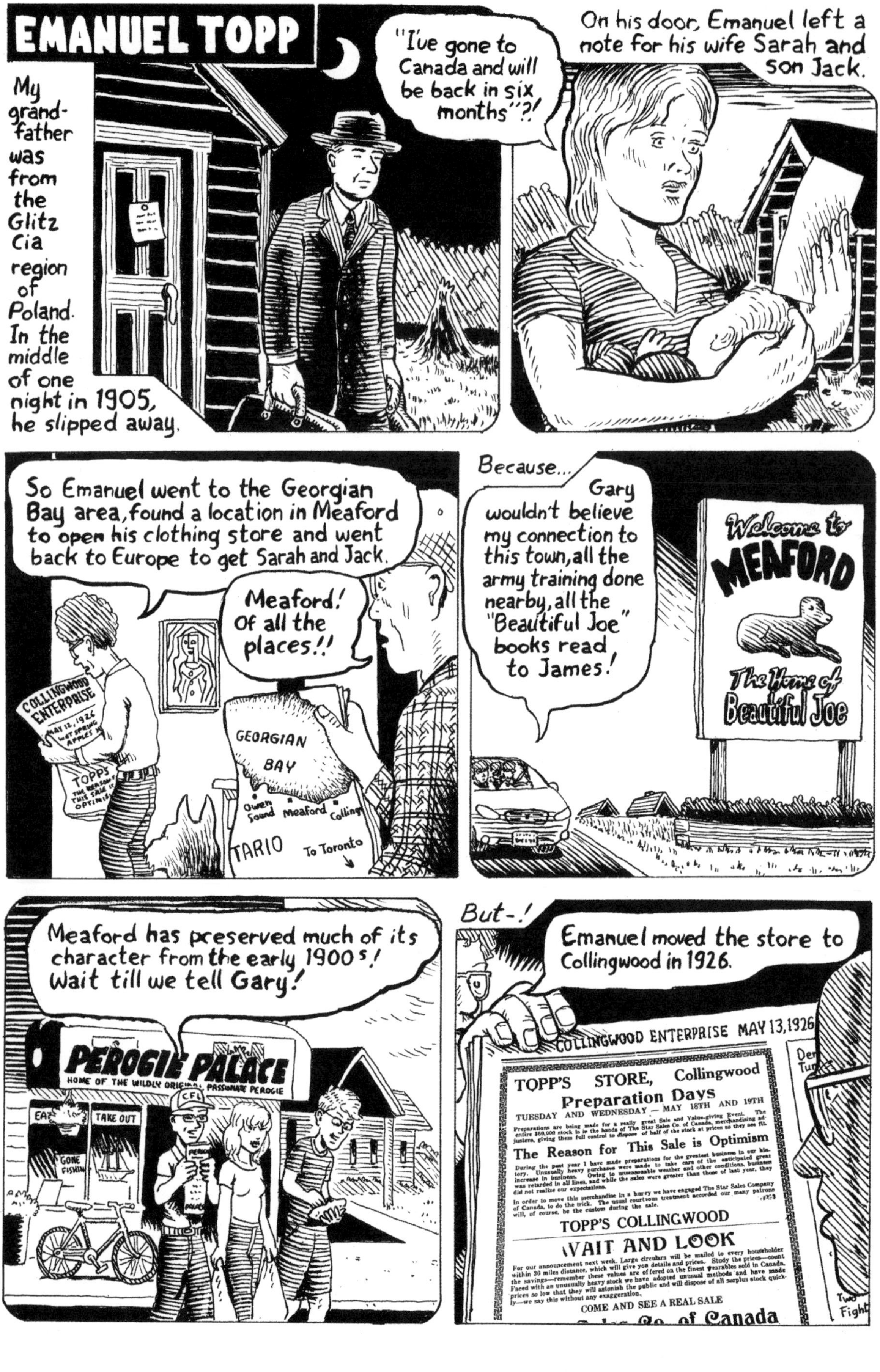
EMANUEL TOPP
My grandfather was from the Glitz Cia region of Poland. In the middle of one night in 1905, he slipped away.
On his door, Emanuel left a note for his wife Sarah and son Jack.
"I've gone to Canada and will be back in six months"?!
So Emanuel went to the Georgian Bay area, found a location in Meaford to open his clothing store and went back to Europe to get Sarah and Jack.
Meaford! Of all the places!!
COLLINGWOOD ENTERPRISE
MAY 12, 1926
GEORGIAN BAY
Owen Sound
Meaford
TARIO
To Toronto
Because...
Gary wouldn't believe my connection to this town, all the army training done nearby, all the "Beautiful Joe" books read to James!
Welcome to MEAFORD
The Home of Beautiful Joe
Meaford has preserved much of its character from the early 1900s! Wait till we tell Gary!
PEROGIE PALACE
HOME OF THE WILDLY ORIGINAL PASSIONATE PEROGIE
TAKE OUT
GONE FISHIN
CFL
But-!
Emanuel moved the store to Collingwood in 1926.
COLLINGWOOD ENTERPRISE MAY 13, 1926
TOPP'S STORE, Collingwood
Preparation Days
TUESDAY AND WEDNESDAY — MAY 18TH AND 19TH
Preparations are being made for a really great Sale and Value-giving Event. The entire $68,000 stock is in the hands of The Star Sales Co. of Canada, merchandising adjusters, giving them full control to dispose of half of the stock at prices as they see fit.
The Reason for This Sale is Optimism
During the past year I have made preparations for the greatest business in our history. Unusually heavy purchases were made to take care of the anticipated great increase in business. Owing to unseasonable weather and other conditions, business was retarded in all lines, and while the sales were greater than those of last year, they did not realize our expectations.
In order to move this merchandise in a hurry we have engaged The Star Sales Company of Canada, to do the trick. The usual courteous treatment accorded our many patrons will, of course, be the custom during the sale.
TOPP'S COLLINGWOOD
WAIT AND LOOK
For our announcement next week. Large circulars will be mailed to every householder within 30 miles distance, which will give you details and prices. Study the prices—count the savings—remember these values are offered on the finest wearables sold in Canada. Faced with an unusually heavy stock we have adopted unusual methods and have made prices so low that they will astonish the public and will dispose of all surplus stock quickly—we say this without any exaggeration.
COME AND SEE A REAL SALE
of Canada
Two
Fight

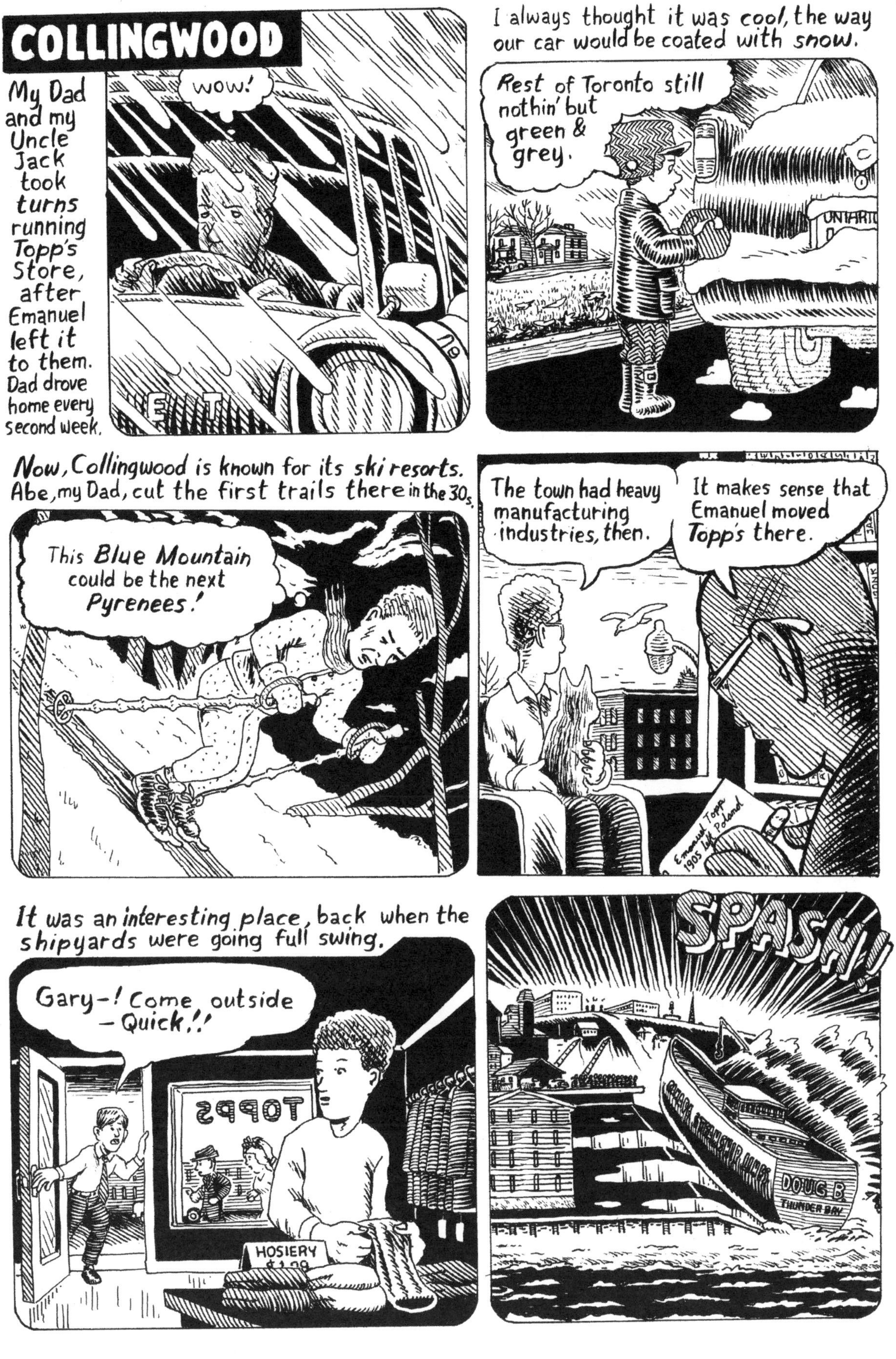
COLLINGWOOD
My Dad and my Uncle Jack took turns running Topp's Store, after Emanuel left it to them. Dad drove home every second week.
wow!
I always thought it was cool, the way our car would be coated with snow.
Rest of Toronto still nothin' but green & grey.
Now, Collingwood is known for its ski resorts. Abe, my Dad, cut the first trails there in the 30s.
This Blue Mountain could be the next Pyrenees!
The town had heavy manufacturing industries, then.
It makes sense that Emanuel moved Topp's there.
Emanuel Topp 1905 left Poland
It was an interesting place, back when the shipyards were going full swing.
Gary-! Come outside —Quick!!
TOPPS
HOSIERY
SPASH!!
DOUG B
THUNDER BAY

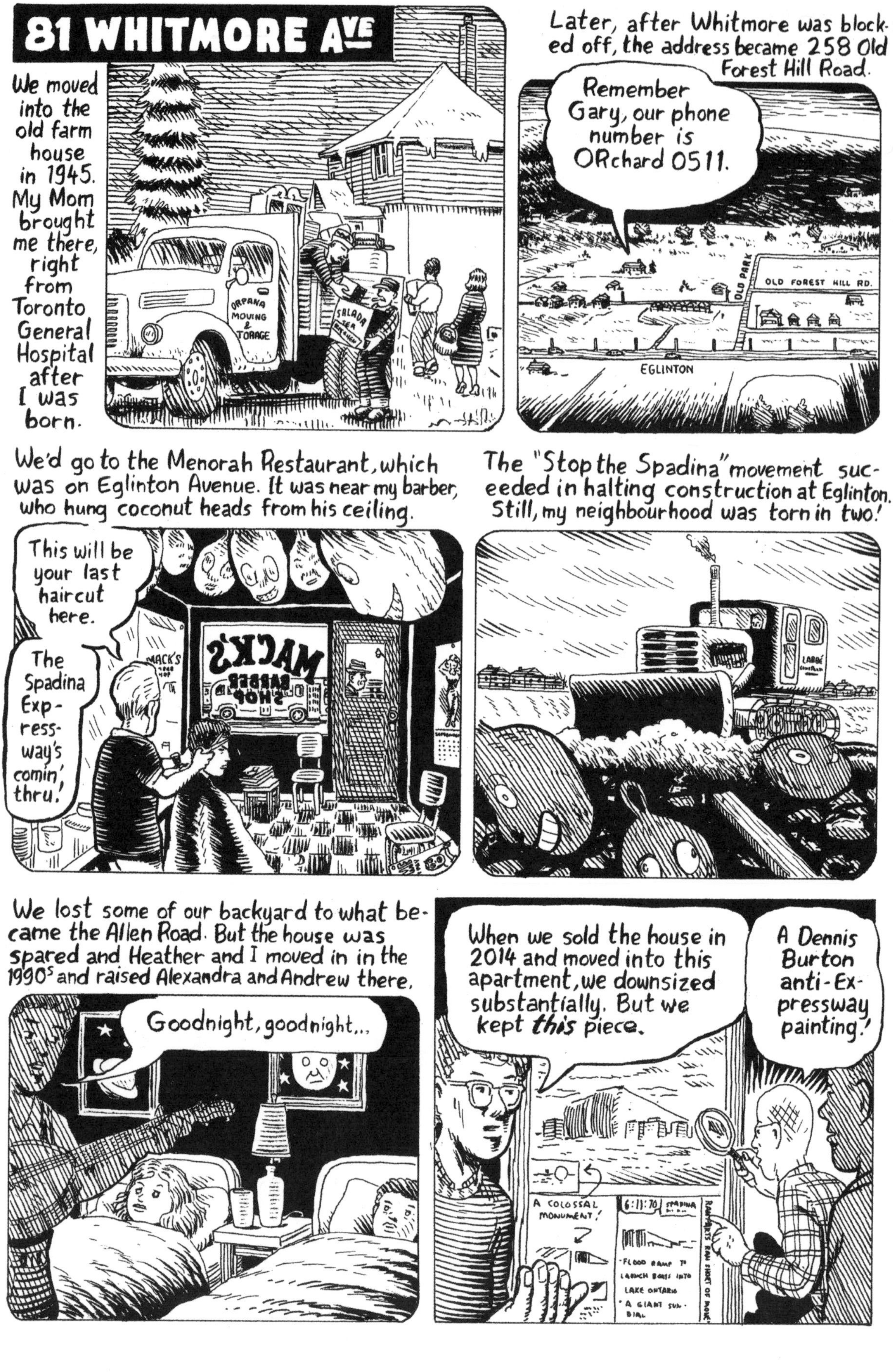
81 WHITMORE AVE
We moved into the old farm house in 1945. My Mom brought me there, right from Toronto General Hospital after I was born.
ORPANA MOVING & TORAGE
SALADA TEA
Later, after Whitmore was blocked off, the address became 258 Old Forest Hill Road.
Remember Gary, our phone number is ORchard 0511.
OLD PARK
OLD FOREST HILL RD.
EGLINTON
We'd go to the Menorah Restaurant, which was on Eglinton Avenue. It was near my barber, who hung coconut heads from his ceiling.
This will be your last haircut here.
The Spadina Expressway's comin' thru!
MACK'S BARBER SHOP
The "Stop the Spadina" movement succeeded in halting construction at Eglinton. Still, my neighbourhood was torn in two!
LABBÉ
We lost some of our backyard to what became the Allen Road. But the house was spared and Heather and I moved in in the 1990s and raised Alexandra and Andrew there.
Goodnight, goodnight...
When we sold the house in 2014 and moved into this apartment, we downsized substantially. But we kept *this* piece.
A Dennis Burton anti-Expressway painting!
A COLOSSAL MONUMENT!
6:11:70
SPADINA
FLOOD RAMP TO LAUNCH BOATS INTO LAKE ONTARIO
A GIANT SUN-DIAL

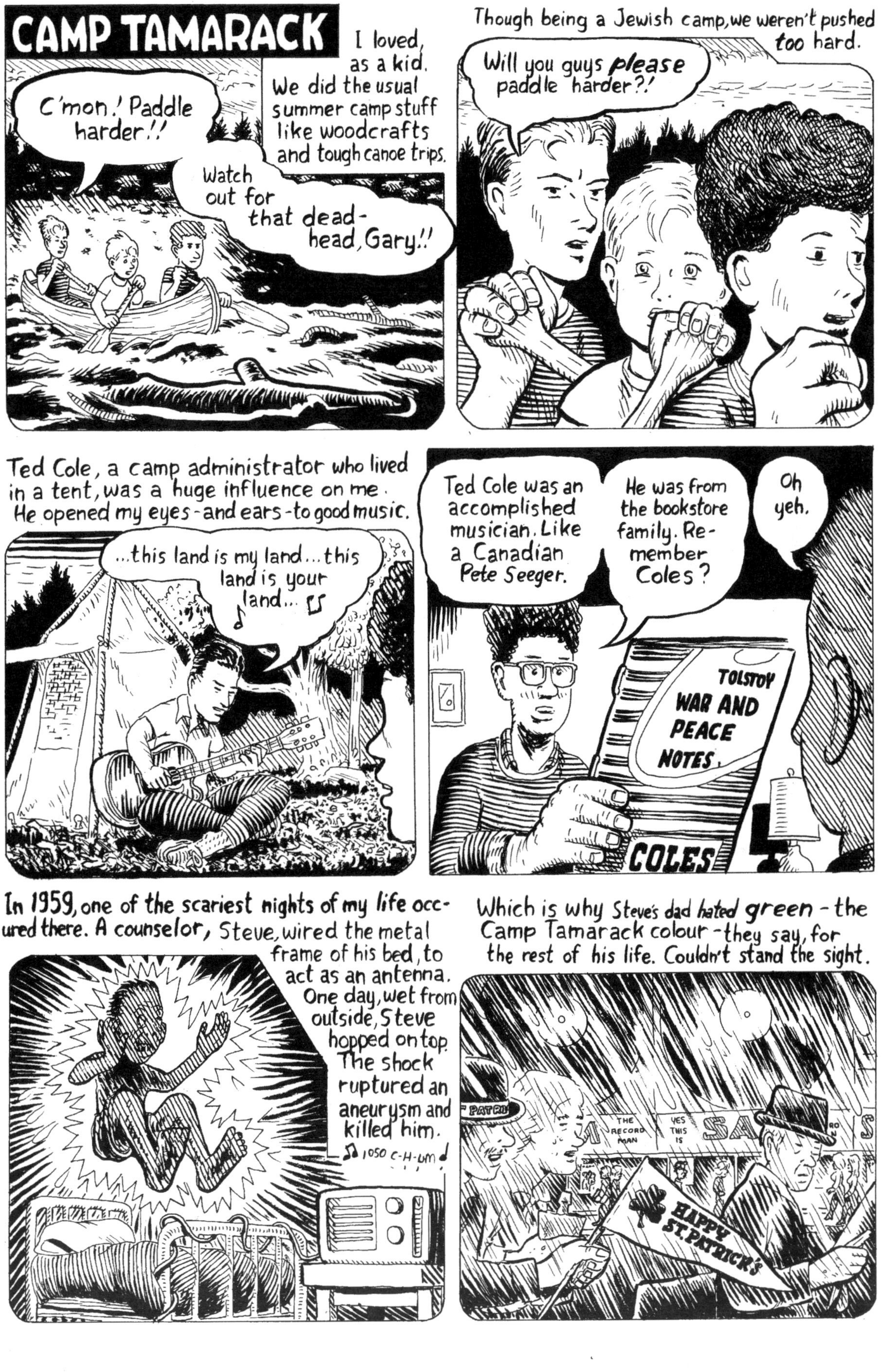
CAMP TAMARACK
I loved, as a kid. We did the usual summer camp stuff like woodcrafts and tough canoe trips.
C'mon! Paddle harder!!
Watch out for that dead-head, Gary!!
Though being a Jewish camp, we weren't pushed too hard.
Will you guys please paddle harder?!
Ted Cole, a camp administrator who lived in a tent, was a huge influence on me. He opened my eyes - and ears - to good music.
...this land is my land... this land is your land...
Ted Cole was an accomplished musician. Like a Canadian Pete Seeger.
He was from the bookstore family. Re-member Coles?
Oh yeh.
TOLSTOY
WAR AND PEACE NOTES
COLES
In 1959, one of the scariest nights of my life occ-ured there. A counselor, Steve, wired the metal frame of his bed, to act as an antenna. One day, wet from outside, Steve hopped on top. The shock ruptured an aneurysm and killed him.
1050 C-H-UM
Which is why Steve's dad hated green - the Camp Tamarack colour - they say, for the rest of his life. Couldn't stand the sight.
THE RECORD MAN
YES THIS IS
HAPPY ST. PATRICK'S

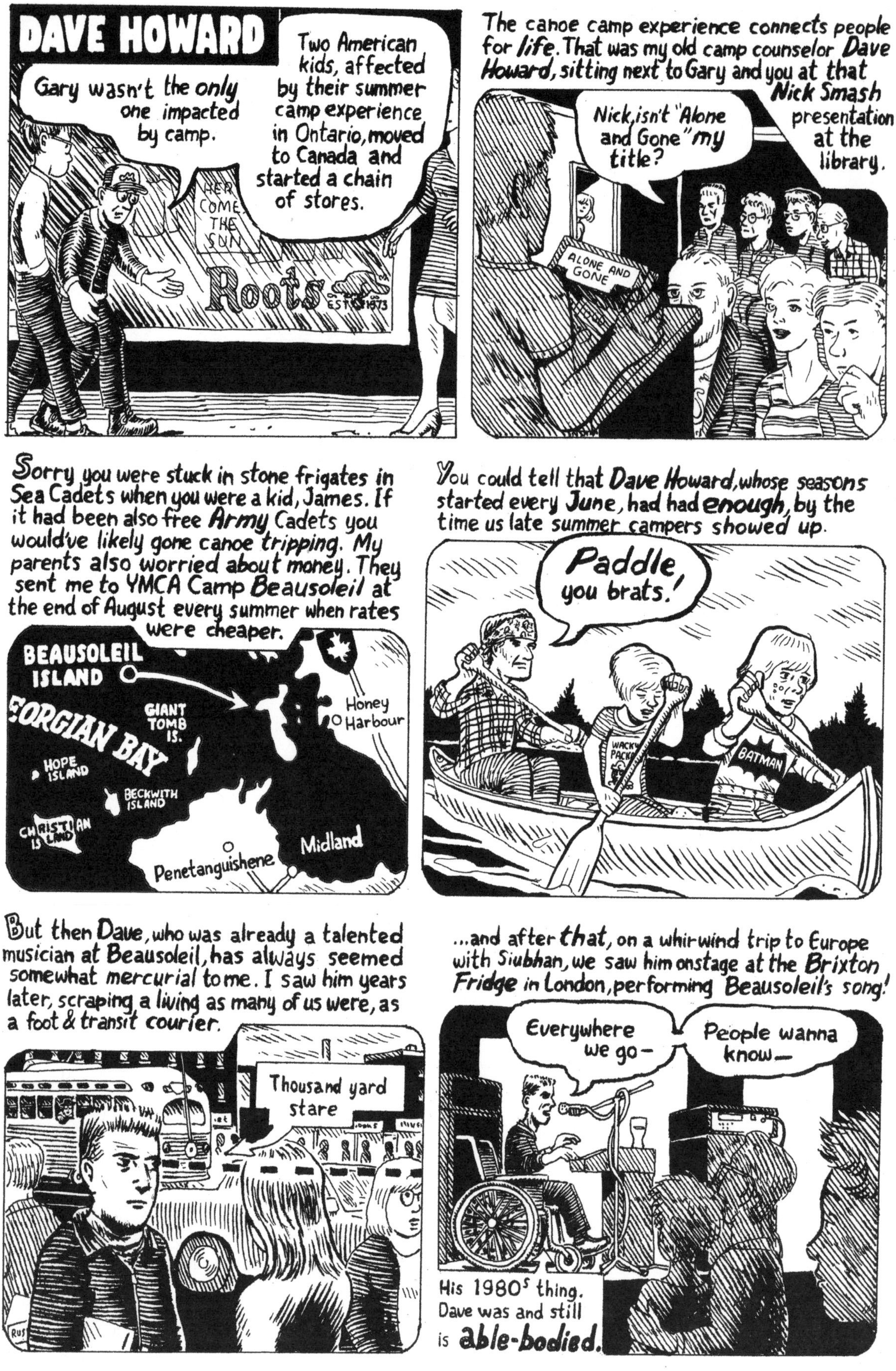
DAVE HOWARD
Gary wasn't the only one impacted by camp.
Two American kids, affected by their summer camp experience in Ontario, moved to Canada and started a chain of stores.
Roots
EST 1973
The canoe camp experience connects people for life. That was my old camp counselor Dave Howard, sitting next to Gary and you at that Nick Smash presentation at the library.
Nick, isn't "Alone and Gone" my title?
ALONE AND GONE
Sorry you were stuck in stone frigates in Sea Cadets when you were a kid, James. If it had been also free Army Cadets you would've likely gone canoe tripping. My parents also worried about money. They sent me to YMCA Camp Beausoleil at the end of August every summer when rates were cheaper.
BEAUSOLEIL ISLAND
EORGIAN BAY
GIANT TOMB IS.
Honey Harbour
HOPE ISLAND
BECKWITH ISLAND
CHRISTIAN ISLAND
Midland
Penetanguishene
You could tell that Dave Howard, whose seasons started every June, had had enough, by the time us late summer campers showed up.
Paddle, you brats!
BATMAN
But then Dave, who was already a talented musician at Beausoleil, has always seemed somewhat mercurial to me. I saw him years later, scraping a living as many of us were, as a foot & transit courier.
Thousand yard stare
...and after that, on a whirlwind trip to Europe with Siubhan, we saw him onstage at the Brixton Fridge in London, performing Beausoleil's song!
Everywhere we go—
People wanna know—
His 1980s thing. Dave was and still is able-bodied.

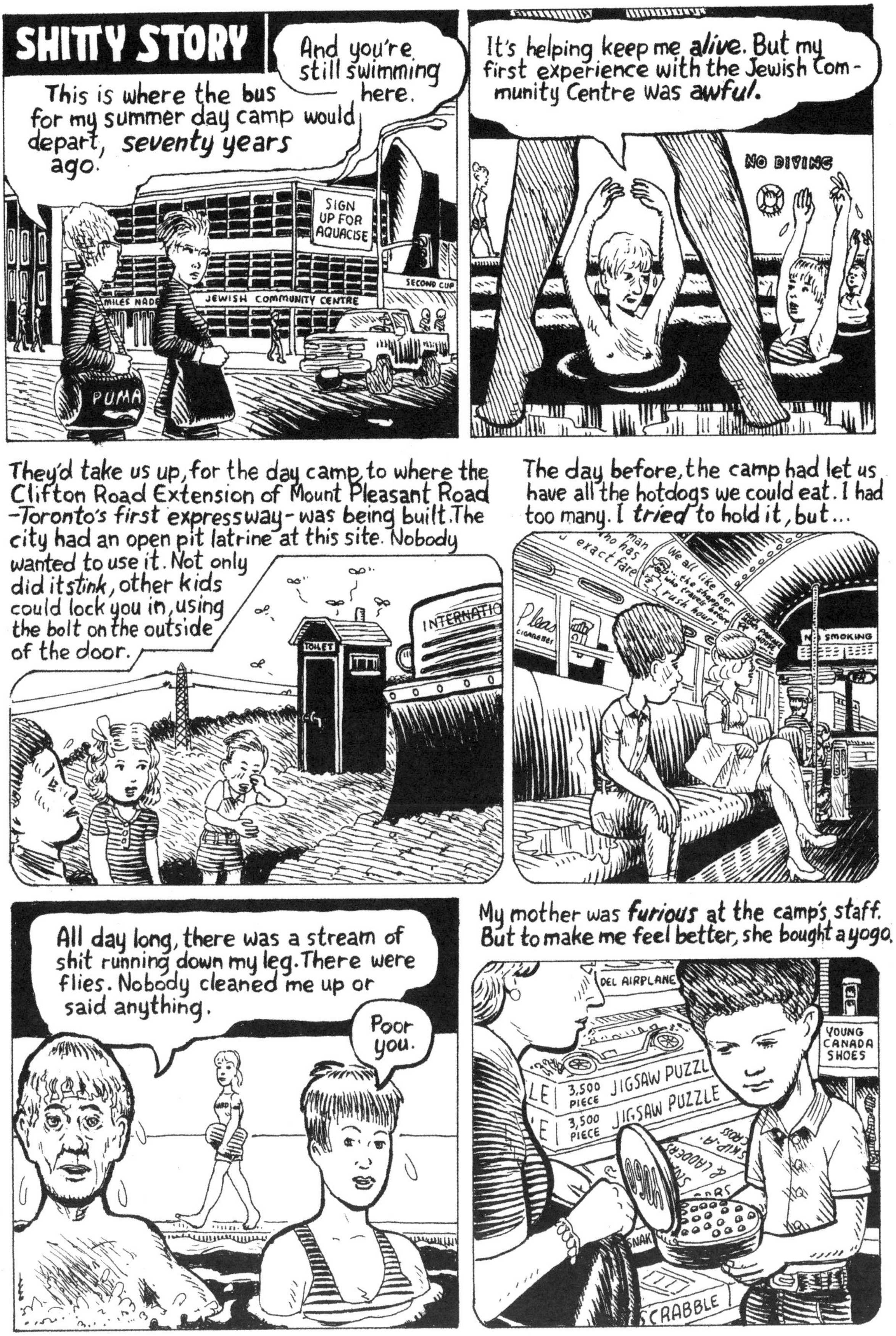
SHITTY STORY
This is where the bus for my summer day camp would depart, *seventy years* ago.
And you're still swimming here.
SIGN UP FOR AQUACISE
MILES NADE
JEWISH COMMUNITY CENTRE
SECOND CUP
PUMA
It's helping keep me *alive*. But my first experience with the Jewish Community Centre was *awful*.
NO DIVING
They'd take us up, for the day camp, to where the Clifton Road Extension of Mount Pleasant Road –Toronto's first expressway– was being built. The city had an open pit latrine at this site. Nobody wanted to use it. Not only did it *stink*, other kids could lock you in, using the bolt on the outside of the door.
TOILET
INTERNATIO
The day before, the camp had let us have all the hotdogs we could eat. I had too many. I *tried* to hold it, but...
NO SMOKING
All day long, there was a stream of shit running down my leg. There were flies. Nobody cleaned me up or said anything.
Poor you.
My mother was *furious* at the camp's staff. But to make me feel better, she bought a yogo.
DEL AIRPLANE
YOUNG CANADA SHOES
3,500 PIECE JIGSAW PUZZLE
3,500 PIECE JIGSAW PUZZLE
SCRABBLE

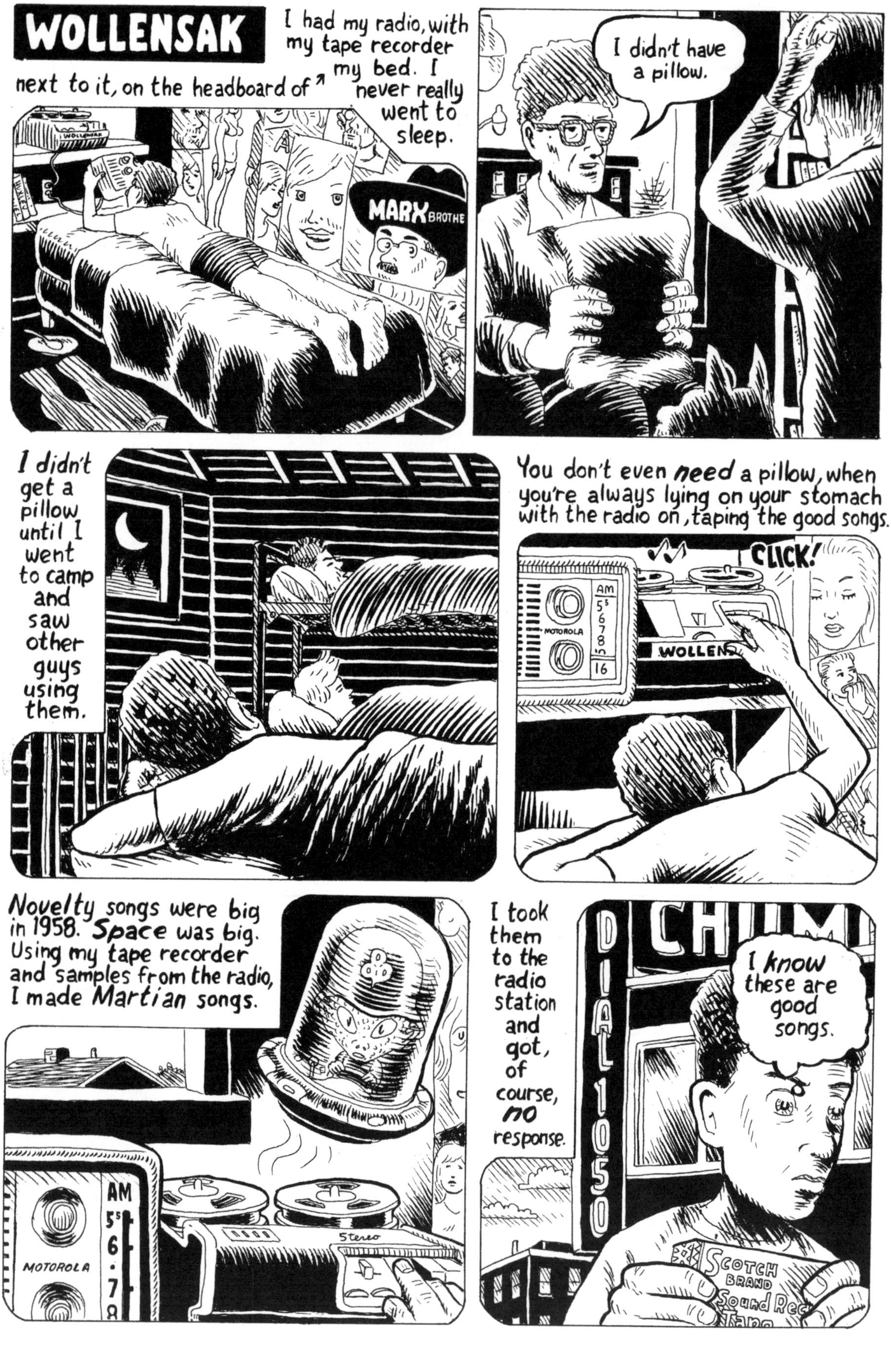
WOLLENSAK
I had my radio, with my tape recorder next to it, on the headboard of my bed. I never really went to sleep.
WOLLENSAK
MARX BROTHE
I didn't have a pillow.
I didn't get a pillow until I went to camp and saw other guys using them.
You don't even *need* a pillow, when you're always lying on your stomach with the radio on, taping the good songs.
CLICK!
AM
MOTOROLA
16
WOLLEN
Novelty songs were big in 1958. *Space* was big. Using my tape recorder and samples from the radio, I made *Martian* songs.
AM
MOTOROLA
Stereo
I took them to the radio station and got, of course, *no* response.
CHUM
DIAL 1050
I *know* these are good songs.
SCOTCH BRAND

THW SALMON*

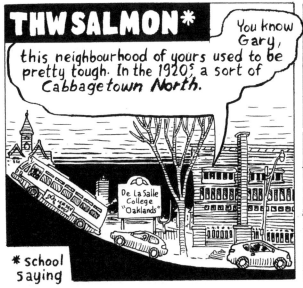

this neighbourhood of yours used to be pretty tough. In the 1920s, a sort of *Cabbagetown North.*

You know Gary,

De La Salle College "Oaklands"

* school saying

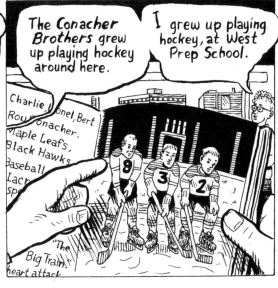

The *Conacher Brothers* grew up playing hockey around here.

I grew up playing hockey, at West Prep School.

Charlie, Lionel, Bert Roy Conacher, Maple Leafs, Black Hawks, Baseball, Lacrosse Sp...

"The Big Train" heart attack

When?

Soon.

We were out there *day* and *night.*

C'mon Teee-deeer!!

SHER-WOOD

One spring, in *the rink's* melting ice, I found a spiffy fountain pen.

Nice!

There was a *rule* at our school that if no one claimed something that you'd returned to Lost and Found within one month, you'd get to keep that item.

But Mr Salmon, the Principal, in the case of the pen, *broke* that *rule.*

He's not going to let me have it! To Hell With Salmon!!

WEST PREP SCHO

FIRE ESCAPE PLAN

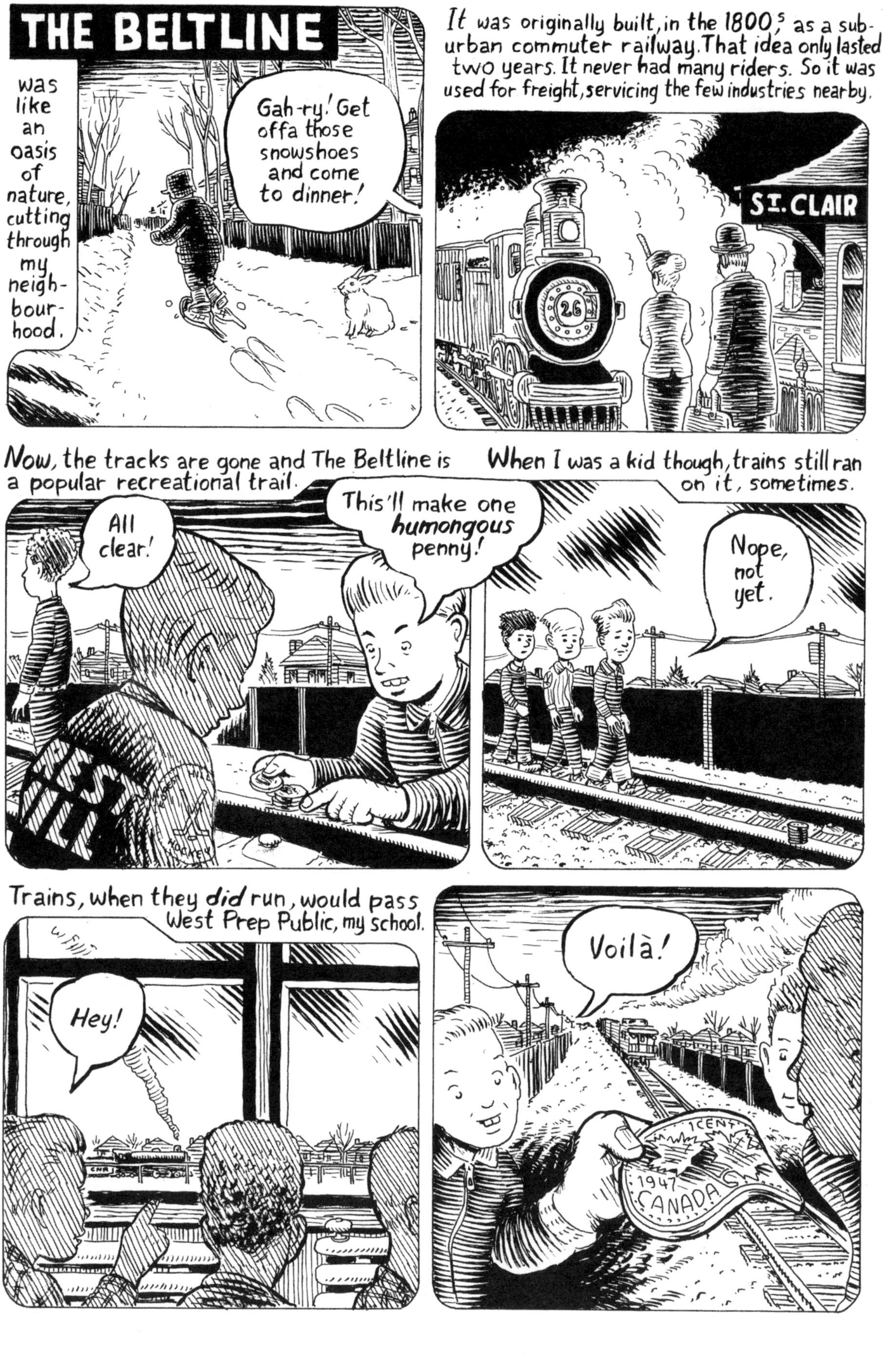
THE BELTLINE
was like an oasis of nature, cutting through my neighbourhood.
Gah-ry! Get offa those snowshoes and come to dinner!
It was originally built, in the 1800s as a suburban commuter railway. That idea only lasted two years. It never had many riders. So it was used for freight, servicing the few industries nearby.
26
ST. CLAIR
Now, the tracks are gone and The Beltline is a popular recreational trail.
All clear!
This'll make one humongous penny!
When I was a kid though, trains still ran on it, sometimes.
Nope, not yet.
Trains, when they did run, would pass West Prep Public, my school.
Hey!
Voilà!
1 CENT
1947
CANADA

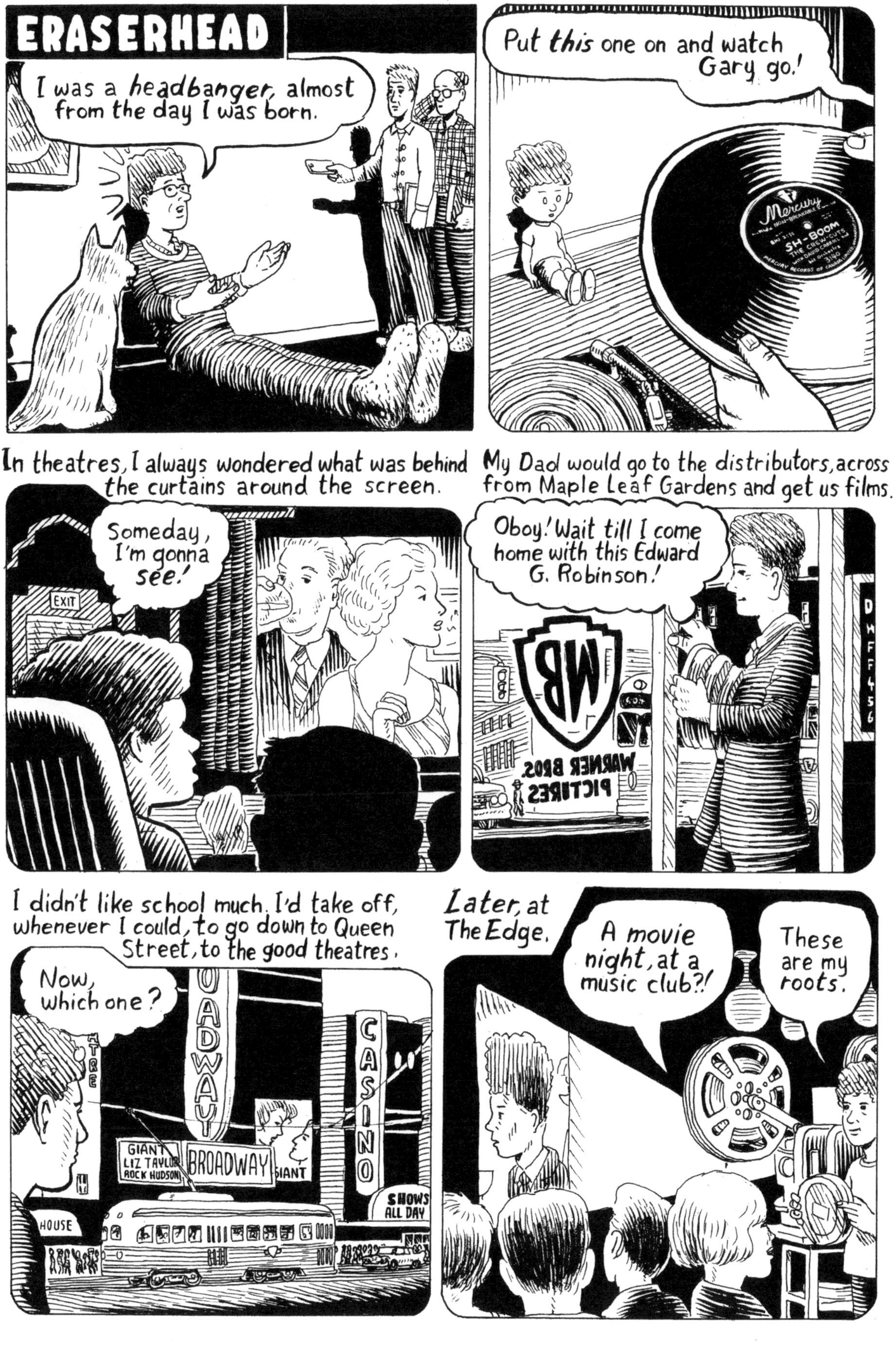
ERASERHEAD
I was a *headbanger*, almost from the day I was born.
Put *this* one on and watch Gary go!
Mercury
SH-BOOM
THE CREW-CUTS
In theatres, I always wondered what was behind the curtains around the screen.
Someday, I'm gonna *see!*
EXIT
My Dad would go to the distributors, across from Maple Leaf Gardens and get us films.
Oboy! Wait till I come home with this Edward G. Robinson!
WB
WARNER BROS. PICTURES
I didn't like school much. I'd take off, whenever I could, to go down to Queen Street, to the good theatres.
Now, which one?
GIANT
LIZ TAYLOR
ROCK HUDSON
BROADWAY
CASINO
SHOWS ALL DAY
HOUSE
Later, at The Edge.
A *movie night*, at a music club?!
These are my *roots*.

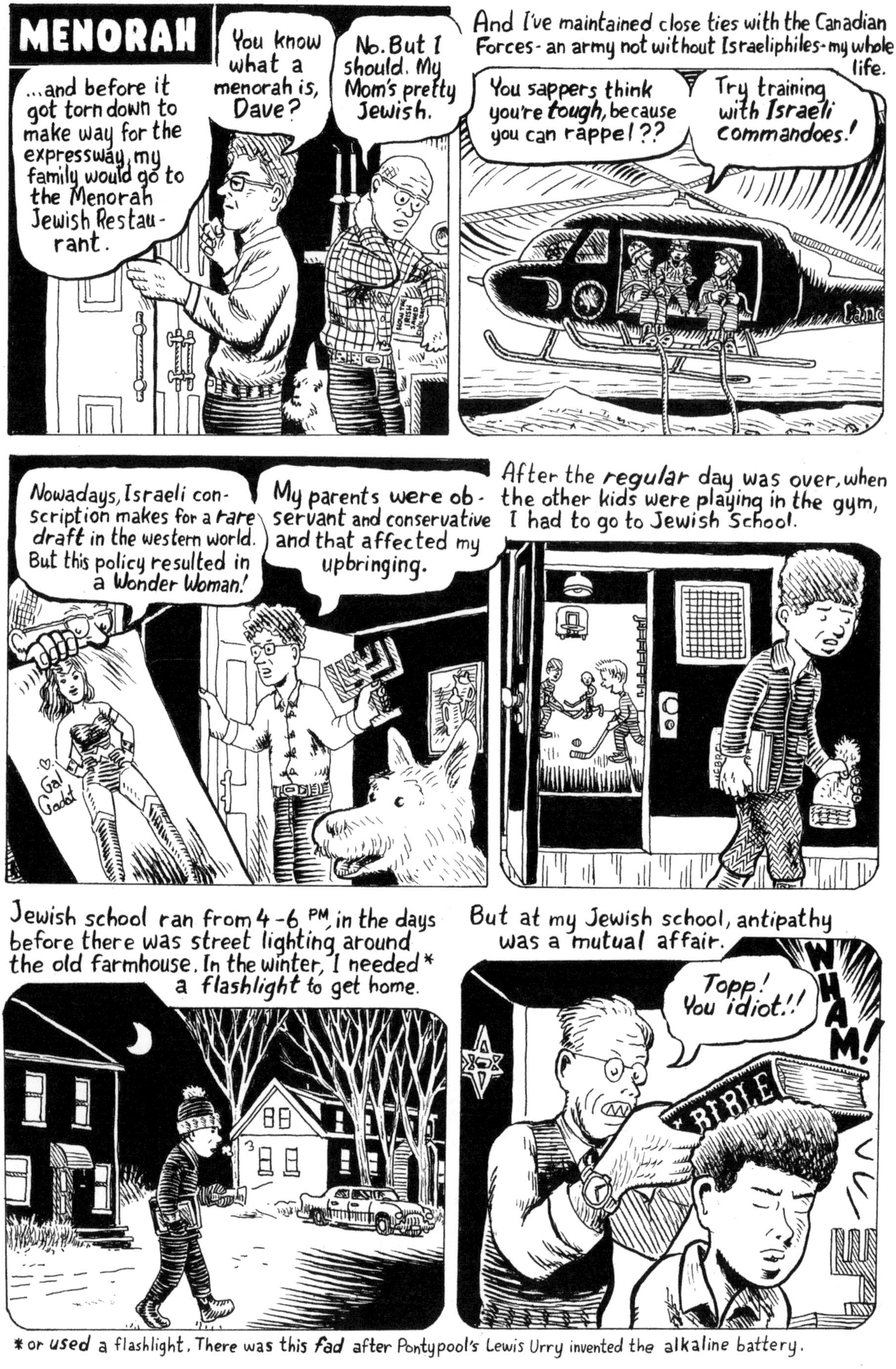
MENORAH
...and before it got torn down to make way for the expressway, my family would go to the Menorah Jewish Restau-rant.
You know what a menorah is, Dave?
No. But I should. My Mom's pretty Jewish.
And I've maintained close ties with the Canadian Forces - an army not without Israeliphiles - my whole life.
You sappers think you're tough, because you can rappel??
Try training with Israeli commandoes!
Nowadays, Israeli con-scription makes for a rare draft in the western world. But this policy resulted in a Wonder Woman!
Gal Gadot
My parents were ob-servant and conservative and that affected my upbringing.
After the regular day was over, when the other kids were playing in the gym, I had to go to Jewish School.
Jewish school ran from 4-6 PM, in the days before there was street lighting around the old farmhouse. In the winter, I needed* a flashlight to get home.
But at my Jewish school, antipathy was a mutual affair.
Topp! You idiot!!
WHAM!
BIBLE

* or used a flashlight. There was this fad after Pontypool's Lewis Urry invented the alkaline battery.

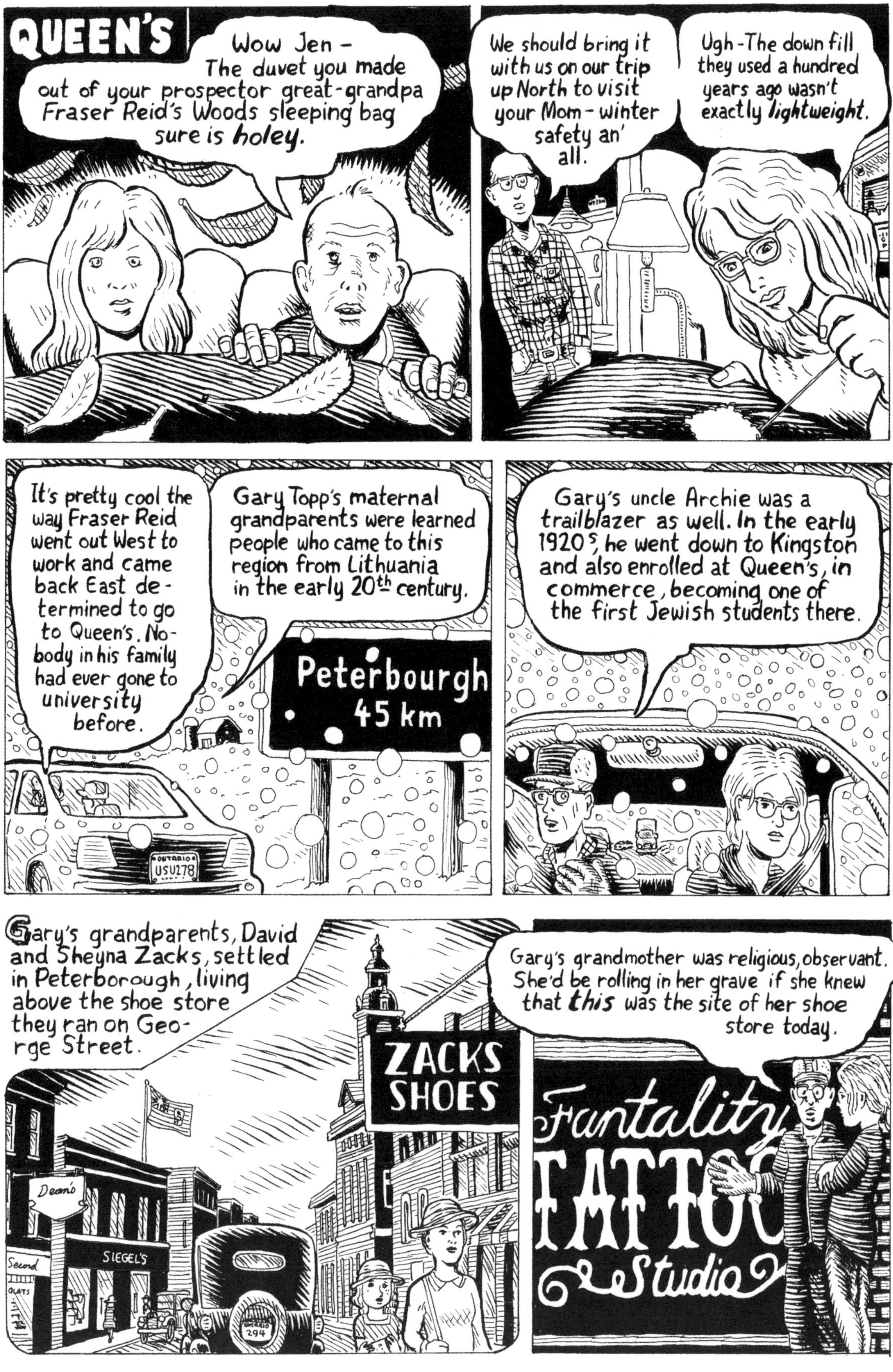
QUEEN'S
Wow Jen - The duvet you made out of your prospector great-grandpa Fraser Reid's Woods sleeping bag sure is holey.
We should bring it with us on our trip up North to visit your Mom - winter safety an' all.
Ugh - The down fill they used a hundred years ago wasn't exactly lightweight.
It's pretty cool the way Fraser Reid went out West to work and came back East determined to go to Queen's. Nobody in his family had ever gone to university before.
Gary Topp's maternal grandparents were learned people who came to this region from Lithuania in the early 20th century.
Peterbourgh 45 km
ONTARIO USU278
Gary's uncle Archie was a trailblazer as well. In the early 1920s, he went down to Kingston and also enrolled at Queen's, in commerce, becoming one of the first Jewish students there.
Gary's grandparents, David and Sheyna Zacks, settled in Peterborough, living above the shoe store they ran on George Street.
ZACKS SHOES
Dean's
SIEGEL'S
Second
ONTARIO 294
Gary's grandmother was religious, observant. She'd be rolling in her grave if she knew that this was the site of her shoe store today.
Fantality TATTOO Studio

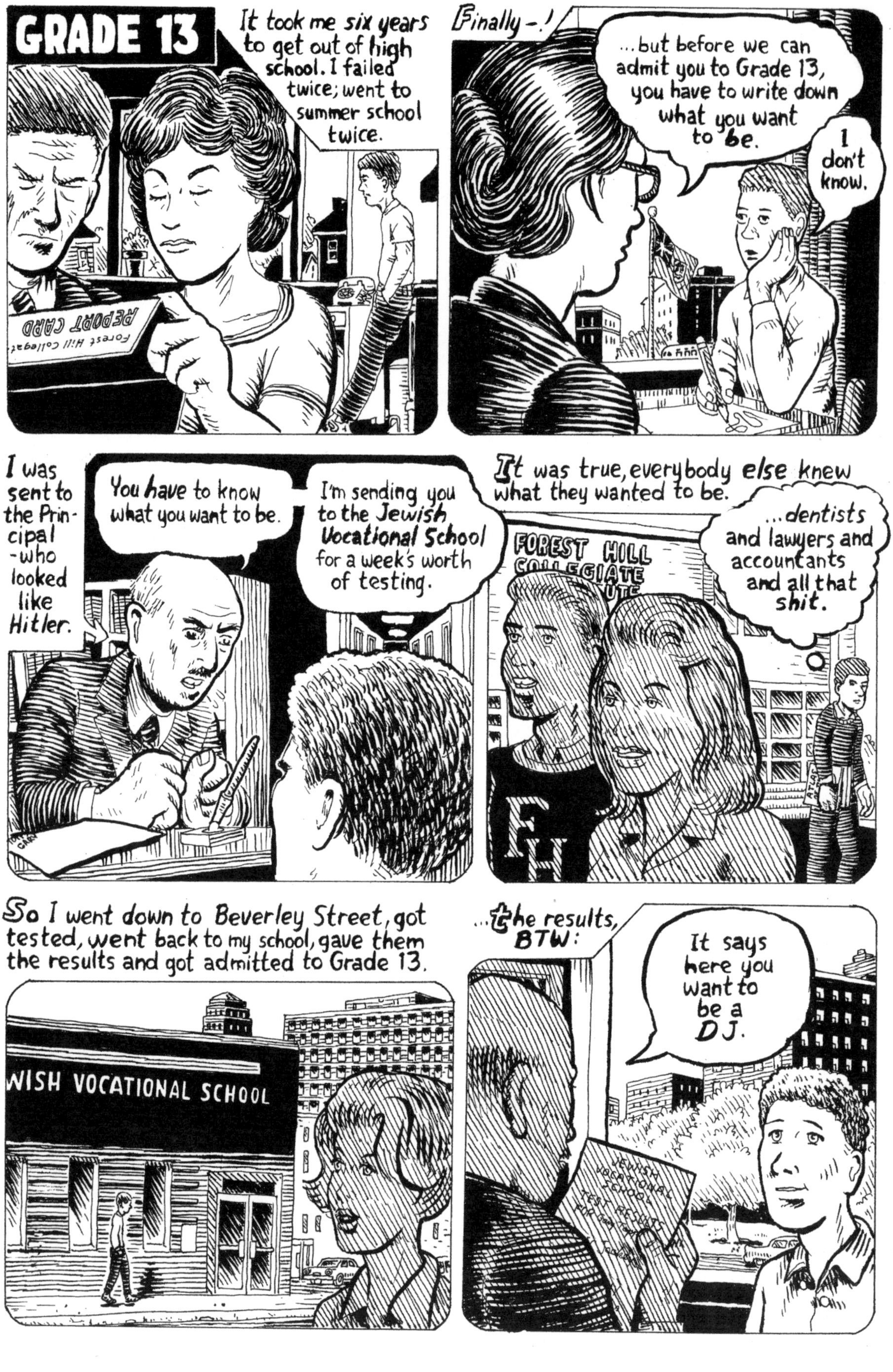
GRADE 13
It took me six years to get out of high school. I failed twice; went to summer school twice.
REPORT CARD
Finally –!
...but before we can admit you to Grade 13, you have to write down what you want to be.
I don't know.
I was sent to the Principal –who looked like Hitler.
You have to know what you want to be.
I'm sending you to the Jewish Vocational School for a week's worth of testing.
It was true, everybody else knew what they wanted to be.
FOREST HILL COLLEGIATE
...dentists and lawyers and accountants and all that shit.
So I went down to Beverley Street, got tested, went back to my school, gave them the results and got admitted to Grade 13.
WISH VOCATIONAL SCHOOL
...the results, BTW:
It says here you want to be a DJ.
JEWISH VOCATIONAL SCHOOL
TEST RESULTS

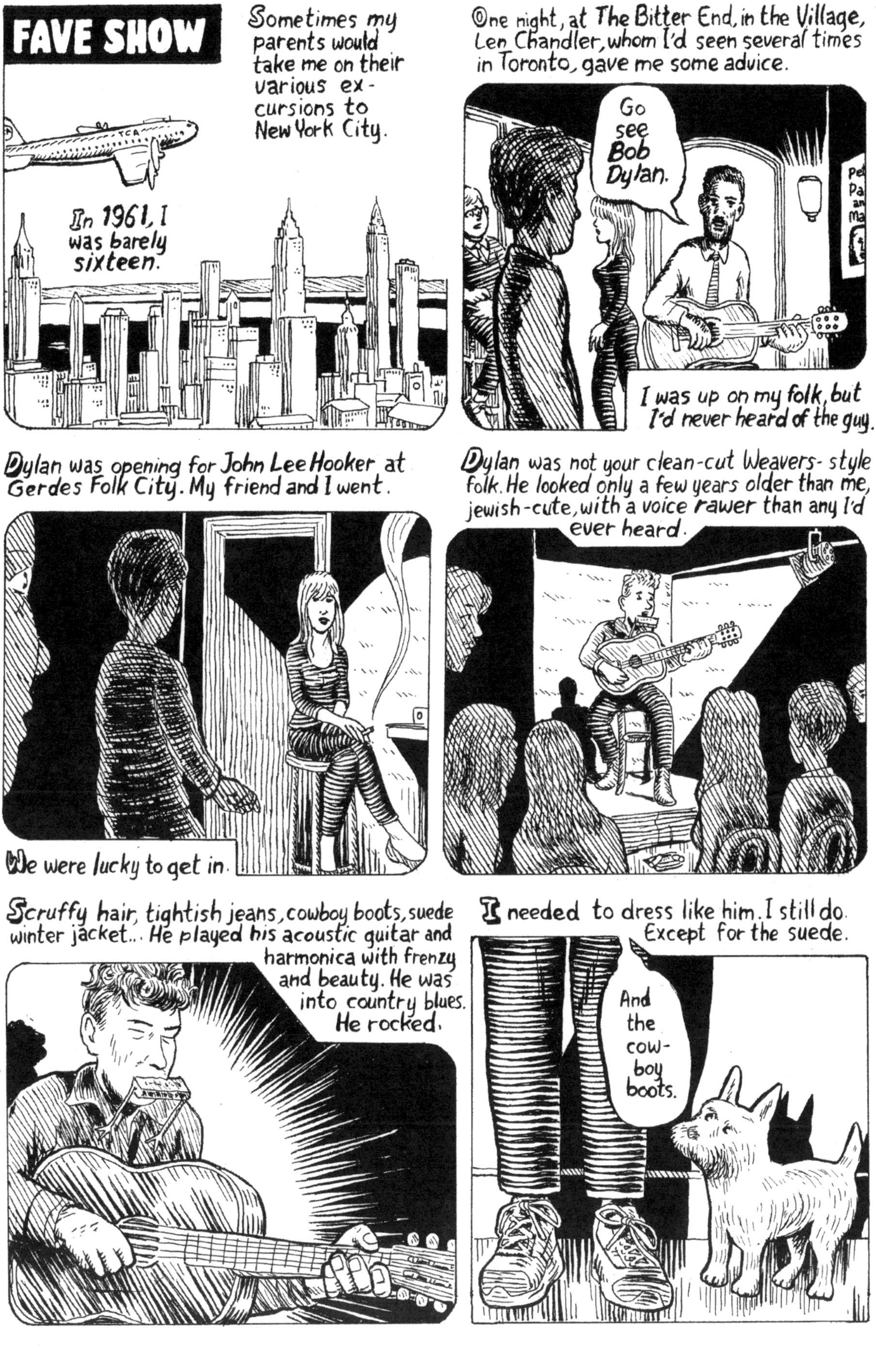
FAVE SHOW
Sometimes my parents would take me on their various excursions to New York City.
In 1961, I was barely sixteen.
One night, at The Bitter End, in the Village, Len Chandler, whom I'd seen several times in Toronto, gave me some advice.
Go see Bob Dylan.
I was up on my folk, but I'd never heard of the guy.
Dylan was opening for John Lee Hooker at Gerdes Folk City. My friend and I went.
We were lucky to get in.
Dylan was not your clean-cut Weavers-style folk. He looked only a few years older than me, jewish-cute, with a voice rawer than any I'd ever heard.
Scruffy hair, tightish jeans, cowboy boots, suede winter jacket... He played his acoustic guitar and harmonica with frenzy and beauty. He was into country blues. He rocked.
I needed to dress like him. I still do. Except for the suede.
And the cowboy boots.

THE CHAIN

Sometimes, I'm *still* feeling for it.

As if it's still there?

That's what we want —

A chain that bonds!

These were the days before tattoo parlours on every corner. This is what we did.

It's on for good.

Good!

Twenty years later—!

It's lasted pretty long, for such a cheap chain!

And then, during a 1992 concert at The Diamond Club, it fell off—!

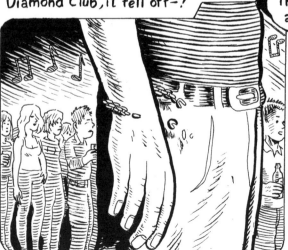

Thanks. But don't worry about a worn out chain.

Here's 'nother piece, Gary.

Things went South after this. My mother had a stroke a week later and I stopped doing shows.

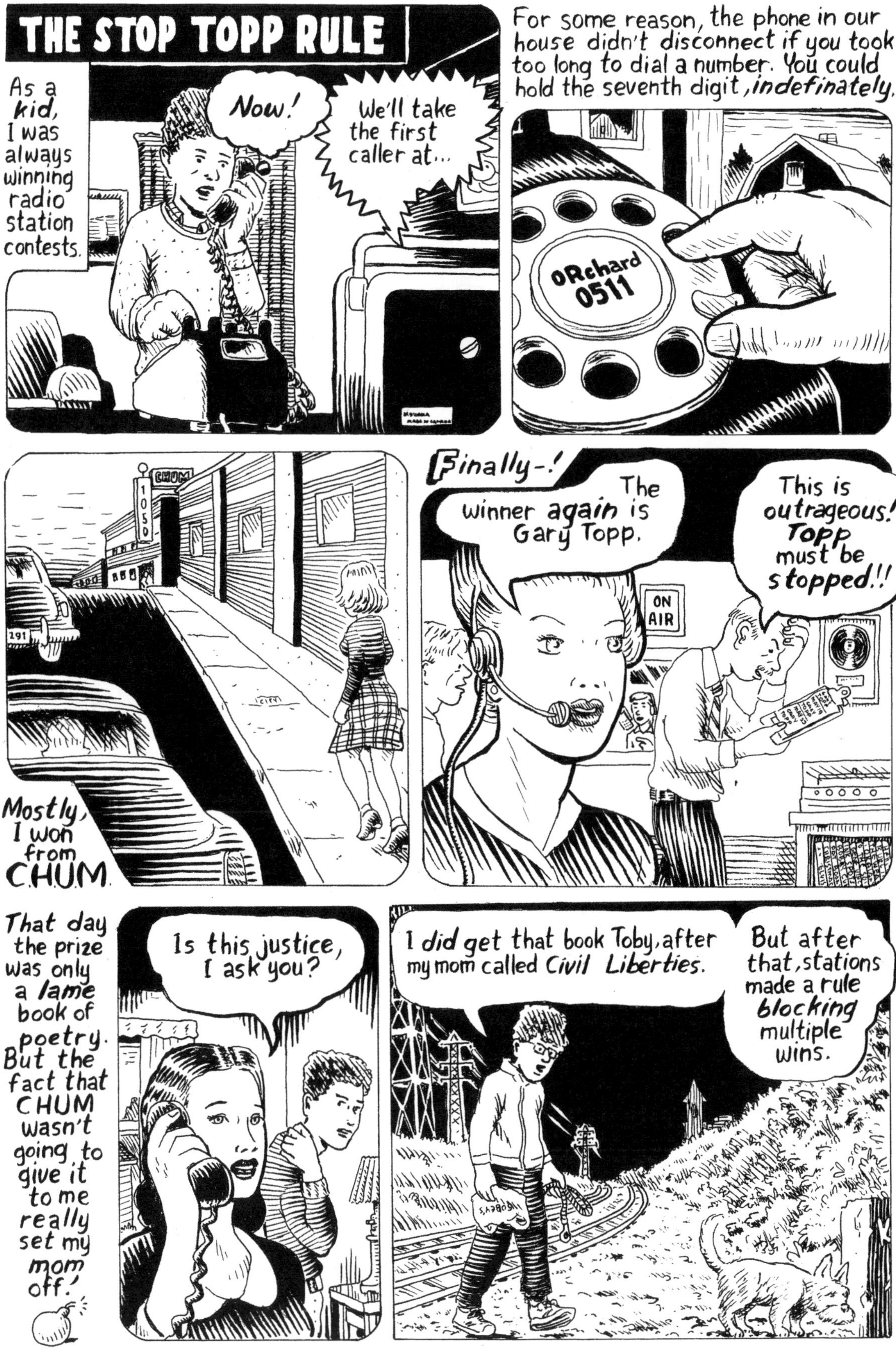
THE STOP TOPP RULE
As a kid, I was always winning radio station contests.
Now!
We'll take the first caller at...
For some reason, the phone in our house didn't disconnect if you took too long to dial a number. You could hold the seventh digit, indefinately.
ORchard 0511
CHUM
1050
Mostly, I won from C.H.U.M.
Finally-!
The winner again is Gary Topp.
ON AIR
This is outrageous! Topp must be stopped!!
That day the prize was only a lame book of poetry. But the fact that CHUM wasn't going to give it to me really set my mom off.
Is this justice, I ask you?
I did get that book Toby, after my mom called Civil Liberties.
But after that, stations made a rule blocking multiple wins.

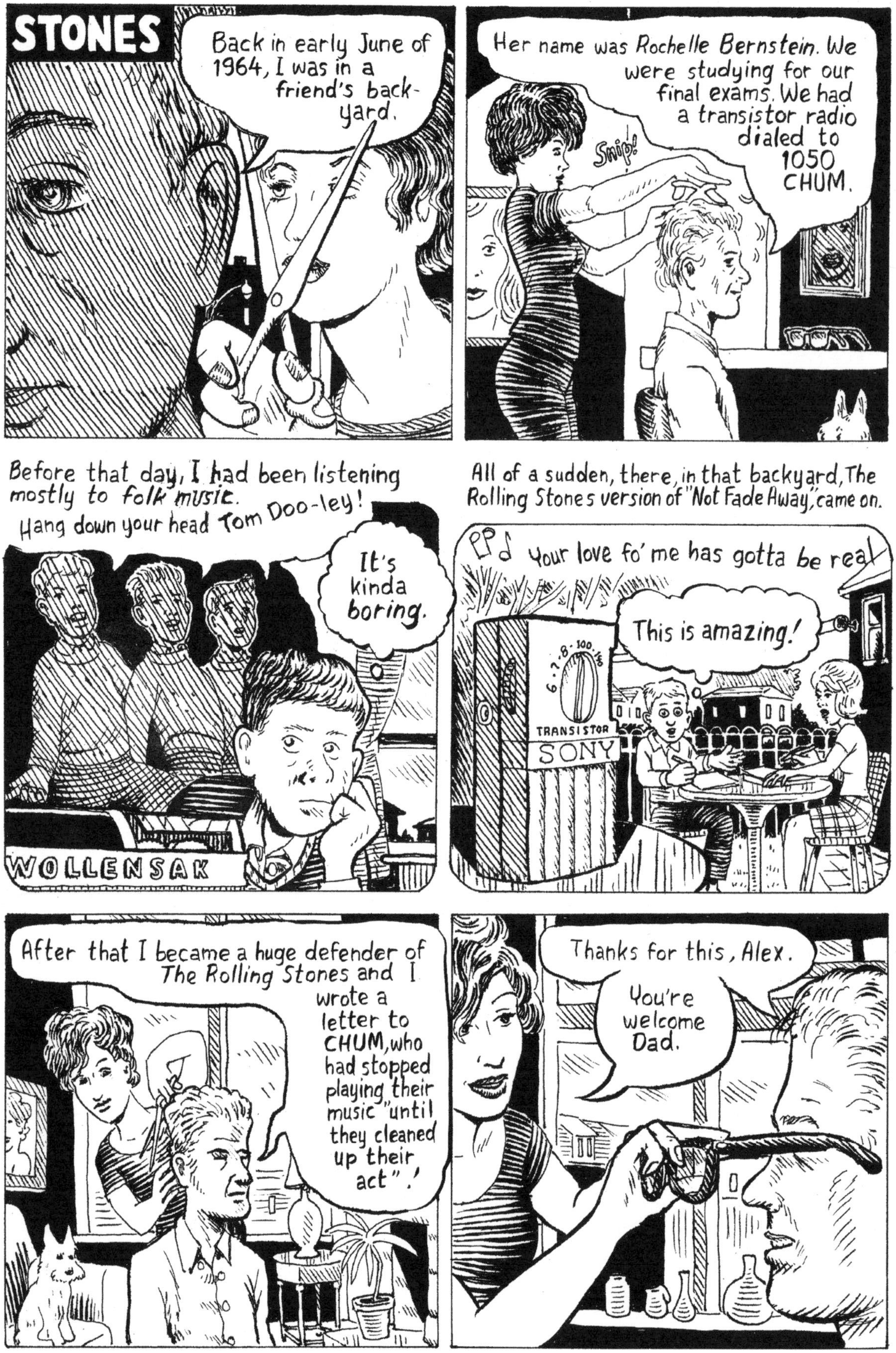
STONES
Back in early June of 1964, I was in a friend's back-yard.
Her name was Rochelle Bernstein. We were studying for our final exams. We had a transistor radio dialed to 1050 CHUM.
Snip!
Before that day, I had been listening mostly to folk music.
Hang down your head Tom Doo-ley!
It's kinda boring.
WOLLENSAK
All of a sudden, there, in that backyard, The Rolling Stones version of "Not Fade Away," came on.
Your love fo' me has gotta be real
This is amazing!
TRANSISTOR
SONY
After that I became a huge defender of The Rolling Stones and I wrote a letter to CHUM, who had stopped playing their music "until they cleaned up their act"!
Thanks for this, Alex.
You're welcome Dad.

Tuesday, Oct. 20/64.

To whom it may concern:

After reading last night's newspaper, I became thoroughly disgusted with the policy of your radio station. The article stated that you would not play any music by "The Rolling Stones", because you did not like what the group stood for. You say that they are not a good influence on the people who listen to your type of music. Do you honestly think that P. J. Proby and his "pony-tail" are a good influence? I seem to remember that "The Platters" were put in jail a few years ago, due to a narcotics charge. You still play their music. Isn't it said that Dean Martin drinks a great deal? Why is his music played? The lives of these performers haven't been pried into. Why then should you discredit "The Stones"?

What do "The Rolling Stones" stand for? It is said that they never wash, that they do not comb their hair, and that they never "fix" themselves up for their live appearances. Do you honestly beliee that they don't wash? Anyways, I don't think that the appearance of a singer makes his song.

Right now you might be saying that I am talking senselessly, and that everything which I have said so far is truthless; you might only be objecting to their "disgusting" sound music. Well then, what do you think about

"—— the bird is the word."
I hope I have the quotation right; if not, you can consult your record library under:

"The Bird" by The Trashmen

I've heard it said at the beginning of "Speak Your Mind" that the opinions expressed are not necessarily those of the station. Why then, should you change this policy concerning

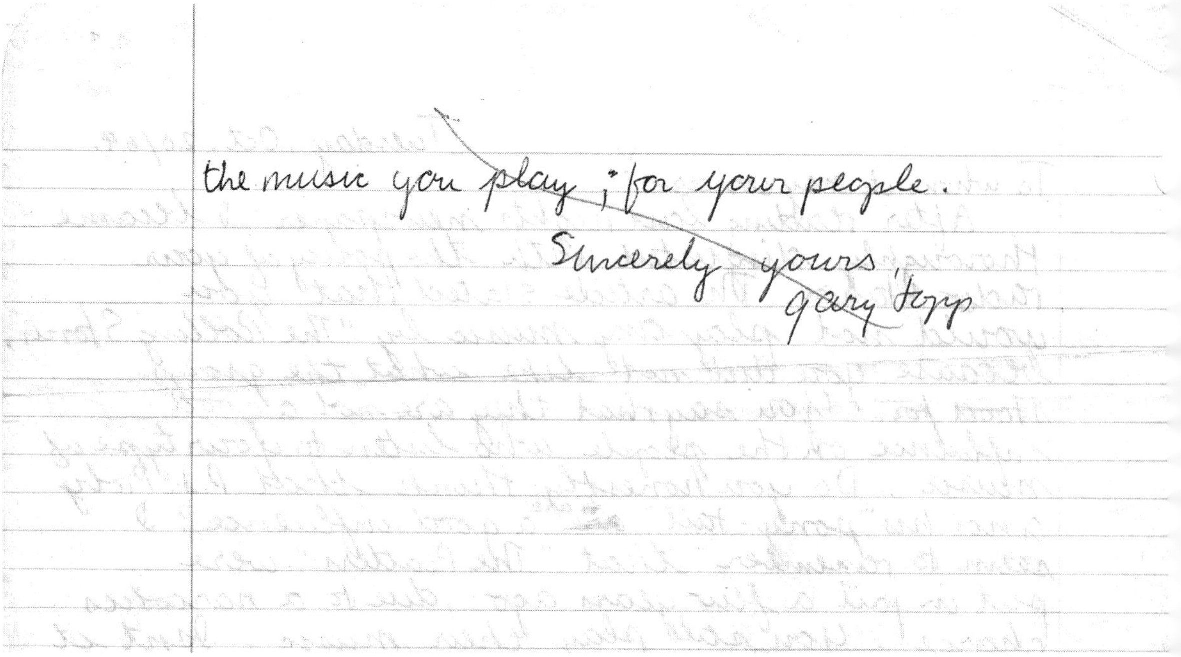
the music you play ; for your people.

Sincerely yours,

gary topp

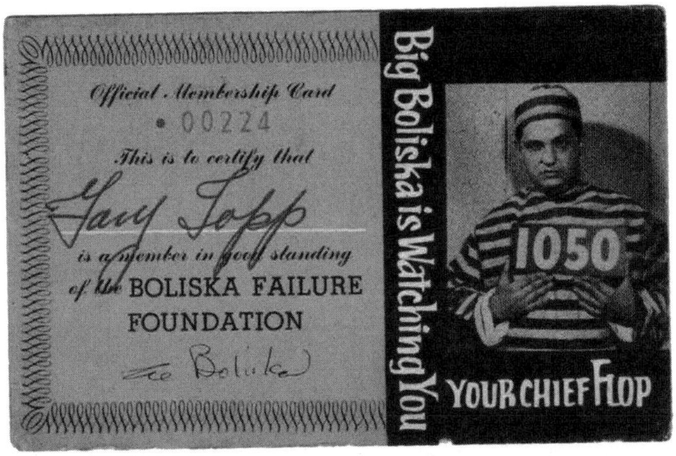

Official Membership Card
• 00224
This is to certify that
Gary Topp
is a member in good standing
of the BOLISKA FAILURE
FOUNDATION
Big Boliska is Watching You
1050
YOUR CHIEF FLOP

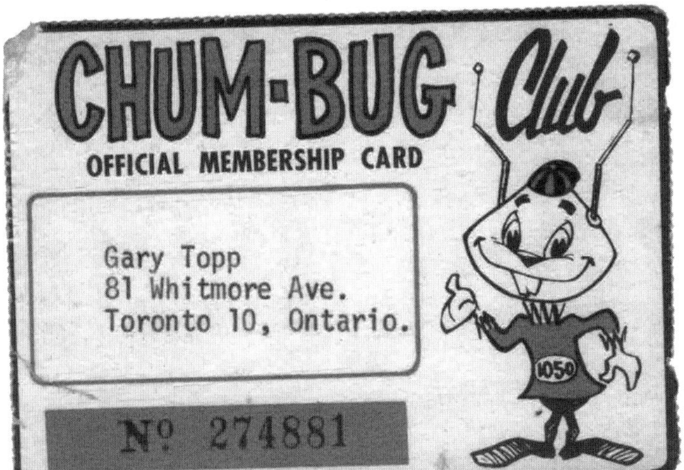

CHUM-BUG Club
OFFICIAL MEMBERSHIP CARD
Gary Topp
81 Whitmore Ave.
Toronto 10, Ontario.
Nº 274881
1050

RADIO CHUM·1050 LTD. · 1331 YONGE STREET, TORONTO 7, ONTARIO · 925-6666

October 27, 1964

Mr. Gary Topp,
81 Whitmore Avenue,
Toronto 10, Ontario.

Dear Gary:

Many entertainers have personal habits that are not
particularly commendable.

In the case of the Rolling Stones, however, we believe
that they or their publicity manager have deliberately
attempted to exploit poor taste to a ridiculous extreme.
I do not recall another phase of the music business in
which the stars boasted that they did not like to
bathe!

If, at any time, CHUM is shown proof that this statement
was publicized in error, or that the Rolling Stones and
their management team have decided to improve the presentation of these young singers to the world, we will
naturally be delighted to feature their music.

Sincerely,

RADIO CHUM - 1050 LTD.,

AS:lh

Allan Slaight,
Program Director.

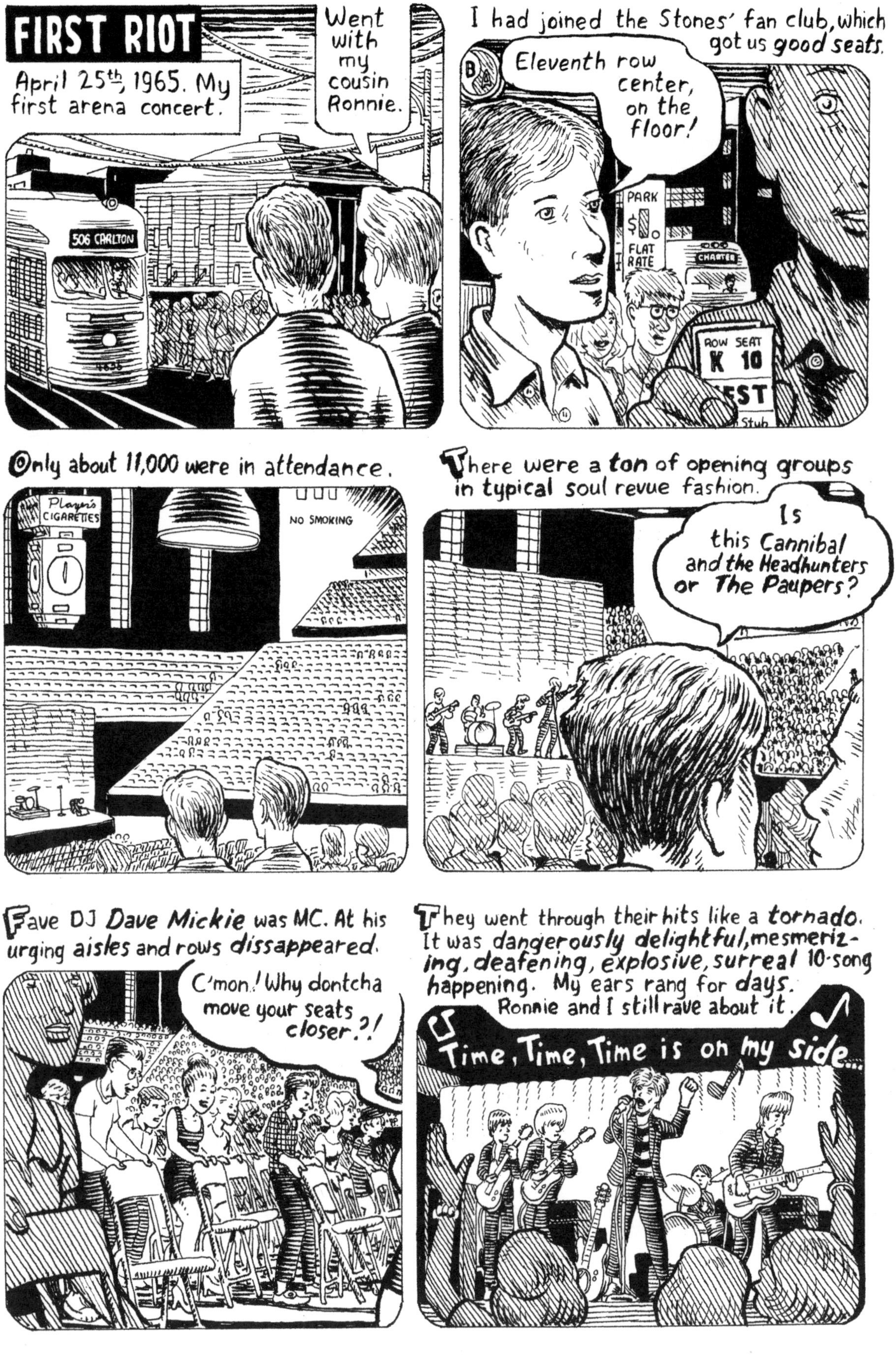
FIRST RIOT
April 25th, 1965. My first arena concert.
Went with my cousin Ronnie.
506 CARLTON
I had joined the Stones' fan club, which got us good seats.
Eleventh row center, on the floor!
PARK $ FLAT RATE
CHARTER
ROW SEAT K 10
Stub
Only about 11,000 were in attendance.
Player's CIGARETTES
NO SMOKING
There were a ton of opening groups in typical soul revue fashion.
Is this Cannibal and the Headhunters or The Paupers?
Fave DJ Dave Mickie was MC. At his urging aisles and rows dissappeared.
C'mon! Why dontcha move your seats closer?!
They went through their hits like a tornado. It was dangerously delightful, mesmerizing, deafening, explosive, surreal 10-song happening. My ears rang for days.
Ronnie and I still rave about it.
Time, Time, Time is on my side...

TORONTO DAILY STAR

BRITAIN'S LATEST SINGING SENSATIONS—THE ROLLING STONES—IN ACTION AT TORONTO'S MAPLE LEAF GARDENS
From left to right they are Bill Wyman, Charlie Watts, Keith Richard, Brian Jones and Mike Jagger

Rolling Stones show violent and vulgar

14 THE GLOBE AND MAIL, MONDAY, SEPTEMBER 27, 1976

POP

—Globe and Mail, Jack Dobson

The Ramones played very loud music in a lyrical style on subjects from cockroaches to glue-sniffing.

Ramones appeal to the morbid

flock to public hangings. Pure mor- [illegible]

get is a rhythmic pulse strong enough to energize the comatose which is something The Ramones provide in spades, they will [illegible] satisfied.

GARY'S STICK
The Leafs won the Stanley Cup in 1962.
A friend of my father's got every player on that team to autograph a stick after the final game.
My dad shellaced it and put it up on my wall.
But one day I needed a stick. So I took it down, taped it up, and used it.
And it got used and used some more and eventually it got wrecked.
Good Stick
Tooth-pick
According to Johnny Ramone:
That stick would be worth a fortune.
BLUE JAYS

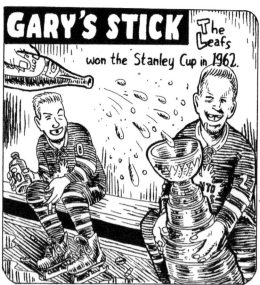

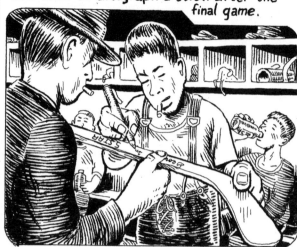

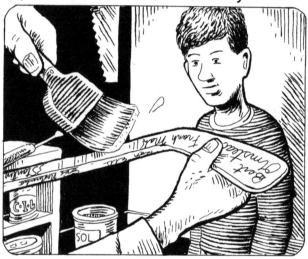

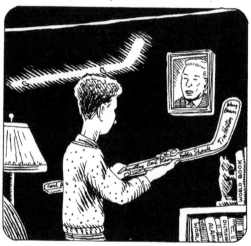

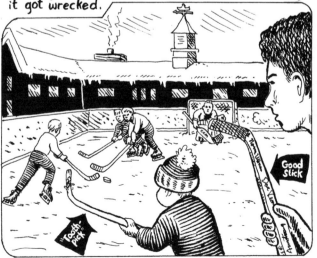

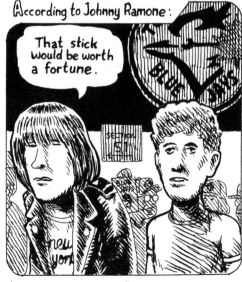

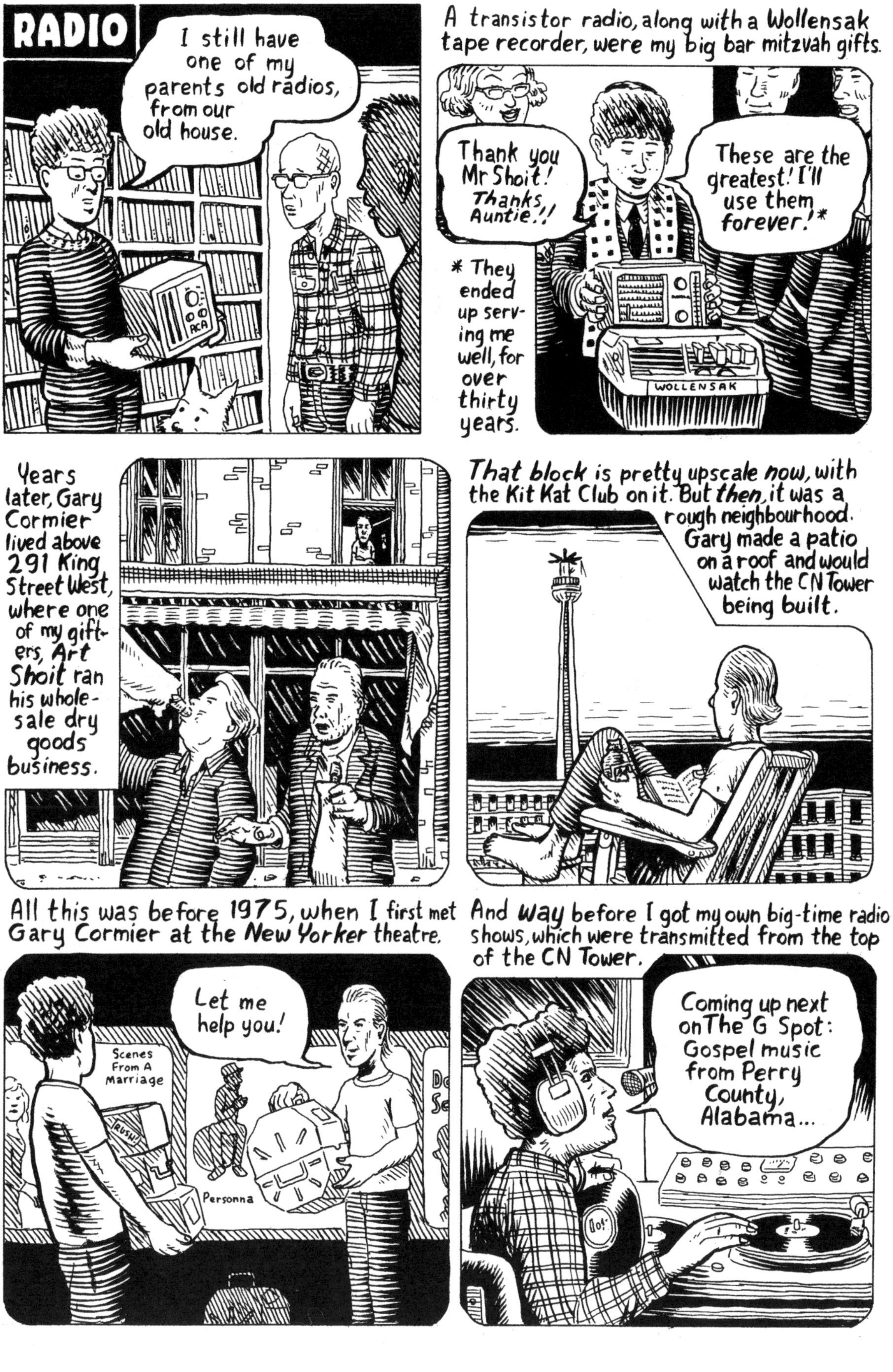
RADIO
I still have one of my parents old radios, from our old house.
RCA
A transistor radio, along with a Wollensak tape recorder, were my big bar mitzvah gifts.
Thank you Mr Shoit! Thanks, Auntie!!
These are the greatest! I'll use them *forever!**
* They ended up serving me well, for over thirty years.
WOLLENSAK
Years later, Gary Cormier lived above 291 King Street West, where one of my gifters, *Art Shoit* ran his wholesale dry goods business.
That block is pretty upscale *now*, with the Kit Kat Club on it. But *then*, it was a rough neighbourhood. Gary made a patio on a roof and would watch the CN Tower being built.
All this was before 1975, when I first met Gary Cormier at the *New Yorker* theatre.
Scenes From A Marriage
RUSH
Let me help you!
Personna
And *way* before I got my own big-time radio shows, which were transmitted from the top of the CN Tower.
Coming up next on The G Spot: Gospel music from Perry County, Alabama...

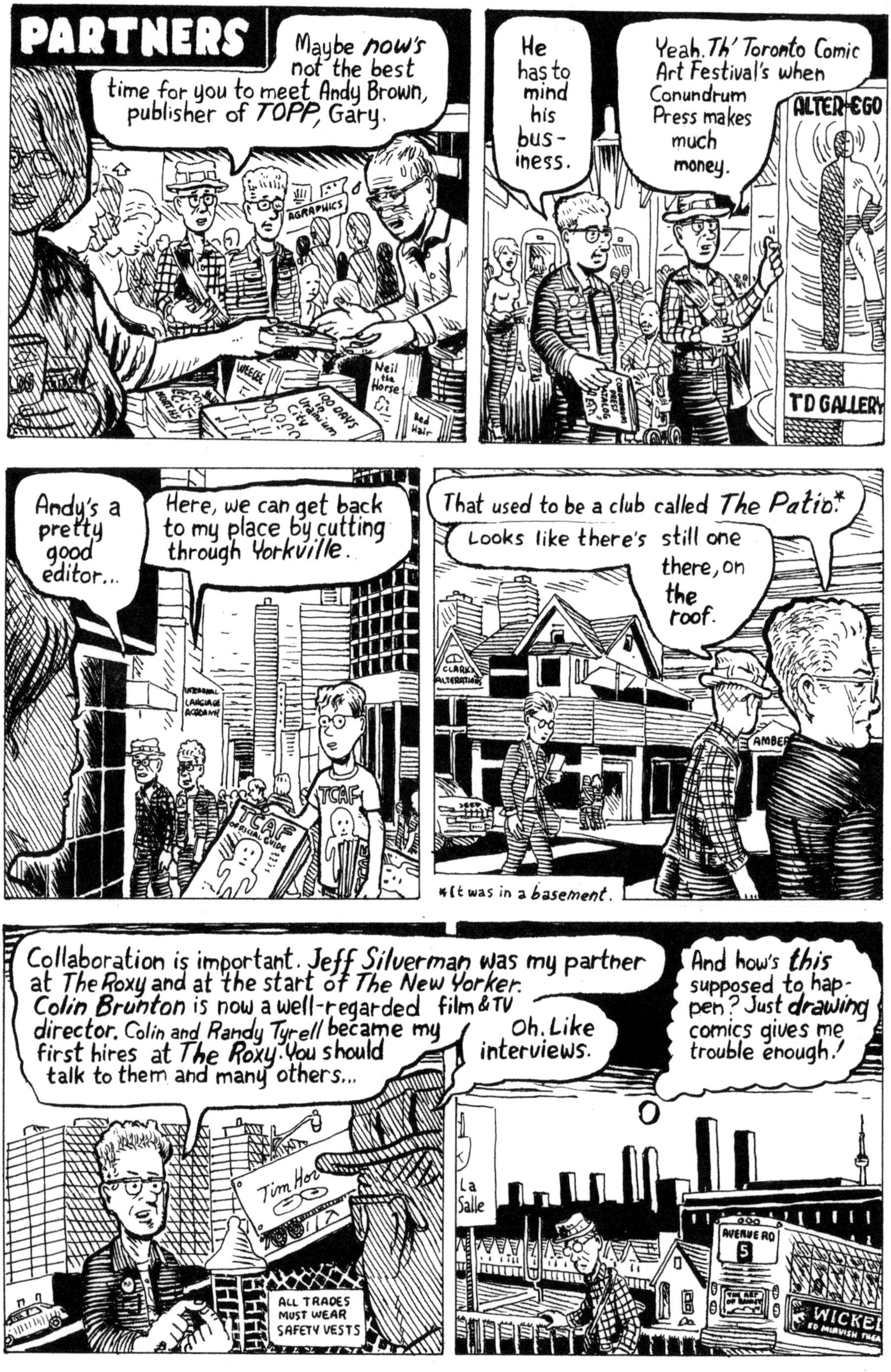
PARTNERS
Maybe now's not the best time for you to meet Andy Brown, publisher of TOPP, Gary.
AGRAPHICS
WEEGEE
Neil the Horse
100 DAYS in Uranium City
Red Hair
He has to mind his bus-iness.
Yeah. Th' Toronto Comic Art Festival's when Conundrum Press makes much money.
ALTER EGO
TD GALLERY
Andy's a pretty good editor...
Here, we can get back to my place by cutting through Yorkville.
TCAF
TCAF OFFICIAL GUIDE
That used to be a club called The Patio.*
Looks like there's still one there, on the roof.
CLARKS ALTERATIONS
AMBER
*It was in a basement.
Collaboration is important. Jeff Silverman was my partner at The Roxy and at the start of The New Yorker. Colin Brunton is now a well-regarded film & TV director. Colin and Randy Tyrell became my first hires at The Roxy. You should talk to them and many others...
Oh. Like interviews.
And how's this supposed to hap-pen? Just drawing comics gives me trouble enough!
Tim Hor
ALL TRADES MUST WEAR SAFETY VESTS
La Salle
AVENUE RD
5
WICKED
ED MIRVISH THEA

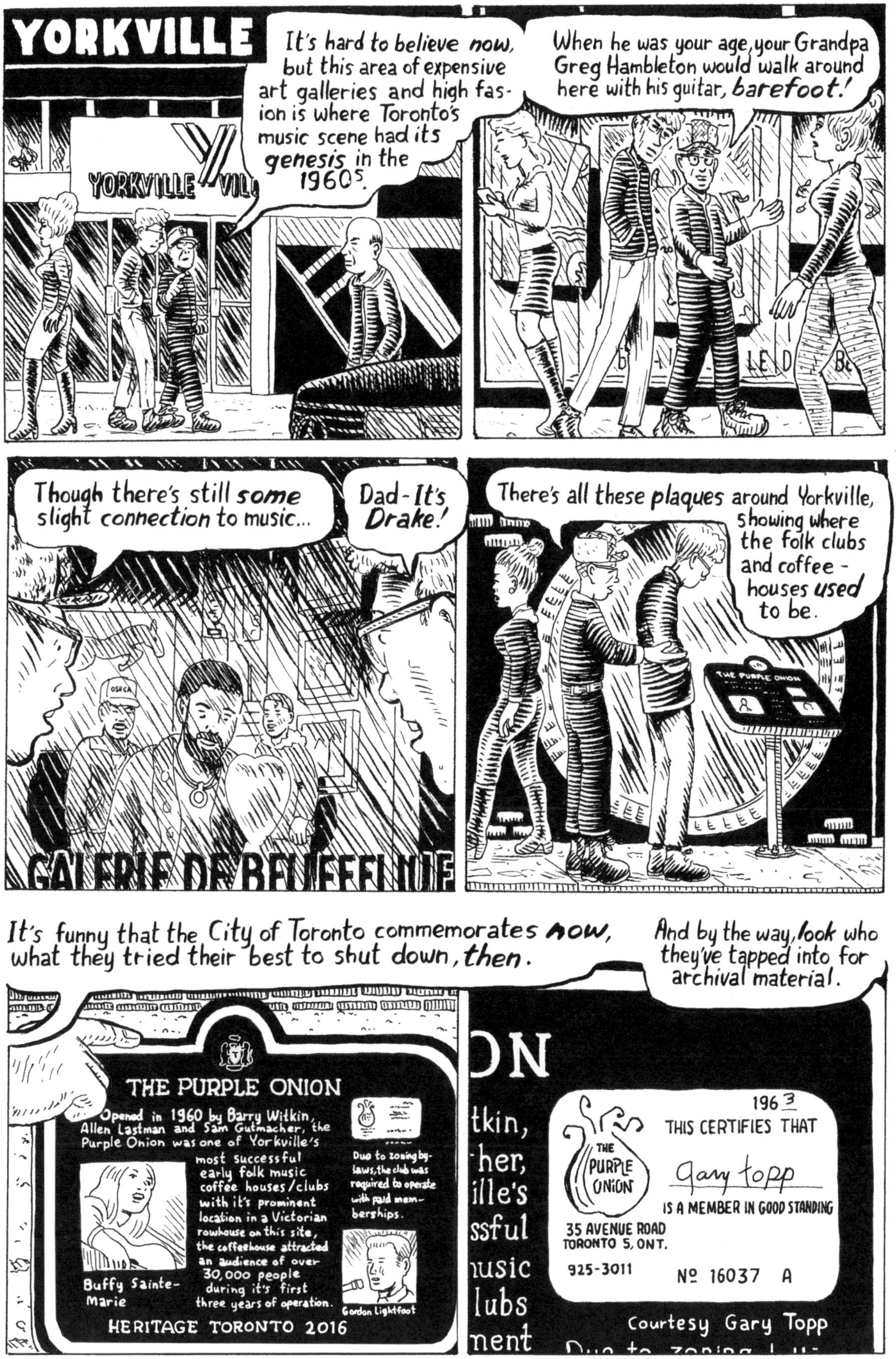
YORKVILLE
YORKVILLE VIL
It's hard to believe now, but this area of expensive art galleries and high fasion is where Toronto's music scene had its genesis in the 1960s.
When he was your age, your Grandpa Greg Hambleton would walk around here with his guitar, barefoot!
Though there's still some slight connection to music...
Dad- It's Drake!
OSHGA
There's all these plaques around Yorkville, showing where the folk clubs and coffee-houses used to be.
THE PURPLE ONION
It's funny that the City of Toronto commemorates now, what they tried their best to shut down, then.
And by the way, look who they've tapped into for archival material.
THE PURPLE ONION
Opened in 1960 by Barry Witkin, Allen Lastman and Sam Gutmacher, the Purple Onion was one of Yorkville's most successful early folk music coffee houses/clubs with it's prominent location in a Victorian rowhouse on this site, the coffeehouse attracted an audience of over 30,000 people during it's first three years of operation.
Buffy Sainte-Marie
Due to zoning by-laws, the club was required to operate with paid memberships.
Gordon Lightfoot
HERITAGE TORONTO 2016
ON
tkin,
-her,
ille's
ssful
nusic
lubs
nent
THE PURPLE ONION
1963
THIS CERTIFIES THAT
Gary Topp
IS A MEMBER IN GOOD STANDING
35 AVENUE ROAD
TORONTO 5, ONT.
925-3011
№ 16037 A
Courtesy Gary Topp

Coffee House News

Publish Your Views It Is Not A Right
It Is A Duty

Vol. 1, No. 1. Apr. 7, 62

Dupont
Macpherson
Pears
Avenue Rd
Yonge
St. George
Bedford
Bloor W.
Bloor E.
N
W
E
S
University
Bay
St. Nicholas
Church
Jarvis
Sherbourne
Wellesley
College
Grenville
Carlton
Hayter
Gerrard
Elizabeth
3½" = 1 mile Scale

Location of Coffee Houses + Clubs

1. Jack & Jill Coffee Bar
2. House of Hambourg Club
3. Fifth Peg Club
4. Voltaire Coffee House
5. Bohemian Embassy Club
6. Ist. Floor Club
7. Chanel Studio Coffee House
8. Purple Onion Club
9. Half Beat Coffee House
10. 71 Yorkville Coffee House
11. Cave Club
12. Cellar Club
13. Village Corner Club
14. Gate of Cleve Club

The Cellar WA 4-9082

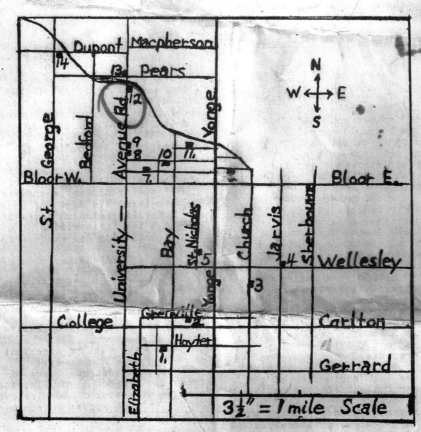

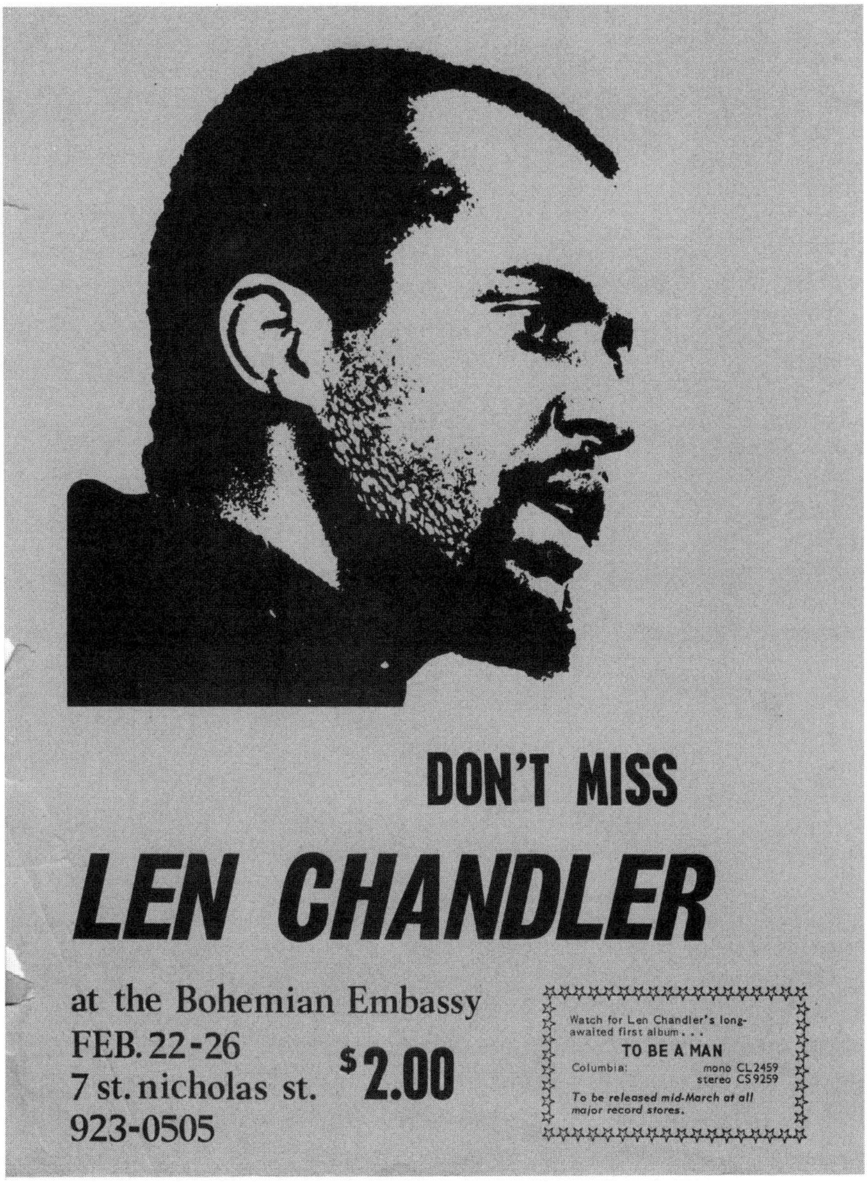
DON'T MISS
LEN CHANDLER
at the Bohemian Embassy
FEB. 22-26
7 st. nicholas st.
923-0505
$2.00
Watch for Len Chandler's long-awaited first album . . .
TO BE A MAN
Columbia: mono CL2459
stereo CS9259
To be released mid-March at all major record stores.

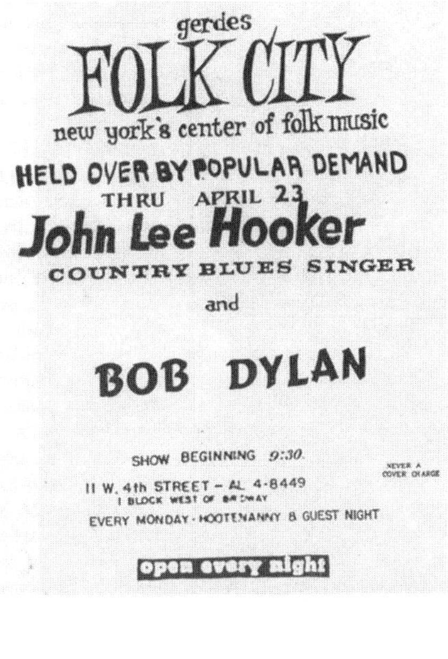
gerdes
FOLK CITY
new york's center of folk music
HELD OVER BY POPULAR DEMAND
THRU APRIL 23
John Lee Hooker
COUNTRY BLUES SINGER
and
BOB DYLAN
SHOW BEGINNING 9:30.
NEVER A COVER CHARGE
11 W. 4th STREET – AL 4-8449
EVERY MONDAY - HOOTENANNY & GUEST NIGHT
open every night

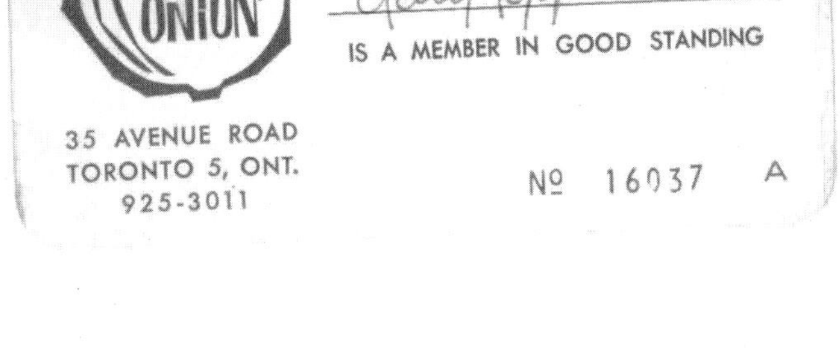
1963
THE PURPLE ONION
THIS CERTIFIES THAT
gary topp
IS A MEMBER IN GOOD STANDING
35 AVENUE ROAD
TORONTO 5, ONT.
925-3011
No 16037 A

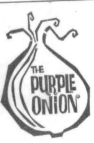

FIRST JOB

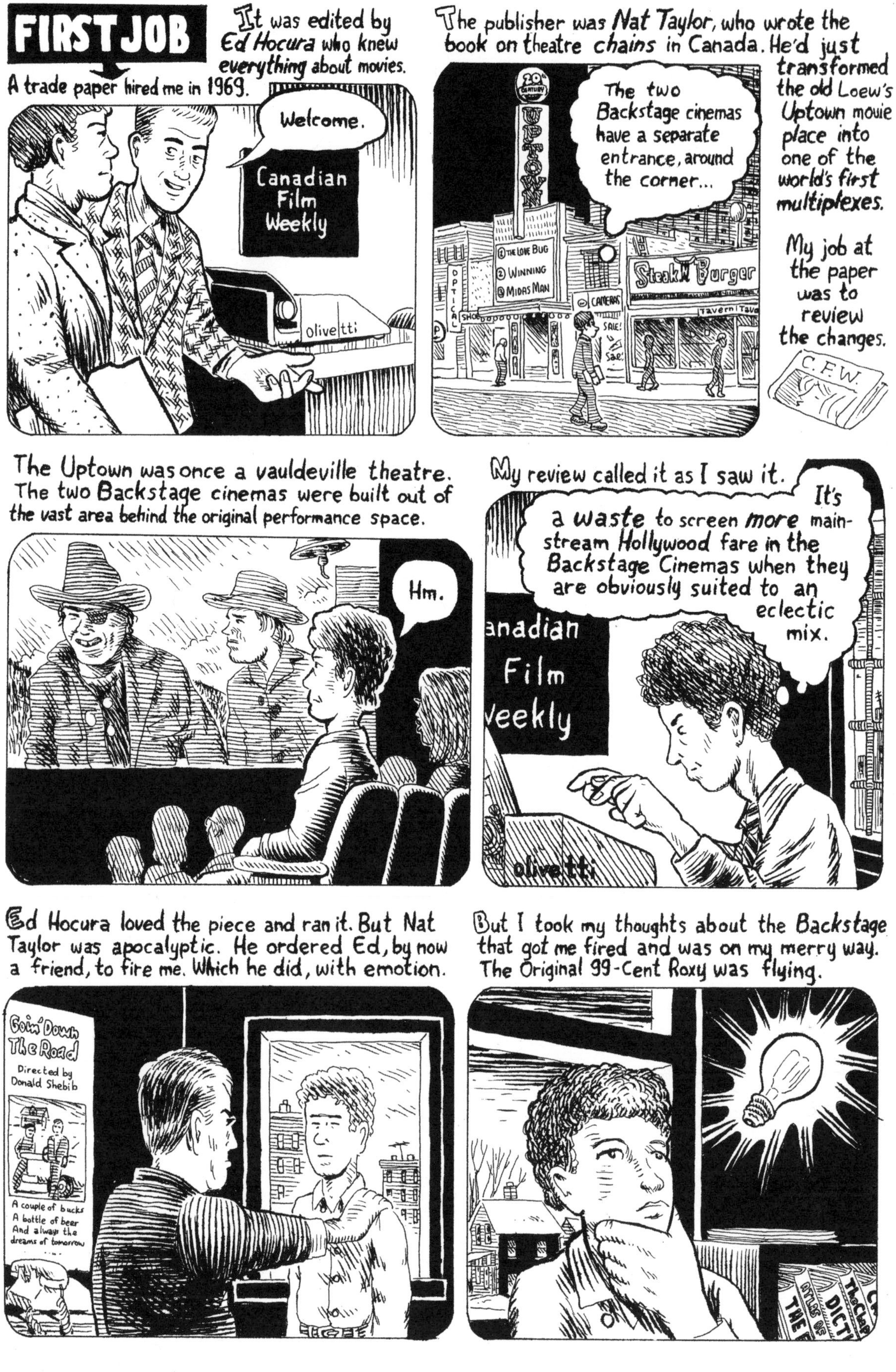
A trade paper hired me in 1969.
It was edited by Ed Hocura who knew everything about movies.
Welcome.
Canadian Film Weekly
olivetti
The publisher was Nat Taylor, who wrote the book on theatre chains in Canada. He'd just transformed the old Loew's Uptown movie place into one of the world's first multiplexes.
The two Backstage cinemas have a separate entrance, around the corner...
UPTOWN
1 THE LOVE BUG
2 WINNING
3 MIDAS MAN
OPTICAL
CAMERAS
Steak n Burger
My job at the paper was to review the changes.
C.F.W.
The Uptown was once a vauldeville theatre. The two Backstage cinemas were built out of the vast area behind the original performance space.
Hm.
My review called it as I saw it.
It's a waste to screen more mainstream Hollywood fare in the Backstage Cinemas when they are obviously suited to an eclectic mix.
anadian Film eekly
olivetti
Ed Hocura loved the piece and ran it. But Nat Taylor was apocalyptic. He ordered Ed, by now a friend, to fire me. Which he did, with emotion.
Goin' Down The Road
Directed by Donald Shebib
A couple of bucks
A bottle of beer
And always the dreams of tomorrow
But I took my thoughts about the Backstage that got me fired and was on my merry way. The Original 99-Cent Roxy was flying.

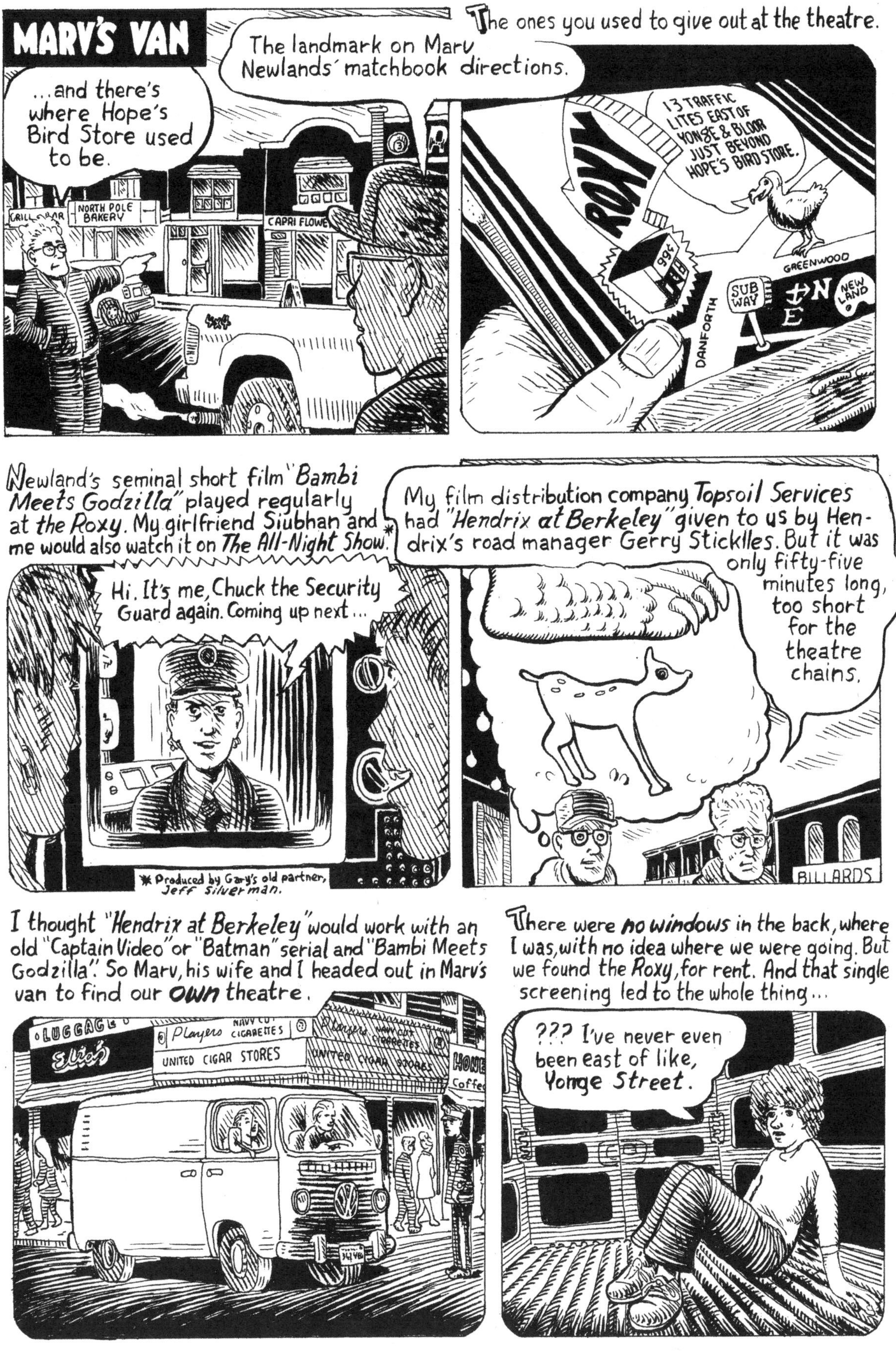
MARV'S VAN
...and there's where Hope's Bird Store used to be.
The landmark on Marv Newlands' matchbook directions.
GRILL BAR
NORTH POLE BAKERY
CAPRI FLOWE
The ones you used to give out at the theatre.
ROXY
13 TRAFFIC LITES EAST OF YONGE & BLOOR JUST BEYOND HOPE'S BIRD STORE.
GREENWOOD
SUB WAY
DANFORTH
NEW LAND
Newland's seminal short film "Bambi Meets Godzilla" played regularly at the Roxy. My girlfriend Siubhan and me would also watch it on The All-Night Show.*
Hi. It's me, Chuck the Security Guard again. Coming up next...
* Produced by Gary's old partner, Jeff Silverman.
My film distribution company Topsoil Services had "Hendrix at Berkeley" given to us by Hendrix's road manager Gerry Sticklles. But it was only fifty-five minutes long, too short for the theatre chains.
BILLARDS
I thought "Hendrix at Berkeley" would work with an old "Captain Video" or "Batman" serial and "Bambi Meets Godzilla". So Marv, his wife and I headed out in Marv's van to find our OWN theatre.
LUGGAGE
Elie's
Players NAVY CUT CIGARETTES
UNITED CIGAR STORES
HONE Coffee
There were no windows in the back, where I was, with no idea where we were going. But we found the Roxy, for rent. And that single screening led to the whole thing...
??? I've never even been east of like, Yonge Street.

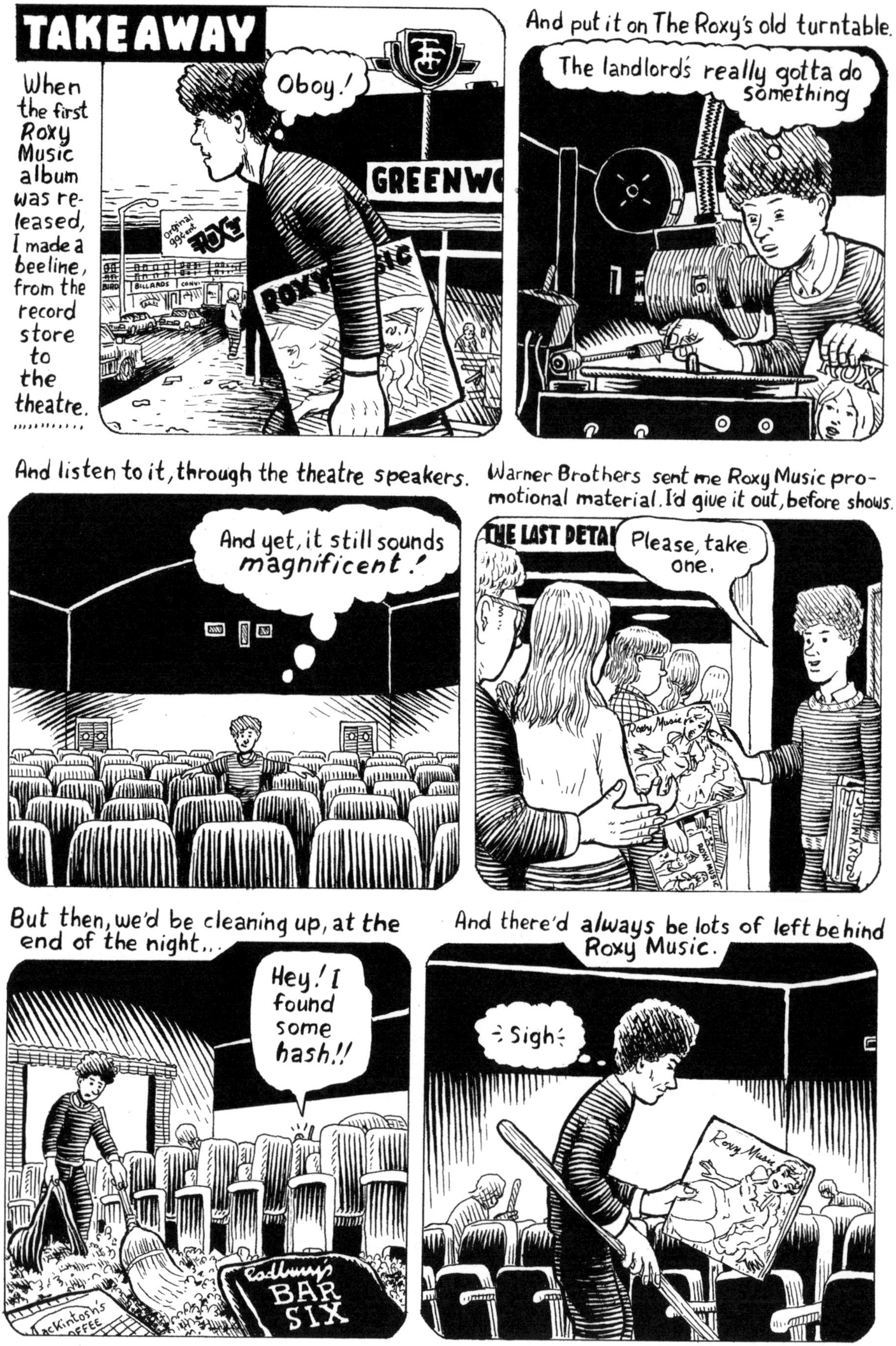
TAKE AWAY
When the first Roxy Music album was released, I made a beeline, from the record store to the theatre. ....
Oboy!
original 99¢ ent ROXY
BILLARDS
GREENWO
And put it on The Roxy's old turntable.
The landlord's really gotta do something
And listen to it, through the theatre speakers.
And yet, it still sounds *magnificent*!
Warner Brothers sent me Roxy Music promotional material. I'd give it out, before shows.
THE LAST DETAI
Please, take one.
Roxy Music
But then, we'd be cleaning up, at the end of the night...
Hey! I found some *hash*!!
Cadbury's BAR SIX
And there'd always be lots of left behind Roxy Music.
Sigh
Roxy Music

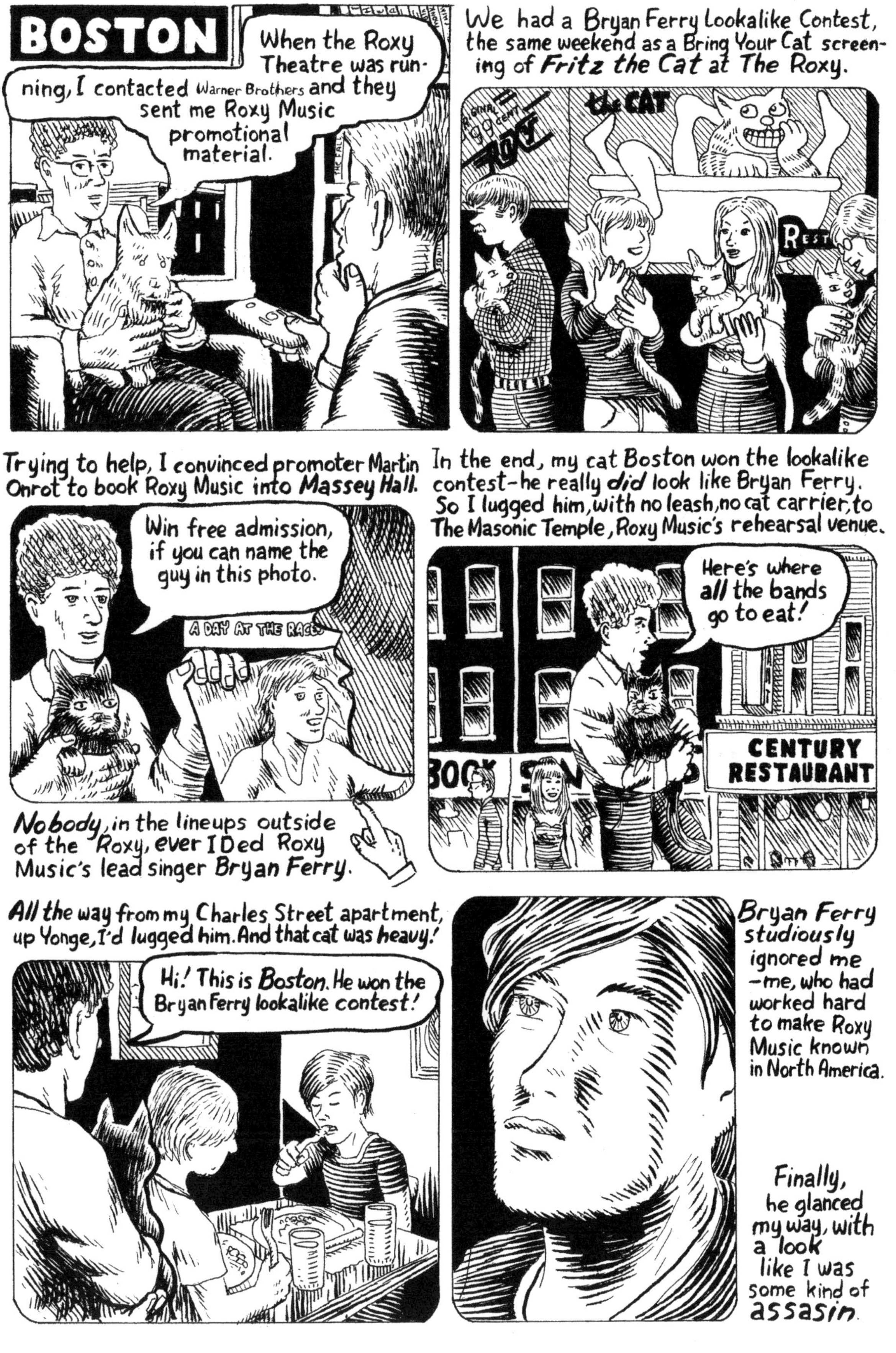

BOSTON
When the Roxy Theatre was running, I contacted Warner Brothers and they sent me Roxy Music promotional material.
We had a Bryan Ferry Lookalike Contest, the same weekend as a Bring Your Cat screening of *Fritz the Cat* at The Roxy.
the CAT
Trying to help, I convinced promoter Martin Onrot to book Roxy Music into *Massey Hall*.
Win free admission, if you can name the guy in this photo.
A DAY AT THE RACES
Nobody, in the lineups outside of the Roxy, ever IDed Roxy Music's lead singer *Bryan Ferry*.
In the end, my cat Boston won the lookalike contest-he really *did* look like Bryan Ferry. So I lugged him, with no leash, no cat carrier, to The Masonic Temple, Roxy Music's rehearsal venue.
Here's where *all* the bands go to eat!
CENTURY RESTAURANT
All the way from my Charles Street apartment, up Yonge, I'd lugged him. And that cat was *heavy*!
Hi! This is *Boston*. He won the Bryan Ferry lookalike contest!
Bryan Ferry studiously ignored me —me, who had worked hard to make Roxy Music known in North America.
Finally, he glanced my way, with a look like I was some kind of assasin.

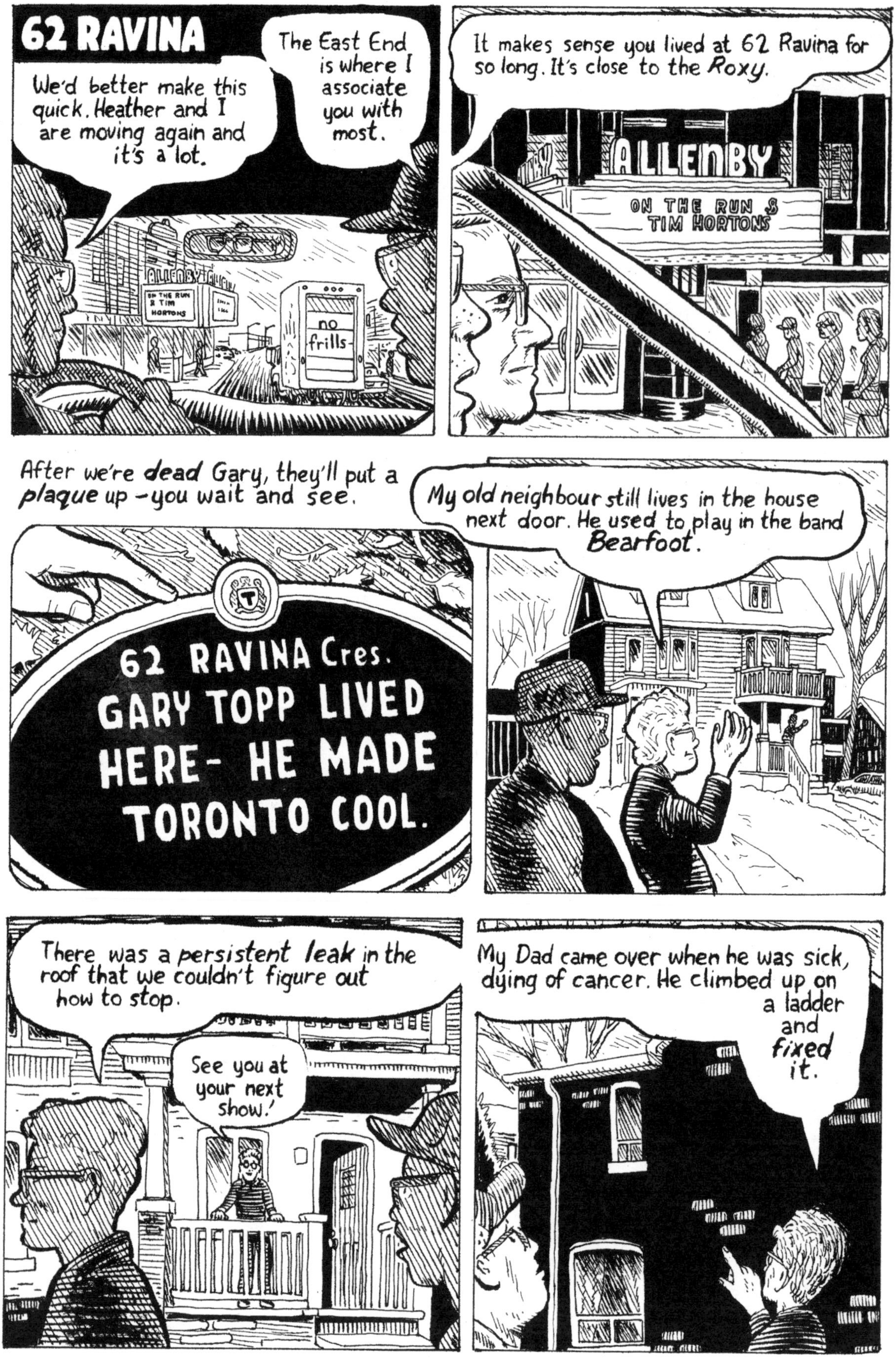
62 RAVINA
We'd better make this quick. Heather and I are moving again and it's a lot.
The East End is where I associate you with most.
ALLENBY
ON THE RUN & TIM HORTONS
no frills
It makes sense you lived at 62 Ravina for so long. It's close to the Roxy.
ALLENBY
ON THE RUN & TIM HORTONS
After we're dead Gary, they'll put a plaque up - you wait and see.
62 RAVINA Cres.
GARY TOPP LIVED HERE- HE MADE TORONTO COOL.
My old neighbour still lives in the house next door. He used to play in the band Bearfoot.
There was a persistent leak in the roof that we couldn't figure out how to stop.
See you at your next show!
My Dad came over when he was sick, dying of cancer. He climbed up on a ladder and fixed it.

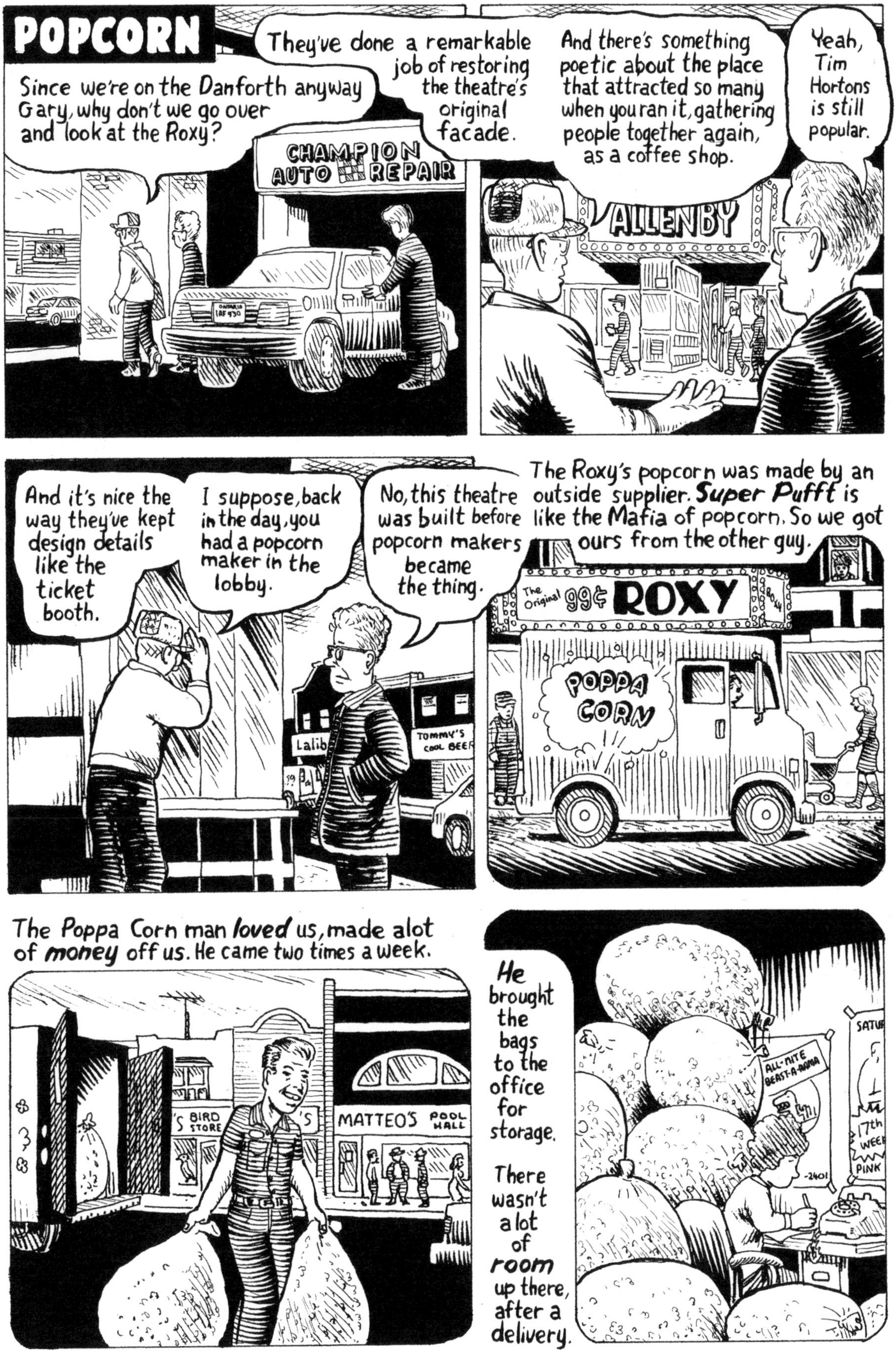
POPCORN
Since we're on the Danforth anyway Gary, why don't we go over and look at the Roxy?
They've done a remarkable job of restoring the theatre's original facade.
CHAMPION AUTO REPAIR
And there's something poetic about the place that attracted so many when you ran it, gathering people together again, as a coffee shop.
Yeah, Tim Hortons is still popular.
ALLENBY
And it's nice the way they've kept design details like the ticket booth.
I suppose, back in the day, you had a popcorn maker in the lobby.
No, this theatre was built before popcorn makers became the thing.
TOMMY'S COOL BEER
The Roxy's popcorn was made by an outside supplier. Super Pufft is like the Mafia of popcorn. So we got ours from the other guy.
The Original 99¢ ROXY
POPPA CORN
The Poppa Corn man loved us, made alot of money off us. He came two times a week.
BIRD STORE
MATTEO'S POOL HALL
He brought the bags to the office for storage.
There wasn't a lot of room up there, after a delivery.
ALL-NITE BEAST-A-RAMA
17th WEEK
PINK

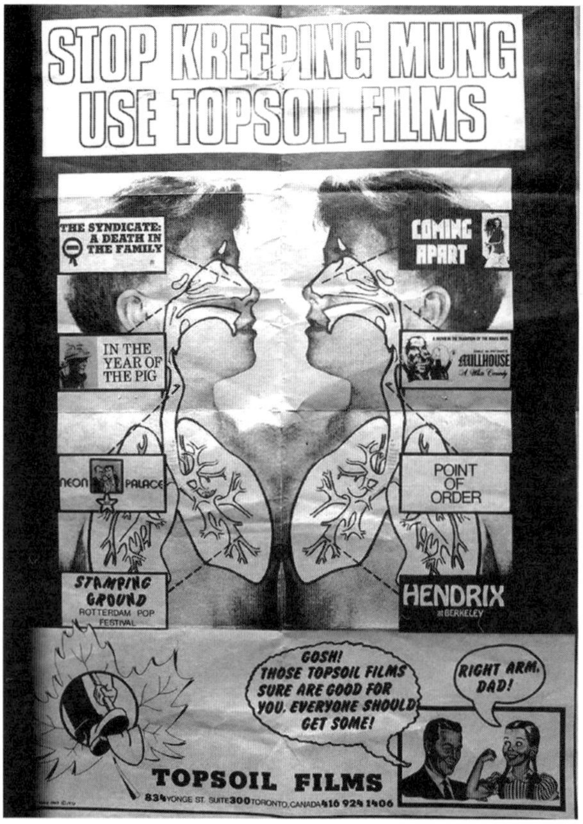
STOP KREEPING MUNG
USE TOPSOIL FILMS
THE SYNDICATE: A DEATH IN THE FAMILY
COMING APART
IN THE YEAR OF THE PIG
MILLHOUSE
NEON PALACE
POINT OF ORDER
STAMPING GROUND
ROTTERDAM POP FESTIVAL
HENDRIX
AT BERKELEY
GOSH! THOSE TOPSOIL FILMS SURE ARE GOOD FOR YOU. EVERYONE SHOULD GET SOME!
RIGHT ARM, DAD!
TOPSOIL FILMS
834 YONGE ST. SUITE 300 TORONTO, CANADA 416 924 1406

Marv Newland

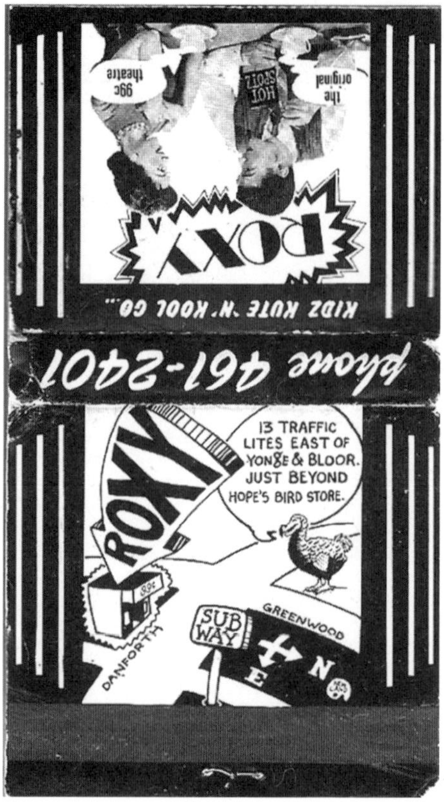
KIDZ KUTE 'N' KOOL CO.
phone 461-2401
ROXY
13 TRAFFIC LITES EAST OF YONGE & BLOOR. JUST BEYOND HOPE'S BIRD STORE.
SUBWAY
GREENWOOD
DANFORTH

Marv Newland

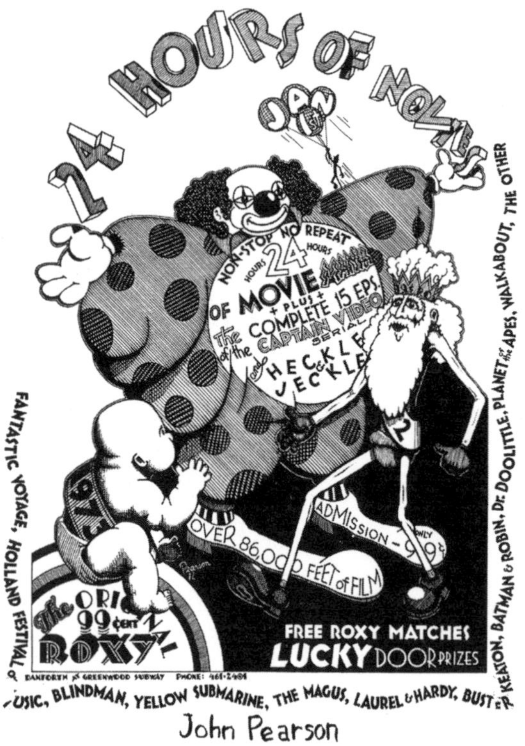
24 HOURS OF MOVIES
NON-STOP NO REPEAT
24 HOURS
OF MOVIE
+ PLUS +
THE COMPLETE 15 EPS. OF THE CAPTAIN VIDEO SERIAL
AND HECKLE & JECKLE
OVER 86,000 FEET of FILM
ADMISSION ONLY 99¢
The ORIGINAL 99¢ ROXY
FREE ROXY MATCHES
LUCKY DOOR PRIZES
DANFORTH AT GREENWOOD SUBWAY PHONE: 461-2401
FANTASTIC VOYAGE, HOLLAND FESTIVAL OF MUSIC, BLINDMAN, YELLOW SUBMARINE, THE MAGUS, LAUREL & HARDY, BUSTER KEATON, BATMAN & ROBIN, Dr. DOOLITTLE, PLANET OF THE APES, WALKABOUT, THE OTHER

John Pearson

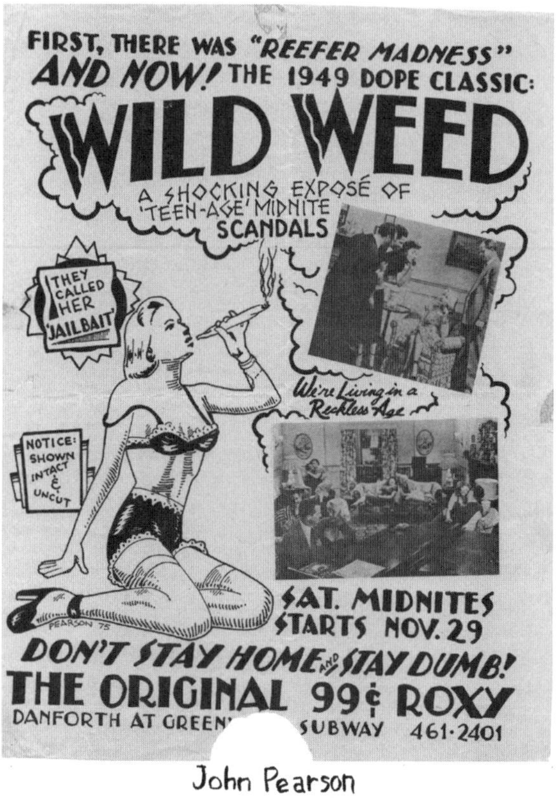
FIRST, THERE WAS "REEFER MADNESS"
AND NOW! THE 1949 DOPE CLASSIC:
WILD WEED
A SHOCKING EXPOSÉ OF TEEN-AGE MIDNITE SCANDALS
THEY CALLED HER 'JAILBAIT'
We're Living in a Reckless Age
NOTICE: SHOWN INTACT & UNCUT
PEARSON 75
SAT. MIDNITES
STARTS NOV. 29
DON'T STAY HOME AND STAY DUMB!
THE ORIGINAL 99¢ ROXY
DANFORTH AT GREEN SUBWAY 461-2401

John Pearson

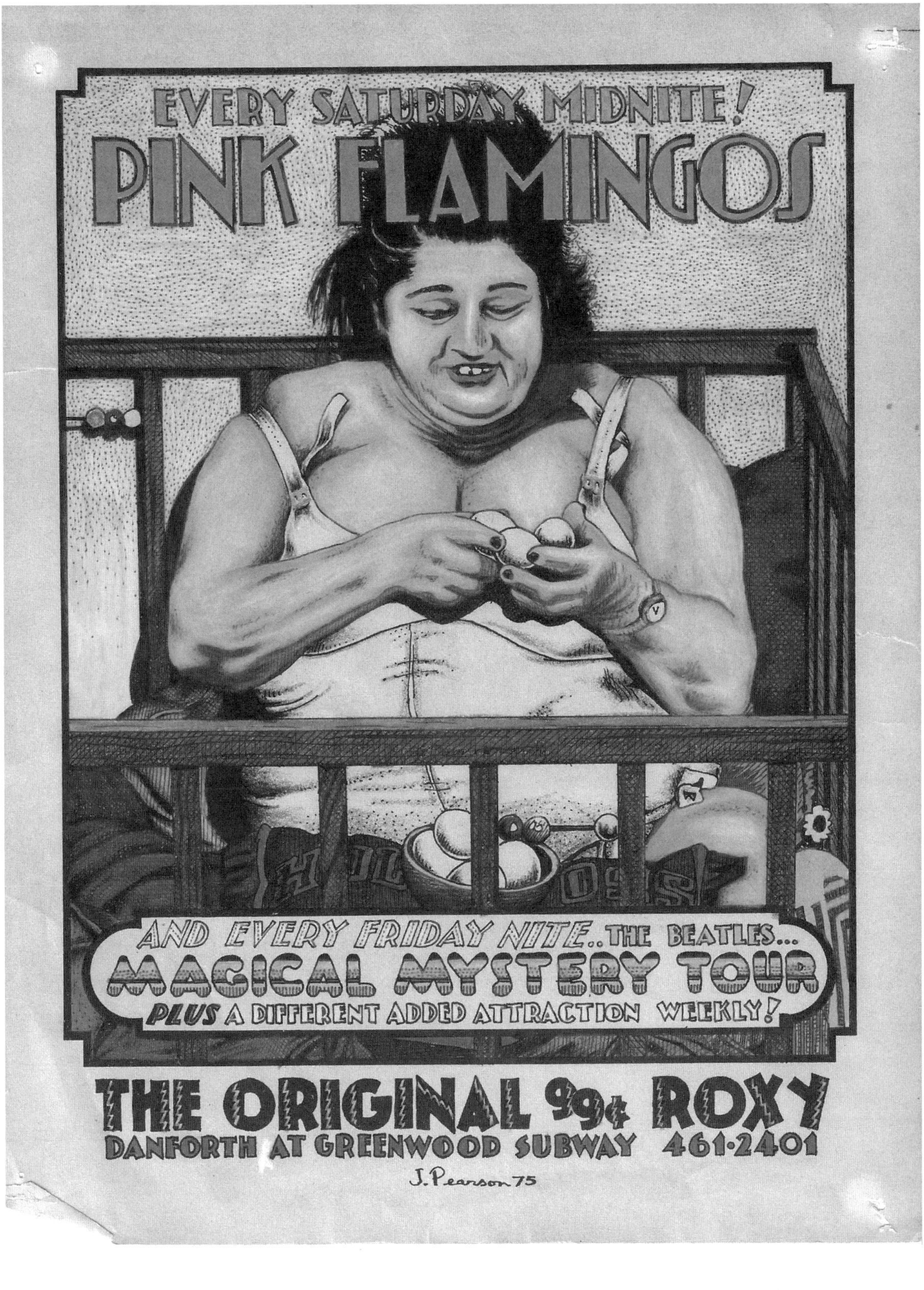
EVERY SATURDAY MIDNITE!
PINK FLAMINGOS
AND EVERY FRIDAY NITE.. THE BEATLES...
MAGICAL MYSTERY TOUR
PLUS A DIFFERENT ADDED ATTRACTION WEEKLY!
THE ORIGINAL 99¢ ROXY
DANFORTH AT GREENWOOD SUBWAY 461·2401
J. Pearson 75

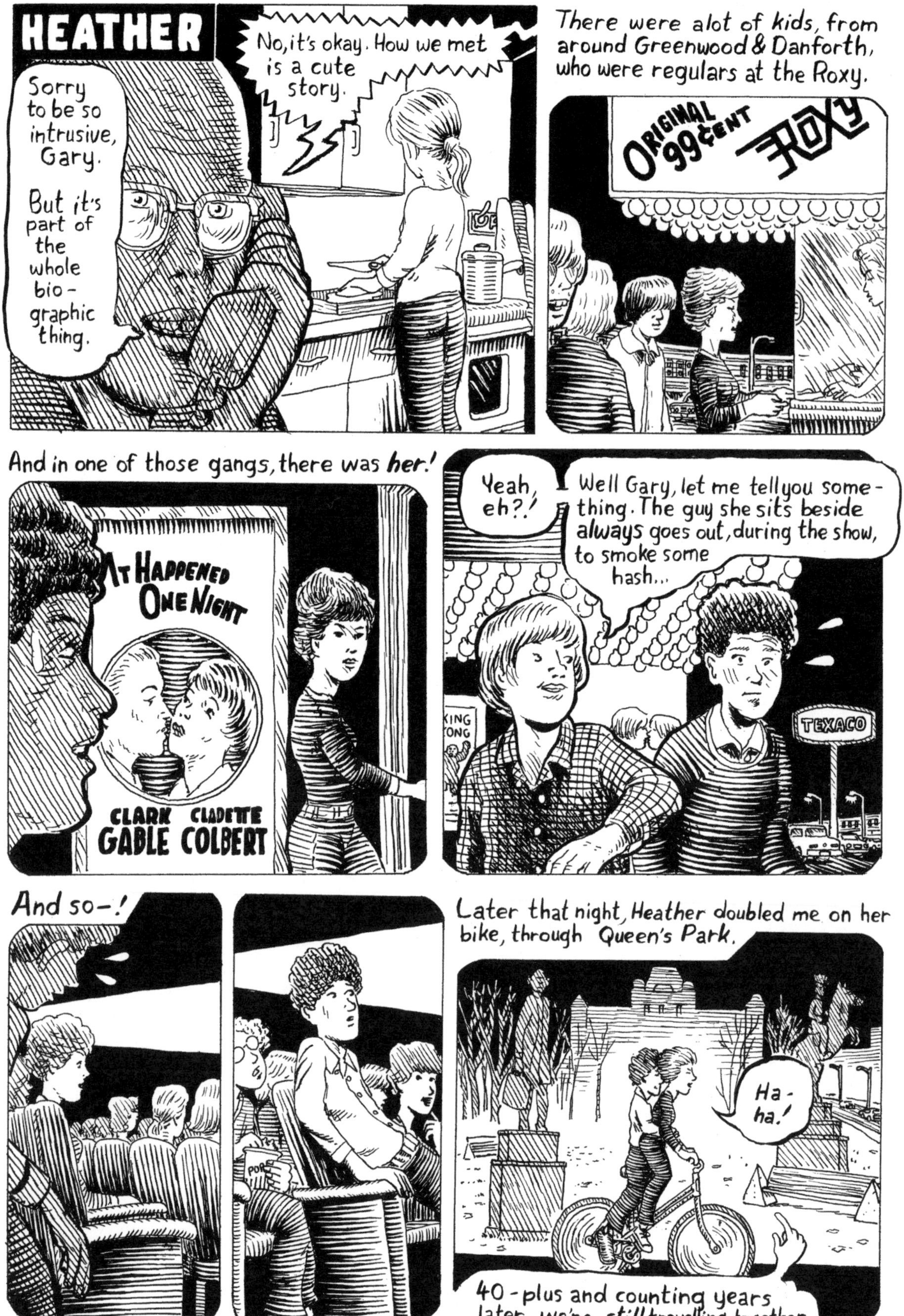
HEATHER
Sorry to be so intrusive, Gary.
But it's part of the whole bio-graphic thing.
No, it's okay. How we met is a cute story.
There were alot of kids, from around Greenwood & Danforth, who were regulars at the Roxy.
ORIGINAL 99¢ENT ROXY
And in one of those gangs, there was *her*!
IT HAPPENED ONE NIGHT
CLARK GABLE CLADETTE COLBERT
Yeah, eh?!
Well Gary, let me tell you some-thing. The guy she sits beside *always* goes out, during the show, to smoke some hash...
KING KONG
TEXACO
And so–!
Later that night, Heather doubled me on her bike, through Queen's Park.
Ha-ha!
40-plus and counting years later, we're *still* travelling together.

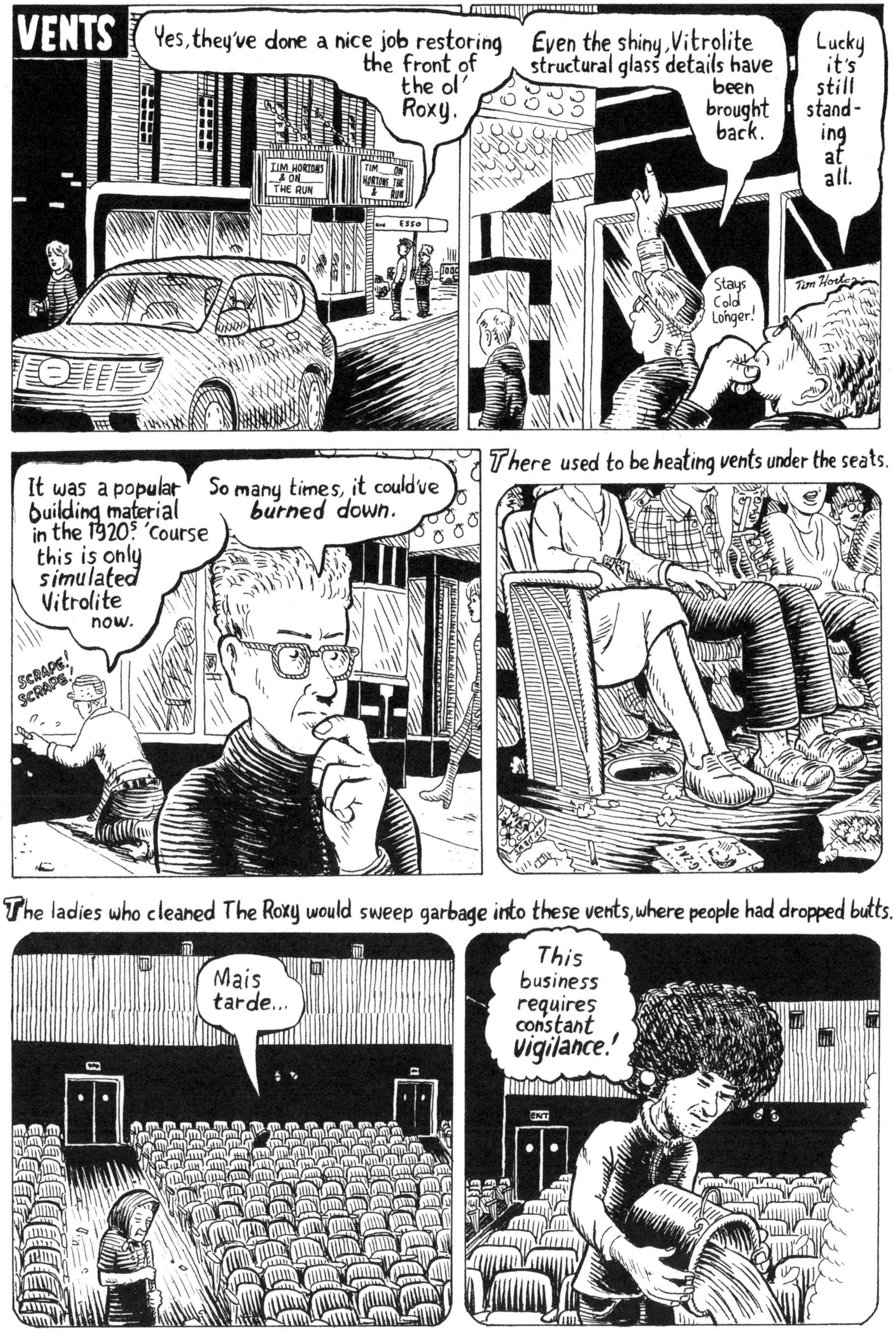
VENTS
Yes, they've done a nice job restoring the front of the ol' Roxy.
TIM HORTONS & ON THE RUN
TIM ON HORTONS THE & RUN
ESSO
Even the shiny, Vitrolite structural glass details have been brought back.
Lucky it's still standing at all.
Stays Cold Longer!
Tim Horto
It was a popular building material in the 1920s. 'Course this is only simulated Vitrolite now.
So many times, it could've burned down.
SCRAPE! SCRAPE!
There used to be heating vents under the seats.
The ladies who cleaned The Roxy would sweep garbage into these vents, where people had dropped butts.
Mais tarde...
This business requires constant vigilance!
EXIT

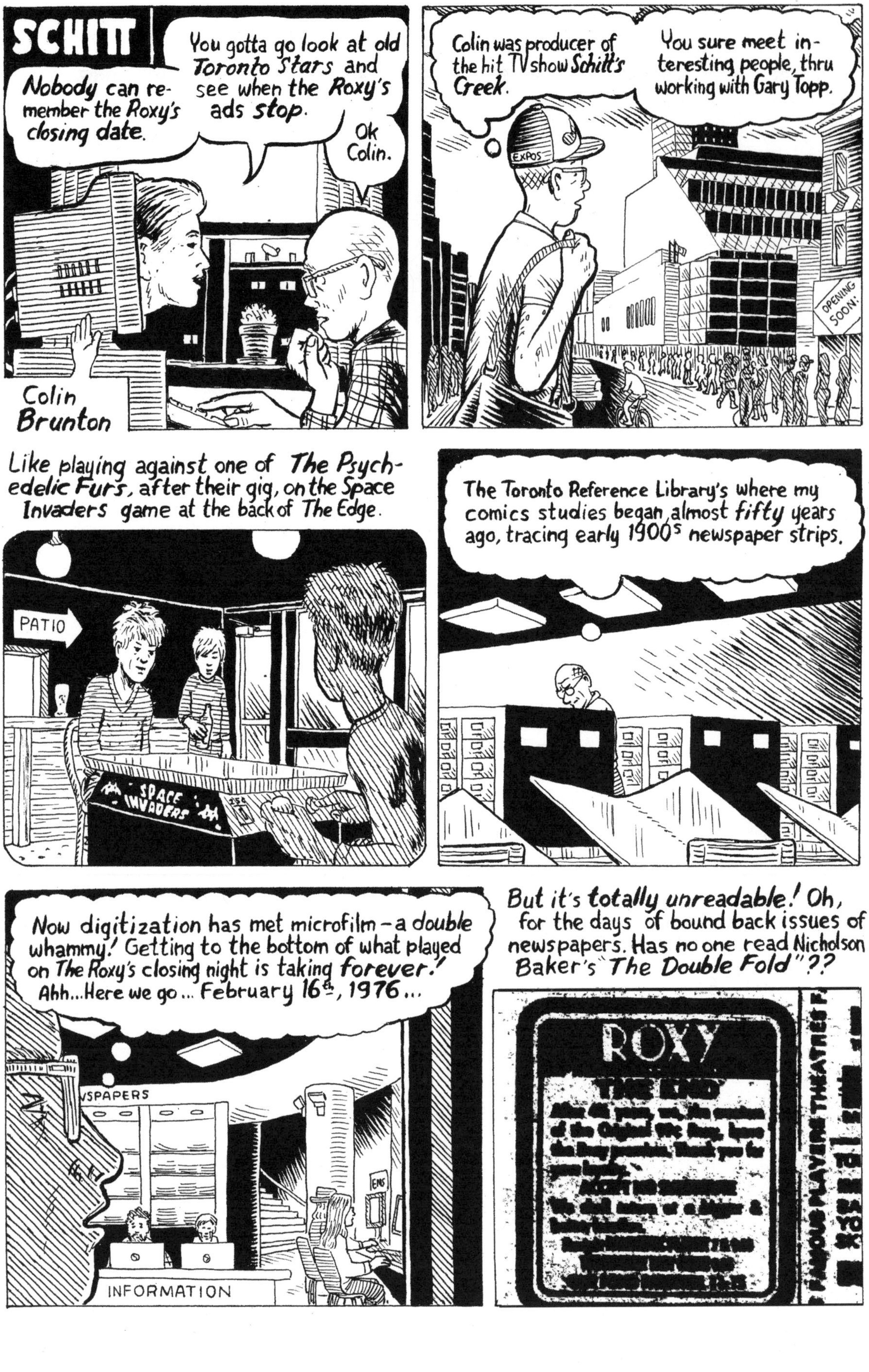
SCHITT
Nobody can remember the Roxy's closing date.
You gotta go look at old Toronto Stars and see when the Roxy's ads stop.
Ok Colin.
Colin Brunton
Colin was producer of the hit TV show Schitt's Creek.
You sure meet interesting people, thru working with Gary Topp.
EXPOS
OPENING SOON:
Like playing against one of The Psychedelic Furs, after their gig, on the Space Invaders game at the back of The Edge.
PATIO
SPACE INVADERS
25¢
The Toronto Reference Library's where my comics studies began, almost fifty years ago, tracing early 1900s newspaper strips.
Now digitization has met microfilm – a double whammy! Getting to the bottom of what played on The Roxy's closing night is taking forever! Ahh... Here we go... February 16th, 1976...
WSPAPERS
INFORMATION
But it's totally unreadable! Oh, for the days of bound back issues of newspapers. Has no one read Nicholson Baker's "The Double Fold"??
ROXY
THE END
FAMOUS PLAYERS THEATRES

The Original 99¢ Roxy Theatre's Closing Night

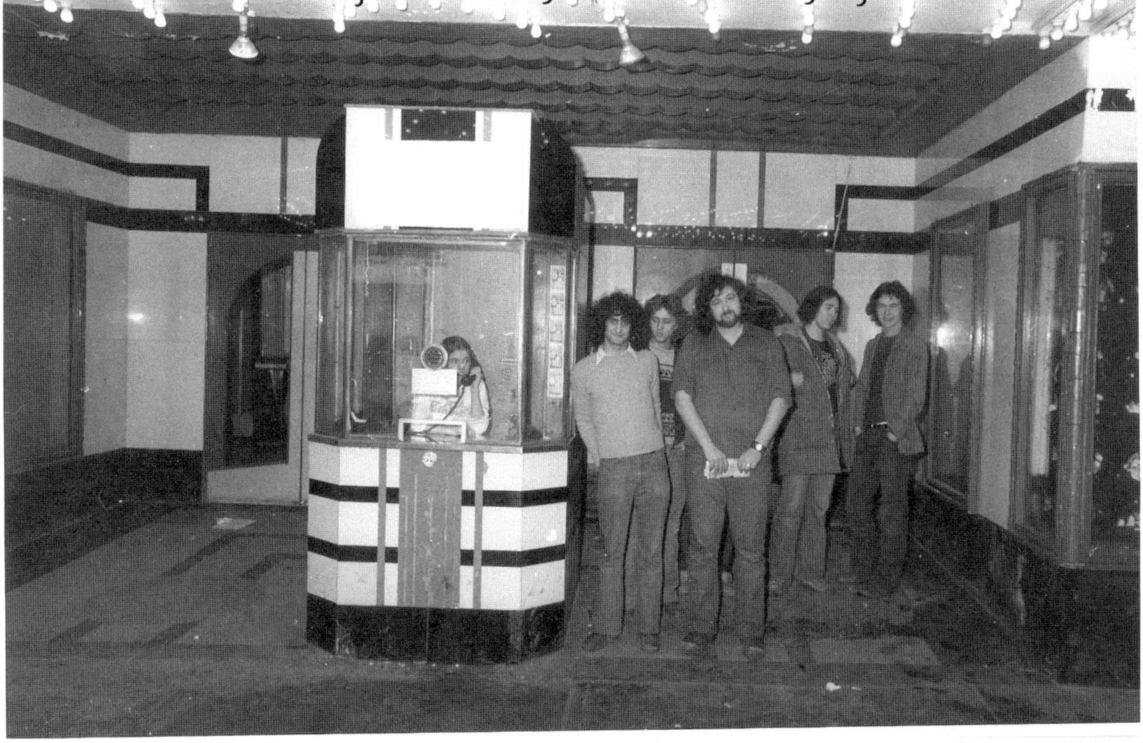

Heather Atwood, Gary Topp, Randy Tyrrell, Jeff Silverman, Leslie Mitchell, Colin Brunton

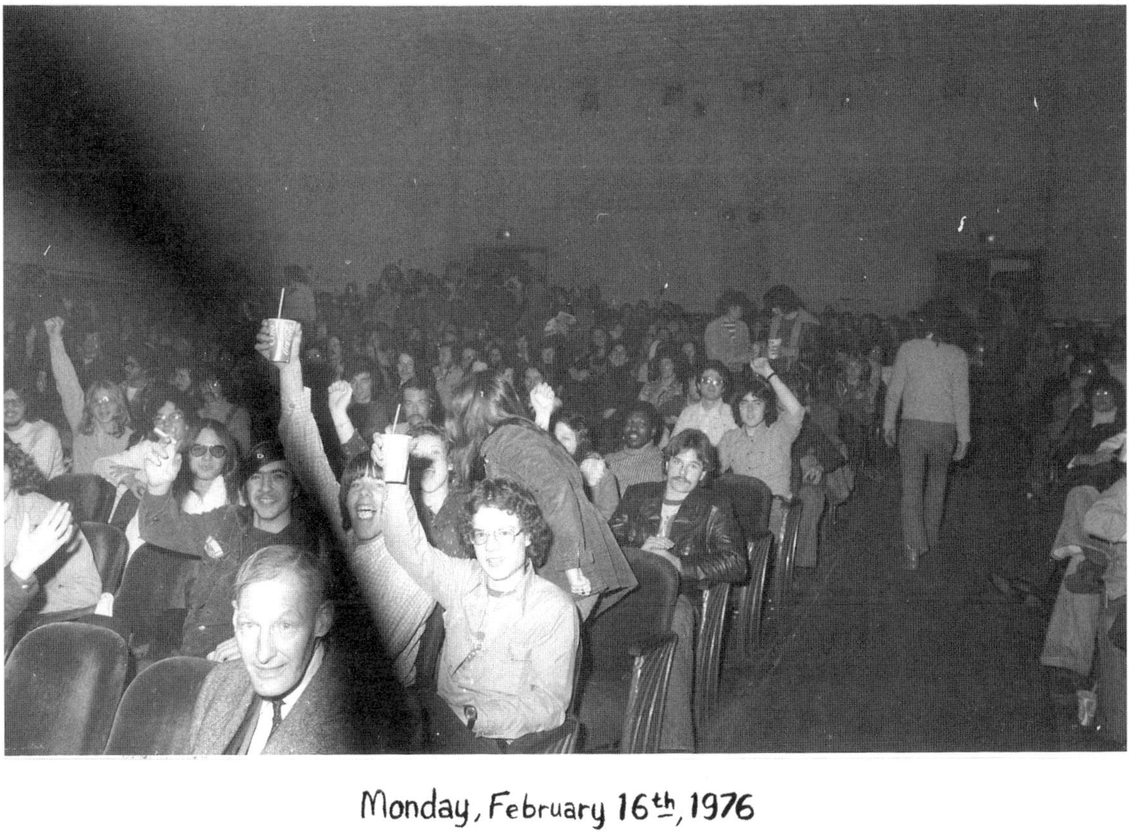

Monday, February 16th, 1976

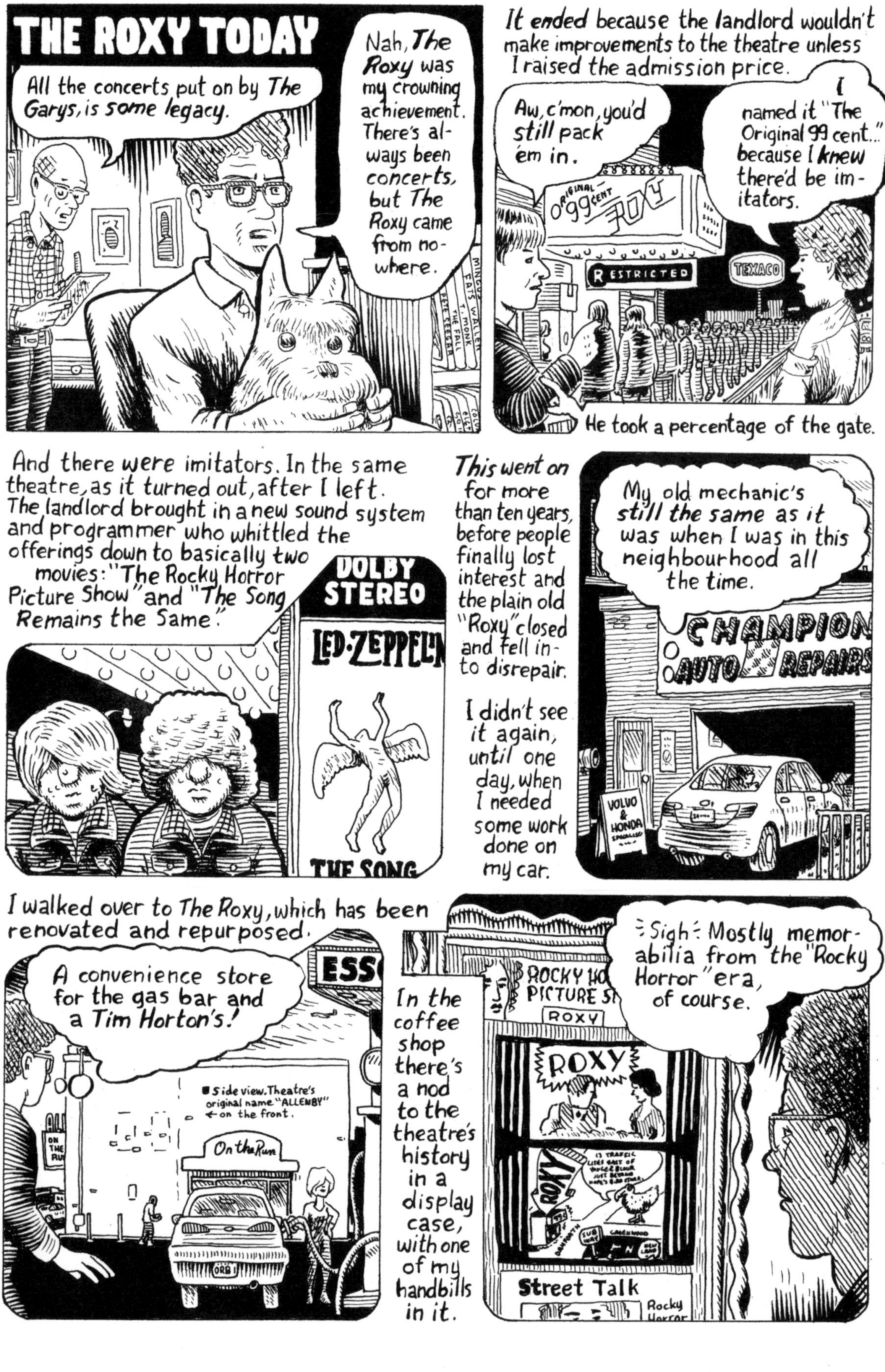

THE ROXY TODAY
All the concerts put on by The Garys, is some legacy.
Nah, The Roxy was my crowning achievement. There's always been concerts, but The Roxy came from nowhere.
MINGUS
FATS WALLER
T. MONK
THE FALL
PETE SEEGER
It ended because the landlord wouldn't make improvements to the theatre unless I raised the admission price.
Aw, c'mon, you'd still pack 'em in.
I named it "The Original 99 cent..." because I knew there'd be imitators.
ORIGINAL 99 CENT ROXY
RESTRICTED
TEXACO
He took a percentage of the gate.
And there were imitators. In the same theatre, as it turned out, after I left. The landlord brought in a new sound system and programmer who whittled the offerings down to basically two movies: "The Rocky Horror Picture Show" and "The Song Remains the Same."
DOLBY STEREO
LED·ZEPPELIN
THE SONG
This went on for more than ten years, before people finally lost interest and the plain old "Roxy" closed and fell into disrepair.
I didn't see it again, until one day, when I needed some work done on my car.
My old mechanic's still the same as it was when I was in this neighbourhood all the time.
CHAMPION AUTO REPAIRS
VOLVO & HONDA
I walked over to The Roxy, which has been renovated and repurposed.
A convenience store for the gas bar and a Tim Horton's!
ESS
Side view. Theatre's original name "ALLENBY" ← on the front.
On the Run
In the coffee shop there's a nod to the theatre's history in a display case, with one of my handbills in it.
Sigh Mostly memorabilia from the "Rocky Horror" era, of course.
ROCKY HO
PICTURE S
ROXY
ROXY
ROXY
Street Talk
Rocky Horror

SMASH

"Everything comes back to Collier," Nick Smash, publisher of the zine *Smash It Up*, once said.

Collier St

Nick and his brother *Simon White* grew up on *Collier Street*, a few doors down from your Mom's *Hambleton* side of the family—some coincidence, huh?

©ut of all your talented relatives who came out of Collier Street, it was *Fergus Hambleton* who got deepest into *The Garys'* music scene. His band *The Sattalites*, played The Edge many times.

Nick has always been movie-star handsome. But, as Dave MacIntosh says, he's never traded in on it. Instead, he documented with his camera.

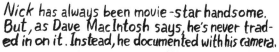

Today, Nick's photos are a *rare glimpse* of a parade that's gone by. *Sometimes* he gathers his files together by hand and punk produces an ISBN#-less book.

Rivoli

This afternoon's book launch event is *here*, at a club that 40 years ago would be *packed*, nites when the band Nick was in, *The Rent Boys*, played.

≥Choke≤ Now we're a bunch of *old farts*.' Nobody cares.'.'

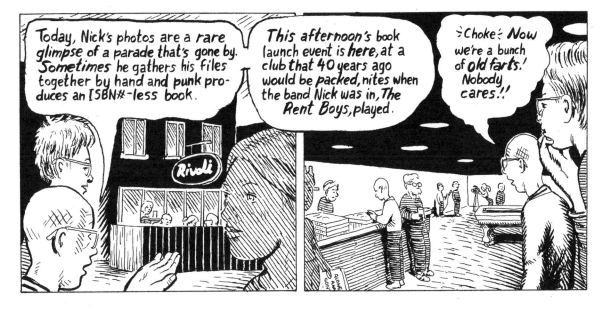

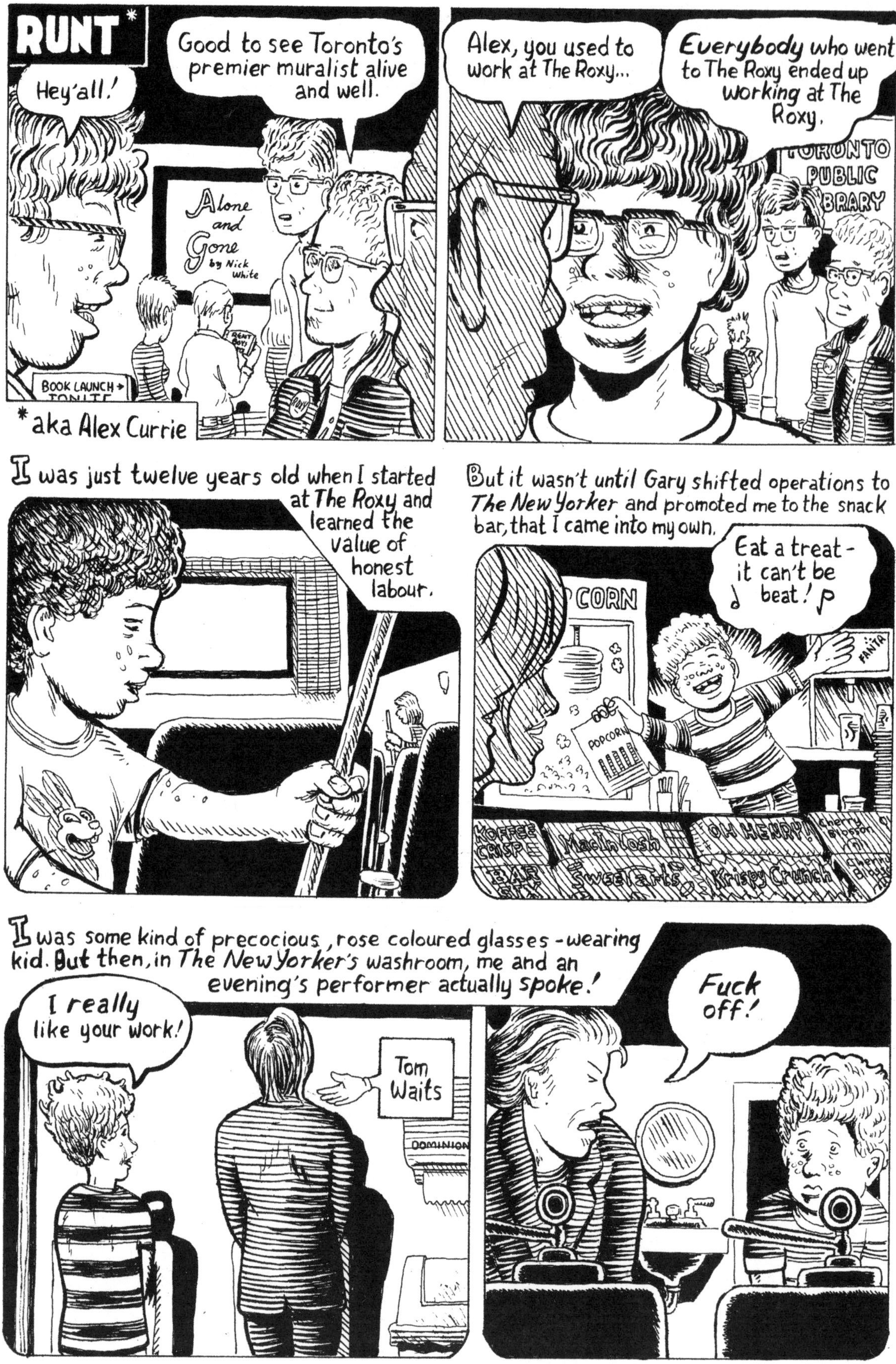
RUNT*
Hey'all!
Good to see Toronto's premier muralist alive and well.
Alone and Gone by Nick White
BOOK LAUNCH →
*aka Alex Currie
Alex, you used to work at The Roxy...
Everybody who went to The Roxy ended up working at The Roxy.
I was just twelve years old when I started at The Roxy and learned the value of honest labour.
But it wasn't until Gary shifted operations to The New Yorker and promoted me to the snack bar, that I came into my own.
Eat a treat - it can't be beat!
CORN
POPCORN
FANTA
KOFFEE CRISP
MacIntosh
OH HENRY!
Cherry Blossom
Sweetarts
Krispy Crunch
I was some kind of precocious, rose coloured glasses-wearing kid. But then, in The New Yorker's washroom, me and an evening's performer actually spoke!
I really like your work!
Tom Waits
DOMINION
Fuck off!

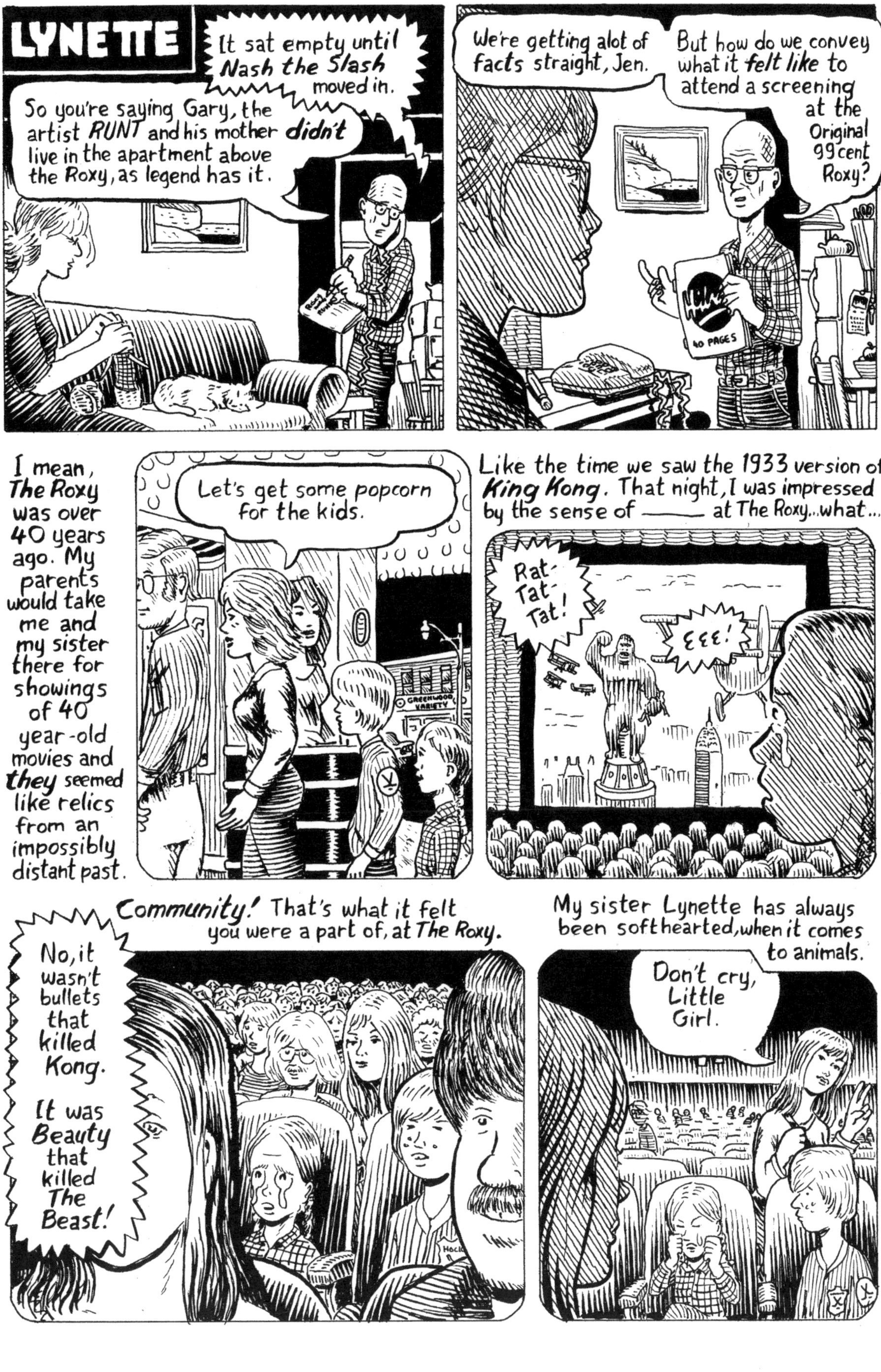

LYNETTE
It sat empty until Nash the Slash moved in.
So you're saying Gary, the artist RUNT and his mother didn't live in the apartment above the Roxy, as legend has it.
We're getting alot of facts straight, Jen.
But how do we convey what it felt like to attend a screening at the Original 99 cent Roxy?
40 PAGES
I mean, The Roxy was over 40 years ago. My parents would take me and my sister there for showings of 40 year-old movies and they seemed like relics from an impossibly distant past.
Let's get some popcorn for the kids.
GREENWOOD VARIETY
Like the time we saw the 1933 version of King Kong. That night, I was impressed by the sense of ——— at The Roxy...what...
Rat-Tat-Tat!
EEE!
Community! That's what it felt you were a part of, at The Roxy.
No, it wasn't bullets that killed Kong.
It was Beauty that killed The Beast!
My sister Lynette has always been softhearted, when it comes to animals.
Don't cry, Little Girl.

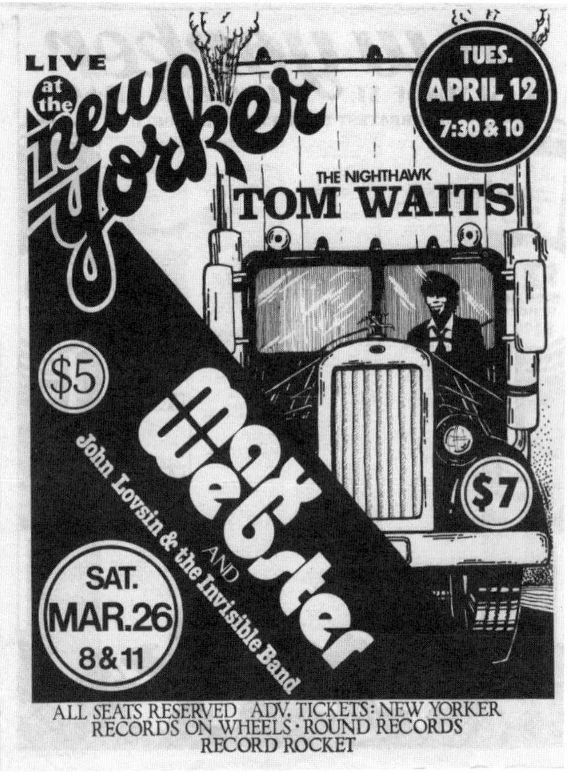
LIVE
at the
new yorker
TUES.
APRIL 12
7:30 & 10
THE NIGHTHAWK
TOM WAITS
$5
Max Webster
AND
John Lovsin & the Invisible Band
$7
SAT.
MAR.26
8&11
ALL SEATS RESERVED ADV. TICKETS: NEW YORKER
RECORDS ON WHEELS · ROUND RECORDS
RECORD ROCKET

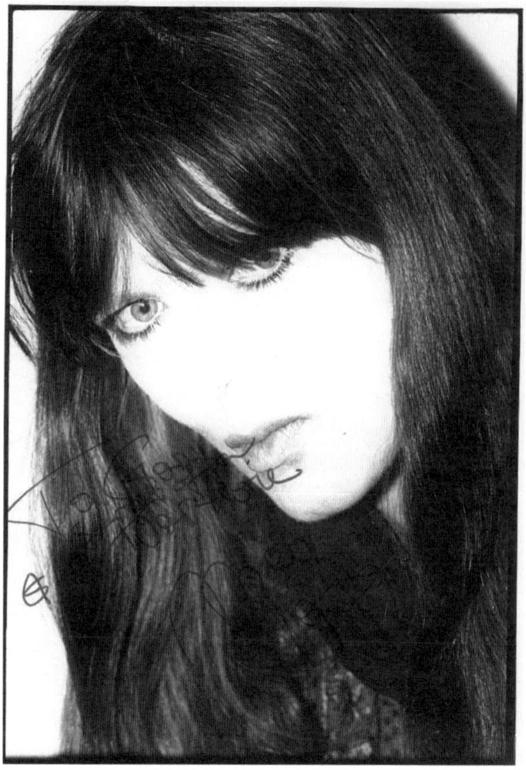

Nico (Photo: Peter Noble)

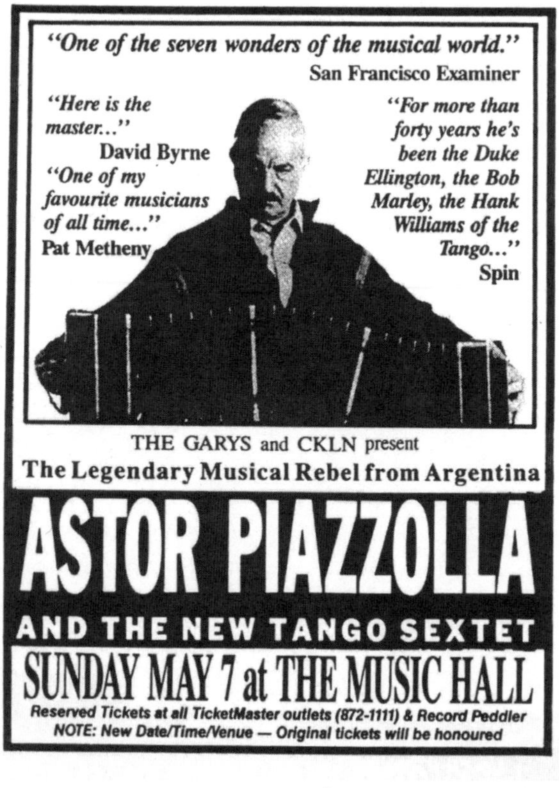
"One of the seven wonders of the musical world."
San Francisco Examiner
"Here is the master..."
David Byrne
"One of my favourite musicians of all time..."
Pat Metheny
"For more than forty years he's been the Duke Ellington, the Bob Marley, the Hank Williams of the Tango..."
Spin
THE GARYS and CKLN present
The Legendary Musical Rebel from Argentina
ASTOR PIAZZOLLA
AND THE NEW TANGO SEXTET
SUNDAY MAY 7 at THE MUSIC HALL
Reserved Tickets at all TicketMaster outlets (872-1111) & Record Peddler
NOTE: New Date/Time/Venue — Original tickets will be honoured

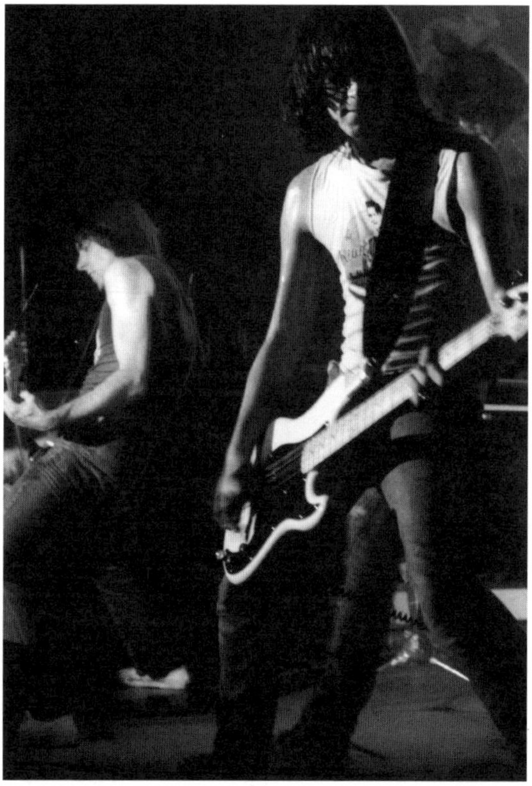

Dee Dee Ramone wears a New Yorker shirt
(Photo: Don Pyle)

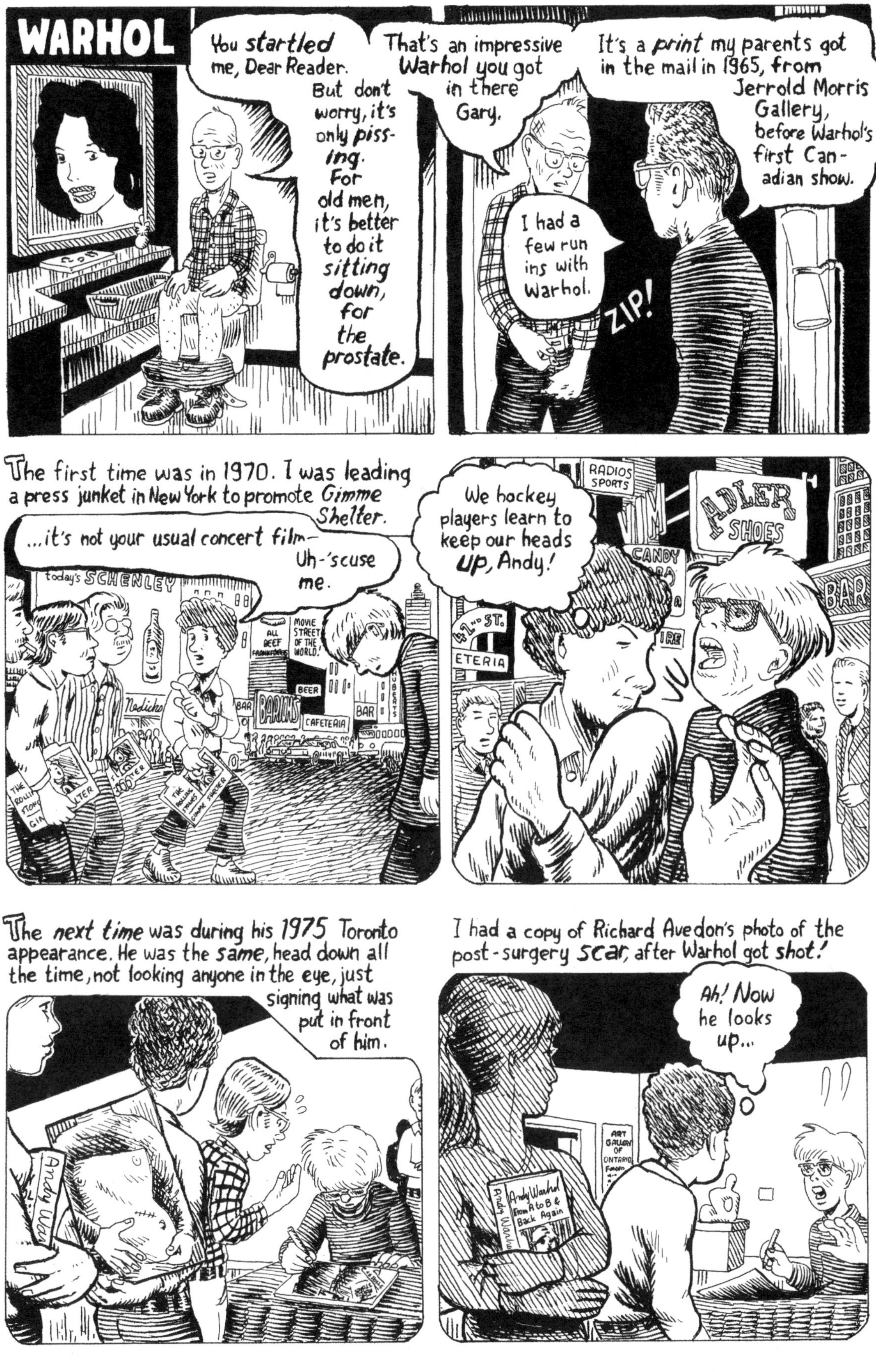

WARHOL
You startled me, Dear Reader.
But don't worry, it's only pissing. For old men, it's better to do it sitting down, for the prostate.
That's an impressive Warhol you got in there Gary.
It's a print my parents got in the mail in 1965, from Jerrold Morris Gallery, before Warhol's first Canadian show.
I had a few run ins with Warhol.
ZIP!
The first time was in 1970. I was leading a press junket in New York to promote Gimme Shelter.
...it's not your usual concert film–
Uh-'scuse me.
today's SCHENLEY
ALL BEEF FRANKFORTERS
MOVIE STREET OF THE WORLD!
BEER
BAR
CAFETERIA
We hockey players learn to keep our heads up, Andy!
RADIOS SPORTS
ADLER SHOES
CANDY
42ND ST.
ETERIA
BAR
The next time was during his 1975 Toronto appearance. He was the same, head down all the time, not looking anyone in the eye, just signing what was put in front of him.
I had a copy of Richard Avedon's photo of the post-surgery scar, after Warhol got shot!
Ah! Now he looks up...
ART GALLERY OF ONTARIO
Andy Warhol From A to B & Back Again

STAGE RITE

Not allowed.

C'mon Jenny, as dresser on this show you have *keys* to the building.

Won't you let Gary and me look around?

Screening movies is okay...

But I want to do *more*.

MUSICAL BIOGRAPHY
PIAF/ DIETRICH
Louise PITRE Jayne LEWIS
Direct Gorde Greenb

After all it was here, at 651 Yonge, that a new phase in Gary Topp's life began.

Gary hired Heather's brother, Blair to come down from *Huntsville* to build a stage.

What *else* do I have to do to get bands in here?

The result was a sturdy concrete structure.

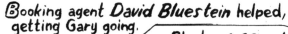

Booking agent *David Bluestein* helped, getting Gary going.

Plenty of **AC** outlets on that stage of yours, for one thing...

new yorker

THE LAST DETAIL

CINE OOKS

Blue also found the contact for the band Gary wanted...

You can get the Ramones, for $5,000.

The Agency

Make it $5,000 for 3 shows in 2 nights.

CLICK! CLICK!

Robbie Rox was the first music act to play *The New Yorker*. And then came the first Canadian appearances of the Ramones.

GABBA GABBA HEY

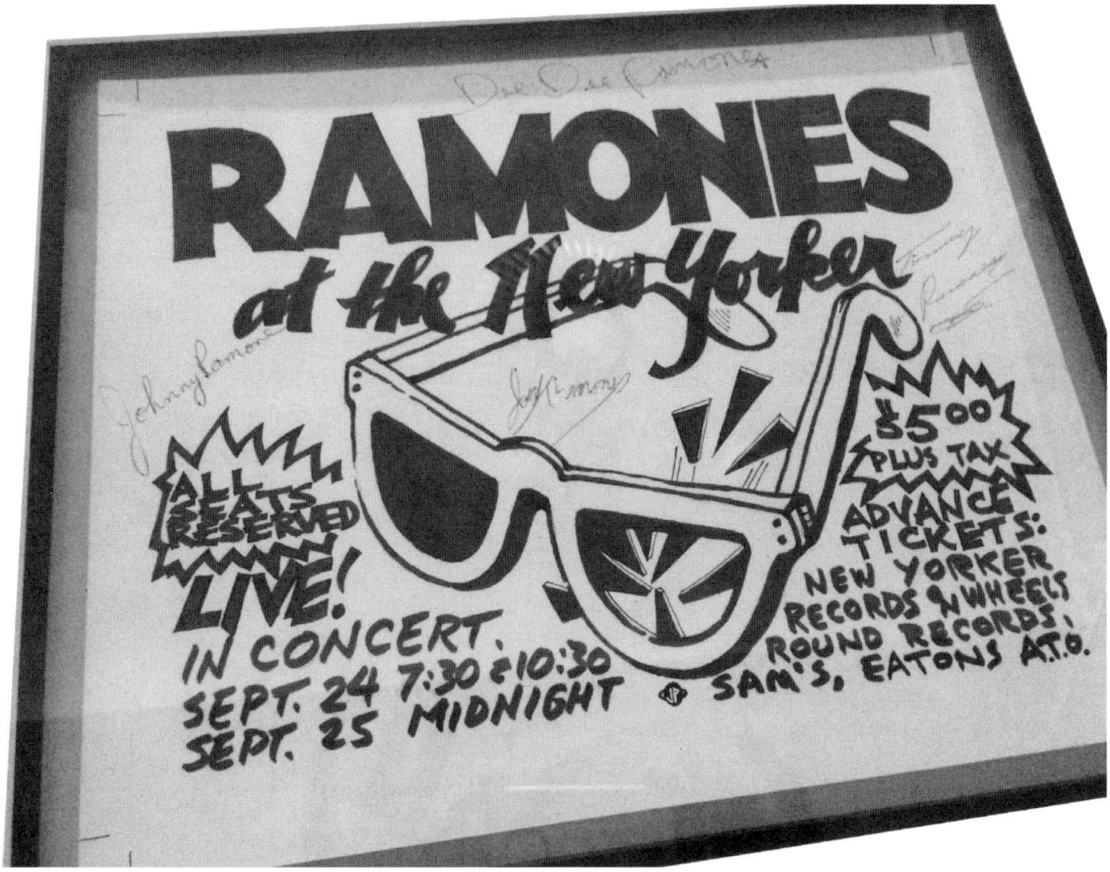
RAMONES
at the New Yorker
ALL SEATS RESERVED
LIVE!
IN CONCERT.
SEPT. 24 7:30 & 10:30
SEPT. 25 MIDNIGHT
$5.00 PLUS TAX
ADVANCE TICKETS:
NEW YORKER
RECORDS 'N WHEELS
ROUND RECORDS,
SAM'S, EATONS A.T.O.

Poster above by John Pearson. First Ramones show in Canada. Signed and hanging in Gary's apartment.

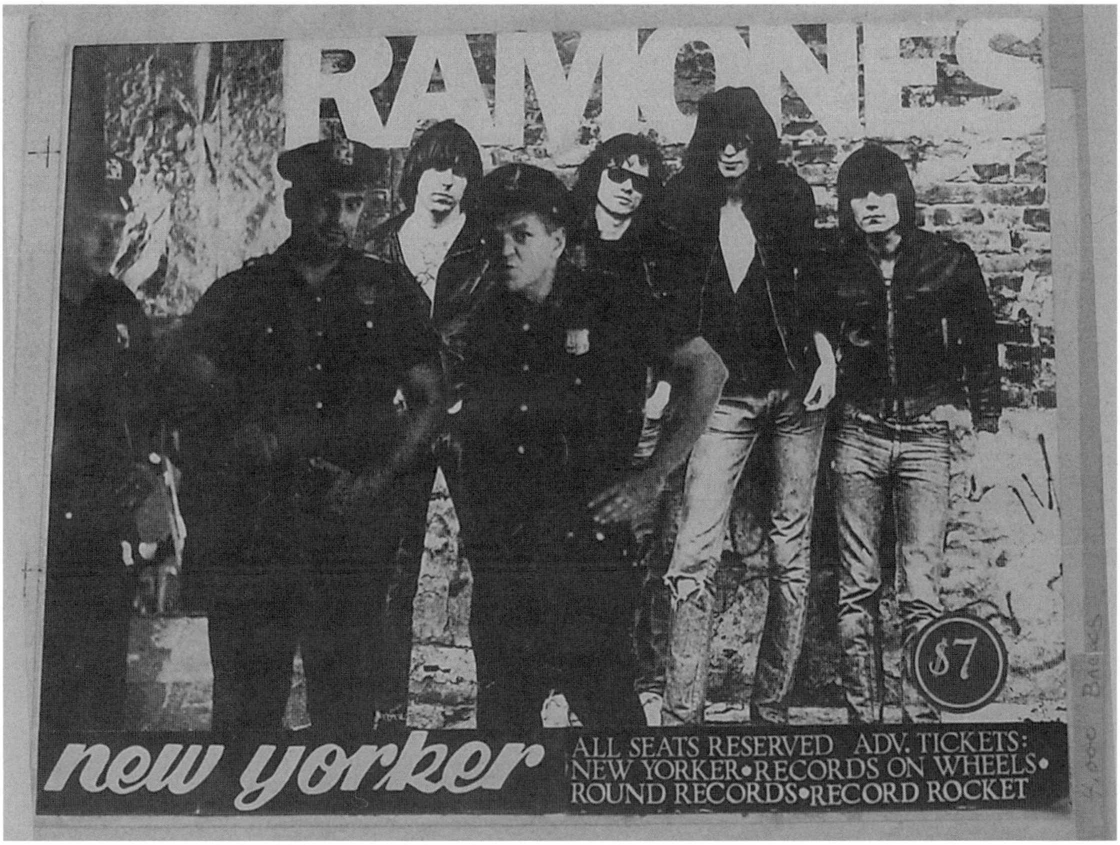
RAMONES
$7
new yorker
ALL SEATS RESERVED ADV. TICKETS:
NEW YORKER•RECORDS ON WHEELS•
ROUND RECORDS•RECORD ROCKET

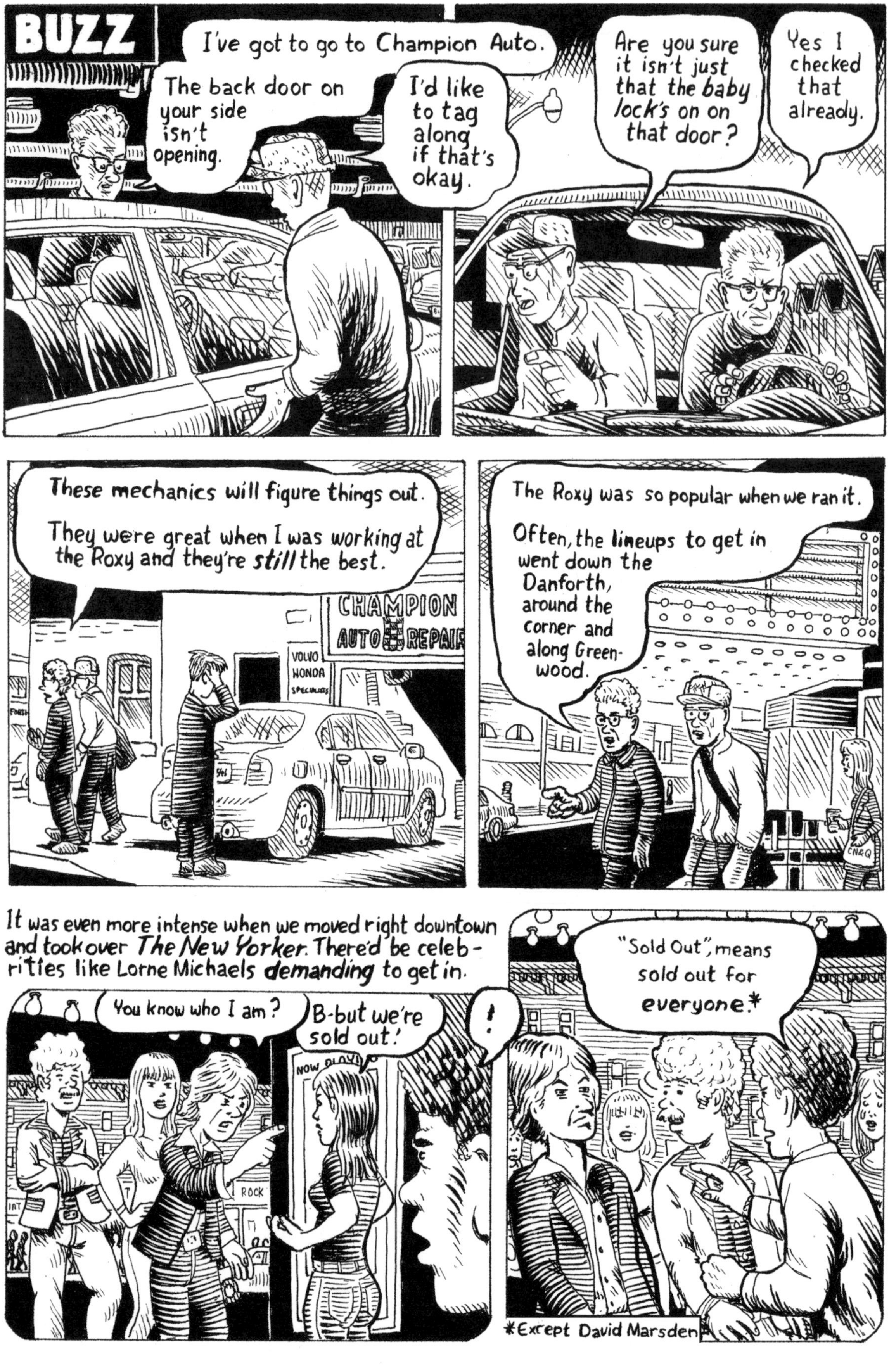

BUZZ
I've got to go to Champion Auto.
The back door on your side isn't opening.
I'd like to tag along if that's okay.
Are you sure it isn't just that the *baby lock's* on on that door?
Yes I checked that already.
These mechanics will figure things out.
They were great when I was *working* at the Roxy and they're *still* the best.
CHAMPION AUTO REPAIR
VOLVO HONDA SPECIALISTS
The Roxy was so popular when we ran it.
Often, the lineups to get in went down the Danforth, around the corner and along Greenwood.
It was even more intense when we moved right downtown and took over *The New Yorker*. There'd be celebrities like Lorne Michaels *demanding* to get in.
You know who I am?
B-but we're sold out!
!
ROCK
"Sold Out", means sold out for **everyone**.*
*Except David Marsden

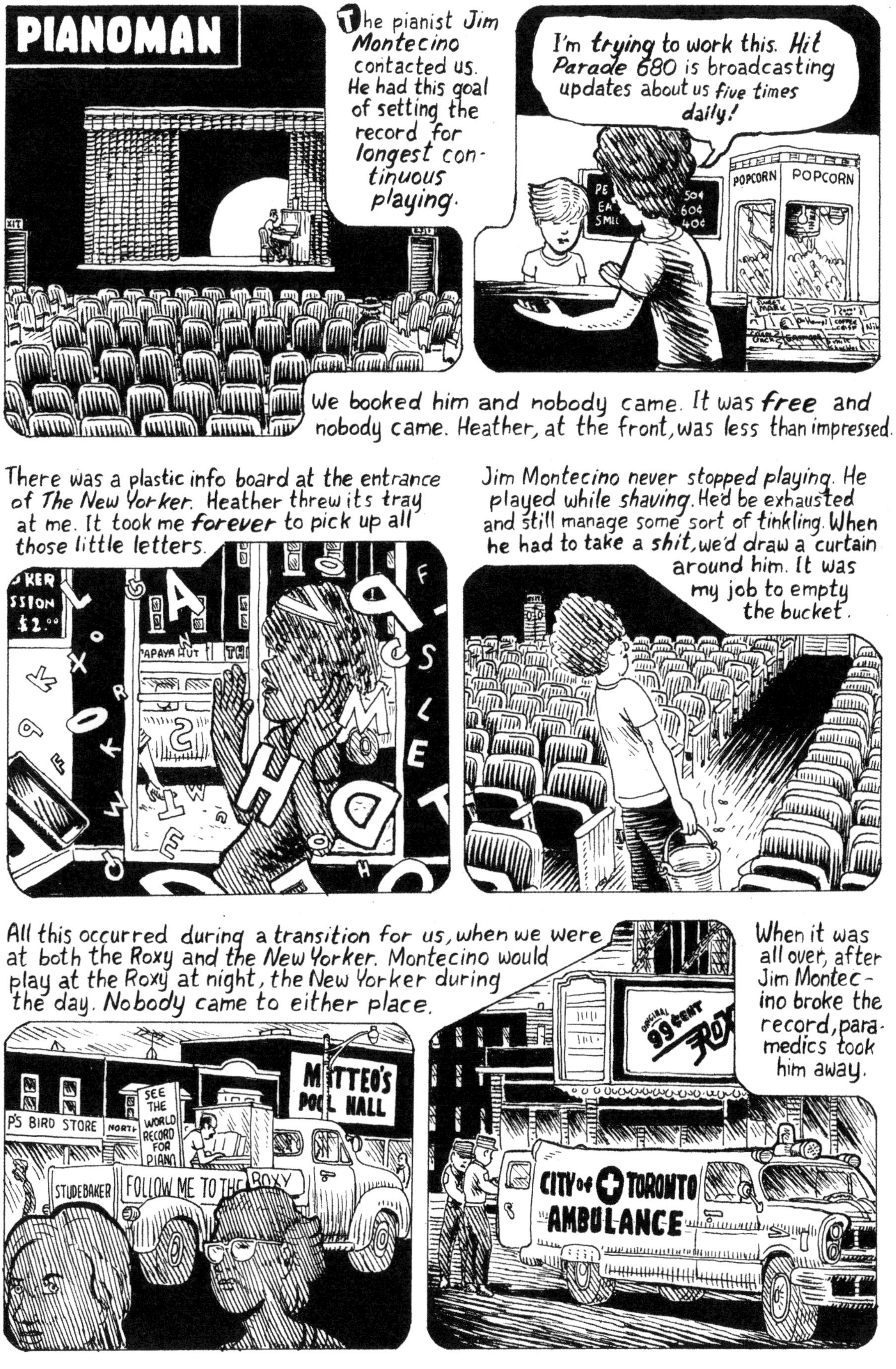
PIANOMAN
The pianist *Jim Montecino* contacted us. He had this goal of setting the record for *longest continuous playing*.
I'm *trying* to work this. *Hit Parade* 680 is broadcasting updates about us *five times daily!*
POPCORN
POPCORN
We booked him and nobody came. It was **free** and nobody came. Heather, at the front, was less than impressed.
There was a plastic info board at the entrance of *The New Yorker*. Heather threw its tray at me. It took me ***forever*** to pick up all those little letters.
PAPAYA HUT
Jim Montecino never stopped *playing*. He played while *shaving*. He'd be exhausted and still manage some sort of *tinkling*. When he had to take a ***shit***, we'd draw a curtain around him. It was my job to empty the bucket.
All this occurred during a *transition* for us, when we were at both the Roxy and the *New Yorker*. Montecino would play at the Roxy at night, the New Yorker during the day. *Nobody* came to either place.
P'S BIRD STORE
MATTEO'S POOL HALL
SEE THE WORLD RECORD FOR PIANO
STUDEBAKER
FOLLOW ME TO THE ROXY
When it was all over, after Jim Montecino broke the record, paramedics took him away.
ORIGINAL 99 CENT ROXY
CITY of TORONTO AMBULANCE

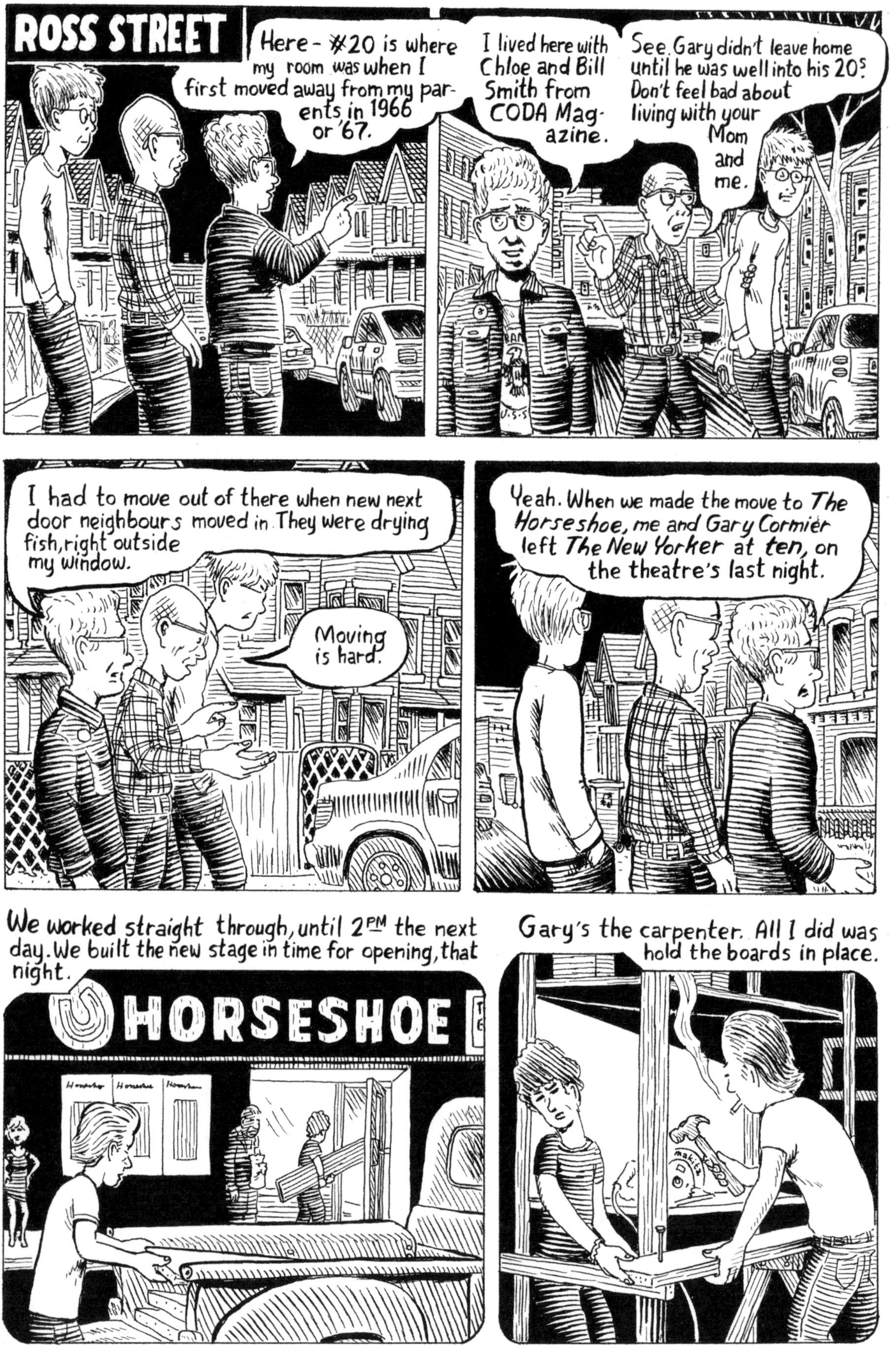
ROSS STREET
Here - #20 is where my room was when I first moved away from my parents in 1966 or '67.
I lived here with Chloe and Bill Smith from CODA Magazine.
See, Gary didn't leave home until he was well into his 20s. Don't feel bad about living with your Mom and me.
I had to move out of there when new next door neighbours moved in. They were drying fish, right outside my window.
Moving is hard.
Yeah. When we made the move to *The Horseshoe*, me and Gary Cormier left *The New Yorker* at *ten*, on the theatre's last night.
We worked straight through, until 2PM the next day. We built the new stage in time for opening, that night.
HORSESHOE
Gary's the carpenter. All I did was hold the boards in place.

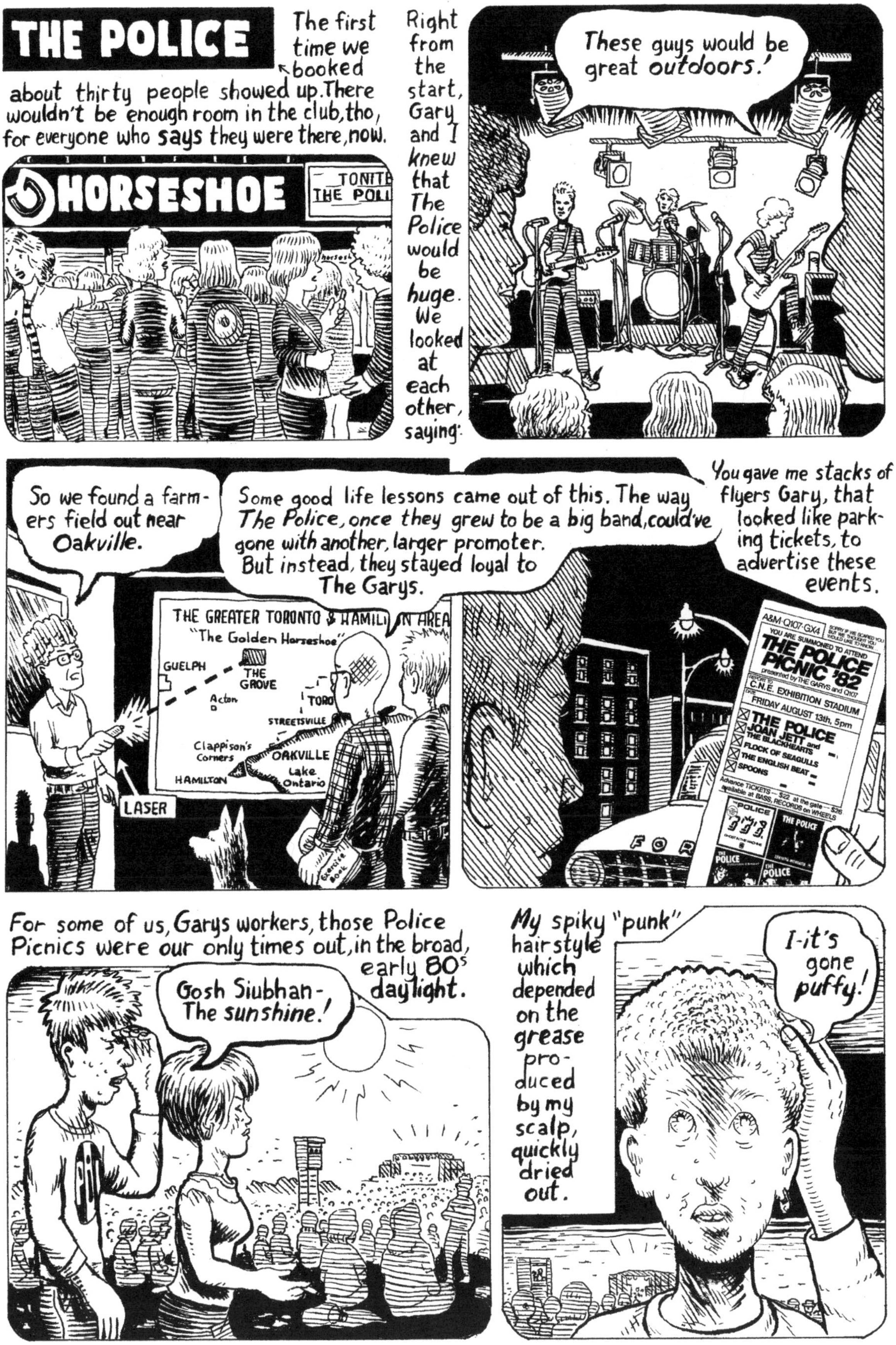
THE POLICE
The first time we booked
about thirty people showed up. There wouldn't be enough room in the club, tho, for everyone who says they were there, now.
HORSESHOE
TONITE THE POLI
Right from the start, Gary and I knew that The Police would be huge. We looked at each other, saying:
These guys would be great outdoors.'
So we found a farmers field out near Oakville.
Some good life lessons came out of this. The way The Police, once they grew to be a big band, could've gone with another, larger promoter. But instead, they stayed loyal to The Garys.
THE GREATER TORONTO & HAMILTON AREA
"The Golden Horseshoe"
GUELPH
THE GROVE
Acton
TORO
STREETSVILLE
Clappison's Corners
OAKVILLE
HAMILTON
Lake Ontario
LASER
Exercise Book
You gave me stacks of flyers Gary, that looked like parking tickets, to advertise these events.
A&M·Q107·GX4
YOU ARE SUMMONED TO ATTEND
THE POLICE PICNIC '82
presented by THE GARYS and Q107
REPORT TO C.N.E. EXHIBITION STADIUM
DATE FRIDAY AUGUST 13th, 5pm
THE POLICE
JOAN JETT and THE BLACKHEARTS
FLOCK OF SEAGULLS
THE ENGLISH BEAT
SPOONS
Advance TICKETS — $22 at the gate — $26
available at BASS, RECORDS on WHEELS
FOR
For some of us, Garys workers, those Police Picnics were our only times out, in the broad, early 80s daylight.
Gosh Siubhan - The sunshine.'
My spiky "punk" hairstyle which depended on the grease produced by my scalp, quickly dried out.
I-it's gone puffy!

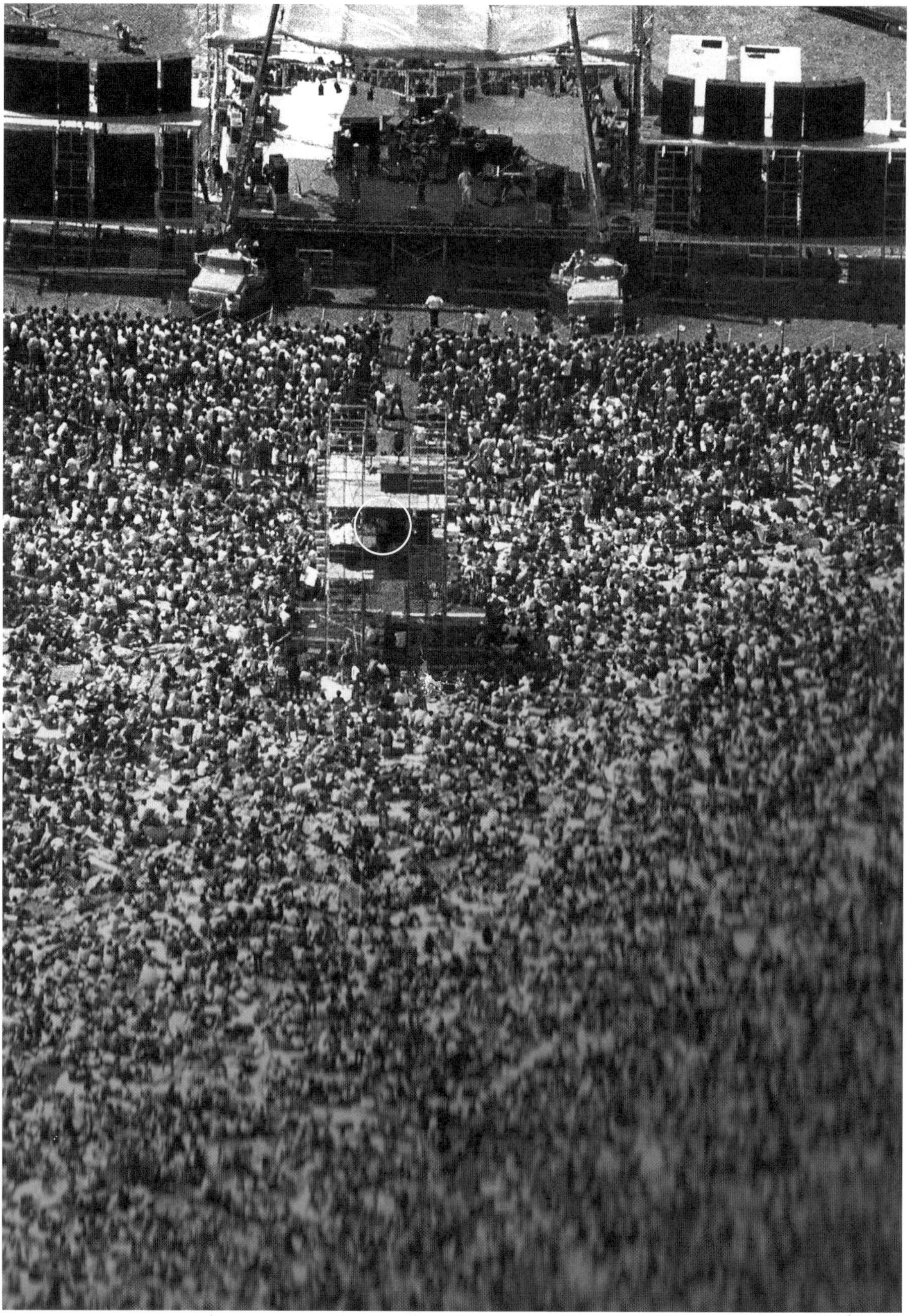

Police Picnic #1 (that's Gary in circle, djing for 10 hours)

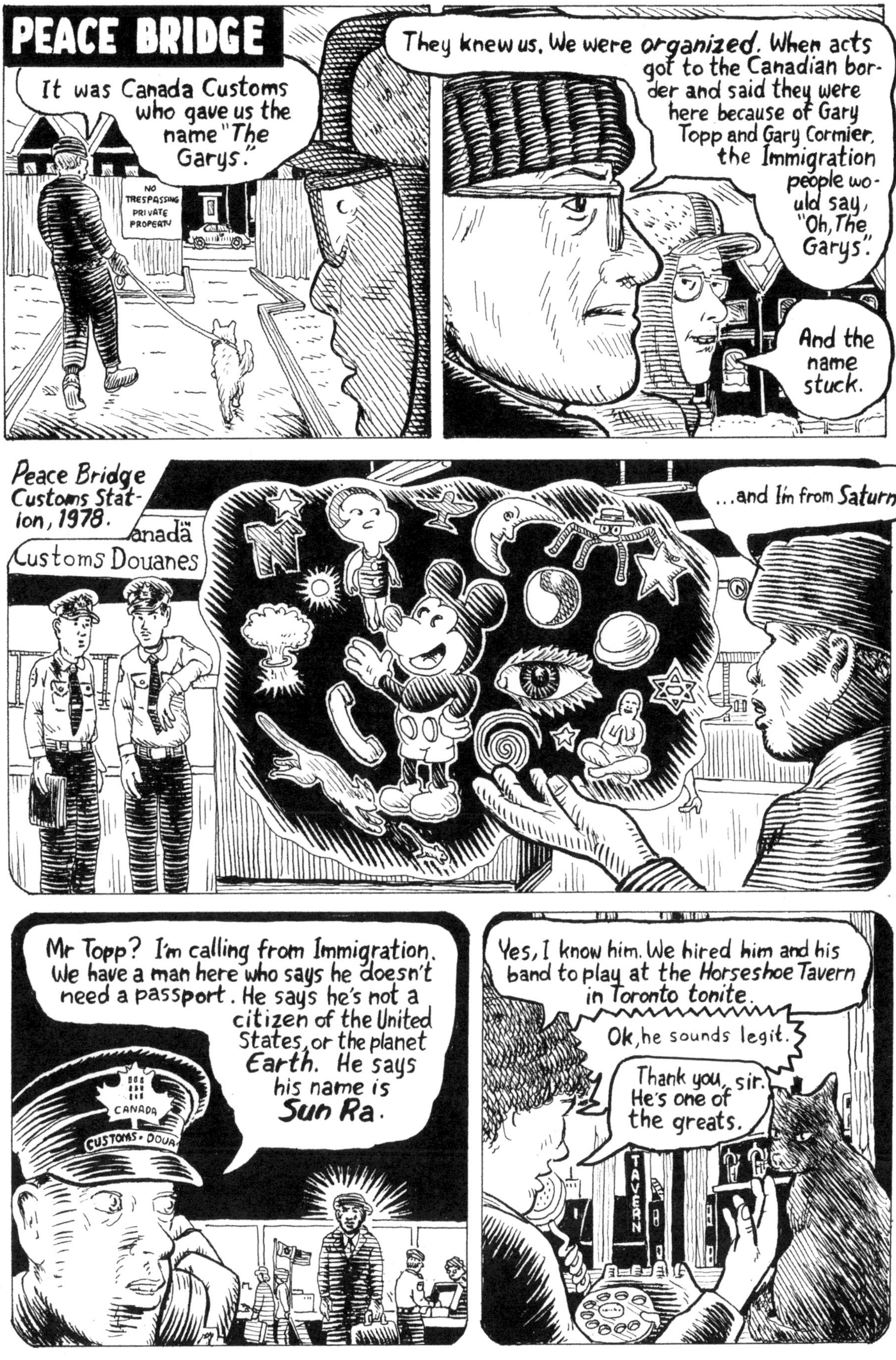
PEACE BRIDGE
It was Canada Customs who gave us the name "The Garys."
NO TRESPASSING PRIVATE PROPERTY
They knew us. We were organized. When acts got to the Canadian border and said they were here because of Gary Topp and Gary Cormier, the Immigration people would say, "Oh, The Garys".
And the name stuck.
Peace Bridge Customs Station, 1978.
Canada Customs Douanes
...and I'm from Saturn!
Mr Topp? I'm calling from Immigration. We have a man here who says he doesn't need a passport. He says he's not a citizen of the United States, or the planet Earth. He says his name is Sun Ra.
CANADA
CUSTOMS • DOUA
Yes, I know him. We hired him and his band to play at the Horseshoe Tavern in Toronto tonite.
Ok, he sounds legit.
Thank you, sir. He's one of the greats.
TAVERN

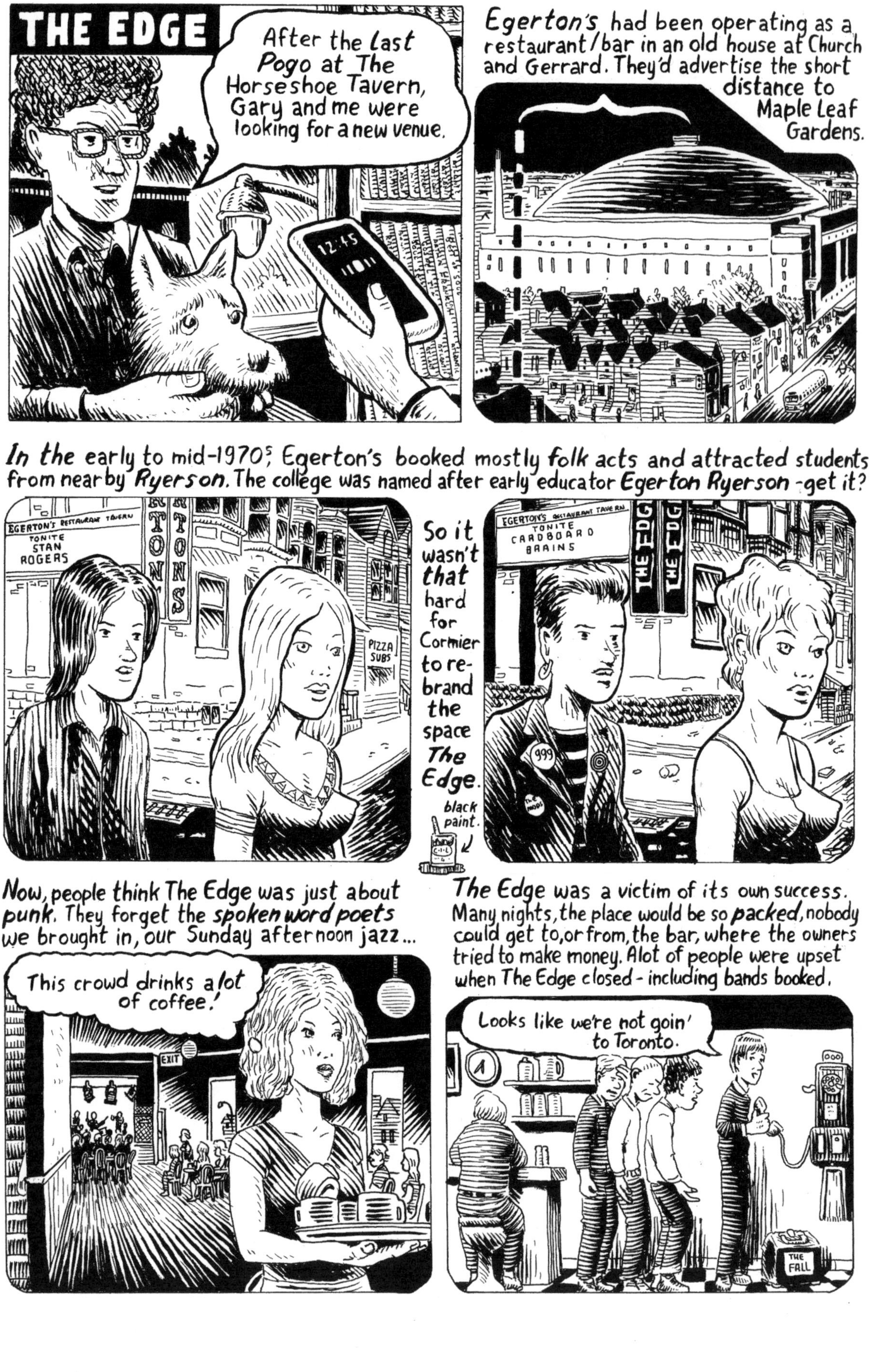
THE EDGE
After the last Pogo at The Horseshoe Tavern, Gary and me were looking for a new venue.
Egerton's had been operating as a restaurant/bar in an old house at Church and Gerrard. They'd advertise the short distance to Maple Leaf Gardens.
In the early to mid-1970s, Egerton's booked mostly folk acts and attracted students from nearby Ryerson. The college was named after early educator Egerton Ryerson - get it?
TONITE
STAN
ROGERS
PIZZA
SUBS
So it wasn't that hard for Cormier to rebrand the space The Edge.
black paint.
TONITE
CARDBOARD
BRAINS
THE EDGE
THE EDGE
999
Now, people think The Edge was just about punk. They forget the spoken word poets we brought in, our Sunday afternoon jazz...
This crowd drinks a lot of coffee!
EXIT
The Edge was a victim of its own success. Many nights, the place would be so packed, nobody could get to, or from, the bar, where the owners tried to make money. Alot of people were upset when The Edge closed - including bands booked.
Looks like we're not goin' to Toronto.
THE FALL

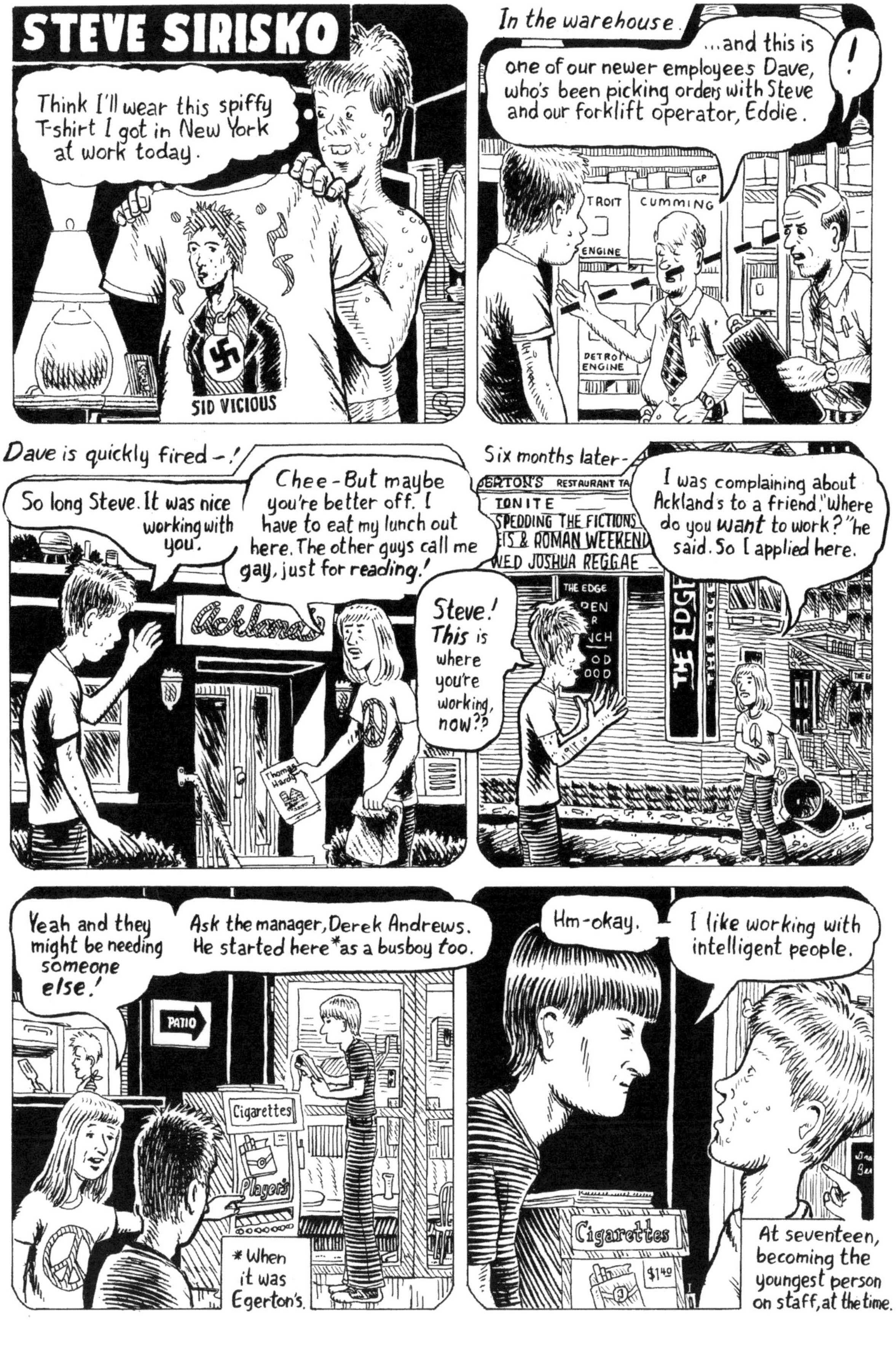
STEVE SIRISKO
Think I'll wear this spiffy T-shirt I got in New York at work today.
SID VICIOUS
In the warehouse.
...and this is one of our newer employees Dave, who's been picking orders with Steve and our forklift operator, Eddie.
!
Dave is quickly fired-!
So long Steve. It was nice working with you.
Chee-But maybe you're better off. I have to eat my lunch out here. The other guys call me gay, just for reading!
Steve! This is where you're working, now??
Thomas Hardy
Six months later-
I was complaining about Ackland's to a friend. "Where do you want to work?" he said. So I applied here.
TONITE
SPEDDING THE FICTIONS
WED JOSHUA REGGAE
THE EDGE
Yeah and they might be needing someone else!
Ask the manager, Derek Andrews. He started here* as a busboy too.
PATIO
Cigarettes
Player's
*When it was Egerton's.
Hm-okay.
I like working with intelligent people.
Cigarettes
At seventeen, becoming the youngest person on staff, at the time.

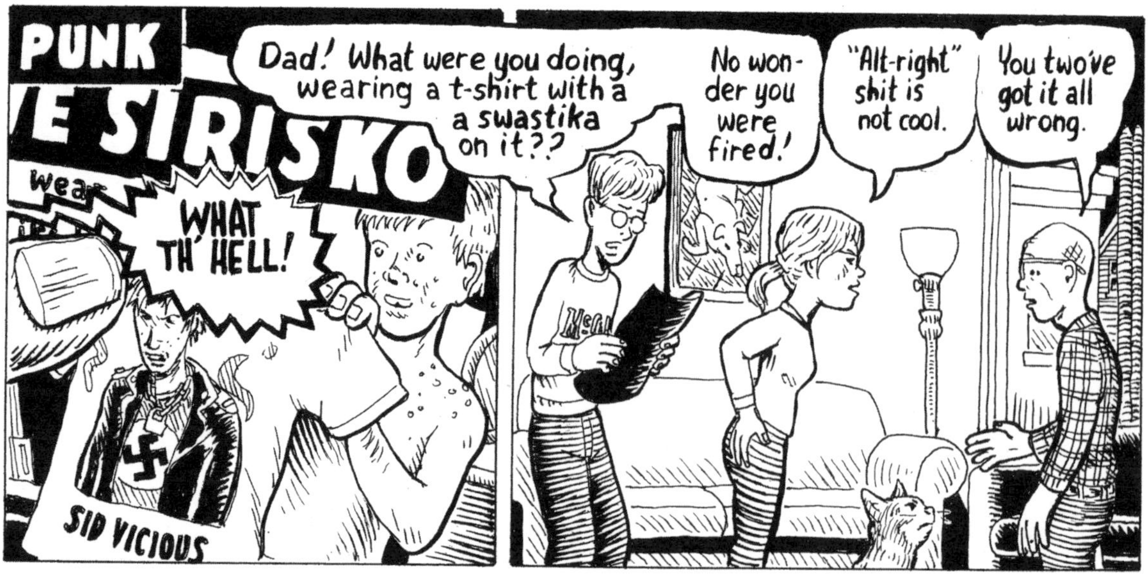
PUNK
E SIRISKO
wear
WHAT TH' HELL!
SID VICIOUS
Dad! What were you doing, wearing a t-shirt with a a swastika on it??
No wonder you were fired!
"Alt-right" shit is not cool.
You two've got it all wrong.

Nobody in those days ever dreamed that someday Nazis would again be taken seriously. For the vast majority of punks, that ideology was a way of saying "I'm stupid and hopeless (please help me)". Punk wasn't particularly political then. Mostly, me and my friends only believed in being *annoying*.

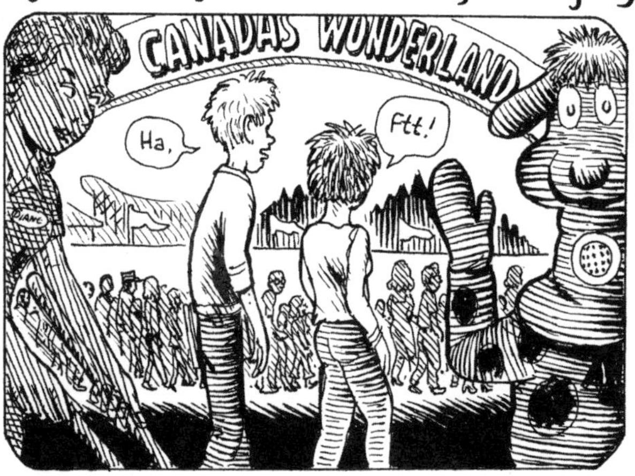
CANADAS WONDERLAND
Ha.
Ftt!

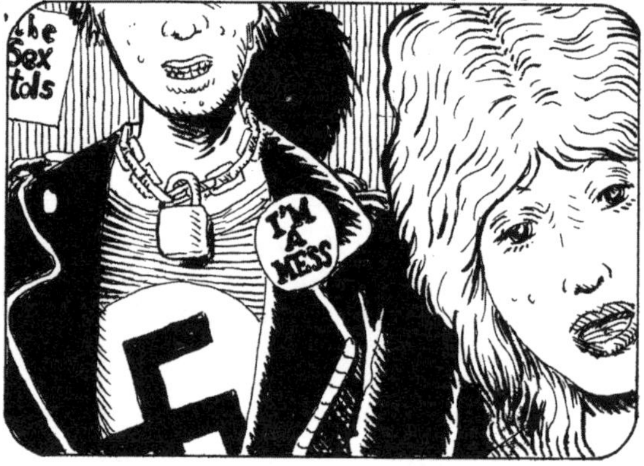
the Sex tols
I'M A MESS

A Sid Vicious t-shirt celebrated the *idiot* in all of us. ↖Sid ↗Nancy

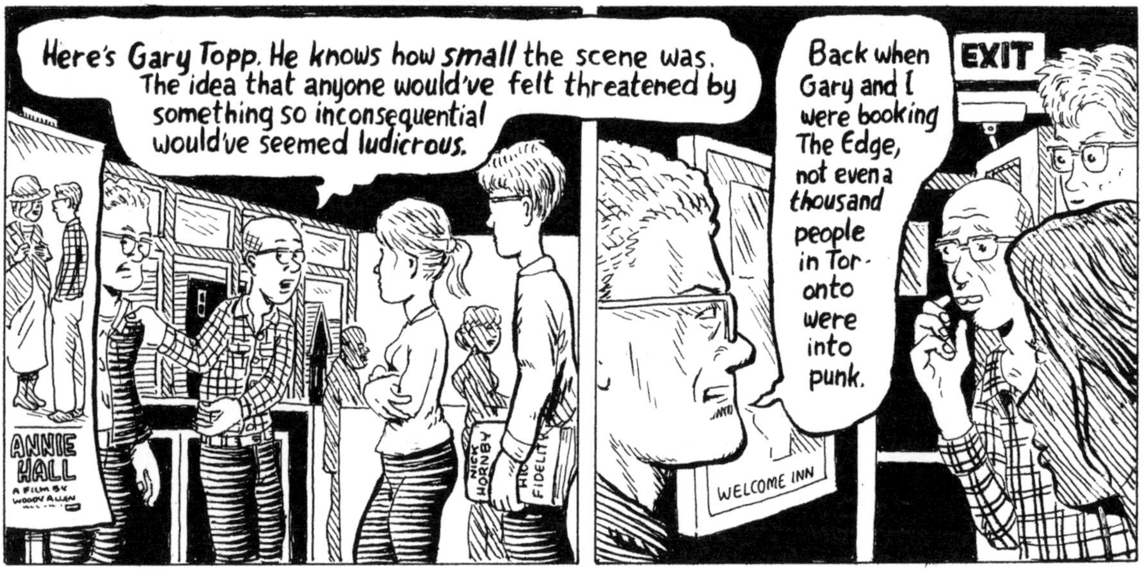
Here's Gary Topp. He knows how *small* the scene was. The idea that anyone would've felt threatened by something so inconsequential would've seemed ludicrous.
ANNIE HALL
A FILM BY WOODY ALLEN
NICK HORNBY
FIDELITY
Back when Gary and I were booking The Edge, not even a *thousand* people in Toronto were into punk.
EXIT
WELCOME INN

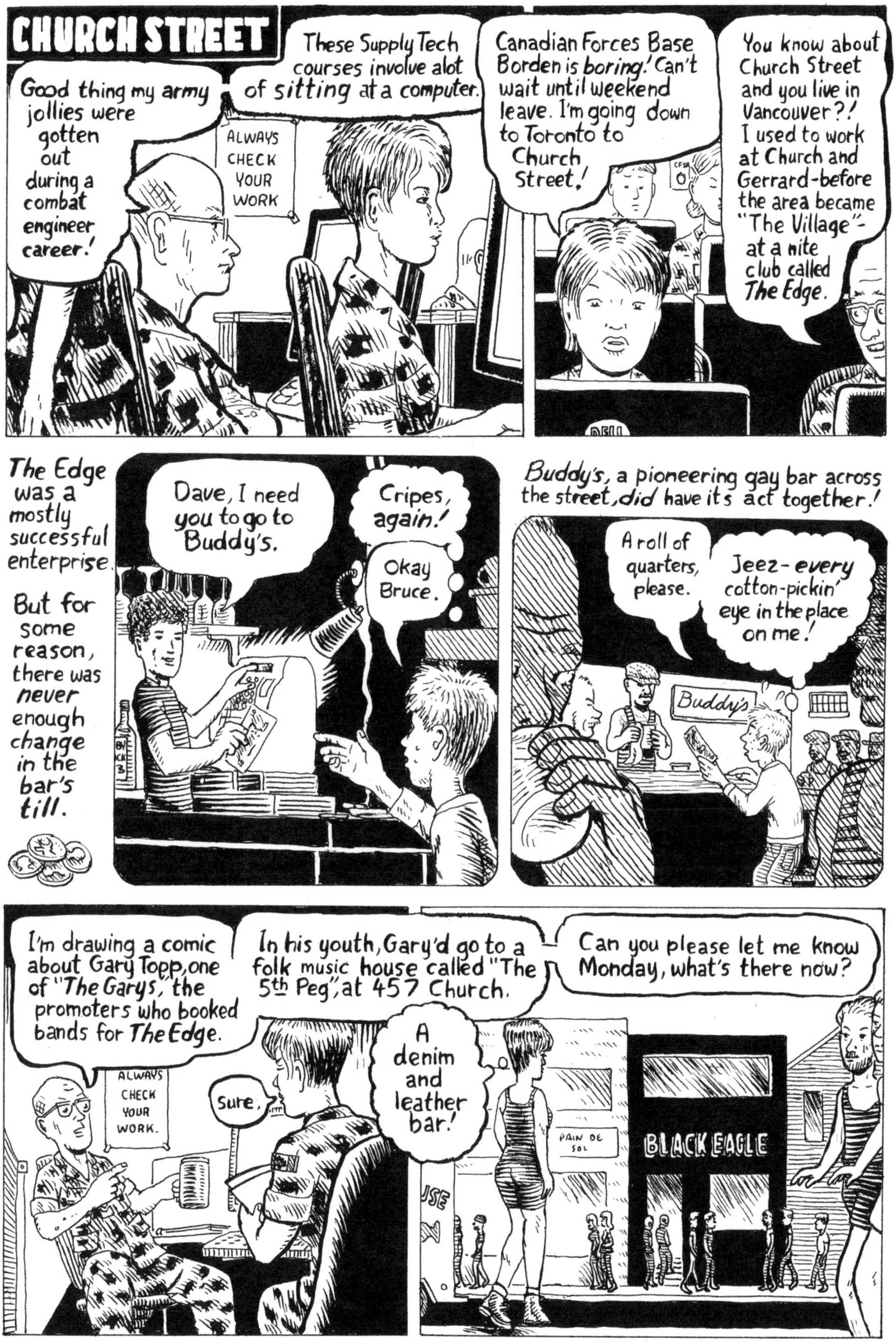
CHURCH STREET
Good thing my army jollies were gotten out during a combat engineer career!
These Supply Tech courses involve alot of sitting at a computer.
ALWAYS CHECK YOUR WORK
Canadian Forces Base Borden is boring! Can't wait until weekend leave. I'm going down to Toronto to Church Street!
You know about Church Street and you live in Vancouver?! I used to work at Church and Gerrard-before the area became "The Village"- at a nite club called The Edge.
The Edge was a mostly successful enterprise.
But for some reason, there was never enough change in the bar's till.
Dave, I need you to go to Buddy's.
Cripes, again!
Okay Bruce.
Buddy's, a pioneering gay bar across the street, did have its act together!
A roll of quarters, please.
Jeez- every cotton-pickin' eye in the place on me!
Buddy's
I'm drawing a comic about Gary Topp, one of "The Garys," the promoters who booked bands for The Edge.
In his youth, Gary'd go to a folk music house called "The 5th Peg", at 457 Church.
Can you please let me know Monday, what's there now?
ALWAYS CHECK YOUR WORK.
Sure.
A denim and leather bar!
PAIN DE SOL
BLACK EAGLE

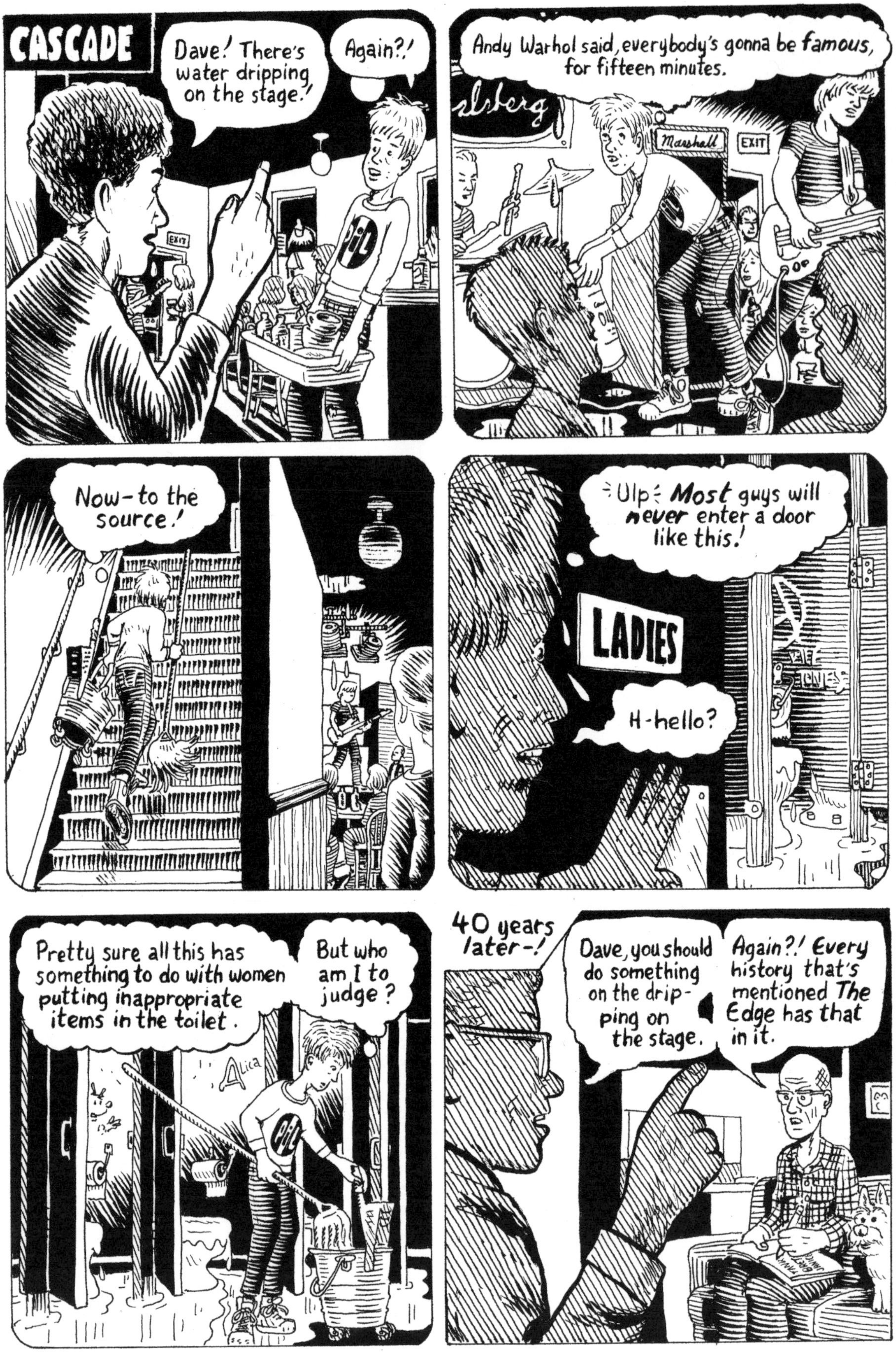
CASCADE
Dave! There's water dripping on the stage!
Again?!
Andy Warhol said, everybody's gonna be famous, for fifteen minutes.
Marshall
EXIT
Now-to the source!
Ulp! Most guys will never enter a door like this!
LADIES
H-hello?
Pretty sure all this has something to do with women putting inappropriate items in the toilet.
But who am I to judge?
40 years later-!
Dave, you should do something on the dripping on the stage.
Again?! Every history that's mentioned The Edge has that in it.

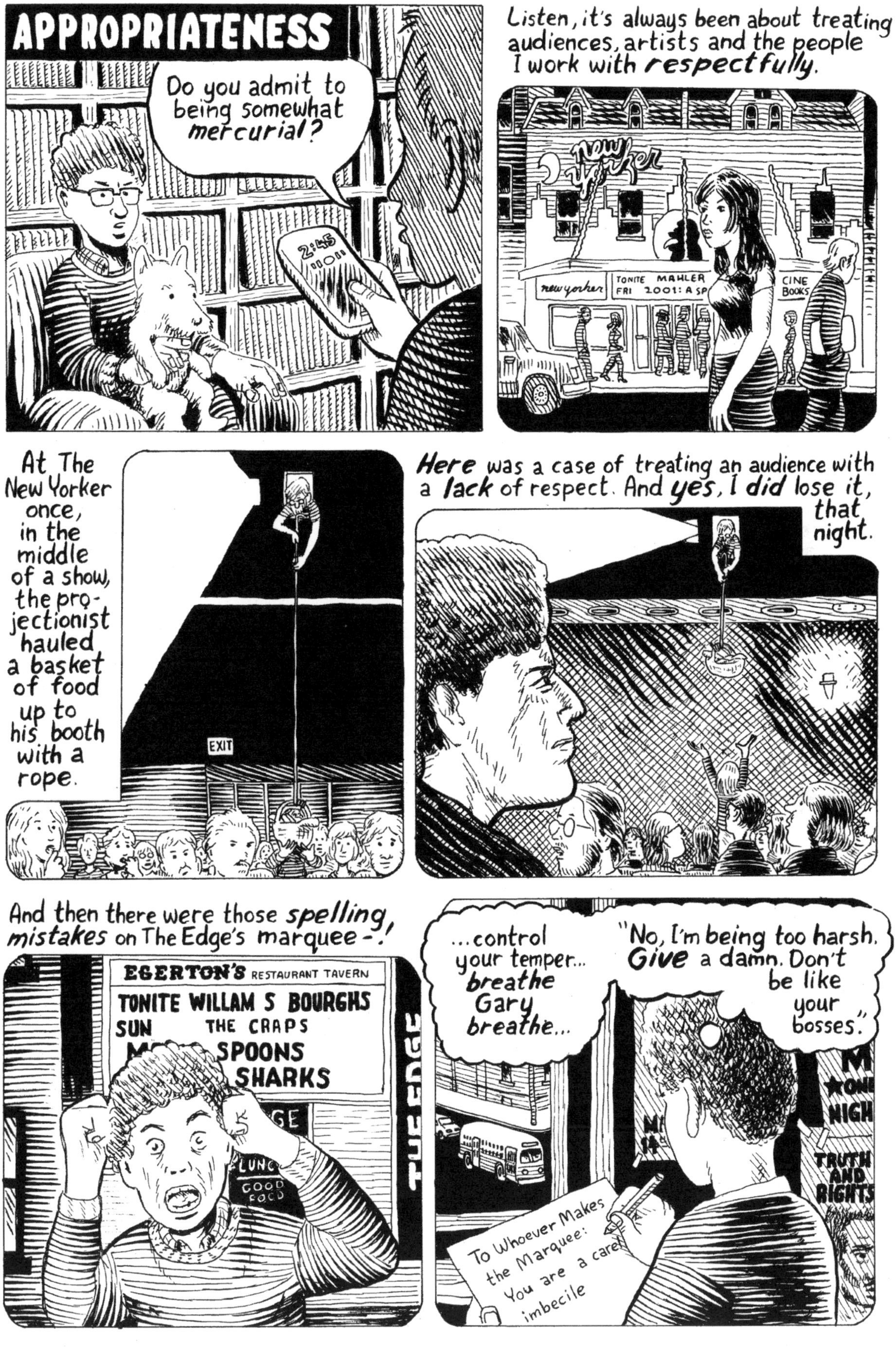

APPROPRIATENESS
Do you admit to being somewhat *mercurial?*
2:45
Listen, it's always been about treating audiences, artists and the people I work with ***respectfully***.
new yorker
new yorker
TONITE MAHLER
FRI 2001: A SP
CINE BOOKS
At The New Yorker once, in the middle of a show, the projectionist hauled a basket of food up to his booth with a rope.
EXIT
Here was a case of treating an audience with a ***lack*** of respect. And ***yes***, ***I did*** lose it, that night.
And then there were those ***spelling mistakes*** on The Edge's marquee -!
EGERTON'S RESTAURANT TAVERN
TONITE WILLAM S BOURGHS
SUN THE CRAPS
SPOONS
SHARKS
THE EDGE
GOOD FOOD
...control your temper... ***breathe*** Gary ***breathe***...
"No, I'm being too harsh. ***Give*** a damn. Don't be like your bosses."
To Whoever Makes the Marquee: You are a care imbecile
TRUTH AND RIGHTS

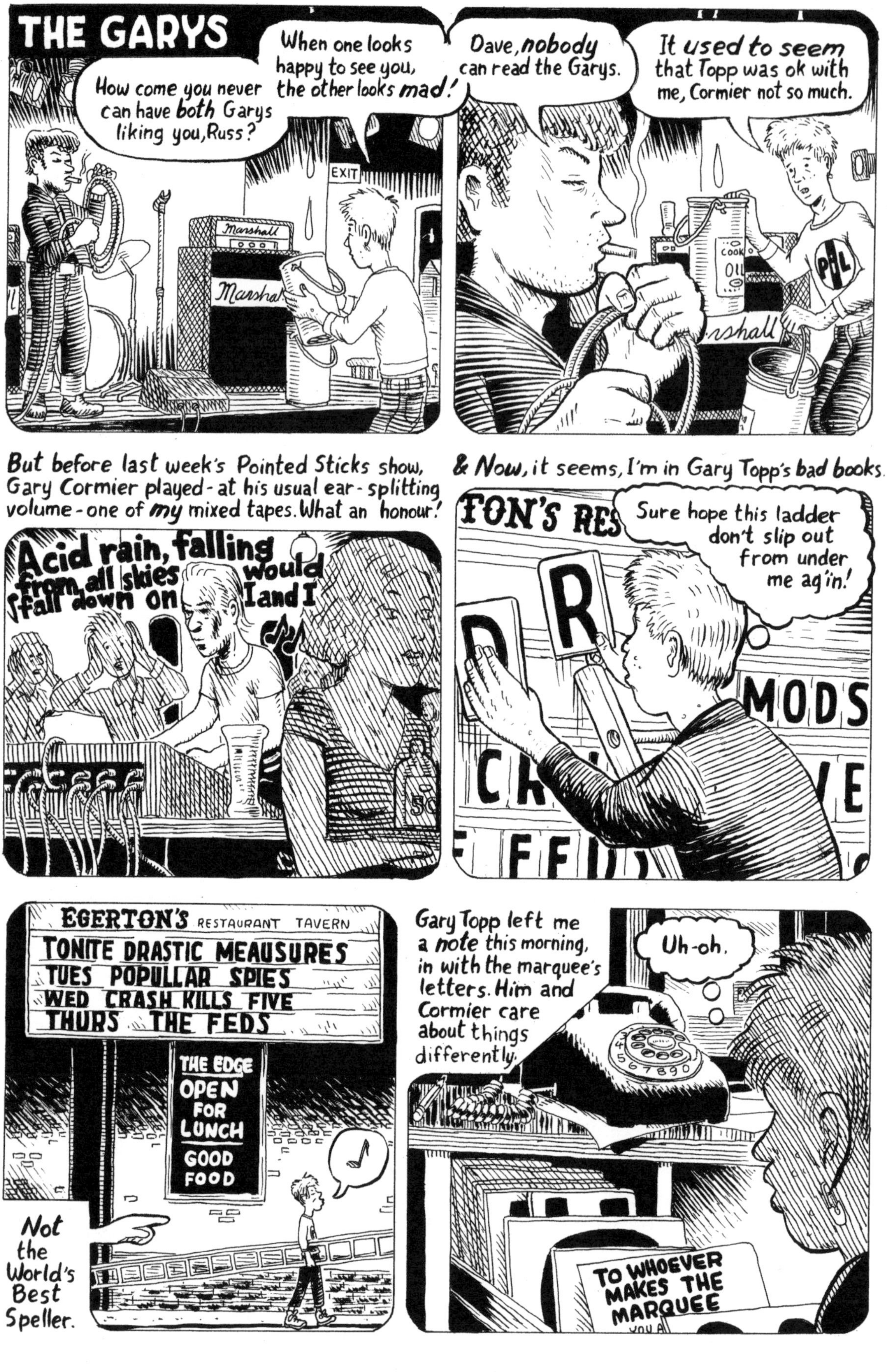
THE GARYS
How come you never can have both Garys liking you, Russ?
When one looks happy to see you, the other looks mad!
EXIT
Marshall
Marshall
Dave, nobody can read the Garys.
It used to seem that Topp was ok with me, Cormier not so much.
COOK OIL
PiL
But before last week's Pointed Sticks show, Gary Cormier played - at his usual ear-splitting volume - one of my mixed tapes. What an honour!
Acid rain, falling from all skies would fall down on I and I
& Now, it seems, I'm in Gary Topp's bad books.
TON'S RES
Sure hope this ladder don't slip out from under me ag'in!
MODS
EGERTON'S RESTAURANT TAVERN
TONITE DRASTIC MEAUSURES
TUES POPULLAR SPIES
WED CRASH KILLS FIVE
THURS THE FEDS
THE EDGE OPEN FOR LUNCH
GOOD FOOD
Not the World's Best Speller.
Gary Topp left me a note this morning, in with the marquee's letters. Him and Cormier care about things differently.
Uh-oh.
TO WHOEVER MAKES THE MARQUEE

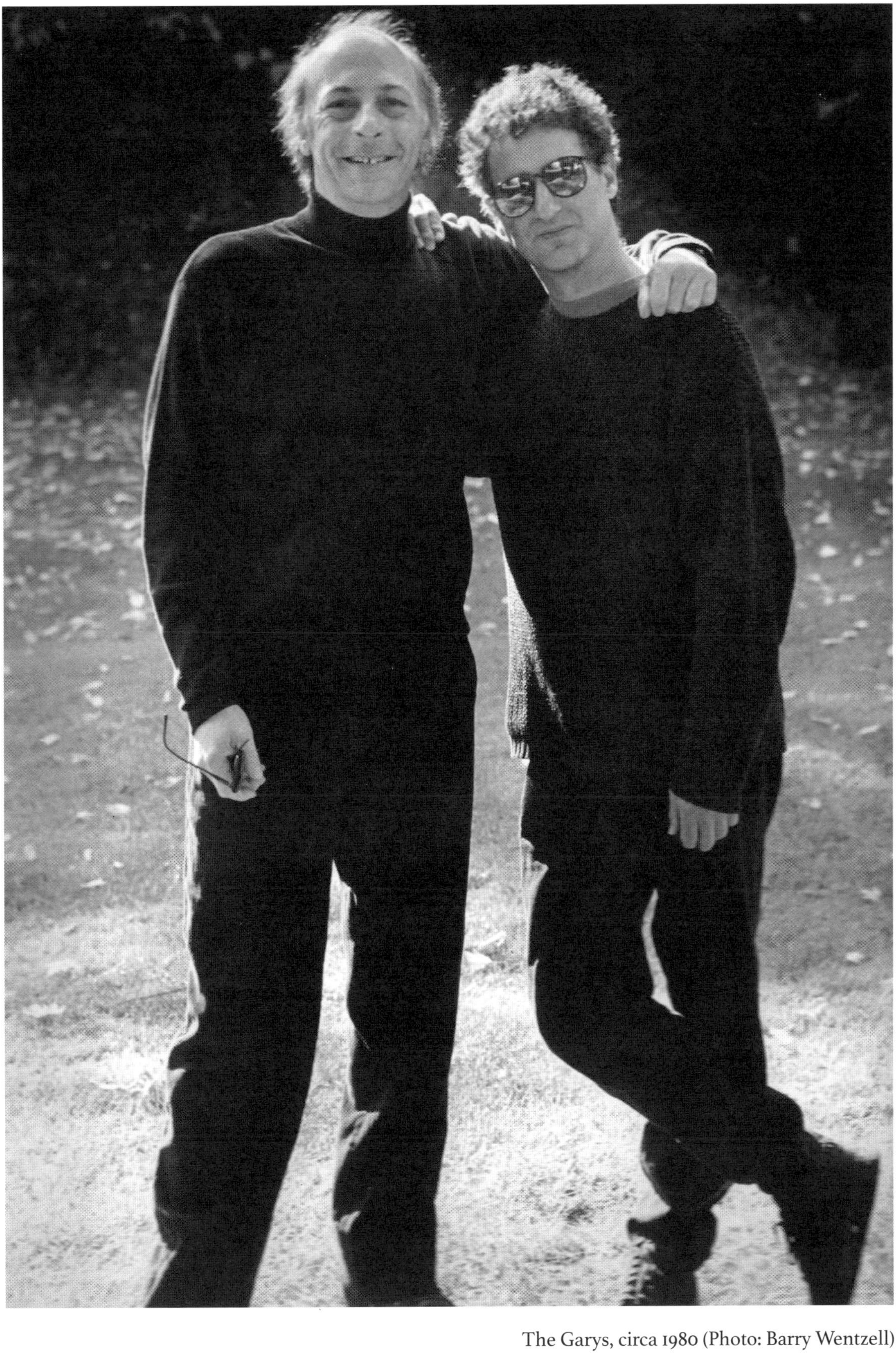

The Garys, circa 1980 (Photo: Barry Wentzell)

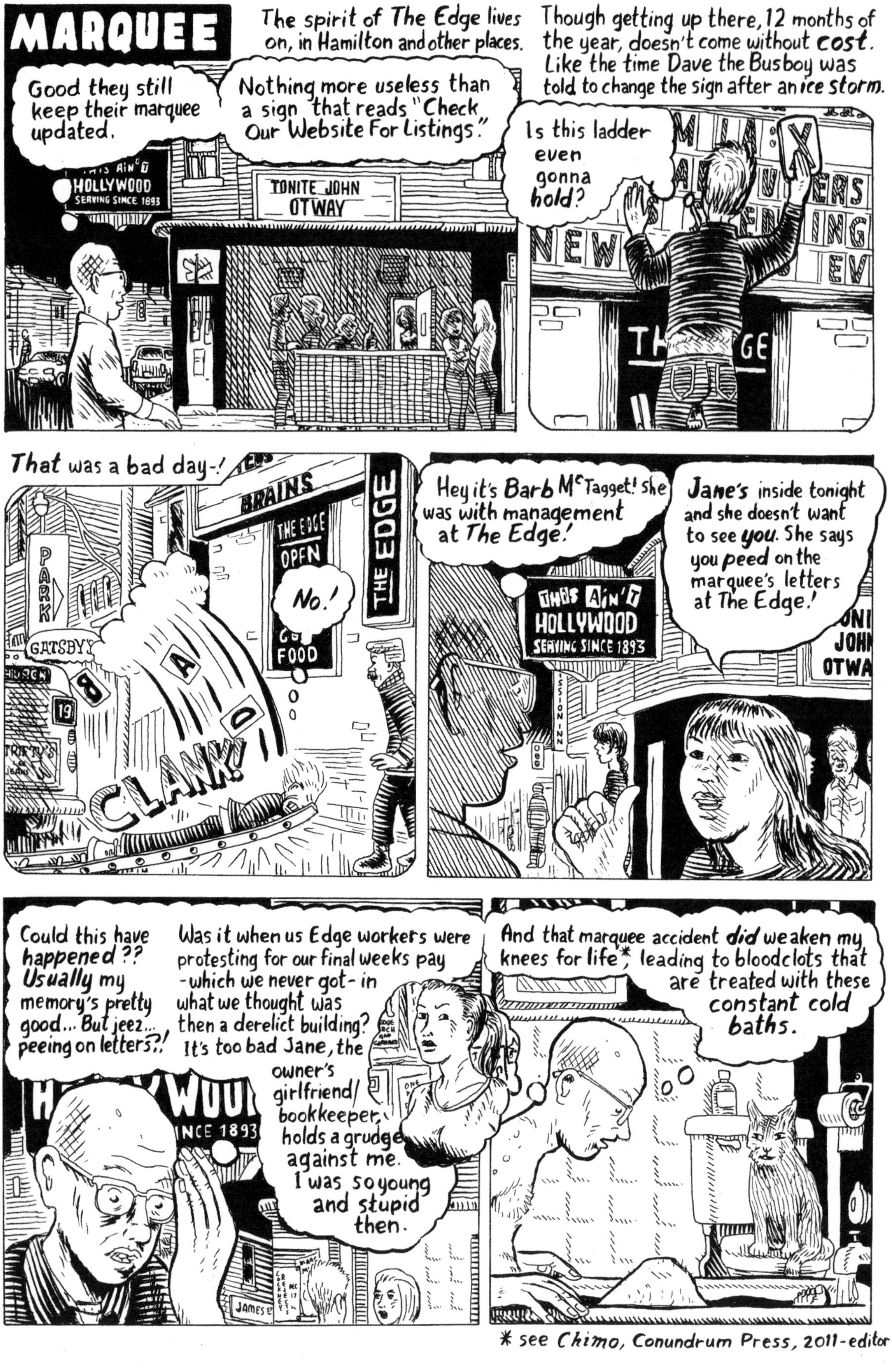
MARQUEE
Good they still keep their marquee updated.
THIS AIN'T HOLLYWOOD SERVING SINCE 1893
The spirit of The Edge lives on, in Hamilton and other places.
Nothing more useless than a sign that reads "Check Our Website For Listings."
TONITE JOHN OTWAY
Though getting up there, 12 months of the year, doesn't come without cost. Like the time Dave the Busboy was told to change the sign after an ice storm.
Is this ladder even gonna hold?
NEW
THE EDGE
That was a bad day-!
BRAINS
THE EDGE
THE EDGE OPEN
FOOD
PARK
GATSBY'S
No.!
B A D
CLANK!
Hey it's Barb McTagget! She was with management at The Edge!
Jane's inside tonight and she doesn't want to see you. She says you peed on the marquee's letters at The Edge!
THIS AIN'T HOLLYWOOD SERVING SINCE 1893
Could this have happened?? Usually my memory's pretty good... But jeez... peeing on letters?!
Was it when us Edge workers were protesting for our final weeks pay -which we never got- in what we thought was then a derelict building? It's too bad Jane, the owner's girlfriend/bookkeeper, holds a grudge against me. I was so young and stupid then.
INCE 1893
JAMES ST
And that marquee accident did weaken my knees for life*, leading to bloodclots that are treated with these constant cold baths.

* see *Chimo*, Conundrum Press, 2011-editor

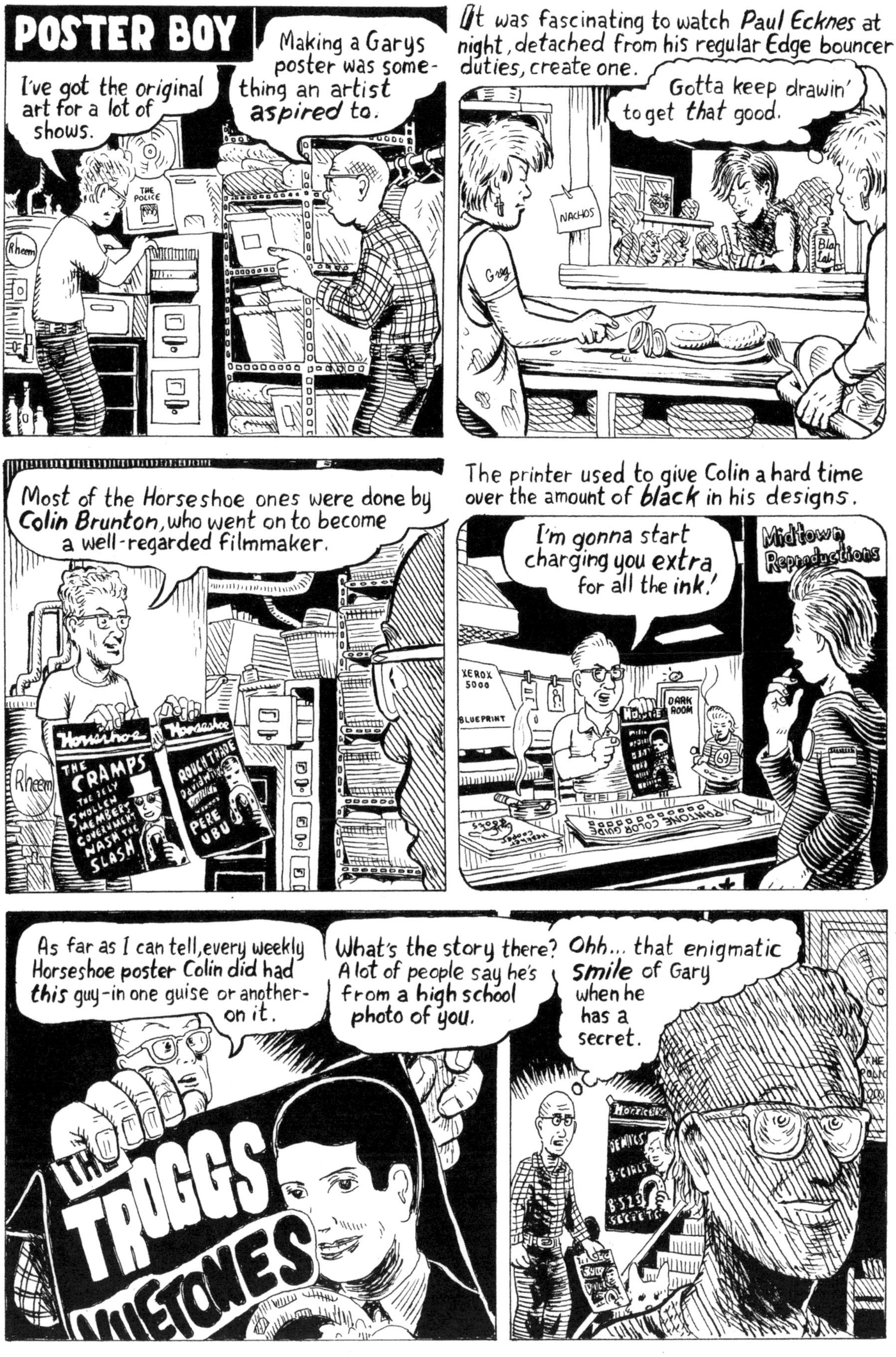
POSTER BOY
I've got the original art for a lot of shows.
Making a Garys poster was something an artist aspired to.
It was fascinating to watch Paul Ecknes at night, detached from his regular Edge bouncer duties, create one.
Gotta keep drawin' to get that good.
NACHOS
Most of the Horseshoe ones were done by Colin Brunton, who went on to become a well-regarded filmmaker.
Horseshoe THE CRAMPS THE FLY SWOLLEN MEMBERS GOVERNMENT NASH THE SLASH
Horseshoe ROUGH TRADE PERE UBU
The printer used to give Colin a hard time over the amount of black in his designs.
I'm gonna start charging you extra for all the ink!
Midtown Reproductions
XEROX 5000
BLUEPRINT
DARK ROOM
PANTONE COLOR GUIDE
As far as I can tell, every weekly Horseshoe poster Colin did had this guy-in one guise or another-on it.
What's the story there? A lot of people say he's from a high school photo of you.
Ohh... that enigmatic smile of Gary when he has a secret.
THE TROGGS
B-GIRLS
B-52'S

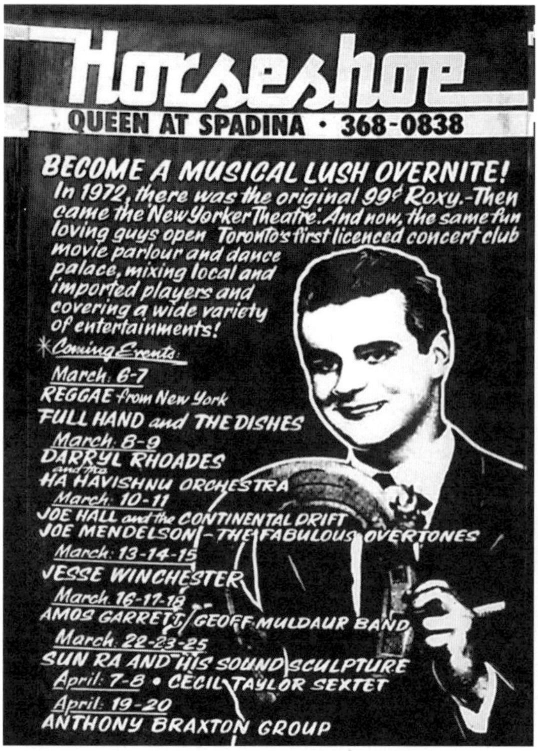
Horseshoe
QUEEN AT SPADINA • 368-0838
BECOME A MUSICAL LUSH OVERNITE!
In 1972, there was the original 99¢ Roxy.-Then came the 'New Yorker Theatre'. And now, the same fun loving guys open Toronto's first licenced concert club movie parlour and dance palace, mixing local and imported players and covering a wide variety of entertainments!
*Coming Events:
March 6-7
REGGAE from New York
FULL HAND and THE DISHES
March 8-9
DARRYL RHOADES and the HA HAVISHNU ORCHESTRA
March 10-11
JOE HALL and the CONTINENTAL DRIFT
JOE MENDELSON - THE FABULOUS OVERTONES
March 13-14-15
JESSE WINCHESTER
March 16-17-18
AMOS GARRETT/GEOFF MULDAUR BAND
March 22-23-25
SUN RA AND HIS SOUND SCULPTURE
April 7-8 • CECIL TAYLOR SEXTET
April 19-20
ANTHONY BRAXTON GROUP

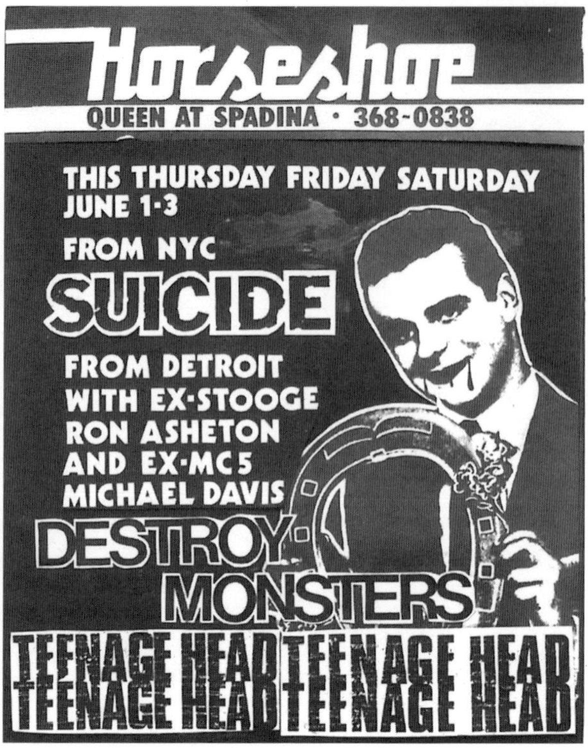
Horseshoe
QUEEN AT SPADINA • 368-0838
THIS THURSDAY FRIDAY SATURDAY
JUNE 1-3
FROM NYC
SUICIDE
FROM DETROIT
WITH EX-STOOGE
RON ASHETON
AND EX-MC5
MICHAEL DAVIS
DESTROY MONSTERS
TEENAGE HEAD TEENAGE HEAD
TEENAGE HEAD TEENAGE HEAD

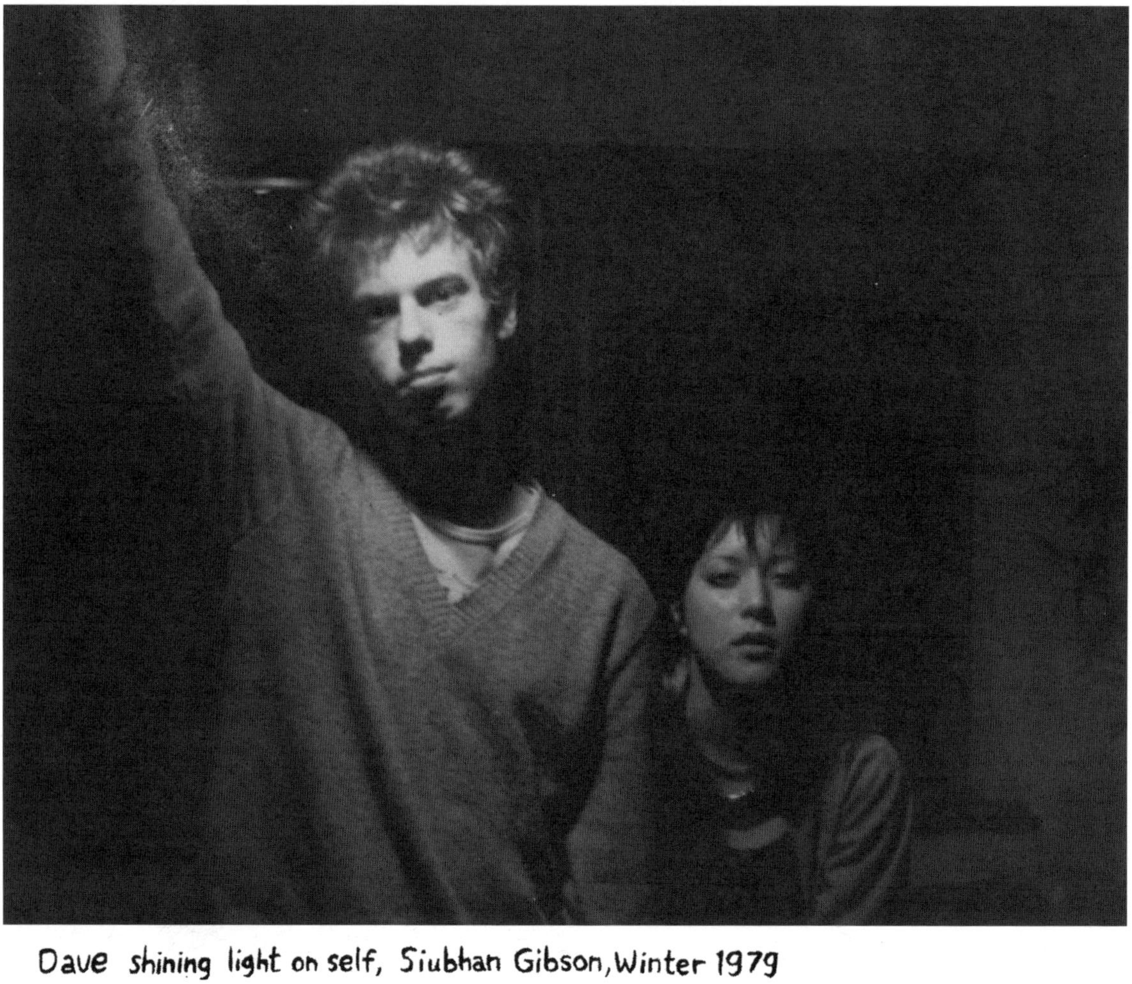

Dave shining light on self, Siubhan Gibson, Winter 1979

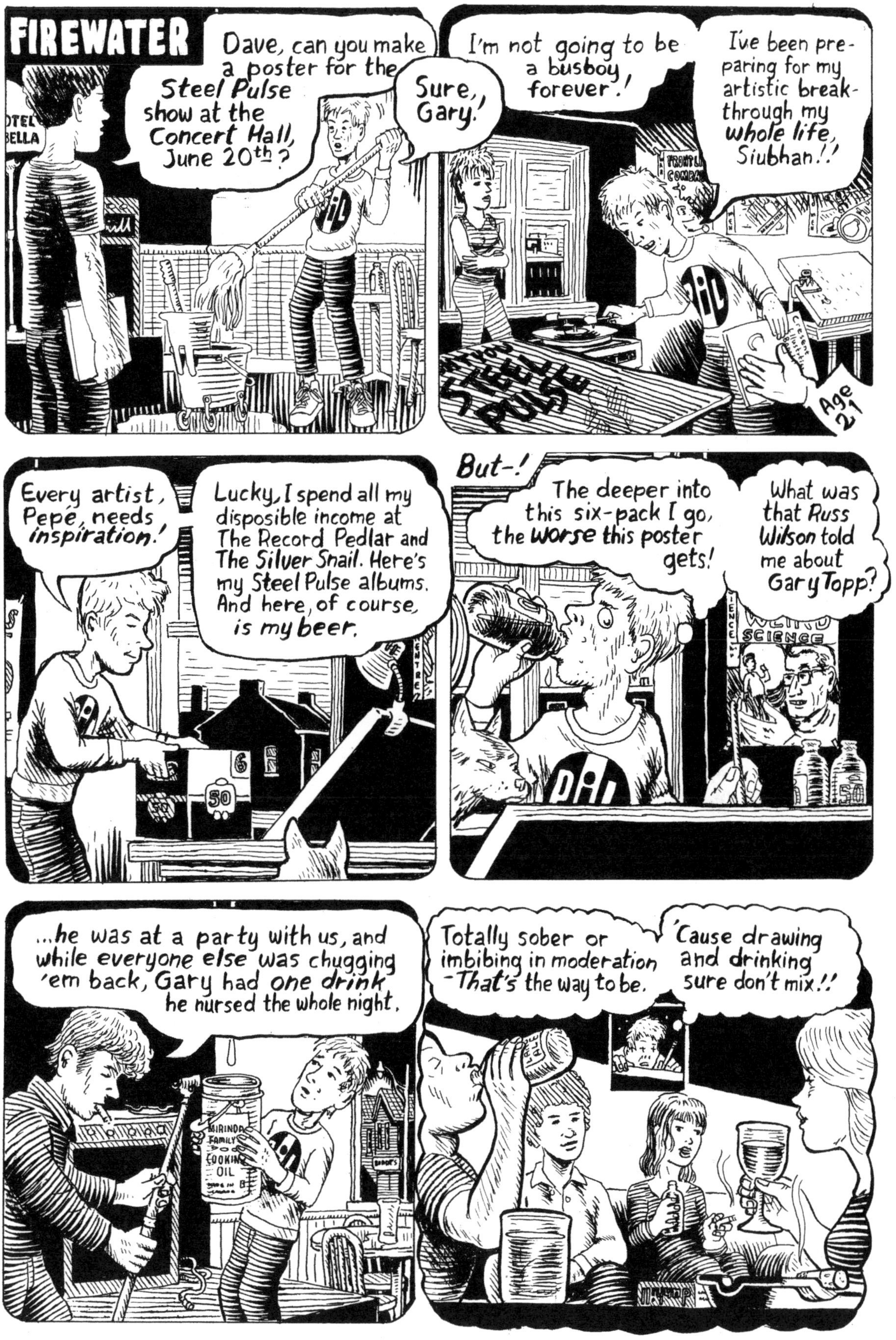
FIREWATER
Dave, can you make a poster for the Steel Pulse show at the Concert Hall, June 20th?
Sure, Gary!
I'm not going to be a busboy forever!
I've been preparing for my artistic breakthrough my whole life, Siubhan!!
Age 21
Every artist, Pepé, needs inspiration!
Lucky, I spend all my disposible income at The Record Pedlar and The Silver Snail. Here's my Steel Pulse albums. And here, of course, is my beer.
But-!
The deeper into this six-pack I go, the worse this poster gets!
What was that Russ Wilson told me about Gary Topp?
...he was at a party with us, and while everyone else was chugging 'em back, Gary had one drink he nursed the whole night.
Totally sober or imbibing in moderation -That's the way to be.
'Cause drawing and drinking sure don't mix!!

Posters by David Collier. Some of his first published art.

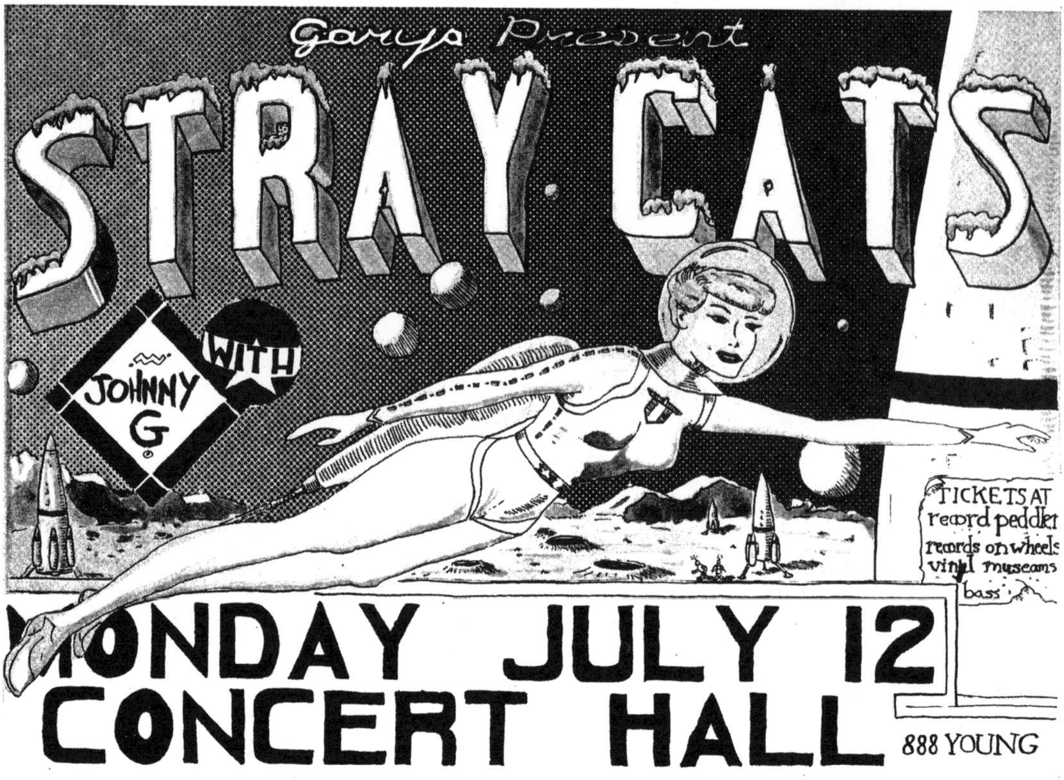
Garys Present
STRAY CATS
WITH
JOHNNY G.
TICKETS AT
record peddler
records on wheels
vinyl museums
bass
MONDAY JULY 12
CONCERT HALL
888 YOUNG

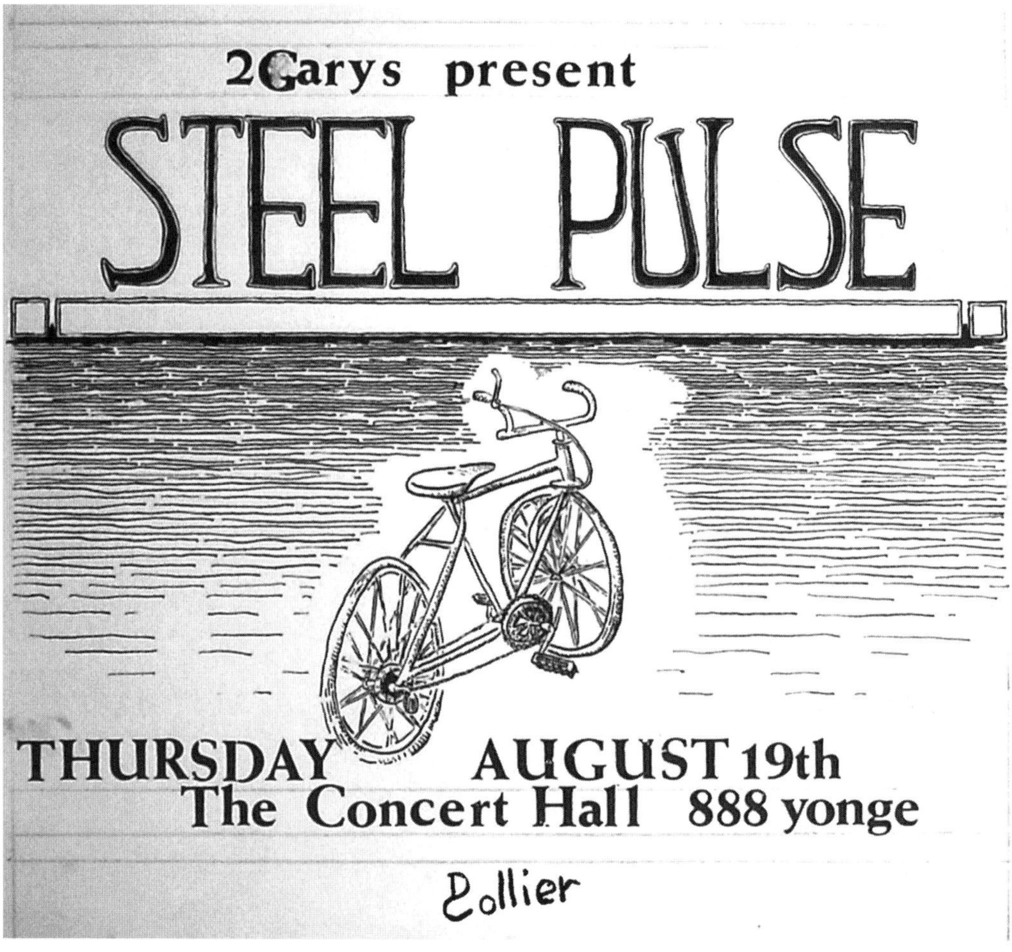
2Garys present
STEEL PULSE
THURSDAY AUGUST 19th
The Concert Hall 888 yonge
Collier

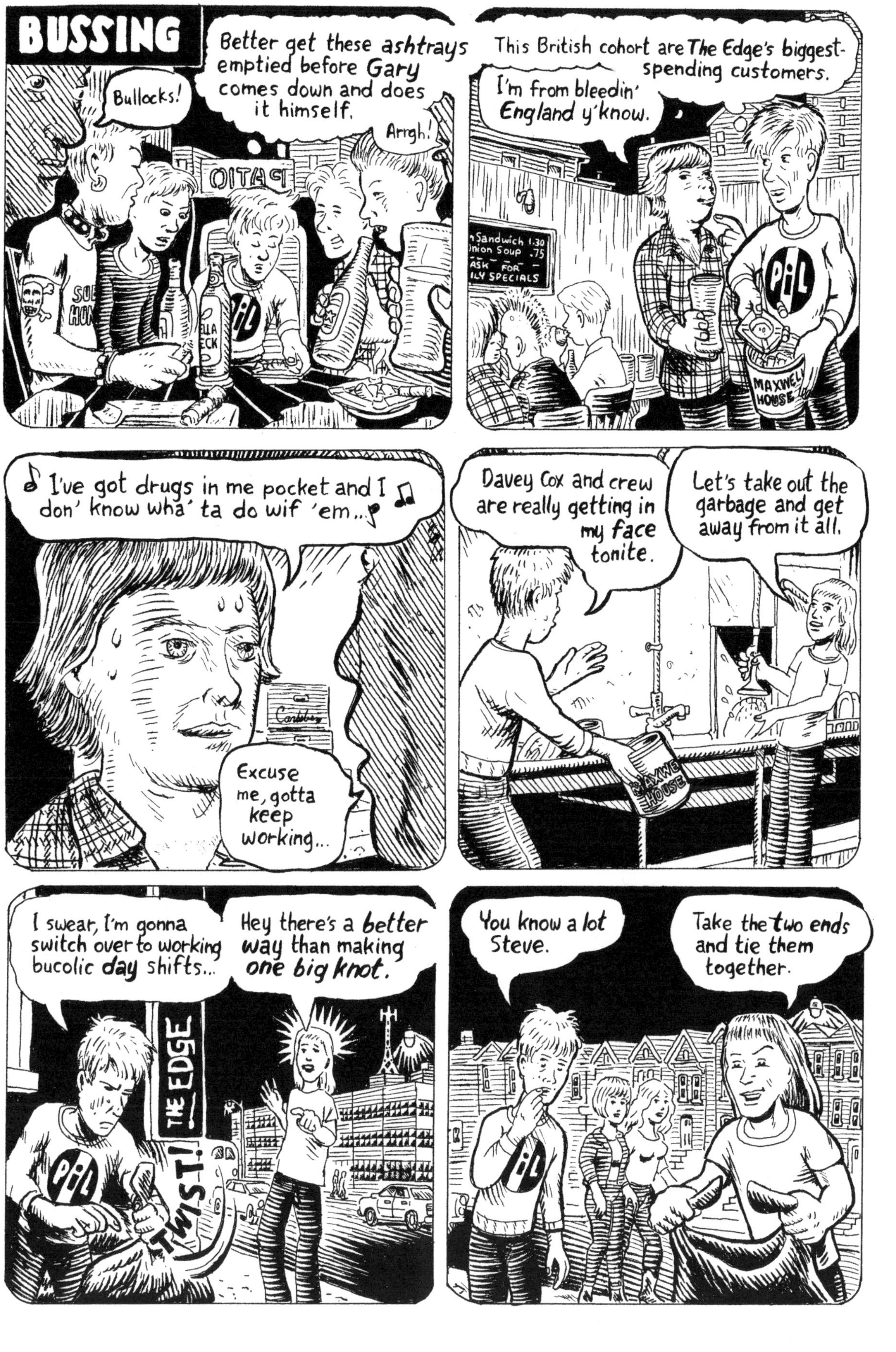

BUSSING
Bullocks!
Better get these ashtrays emptied before Gary comes down and does it himself.
Arrgh!
This British cohort are The Edge's biggest-spending customers.
I'm from bleedin' England y'know.
Sandwich 1.30
Onion Soup .75
ASK FOR
LY SPECIALS
MAXWELL HOUSE
I've got drugs in me pocket and I don' know wha' ta do wif 'em...
Excuse me, gotta keep working...
Davey Cox and crew are really getting in my face tonite.
Let's take out the garbage and get away from it all.
I swear, I'm gonna switch over to working bucolic day shifts...
Hey there's a better way than making one big knot.
THE EDGE
TWIST!
You know a lot Steve.
Take the two ends and tie them together.

BABYSLITTERS

At The Edge, there were these girls Regan and Karen, even younger than *me* who'd hang out at my busboy station.

Enjoy being young and handsome while you can, James.

When you're old like me, you become *invisible*.

We've renamed our band: we're now *The Babyslitters*.

Uh-

They had a *mentor*, an older -like maybe age *25*-woman who pierced my ear one night using a *potato* as a base.

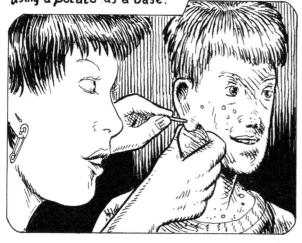

Then, with no place to go, we all spent a cold night trying to sleep on the porch of a house.

How close is she gonna let me come??

The older woman *friend*.

Last time Karen and me spoke, it was a few years later. We both had started getting our poetry and comics published. An acquaintance of hers had made unwanted advances the previous night.

And then he-he-

I know *you'd* never try something like that, Dave.

But it could happen. How I *yearned* for her friend, on the porch, that night.

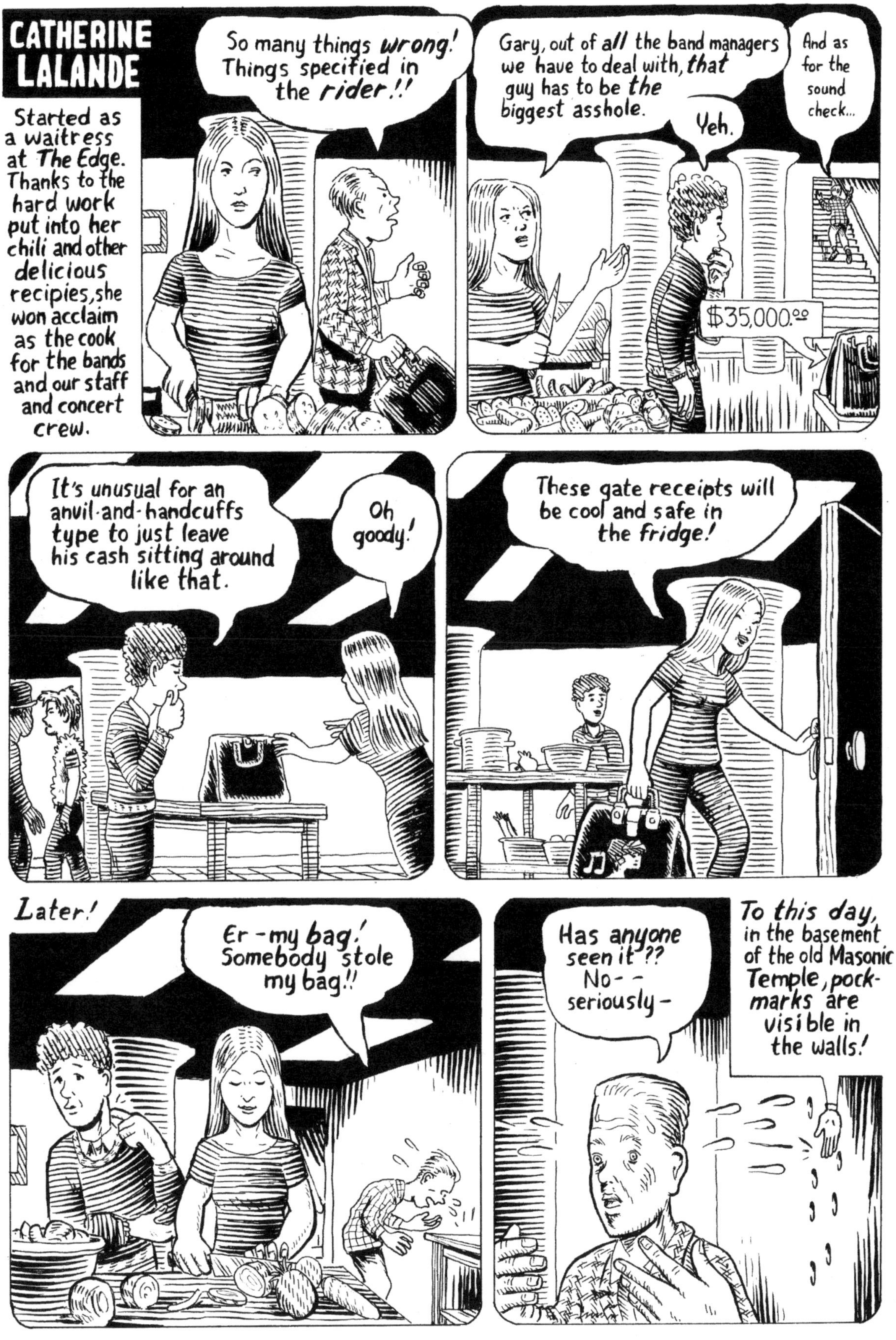
CATHERINE LALANDE
Started as a waitress at The Edge. Thanks to the hard work put into her chili and other delicious recipies, she won acclaim as the cook for the bands and our staff and concert crew.
So many things wrong! Things specified in the rider!!
Gary, out of all the band managers we have to deal with, that guy has to be the biggest asshole.
Yeh.
And as for the sound check...
$35,000.00
It's unusual for an anvil-and-handcuffs type to just leave his cash sitting around like that.
Oh goody!
These gate receipts will be cool and safe in the fridge!
Later!
Er-my bag! Somebody stole my bag!!
Has anyone seen it?? No-- seriously-
To this day, in the basement of the old Masonic Temple, pock-marks are visible in the walls!

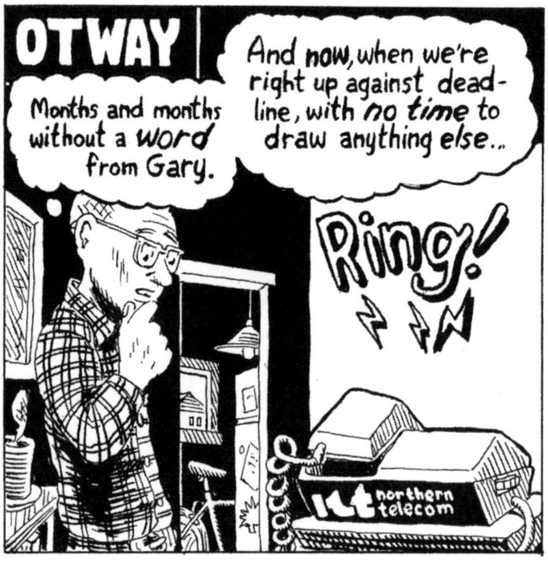
OTWAY
Months and months without a *word* from Gary.
And *now*, when we're right up against dead-line, with *no time* to draw anything else..
Ring!
northern telecom

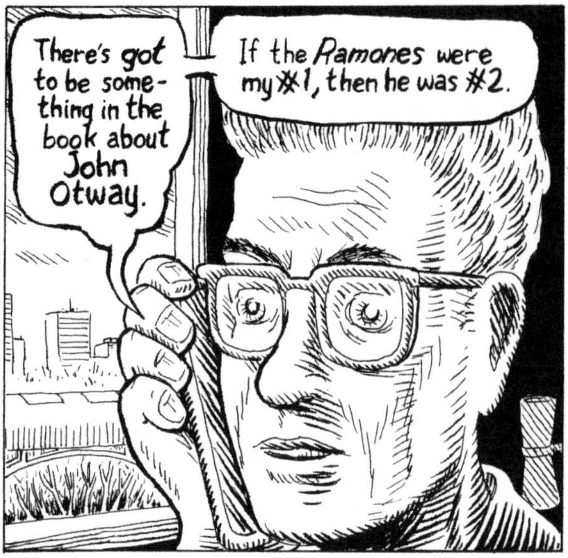
There's *got* to be some-thing in the book about John Otway.
If the *Ramones* were my #1, then he was #2.

*H*eather and I first saw him at London's Victoria Palace Theatre on December 16th, 1977.

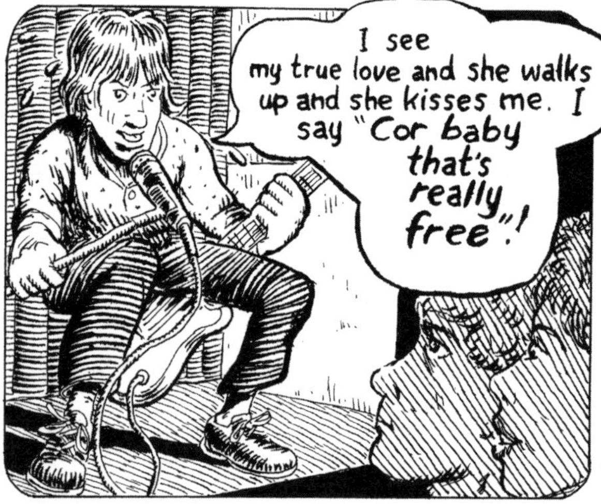
I see my true love and she walks up and she kisses me. I say "*Cor baby that's really free*"!

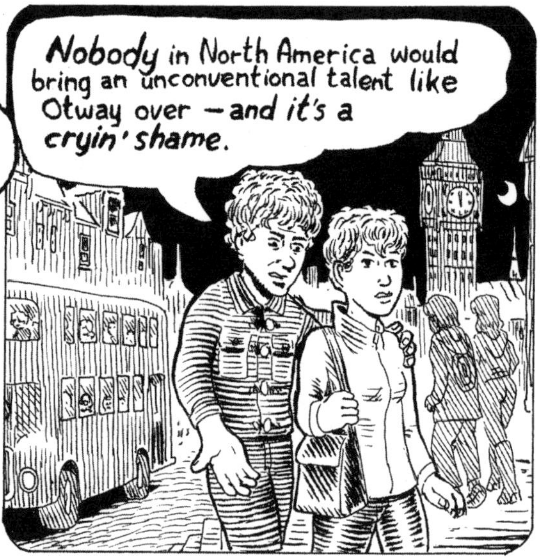
Nobody in North America would bring an unconventional talent like Otway over — *and it's* a *cryin' shame*.

*O*tway never appealed to the mainstream. At The Police Picnic people pelted him and Wild Willy Barrett with pieces of *watermelon* Heather was selling.

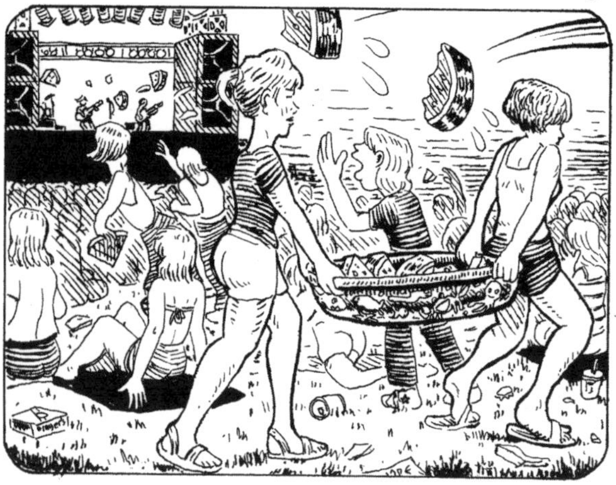

*A*nd yet *forty years later*, Otway is the *lone voice* still playing in the spirit of those times. He'll have his 5,000th gig, Easter weekend, 2021. The last time he crossed the Atlantic, a bus load of his fans came with him.

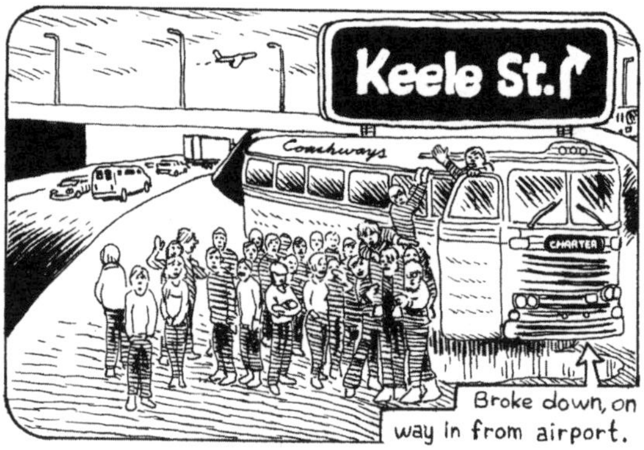
Keele St.
Coachways
CHARTER

Broke down, on way in from airport.

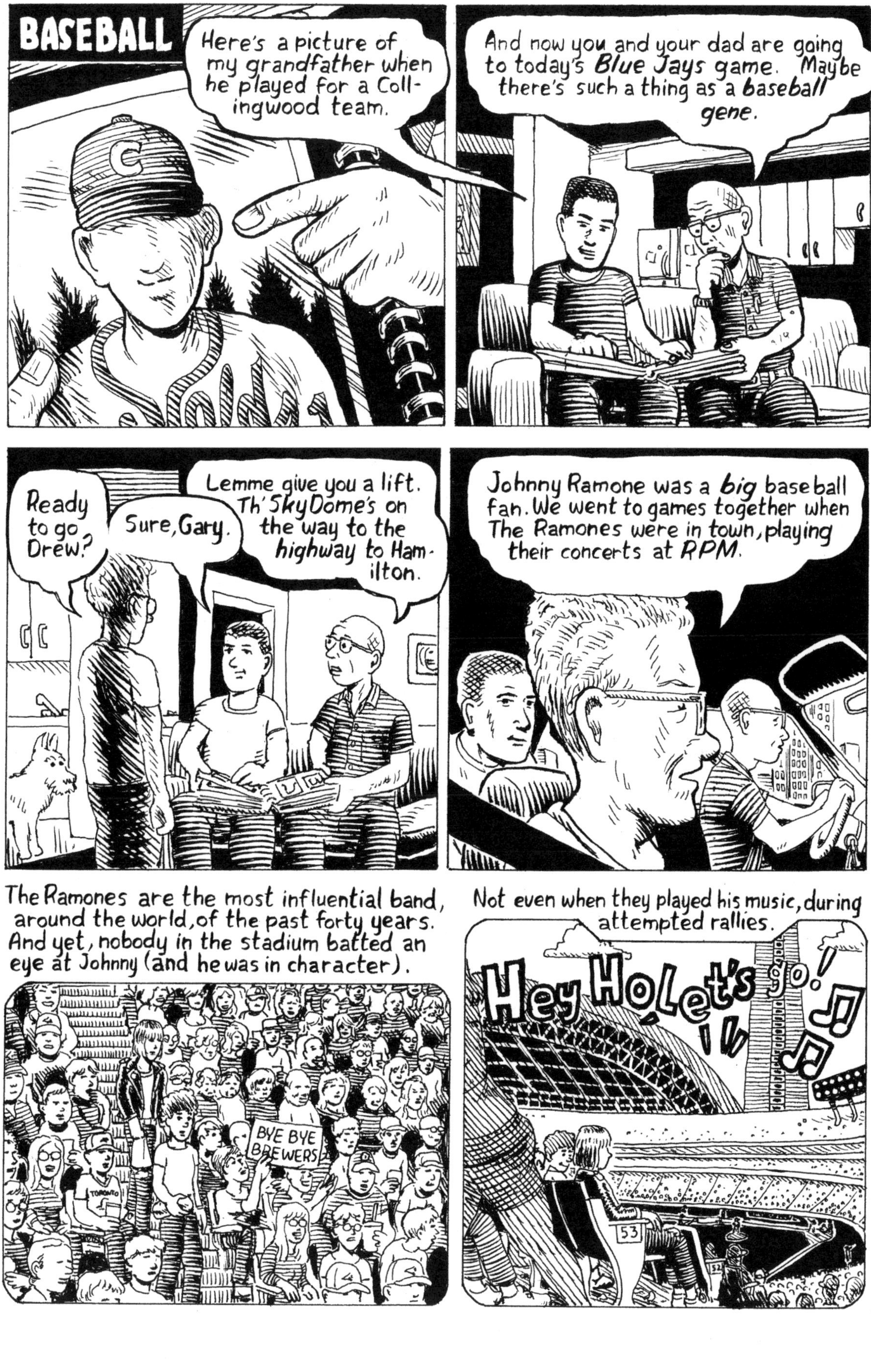
BASEBALL
Here's a picture of my grandfather when he played for a Coll-ingwood team.
And now you and your dad are going to today's Blue Jays game. Maybe there's such a thing as a baseball gene.
Ready to go Drew?
Sure, Gary.
Lemme give you a lift. Th' SkyDome's on the way to the highway to Ham-ilton.
Johnny Ramone was a big baseball fan. We went to games together when The Ramones were in town, playing their concerts at RPM.
The Ramones are the most influential band, around the world, of the past forty years. And yet, nobody in the stadium batted an eye at Johnny (and he was in character).
BYE BYE BREWERS
TORONTO
Not even when they played his music, during attempted rallies.
Hey Ho Let's go!
53
52

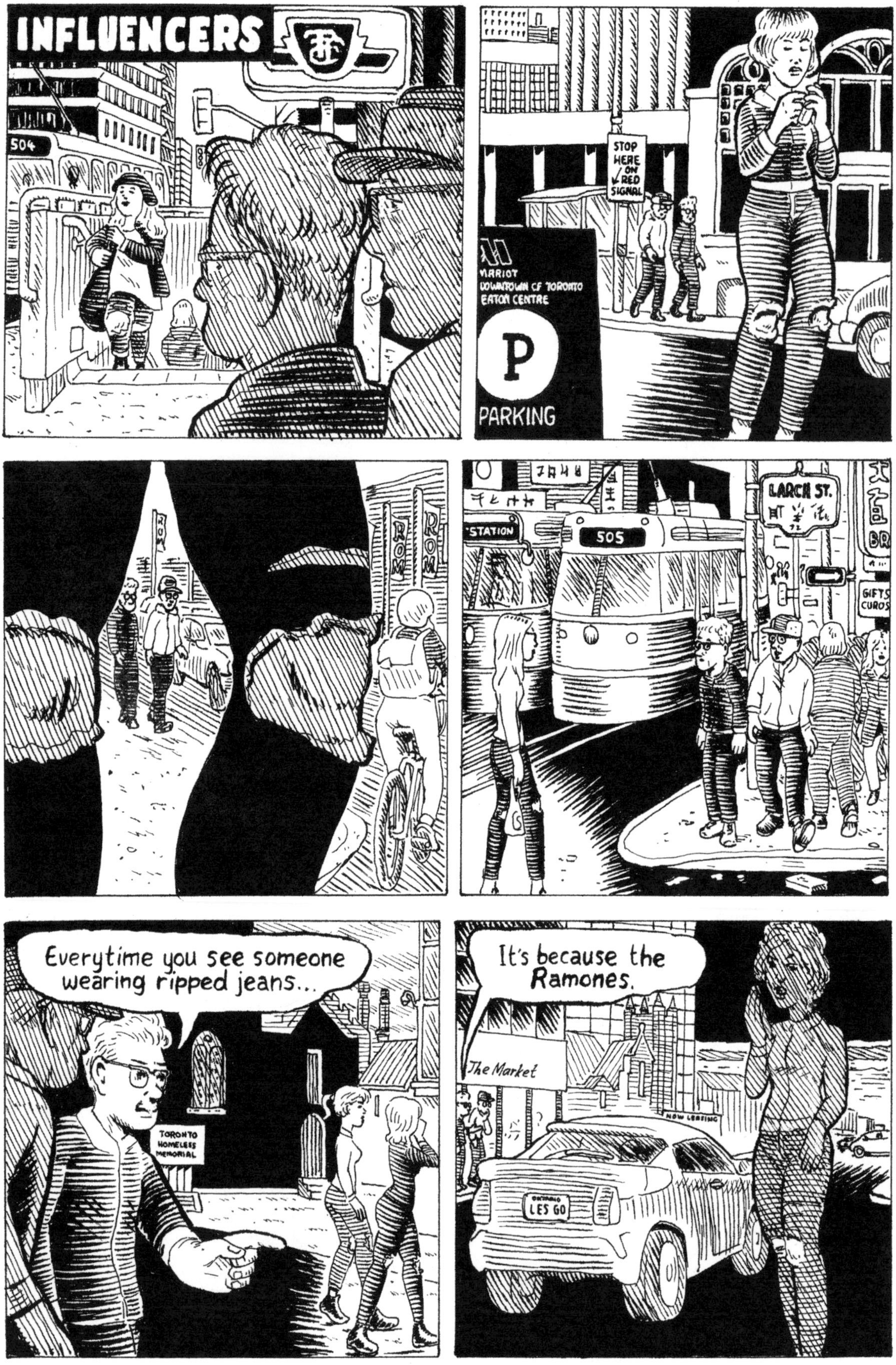
INFLUENCERS
504
STOP HERE ON RED SIGNAL
MARIOT DOWNTOWN OF TORONTO EATON CENTRE
P
PARKING
ROM
ROM
STATION
505
LARCH ST.
Everytime you see someone wearing ripped jeans...
TORONTO HOMELESS MEMORIAL
It's because the *Ramones*.
The Market
NOW LEASING
ONTARIO
LES GO

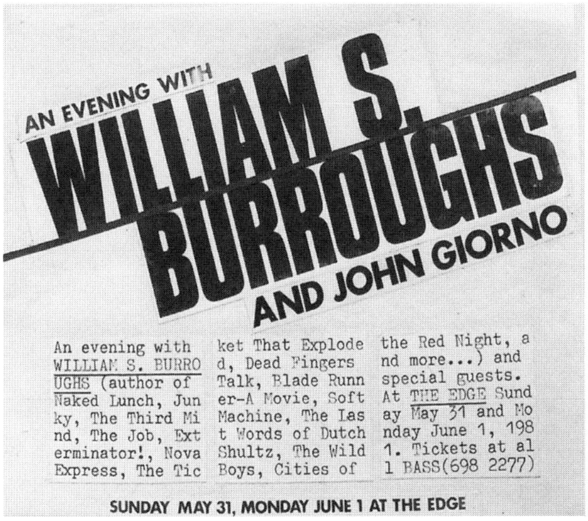
AN EVENING WITH
WILLIAM S. BURROUGHS
AND JOHN GIORNO
An evening with WILLIAM S. BURROUGHS (author of Naked Lunch, Junky, The Third Mind, The Job, Exterminator!, Nova Express, The Ticket That Exploded, Dead Fingers Talk, Blade Runner-A Movie, Soft Machine, The Last Words of Dutch Shultz, The Wild Boys, Cities of the Red Night, and more...) and special guests. At THE EDGE Sunday May 31 and Monday June 1, 1981. Tickets at all BASS(698 2277)
SUNDAY MAY 31, MONDAY JUNE 1 AT THE EDGE

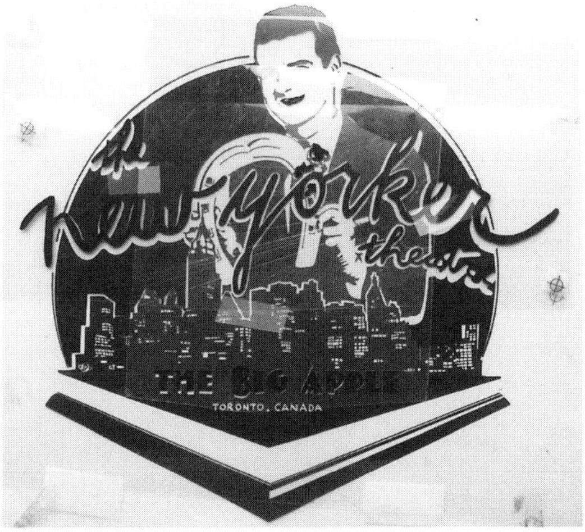
the new yorker theatre
THE BIG APPLE
TORONTO, CANADA

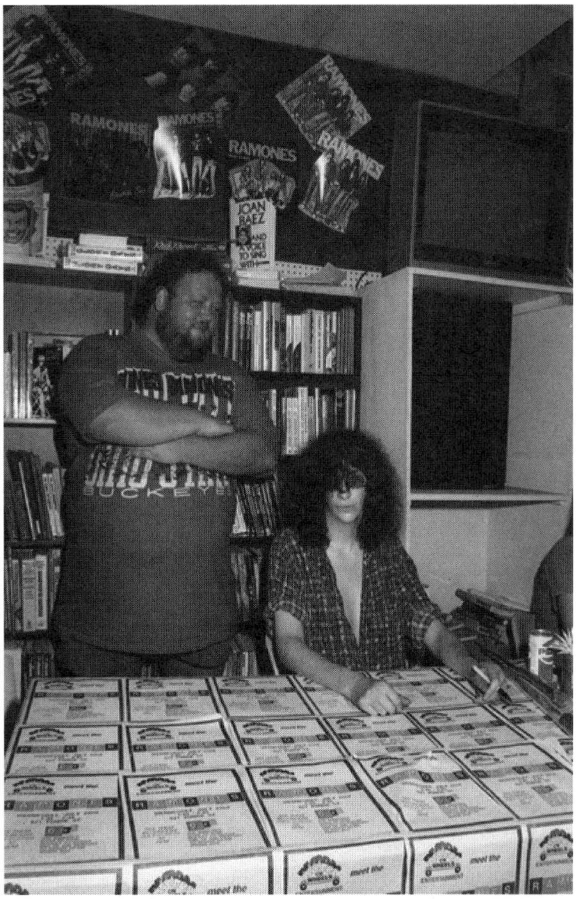
RAMONES
meet the

Dave “Tank” Roberts with Joey Ramone
at Records on Wheels (RIP Rosie)

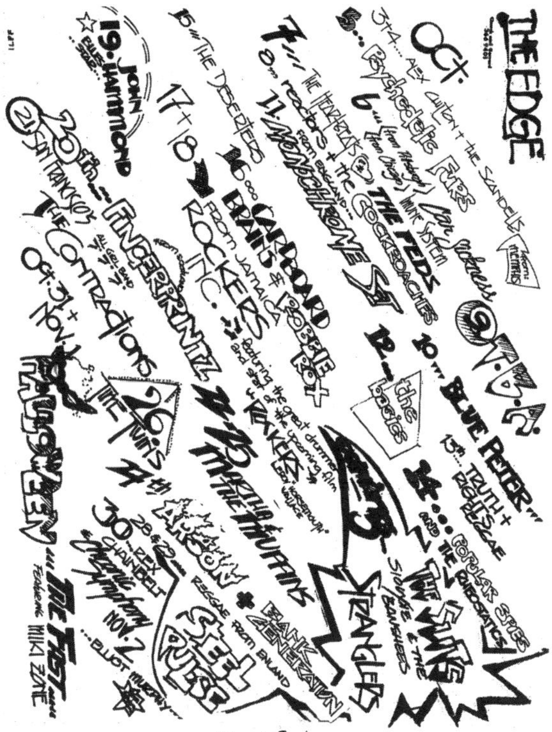
THE EDGE
OCT.
BLUE PETER
THE FEDS
THE COCKROACHES
STRANGLERS

Paul Ecknes

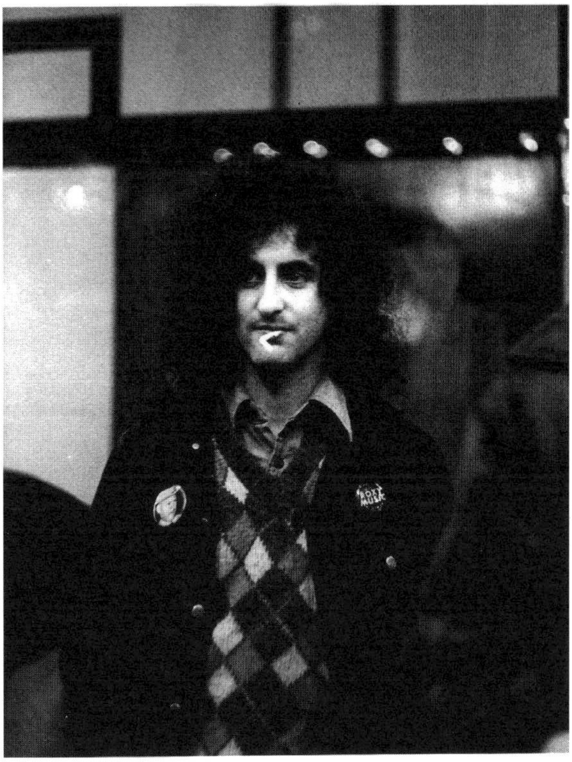

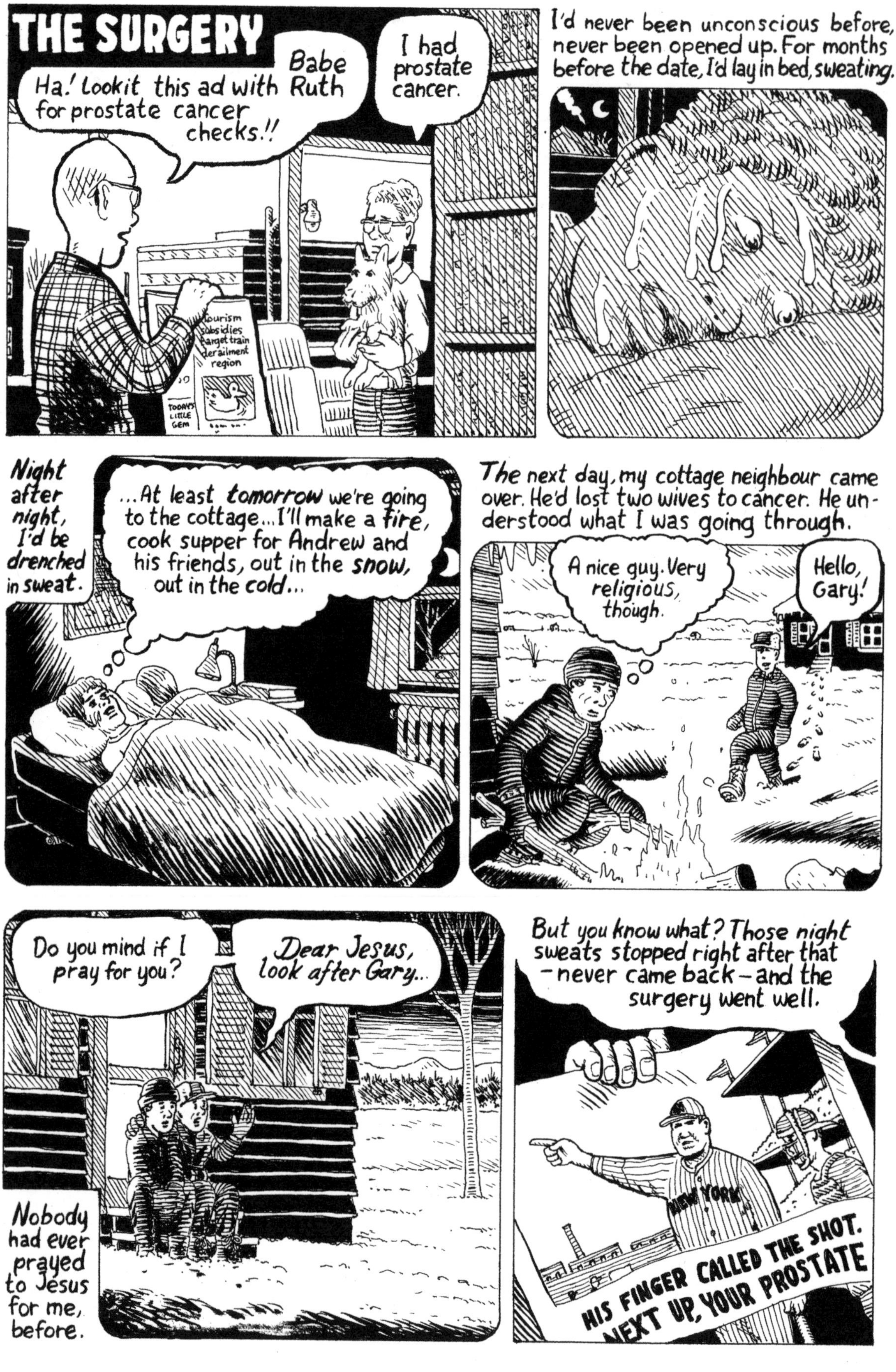

THE SURGERY
Ha! Lookit this ad with Babe Ruth for prostate cancer checks!!
I had prostate cancer.
Tourism subsidies target train derailment region
TODAY'S LITTLE GEM
I'd never been unconscious before, never been opened up. For months before the date, I'd lay in bed, sweating.
Night after night, I'd be drenched in sweat.
...At least tomorrow we're going to the cottage...I'll make a fire, cook supper for Andrew and his friends, out in the snow, out in the cold...
The next day, my cottage neighbour came over. He'd lost two wives to cancer. He understood what I was going through.
A nice guy. Very religious, though.
Hello, Gary!
Do you mind if I pray for you?
Dear Jesus, look after Gary...
Nobody had ever prayed to Jesus for me, before.
But you know what? Those night sweats stopped right after that – never came back – and the surgery went well.
NEW YORK
HIS FINGER CALLED THE SHOT.
NEXT UP, YOUR PROSTATE

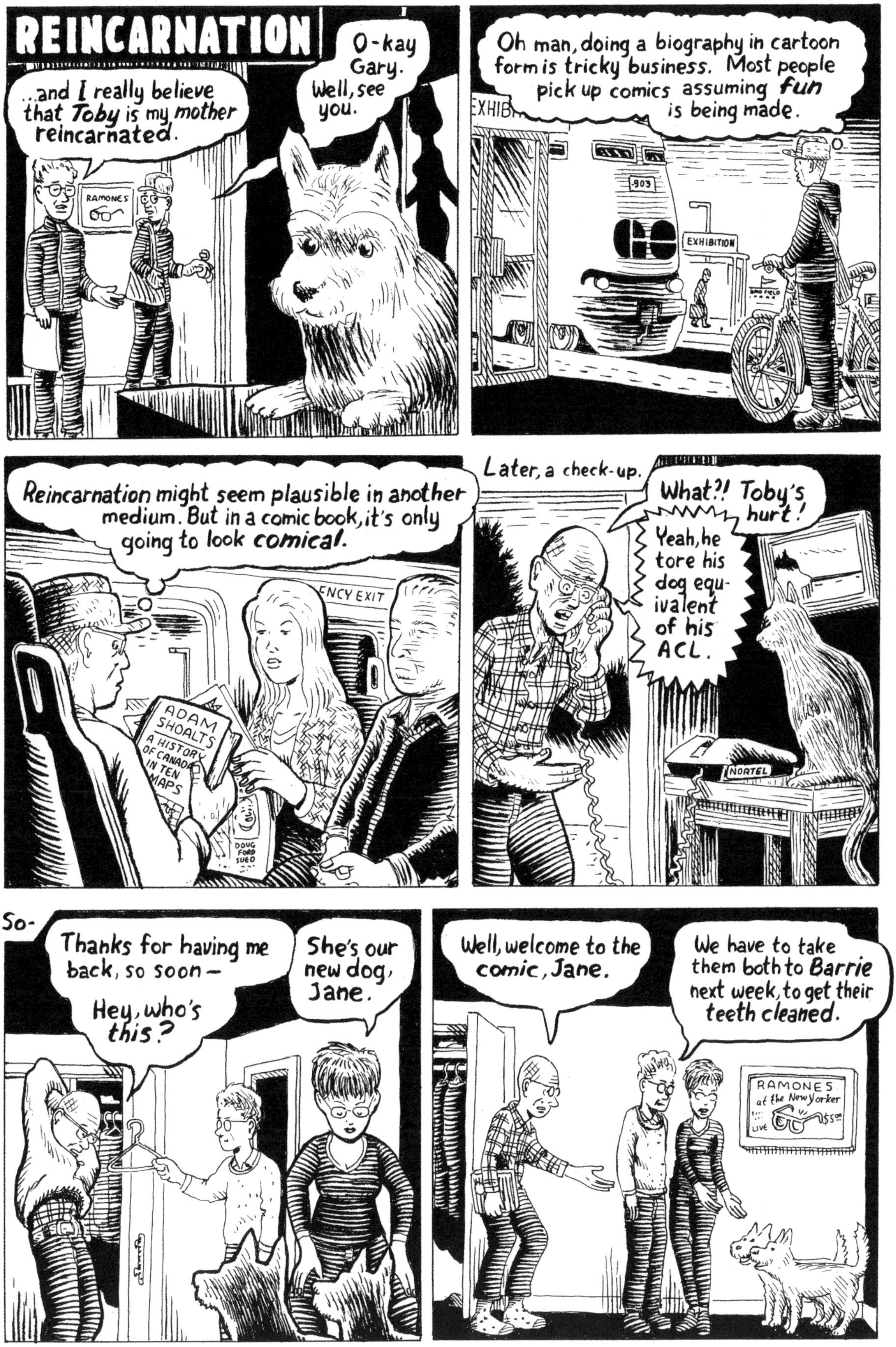
REINCARNATION
...and I really believe that Toby is my mother reincarnated.
RAMONES
O-kay Gary. Well, see you.
Oh man, doing a biography in cartoon form is tricky business. Most people pick up comics assuming fun is being made.
EXHIBITION
903
Reincarnation might seem plausible in another medium. But in a comic book, it's only going to look comical.
ENCY EXIT
ADAM SHOALTS A HISTORY OF CANADA IN TEN MAPS
DOUG FORD SUED
Later, a check-up.
What?! Toby's hurt!
Yeah, he tore his dog equivalent of his ACL.
NORTEL
So-
Thanks for having me back, so soon —
Hey, who's this?
She's our new dog, Jane.
Well, welcome to the comic, Jane.
We have to take them both to Barrie next week, to get their teeth cleaned.
RAMONES at the New Yorker
LIVE
$5.00

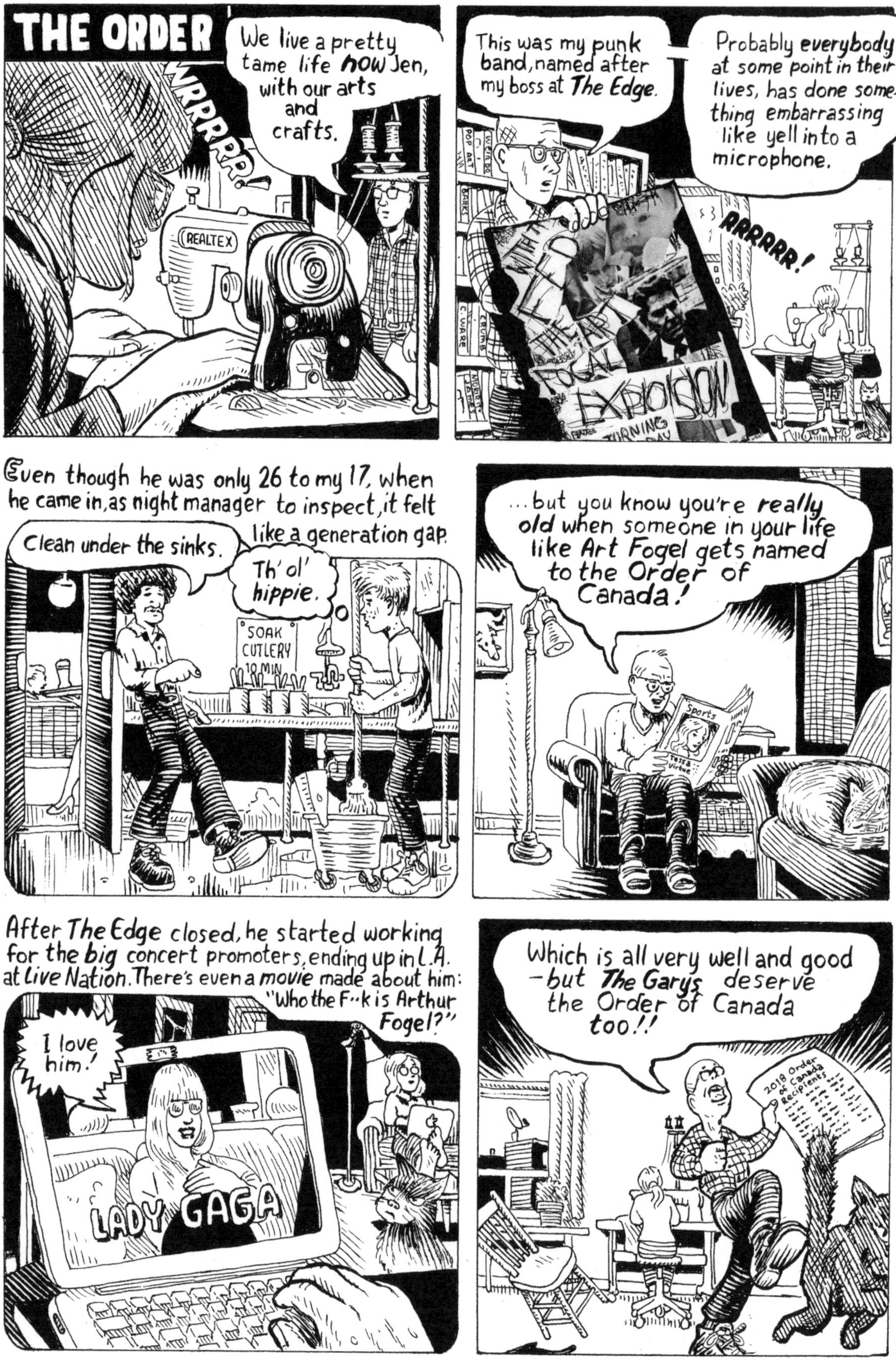
THE ORDER
We live a pretty tame life **now** Jen, with our arts and crafts.
WRRRRRR!
REALTEX
This was my punk band, named after my boss at *The Edge.*
Probably **everybody** at some point in their lives, has done something embarrassing like yell into a microphone.
ARRRRRR!
POP ART
BARKS
C. WARE
CRUMB
Even though he was only 26 to my 17, when he came in, as night manager to inspect, it felt like a generation gap.
Clean under the sinks.
Th' ol' **hippie**.
SOAK CUTLERY 10 MIN
...but you know you're **really old** when someone in your life like *Art Fogel* gets named to the Order of Canada!
Sports
Tessa Virtue
After **The Edge** closed, he started working for the **big** concert promoters, ending up in L.A. at *Live Nation*. There's even a *movie* made about him: "Who the F--k is Arthur Fogel?"
I love him!
LADY GAGA
Which is all very well and good —*but* **The Garys** deserve the Order of Canada too!!
2018 Order of Canada Recipients

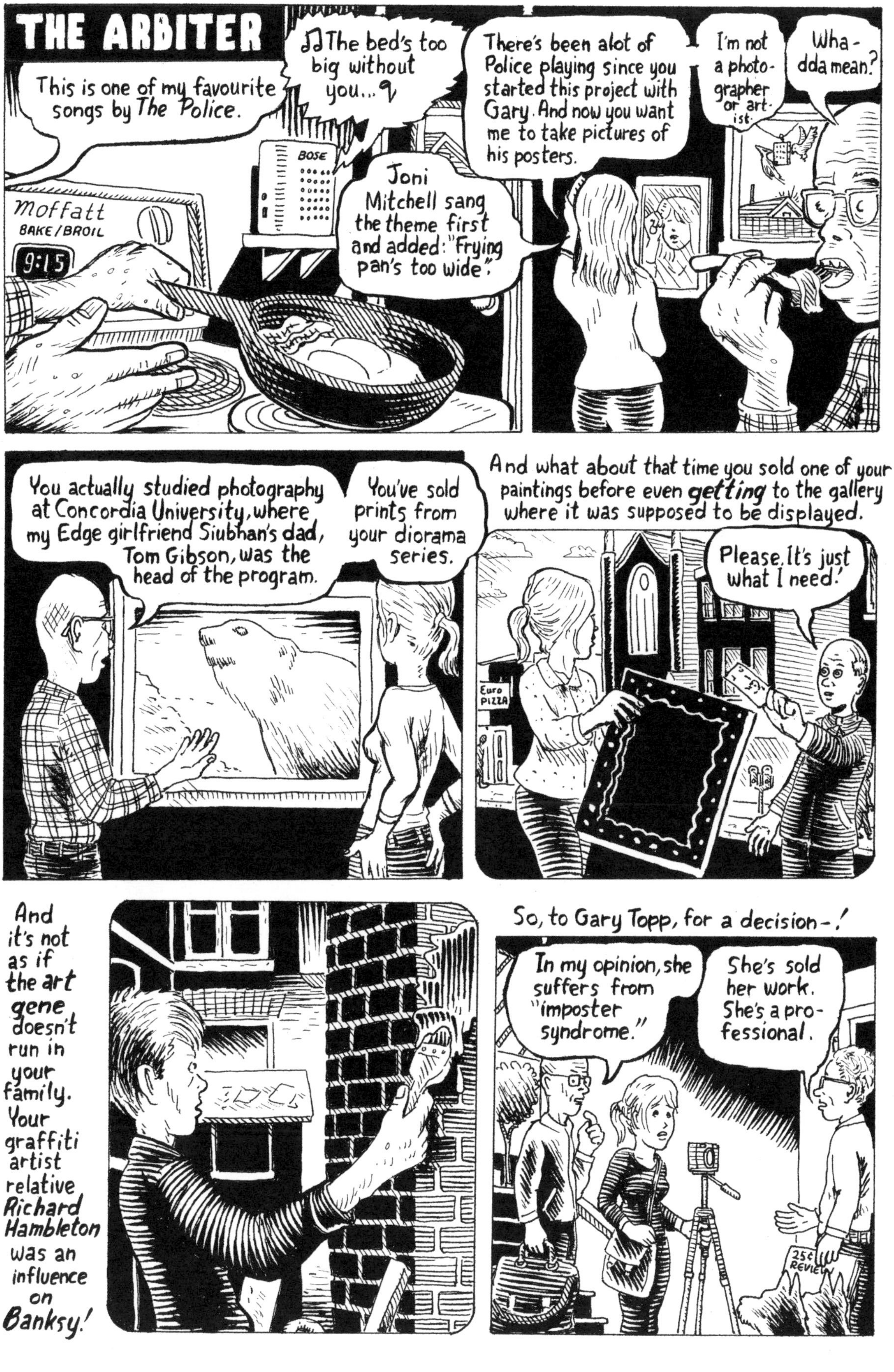
THE ARBITER
This is one of my favourite songs by The Police.
♫The bed's too big without you...♪
Moffatt
BAKE/BROIL
9:15
BOSE
Joni Mitchell sang the theme first and added: "Frying pan's too wide".
There's been alot of Police playing since you started this project with Gary. And now you want me to take pictures of his posters.
I'm not a photographer or artist.
Whadda mean?
You actually studied photography at Concordia University, where my Edge girlfriend Siubhan's dad, Tom Gibson, was the head of the program.
You've sold prints from your diorama series.
And what about that time you sold one of your paintings before even getting to the gallery where it was supposed to be displayed.
Please. It's just what I need!
Euro PIZZA
And it's not as if the art gene doesn't run in your family. Your graffiti artist relative Richard Hambleton was an influence on Banksy!
So, to Gary Topp, for a decision—!
In my opinion, she suffers from "imposter syndrome."
She's sold her work. She's a professional.

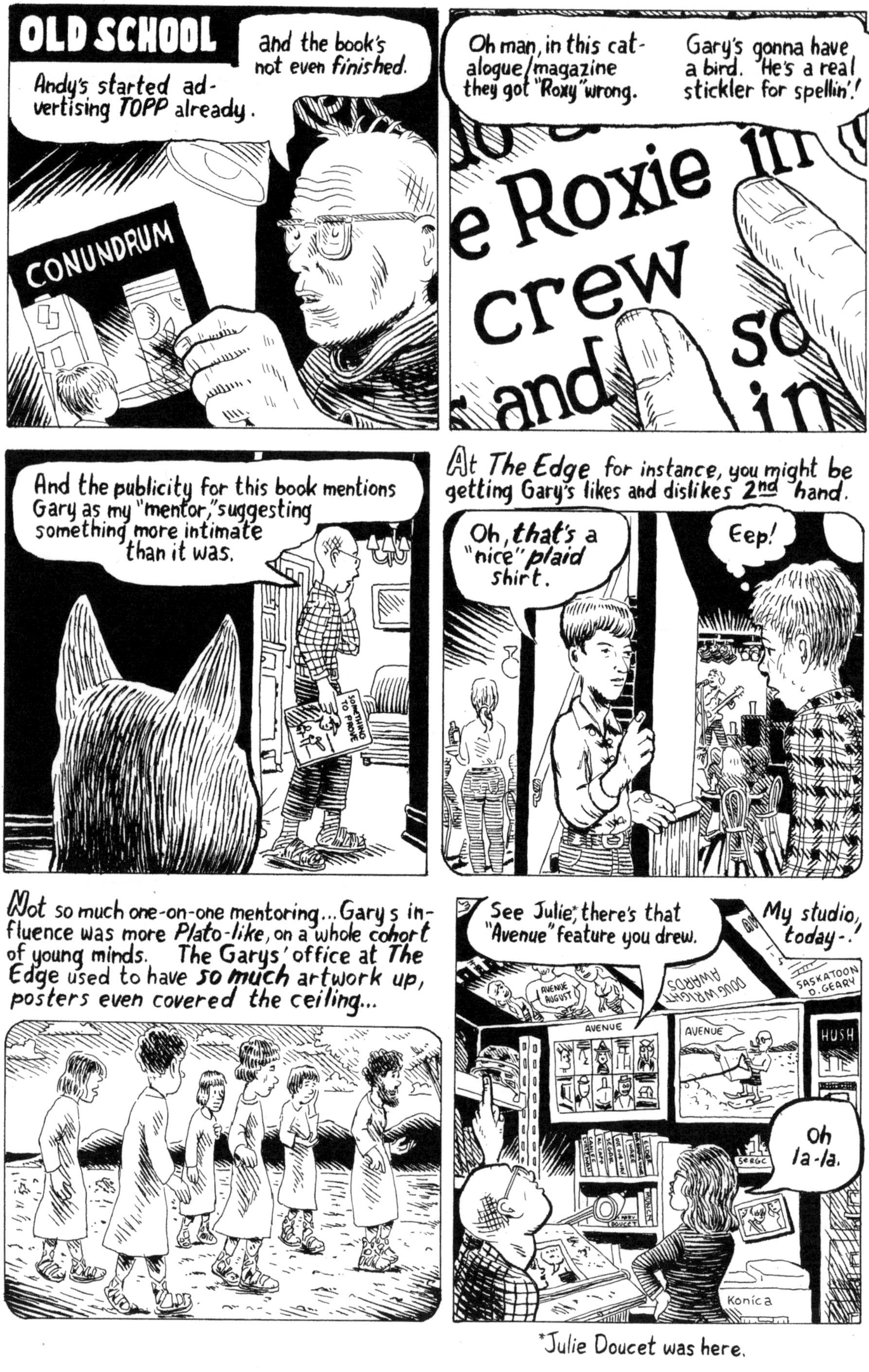
OLD SCHOOL
Andy's started advertising TOPP already.
and the book's not even *finished*.
CONUNDRUM
Oh man, in this catalogue/magazine they got "Roxy" wrong.
Gary's gonna have a bird. He's a real stickler for spellin'!
e Roxie in
crew
and so
And the publicity for this book mentions Gary as my "mentor," suggesting something more intimate than it was.
SOMETHING TO PROVE
At *The Edge* for instance, you might be getting Gary's likes and dislikes 2nd hand.
Oh, *that's* a "nice" *plaid* shirt.
Eep!
Not so much one-on-one mentoring... Gary's influence was more *Plato-like*, on a whole *cohort* of young minds. The Garys' office at *The Edge* used to have **so much** artwork up, posters even covered the ceiling...
See Julie,* there's that "Avenue" feature you drew.
My studio, today-!
DOUG WRIGHT AWARDS
SASKATOON D. GEARY
AVENUE AUGUST
AVENUE
AVENUE
HUSH
Oh la-la.
Konica

*Julie Doucet was here.

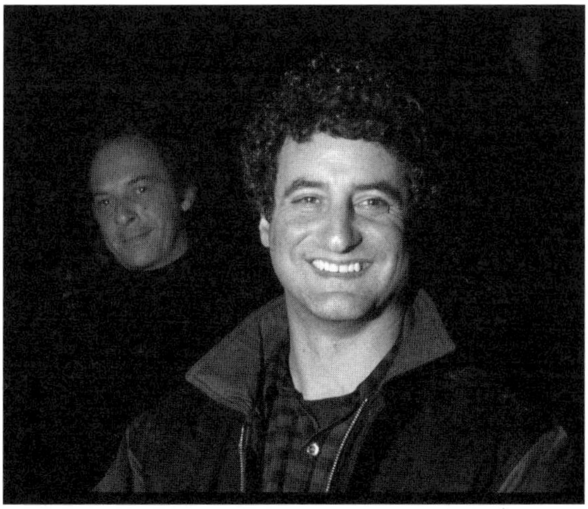

Gary and Gary at Massey Hall
(Photo: Viliam Hrubovcak / Jolie Fejer)

New Music video offends reader

NOW:

I am writing to you because you are Toronto's entertainment weekly and what I have to say concerns entertainment video and enterpreneurial arts going on in the city of Toronto.

Saturday night, July 2, I viewed what must be the most tasteless, boring and disgraceful video ever to be broadcast in this town, on Channel 79, The New Music. I couldn't believe what I was seeing!

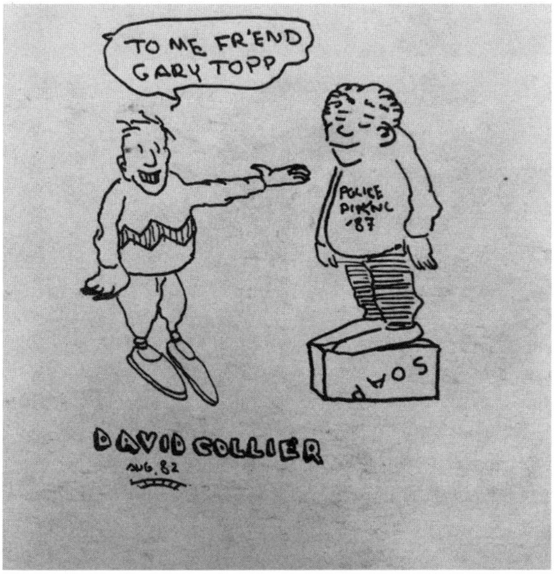
TO ME FR'END GARY TOPP
POLICE PICNIC '87
SOAP
DAVID COLLIER
AUG. 82

Sly video right on says reader

NOW:

[redacted]'s letter expressing indignation following the CITY TV video use of Sly Stone's song warrants some comment. To understand what the video was attempting necessitates knowing exactly what the title of the song is. It is *not* "Thank You For Letting Me Be Myself Again"; it is specifically "I Wanna Thank You For Letting Me Be Mice Elf Again". In fact it is a counter culture poem

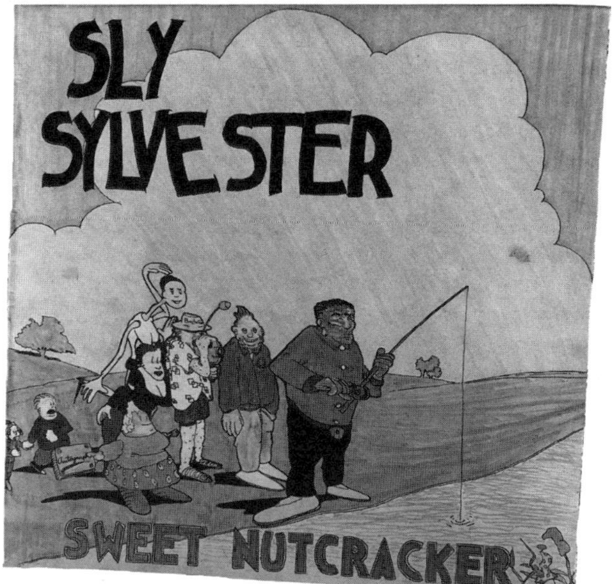
SLY SYLVESTER
SWEET NUTCRACKER

Following a scam of a Sly and the Family Stone concert (without the Family Stone) we made a sarcastic video. Superstar Sly Sylvester had a terrible fishing accident, lost his torso from the chest down and lived the rest of his life as a nutcracker in a bowl of nuts. One day, Gary shot a video for him as CFNY DJ Tim Keele who helped Sly do what he loved best, singing one of his biggest hits, "Thank you falettinme be mice elf again". The actual nutcracker was an artifact from apartheid South Africa and the silly video was meant as sarcasm against racism. Much Music liked it, aired it on national TV and received more complaints than it ever had. The Garys won several Black Music Awards and are not racist. For the video Dave drew the front and back of the album cover (featured here).

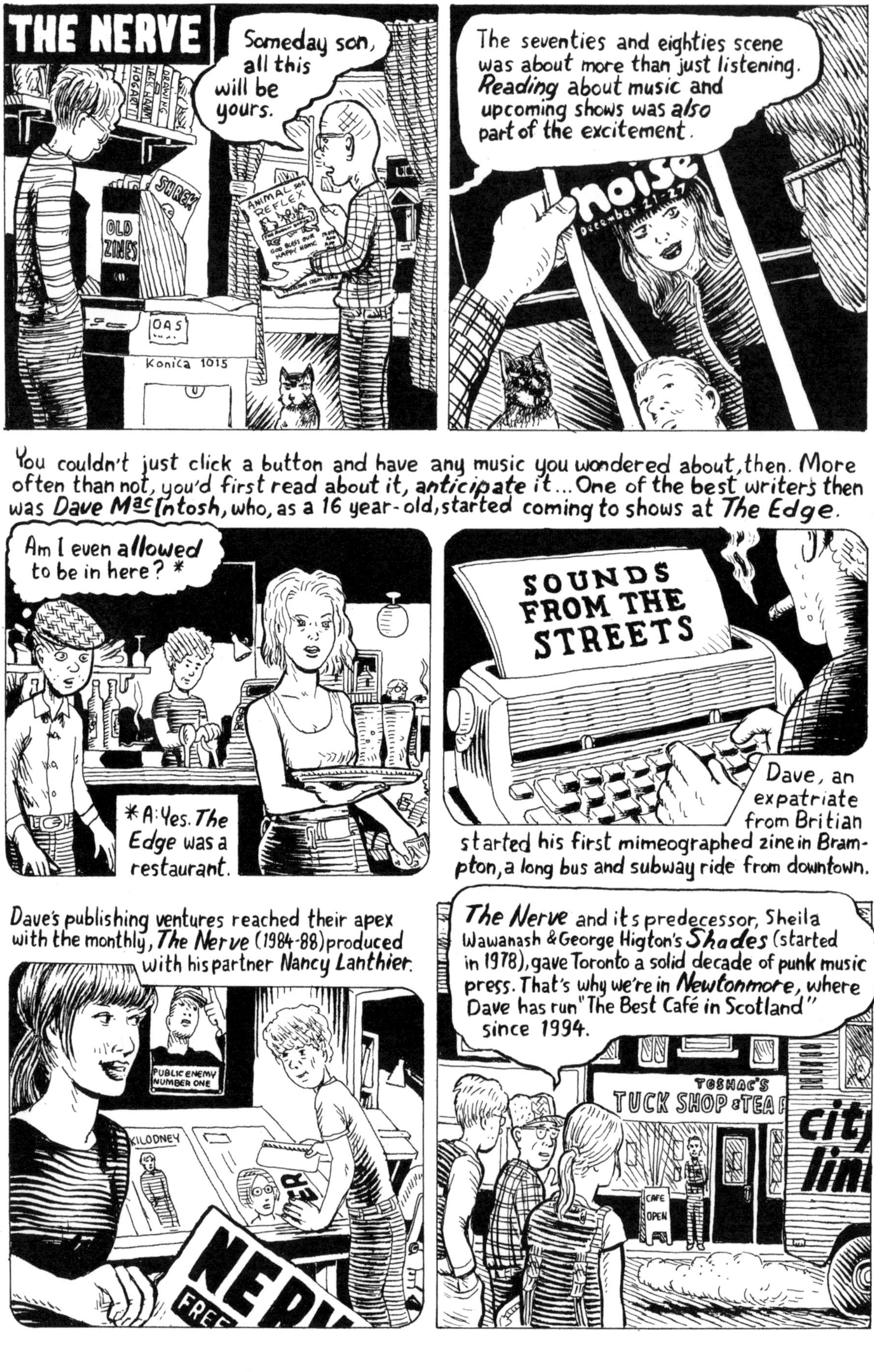
THE NERVE
Someday son, all this will be yours.
The seventies and eighties scene was about more than just listening. Reading about music and upcoming shows was also part of the excitement.
noise
December 21-27
OLD ZINES
SHREK
ANIMAL SOS REFLEX
Konica 1015
You couldn't just click a button and have any music you wondered about, then. More often than not, you'd first read about it, anticipate it... One of the best writers then was Dave MacIntosh, who, as a 16 year-old, started coming to shows at The Edge.
Am I even allowed to be in here? *
* A: Yes. The Edge was a restaurant.
SOUNDS FROM THE STREETS
Dave, an expatriate from Britian started his first mimeographed zine in Brampton, a long bus and subway ride from downtown.
Dave's publishing ventures reached their apex with the monthly, The Nerve (1984-88) produced with his partner Nancy Lanthier.
PUBLIC ENEMY NUMBER ONE
KILODNEY
NERV
FREE
The Nerve and its predecessor, Sheila Wawanash & George Higton's Shades (started in 1978), gave Toronto a solid decade of punk music press. That's why we're in Newtonmore, where Dave has run "The Best Café in Scotland" since 1994.
TOSHAC'S
TUCK SHOP & TEA
CAFE OPEN
city link

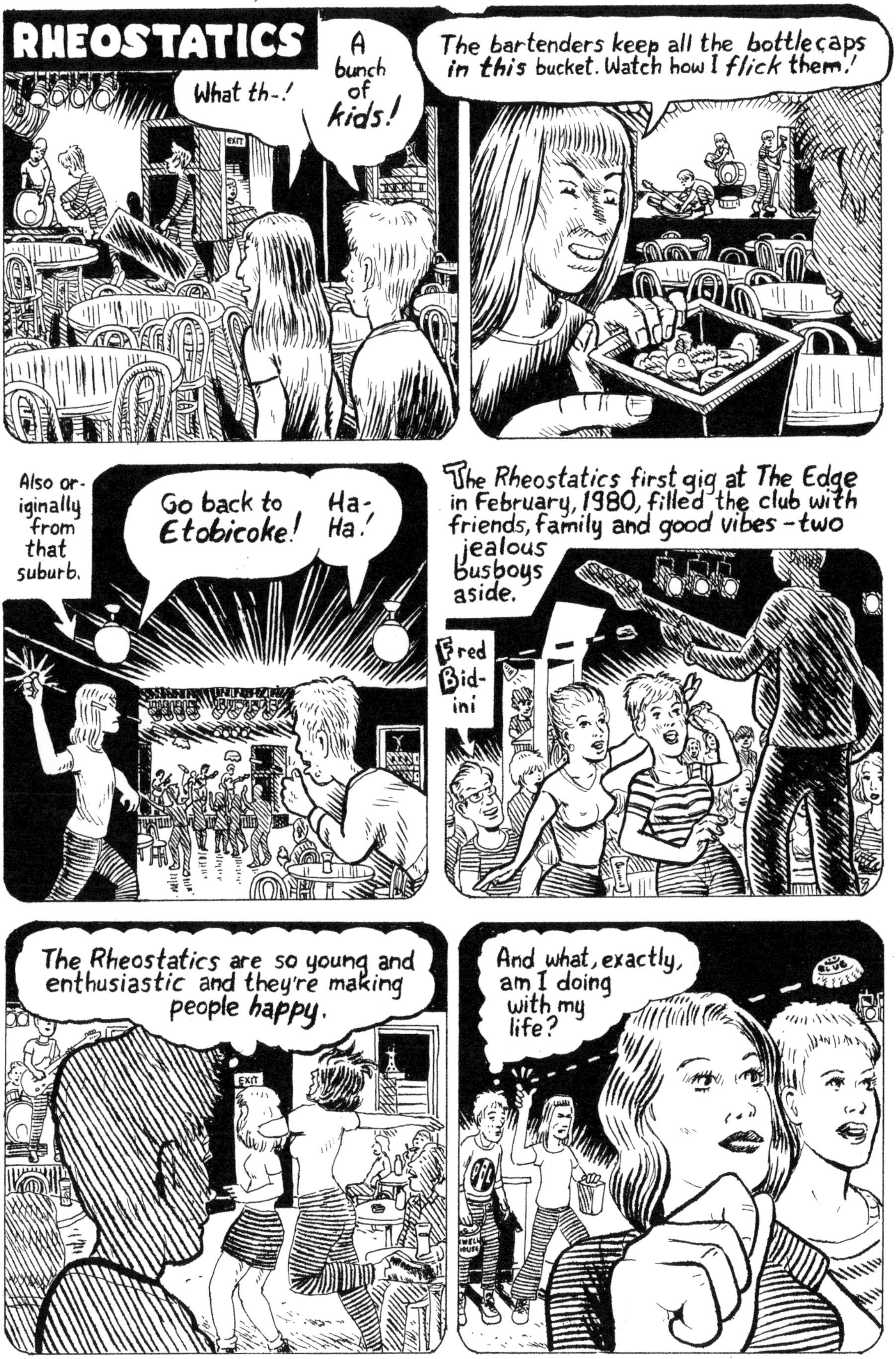
RHEOSTATICS
What th-!
A bunch of kids!
EXIT
The bartenders keep all the bottlecaps in this bucket. Watch how I flick them!
Also originally from that suburb.
Go back to Etobicoke!
Ha-Ha!
The Rheostatics first gig at The Edge in February, 1980, filled the club with friends, family and good vibes – two jealous busboys aside.
Fred Bidini
The Rheostatics are so young and enthusiastic and they're making people happy.
EXIT
And what, exactly, am I doing with my life?
BLUE

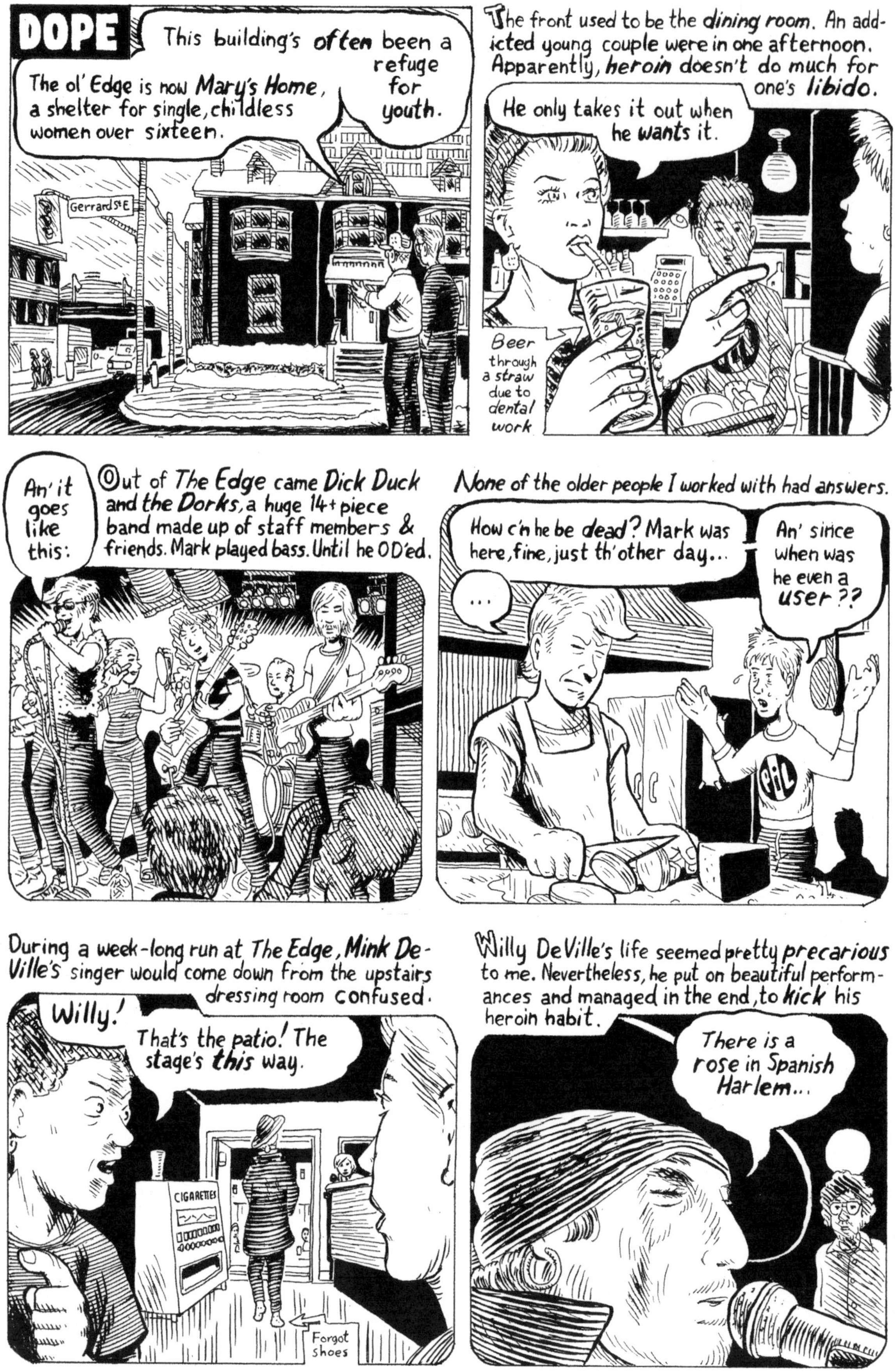
DOPE
The ol' Edge is now Mary's Home, a shelter for single, childless women over sixteen.
This building's often been a refuge for youth.
Gerrard St E
The front used to be the dining room. An addicted young couple were in one afternoon. Apparently, heroin doesn't do much for one's libido.
He only takes it out when he wants it.
Beer through a straw due to dental work
An' it goes like this:
Out of The Edge came Dick Duck and the Dorks, a huge 14+ piece band made up of staff members & friends. Mark played bass. Until he OD'ed.
None of the older people I worked with had answers.
How c'n he be dead? Mark was here, fine, just th'other day...
An' since when was he even a user??
...
PiL
During a week-long run at The Edge, Mink DeVille's singer would come down from the upstairs dressing room confused.
Willy!
That's the patio! The stage's this way.
CIGARETTES
Forgot shoes
Willy DeVille's life seemed pretty precarious to me. Nevertheless, he put on beautiful performances and managed in the end, to kick his heroin habit.
There is a rose in Spanish Harlem...

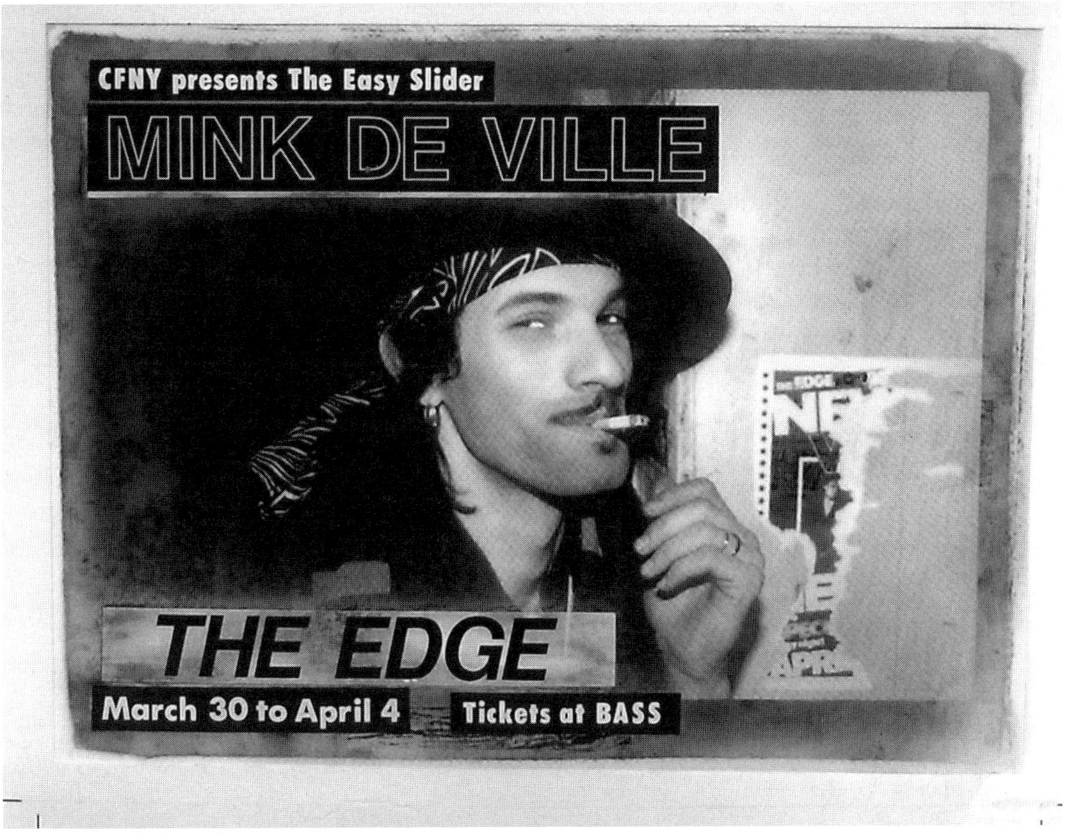

CFNY presents The Easy Slider
MINK DE VILLE
THE EDGE
March 30 to April 4
Tickets at BASS

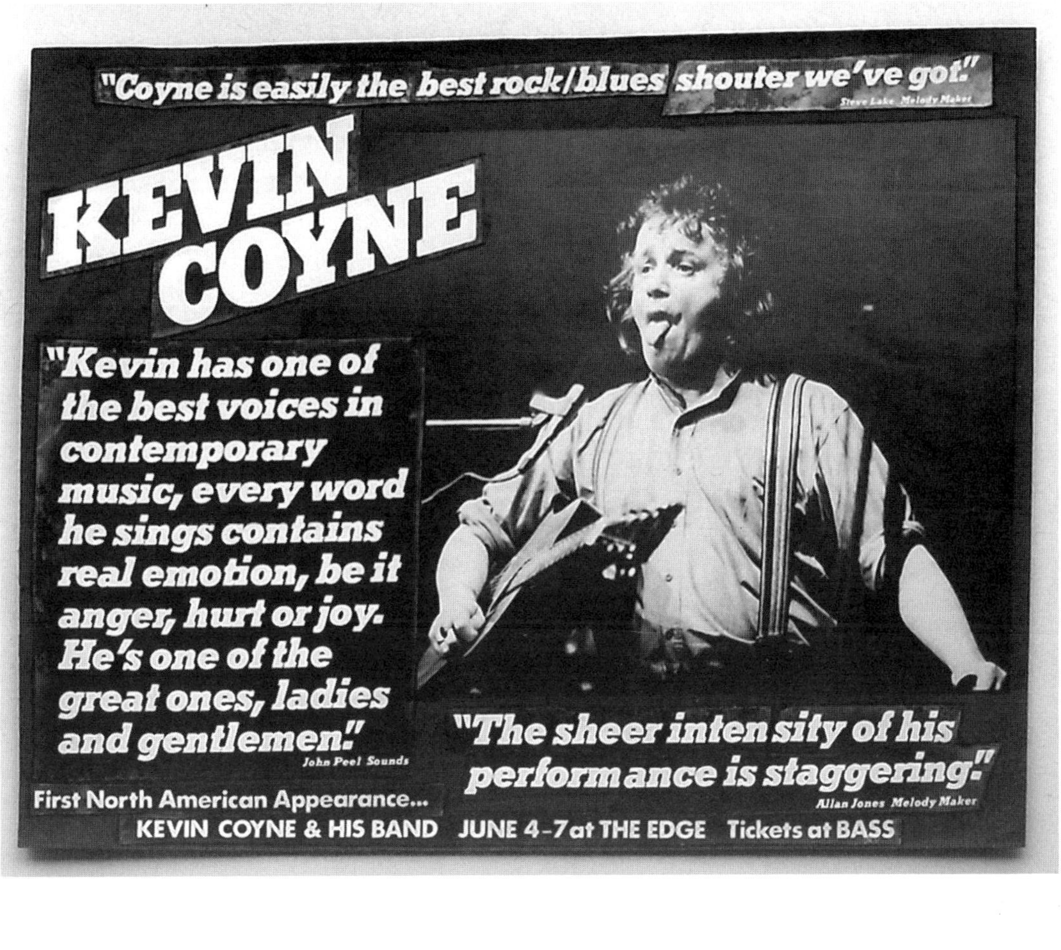

"Coyne is easily the best rock/blues shouter we've got."
Steve Lake Melody Maker
KEVIN COYNE
"Kevin has one of the best voices in contemporary music, every word he sings contains real emotion, be it anger, hurt or joy. He's one of the great ones, ladies and gentlemen."
John Peel Sounds
"The sheer intensity of his performance is staggering."
Allan Jones Melody Maker
First North American Appearance...
KEVIN COYNE & HIS BAND JUNE 4-7 at THE EDGE Tickets at BASS

PHOTOS BY P.L. NOBLE

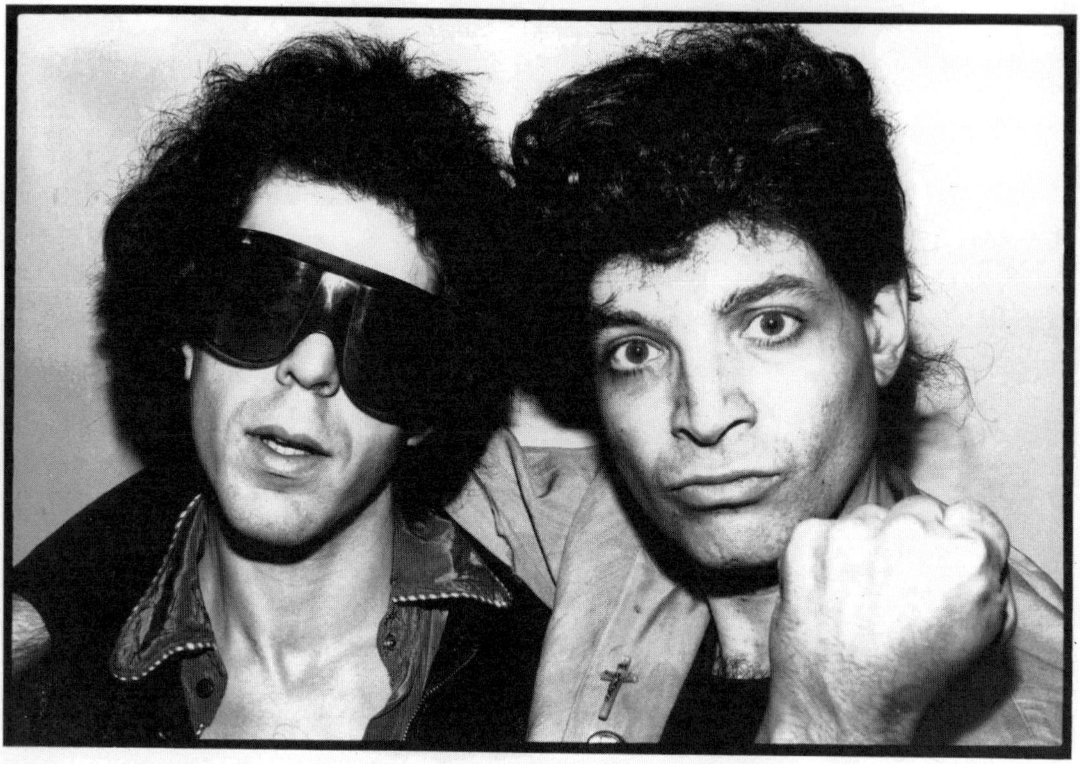

Suicide

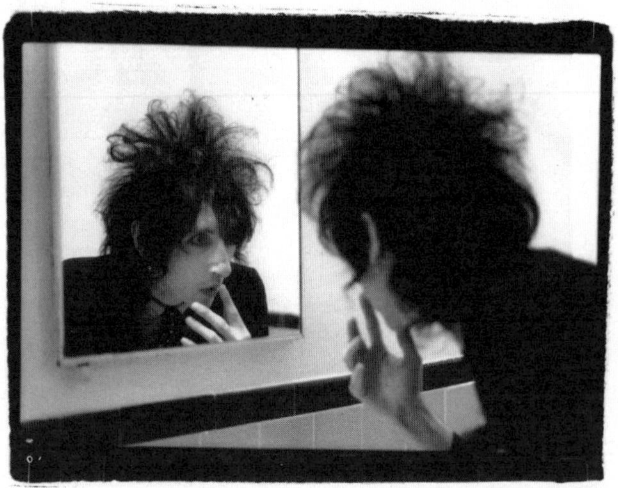

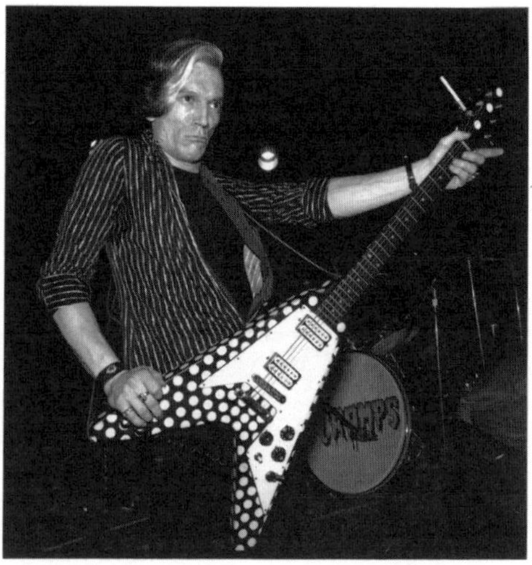
CRAMPS

Brian Gregory (Cramps)

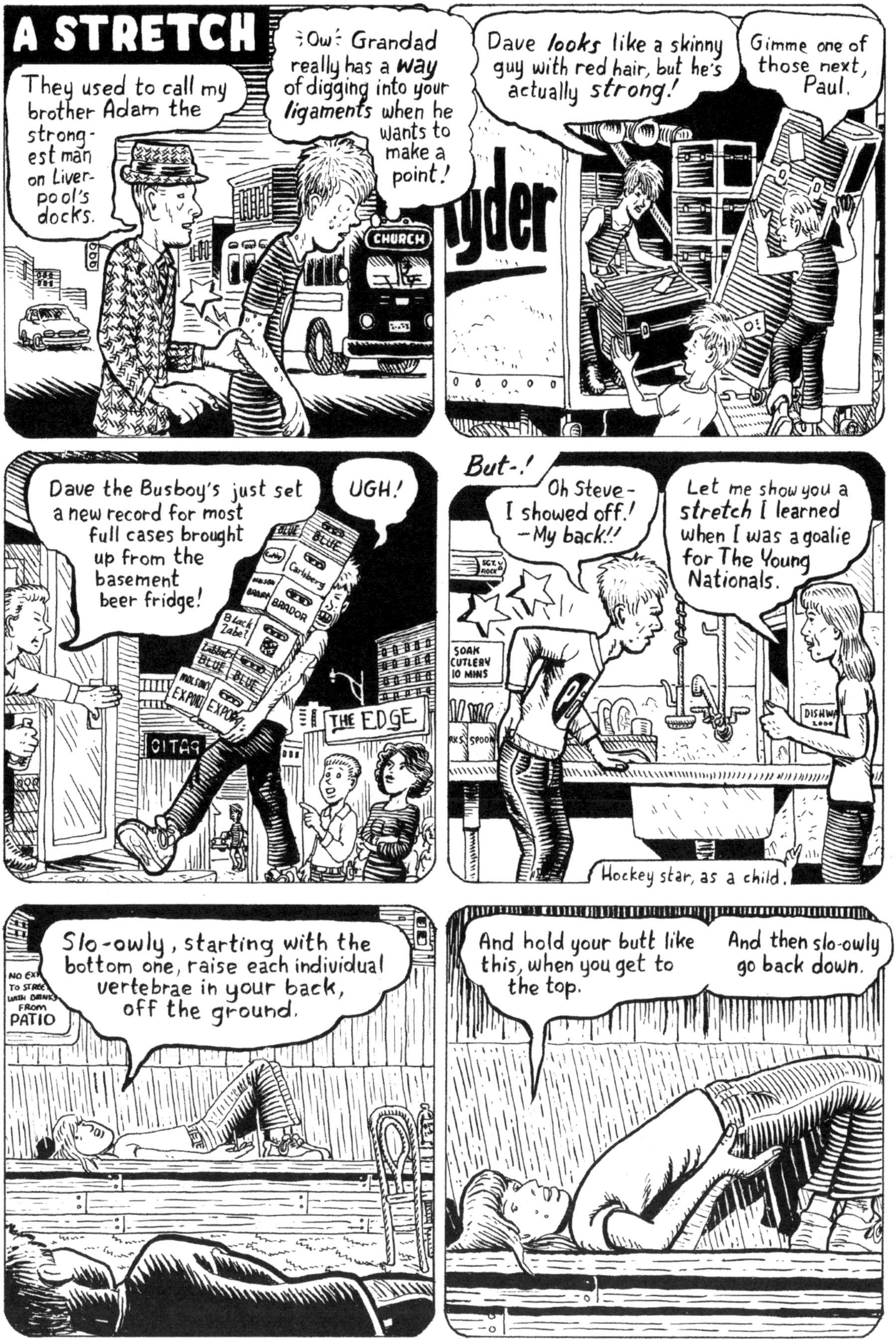
A STRETCH
They used to call my brother Adam the strongest man on Liverpool's docks.
Ow Grandad really has a way of digging into your ligaments when he wants to make a point!
CHURCH
Dave looks like a skinny guy with red hair, but he's actually strong!
Gimme one of those next, Paul.
Dave the Busboy's just set a new record for most full cases brought up from the basement beer fridge!
UGH!
BLUE
Carlsberg
BRADOR
Black Label
Labatt's BLUE
MOLSON EXPORT
THE EDGE
But-!
Oh Steve- I showed off! -My back!!
Let me show you a stretch I learned when I was a goalie for The Young Nationals.
SOAK CUTLERY 10 MINS
Hockey star, as a child.
Slo-owly, starting with the bottom one, raise each individual vertebrae in your back, off the ground.
PATIO
And hold your butt like this, when you get to the top.
And then slo-owly go back down.

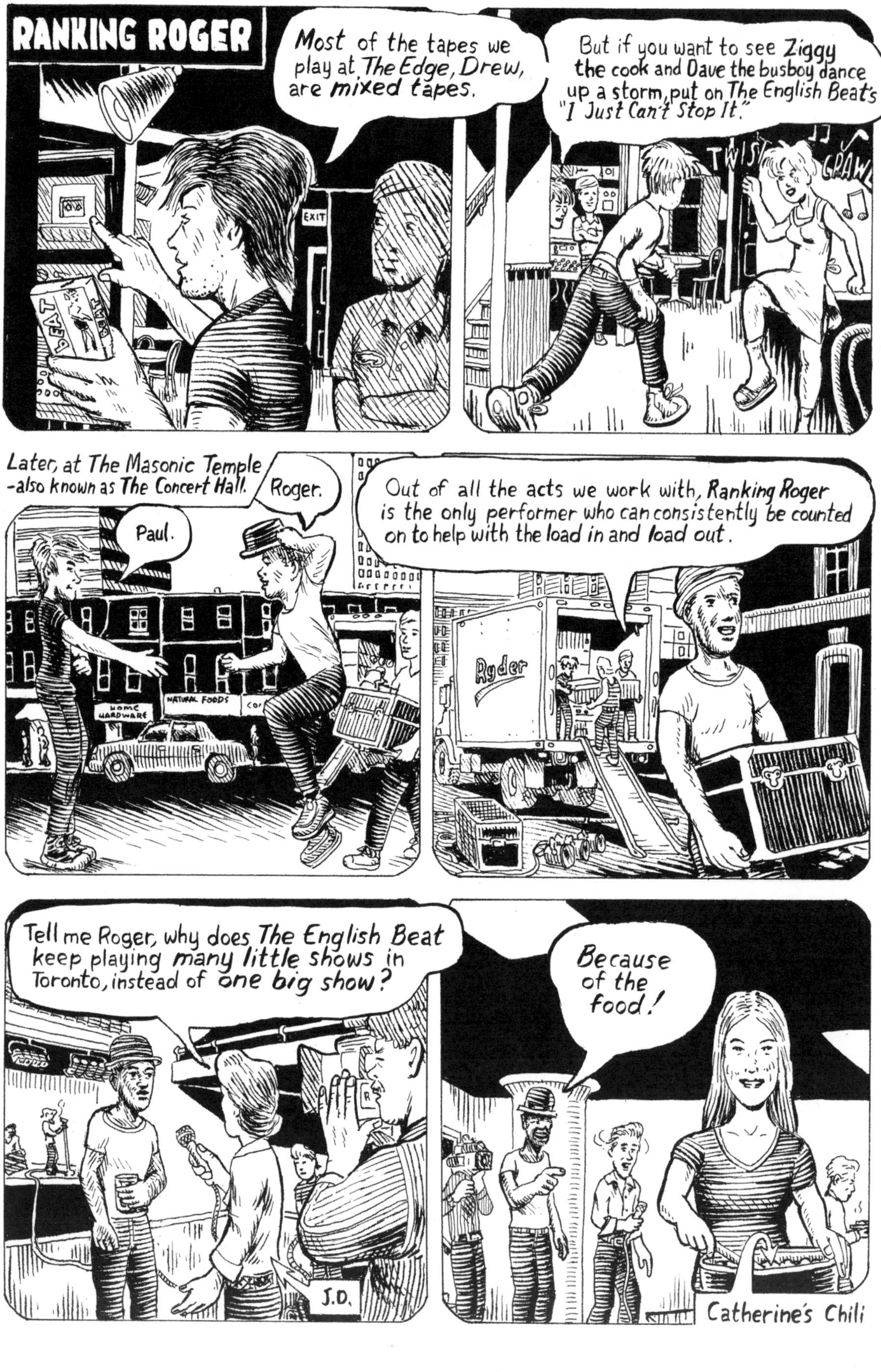
RANKING ROGER
Most of the tapes we play at The Edge, Drew, are mixed tapes.
But if you want to see Ziggy the cook and Dave the busboy dance up a storm, put on The English Beat's "I Just Can't Stop It."
BEAT
TWIST
GRAWL
EXIT
Later, at The Masonic Temple -also known as The Concert Hall.
Roger.
Paul.
Out of all the acts we work with, Ranking Roger is the only performer who can consistently be counted on to help with the load in and load out.
HOME HARDWARE
NATURAL FOODS
Ryder
Tell me Roger, why does The English Beat keep playing many little shows in Toronto, instead of one big show?
J.D.
Because of the food!
Catherine's Chili

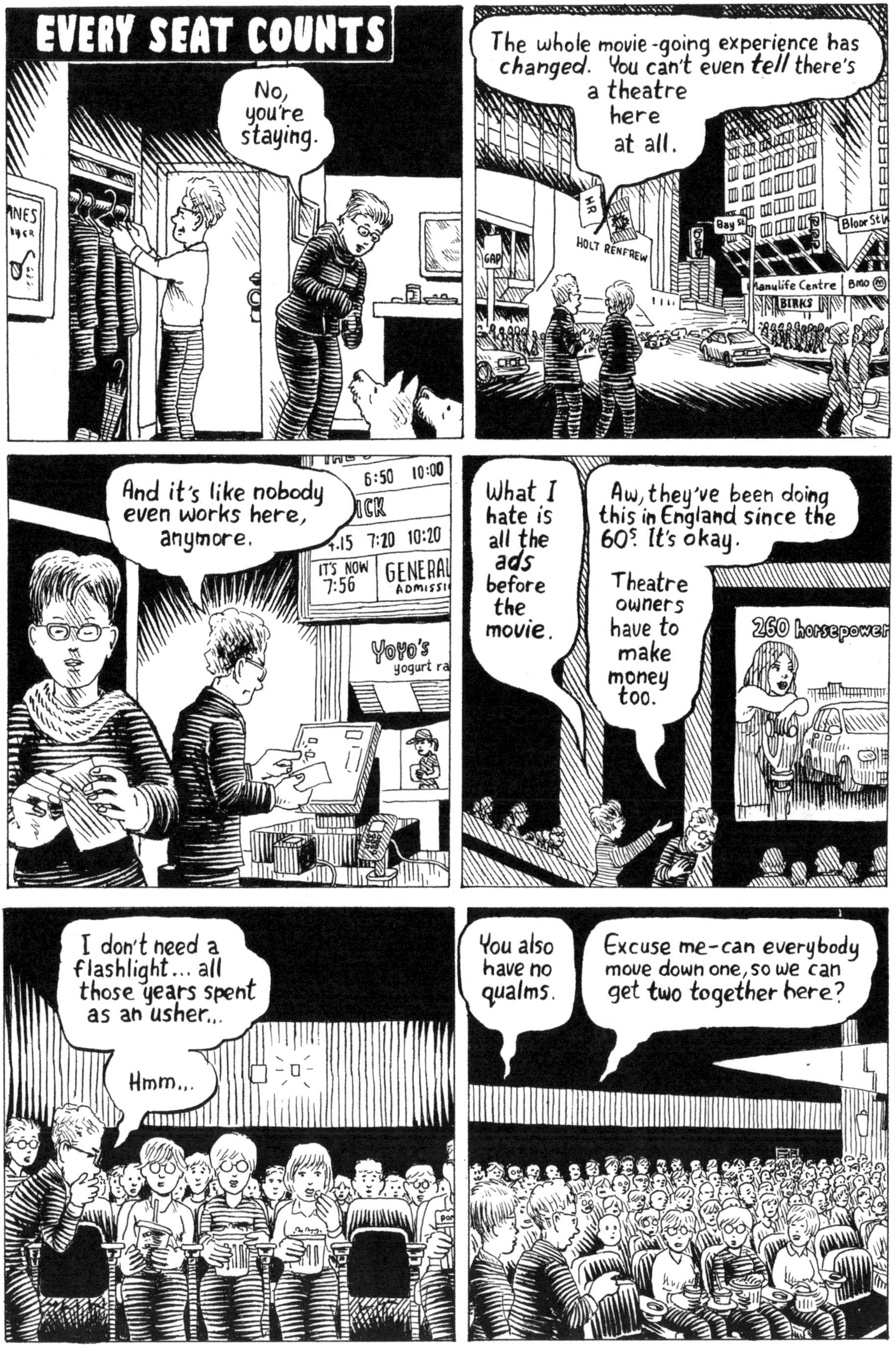
EVERY SEAT COUNTS
No, you're staying.
The whole movie-going experience has changed. You can't even tell there's a theatre here at all.
HR
HOLT RENFREW
GAP
Bay St
Bloor St W
Manulife Centre
BMO
BIRKS
And it's like nobody even works here, anymore.
6:50 10:00
4:15 7:20 10:20
IT'S NOW 7:56
GENERAL
Yoyo's
What I hate is all the ads before the movie.
Aw, they've been doing this in England since the 60s. It's okay.
Theatre owners have to make money too.
260 horsepower
I don't need a flashlight... all those years spent as an usher...
Hmm...
You also have no qualms.
Excuse me—can everybody move down one, so we can get two together here?

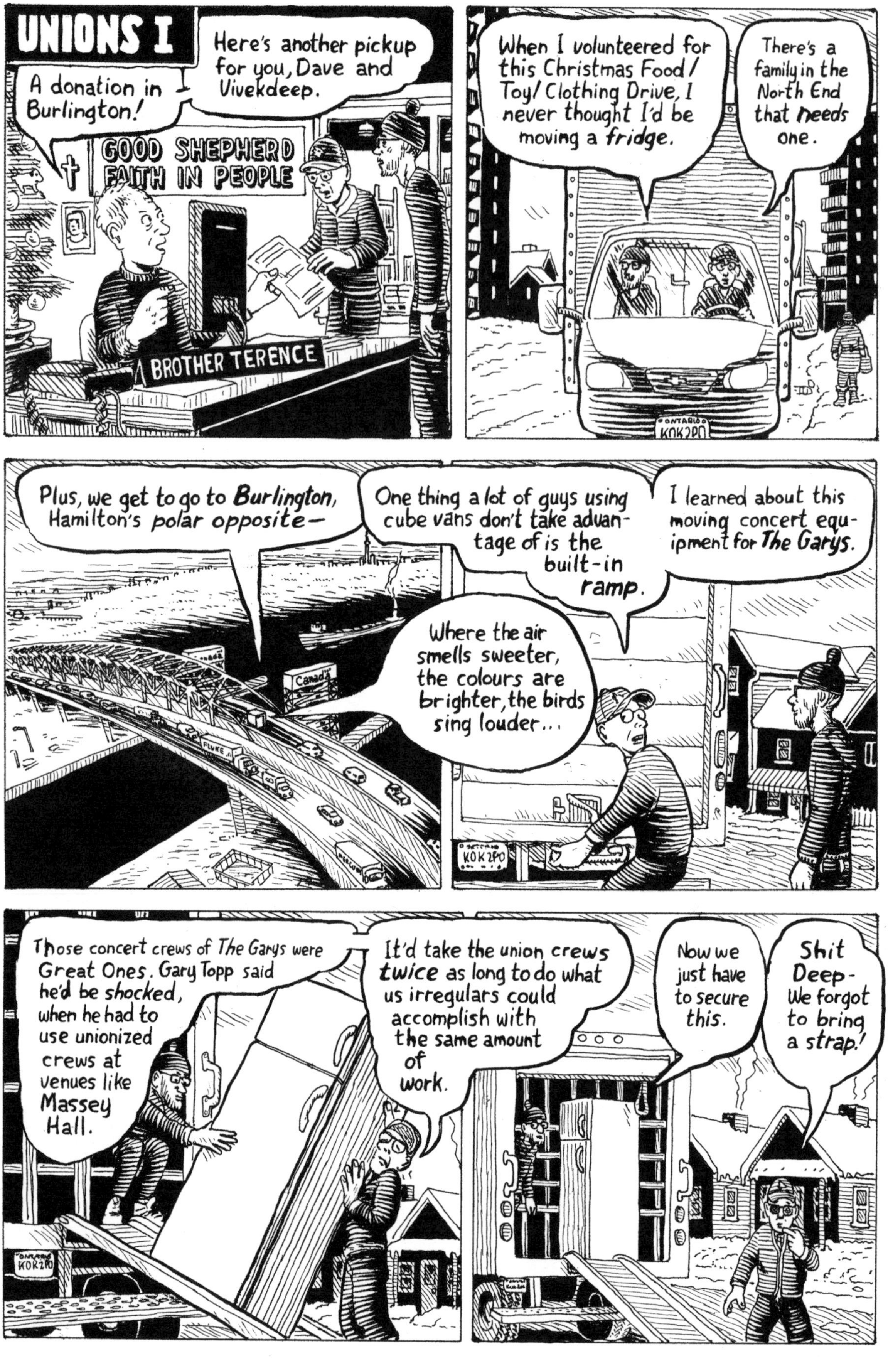
UNIONS I
A donation in Burlington!
Here's another pickup for you, Dave and Vivekdeep.
GOOD SHEPHERD FAITH IN PEOPLE
BROTHER TERENCE
When I volunteered for this Christmas Food/Toy/Clothing Drive, I never thought I'd be moving a *fridge*.
There's a family in the North End that *needs* one.
ONTARIO KOK 2PO
Plus, we get to go to *Burlington*, Hamilton's *polar opposite*—
Where the air smells sweeter, the colours are brighter, the birds sing louder...
Canada
One thing a lot of guys using cube vans don't take advantage of is the built-in **ramp**.
I learned about this moving concert equipment for *The Garys*.
KOK 2PO
Those concert crews of *The Garys* were Great Ones. Gary Topp said he'd be *shocked*, when he had to use unionized crews at venues like Massey Hall.
It'd take the union crews *twice* as long to do what us irregulars could accomplish with the same amount of work.
Now we just have to secure this.
Shit Deep- We forgot to bring a *strap*!

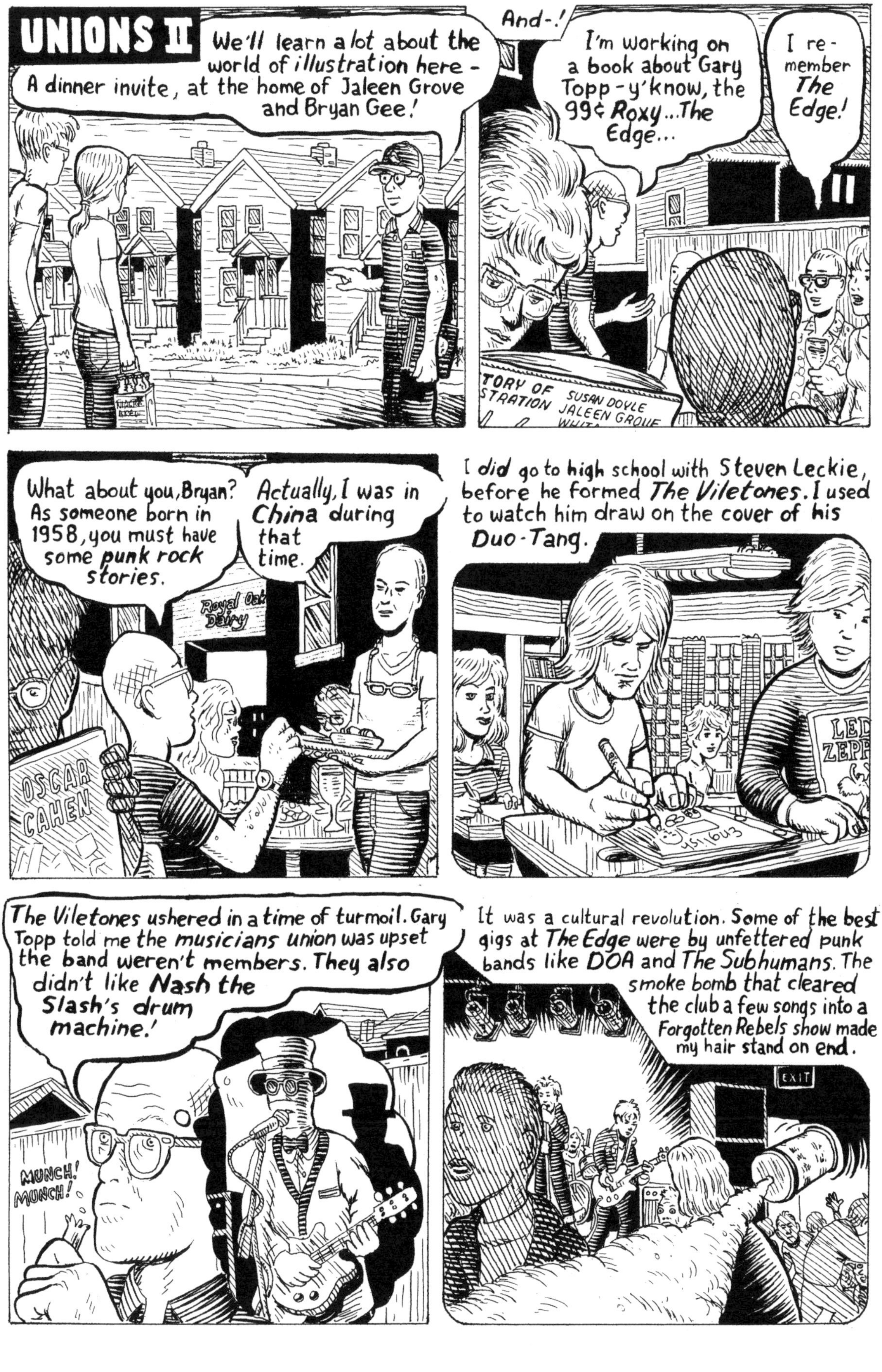
UNIONS II
We'll learn a lot about the world of illustration here - A dinner invite, at the home of Jaleen Grove and Bryan Gee!
And-!
I'm working on a book about Gary Topp - y'know, the 99¢ Roxy...The Edge...
I re-member The Edge!
TORY OF STRATION SUSAN DOYLE JALEEN GROVE
What about you, Bryan? As someone born in 1958, you must have some punk rock stories.
Actually, I was in China during that time.
Royal Oak Dairy
OSCAR CAHEN
I did go to high school with Steven Leckie, before he formed The Viletones. I used to watch him draw on the cover of his Duo-Tang.
LED ZEPP
The Viletones ushered in a time of turmoil. Gary Topp told me the musicians union was upset the band weren't members. They also didn't like Nash the Slash's drum machine!
MUNCH! MUNCH!
It was a cultural revolution. Some of the best gigs at The Edge were by unfettered punk bands like DOA and The Subhumans. The smoke bomb that cleared the club a few songs into a Forgotten Rebels show made my hair stand on end.
EXIT

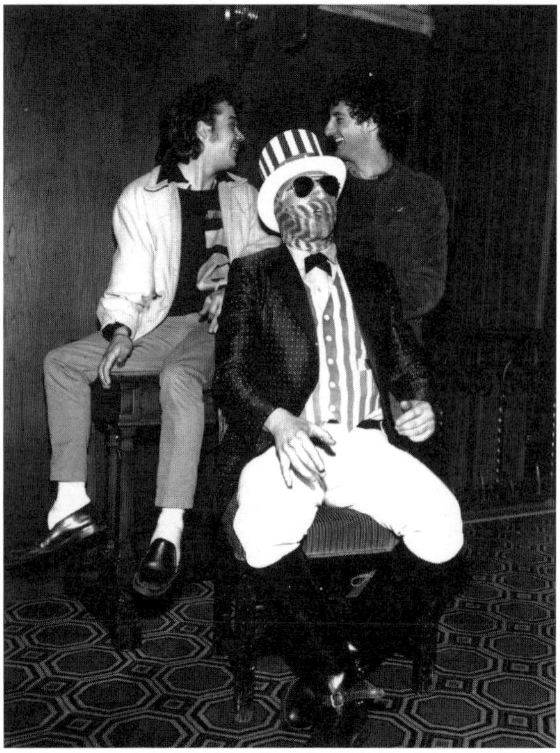

Russ Wilson, Nash the Slash, Gary

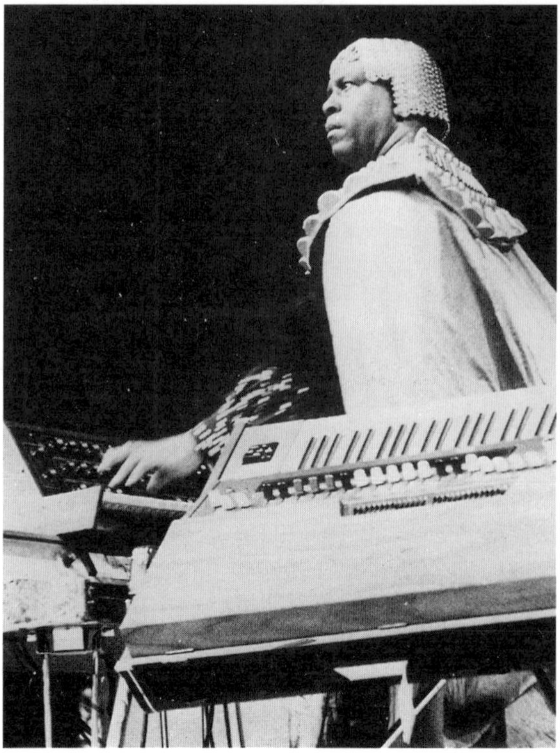

Sun Ra at The Horseshoe

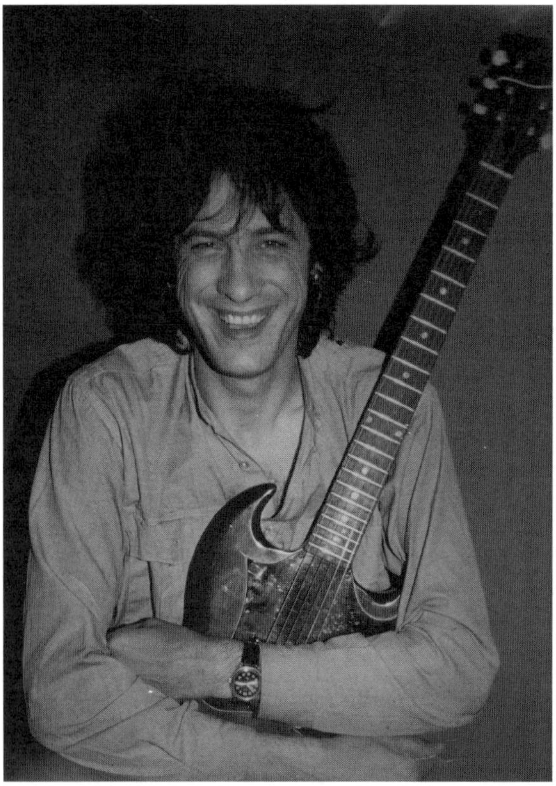

John Otway at The Edge
(Photo: Anita Alksnis)

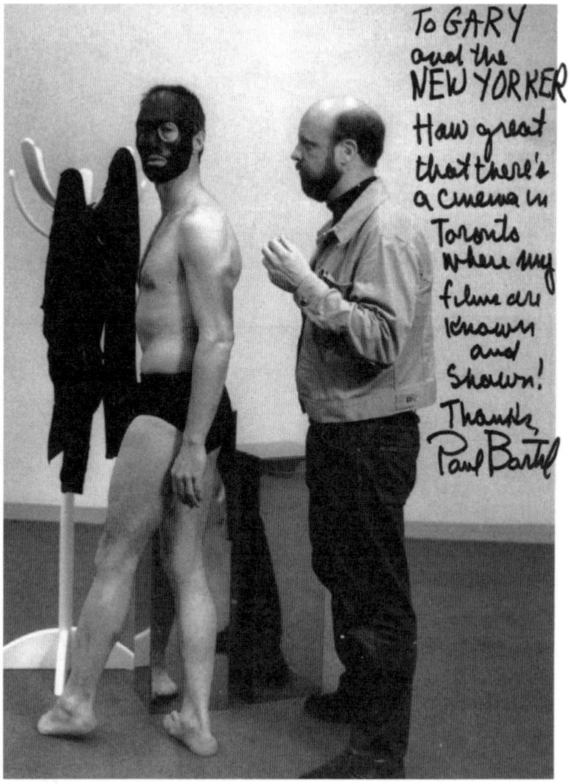
To GARY
and the
NEW YORKER
How great
that there's
a cinema in
Toronto
where my
films are
known
and
shown!
Thanks,
Paul Bartel

Paul Bartel (1938-2000), American director of 11 low-budget films (*Death Race 2000, Eating Raoul*) and actor in over 90 films and TV episodes

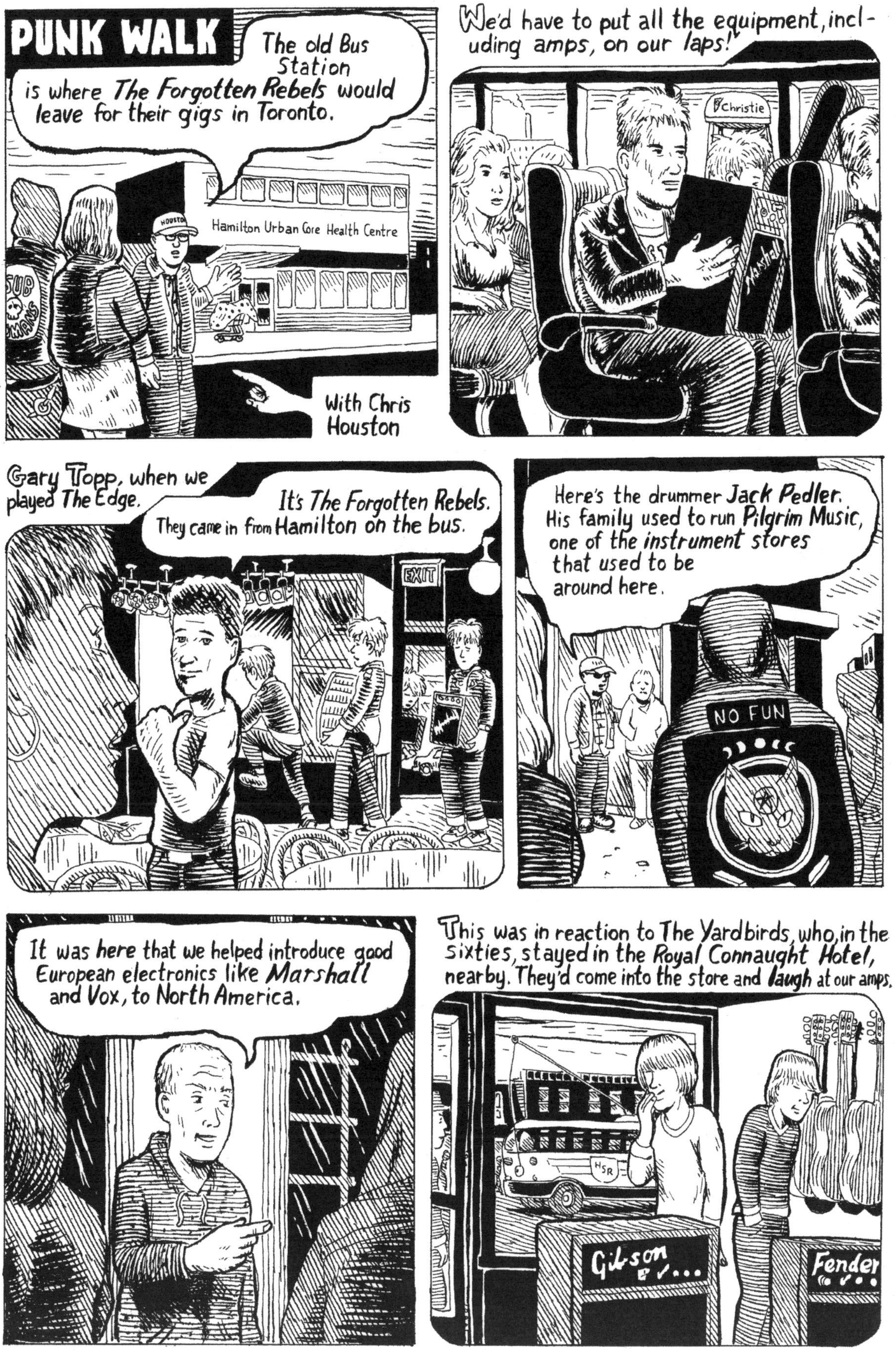

PUNK WALK
The old Bus Station is where The Forgotten Rebels would leave for their gigs in Toronto.
HOUSTON
Hamilton Urban Core Health Centre
SUB HUMANS
With Chris Houston
We'd have to put all the equipment, including amps, on our laps!
Christie
Gary Topp, when we played The Edge.
It's The Forgotten Rebels. They came in from Hamilton on the bus.
EXIT
Here's the drummer Jack Pedler. His family used to run Pilgrim Music, one of the instrument stores that used to be around here.
NO FUN
It was here that we helped introduce good European electronics like Marshall and Vox, to North America.
This was in reaction to The Yardbirds, who, in the sixties, stayed in the Royal Connaught Hotel, nearby. They'd come into the store and laugh at our amps.
HSR
Gibson
Fender

FEDS

So many *talented* people worked at *The Edge*. Like the singer/songwriter/guitarist *Phil Smith*.

THE FEDS
THIS SIDE
Sex RECORDS
TIME 2:50
THE GODS
(Smith/Gregg)
© Copyright 1980
BLOOD MUSIC

Phil was the *coolest* bartender. He had this *loose-limbed* way of entering amounts into the till from a distance.

$1.50

Ka-Cheng!

Dave the Busboy you don't want to know about. It *pains* me *now*, to draw a picture of after hours *beer chugging*, right from the *draft tap.*

DRAFT

Late one night/early morning, Phil and me realized we *both* had the next day off—!

Yeah!

Y'know shumpsthin'— we oughta go to *New York Shitty right now!*

As if we weren't *drunk enough*, we took a bottle of wine for the bus ride. It was *ugly* at the Border.

Ha! Lookit th' picture of *Reagan!*

Wotta sacka-maroon...

The U.S. border agents put Phil and me in a taxi that took us over the *Rainbow Bridge* back to Canada. One of them kicked me in the ass *so hard*, my nuts still hurt to think about it.

TAXI

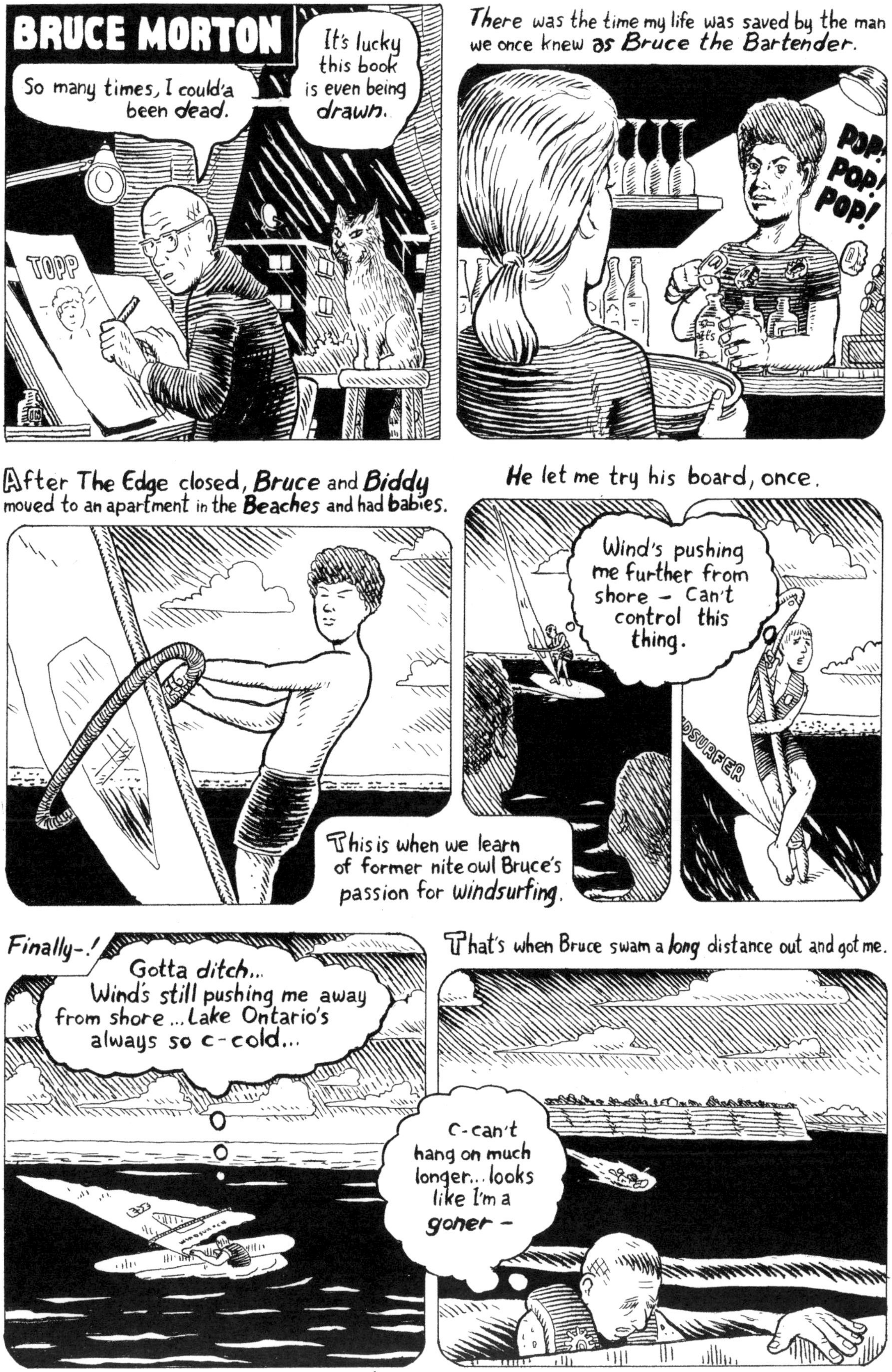
BRUCE MORTON
So many times, I could'a been dead.
It's lucky this book is even being drawn.
TOPP
There was the time my life was saved by the man we once knew as Bruce the Bartender.
POP! POP! POP!
After The Edge closed, Bruce and Biddy moved to an apartment in the Beaches and had babies.
This is when we learn of former nite owl Bruce's passion for windsurfing.
He let me try his board, once.
Wind's pushing me further from shore - Can't control this thing.
WINDSURFER
Finally-!
Gotta ditch... Wind's still pushing me away from shore ... Lake Ontario's always so c-cold...
That's when Bruce swam a long distance out and got me.
C-can't hang on much longer... looks like I'm a goner -

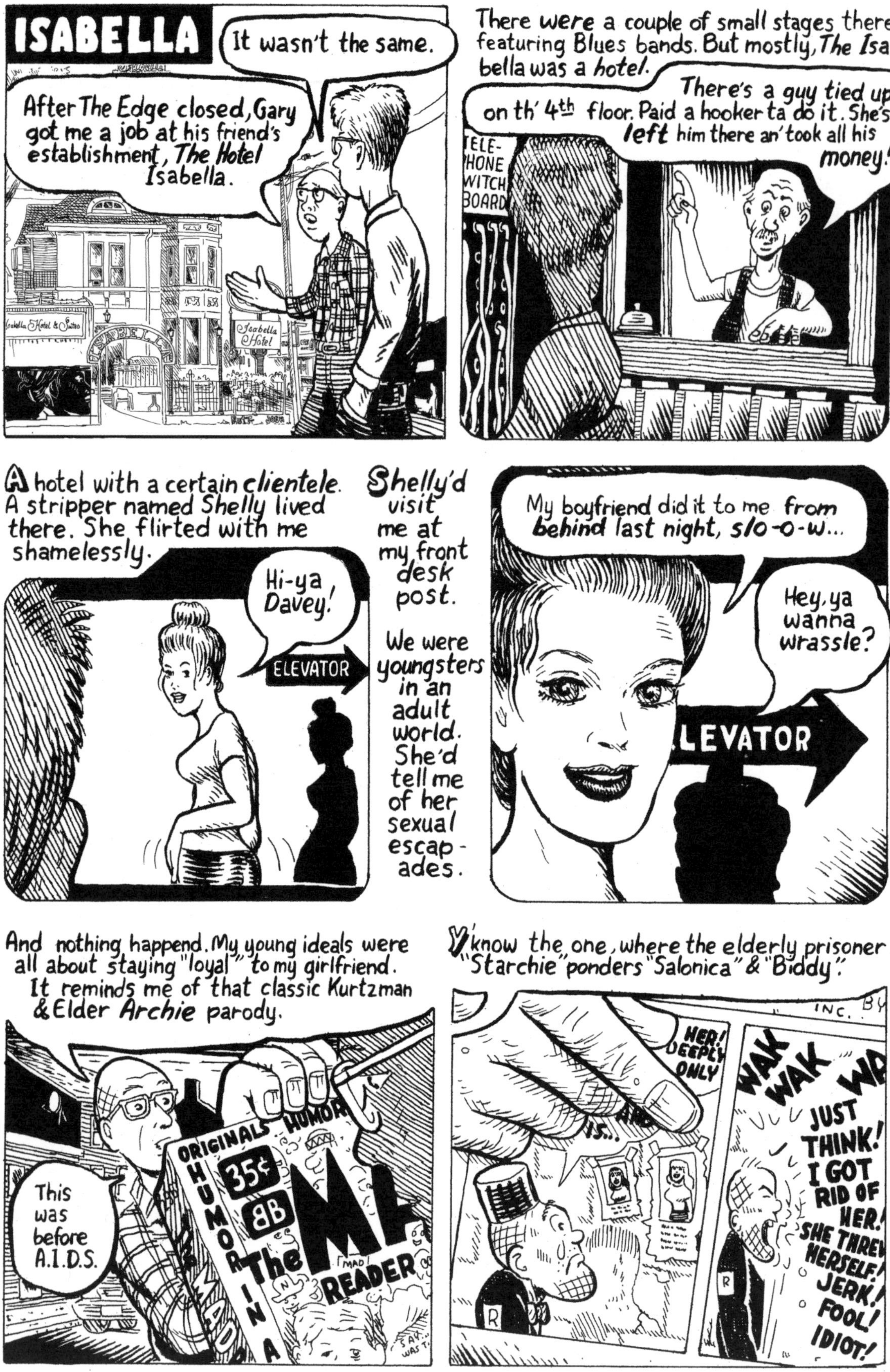
ISABELLA
It wasn't the same.
After The Edge closed, Gary got me a job at his friend's establishment, The Hotel Isabella.
Isabella Hotel & Suites
ISABELLA
Isabella Hotel
There were a couple of small stages there, featuring Blues bands. But mostly, The Isabella was a hotel.
There's a guy tied up on th' 4th floor. Paid a hooker ta do it. She's left him there an' took all his money!
TELE-PHONE SWITCH BOARD
A hotel with a certain clientele. A stripper named Shelly lived there. She flirted with me shamelessly.
Hi-ya Davey!
ELEVATOR
Shelly'd visit me at my front desk post.
We were youngsters in an adult world. She'd tell me of her sexual escapades.
My boyfriend did it to me from behind last night, slo-o-w...
Hey, ya wanna wrassle?
ELEVATOR
And nothing happend. My young ideals were all about staying "loyal" to my girlfriend. It reminds me of that classic Kurtzman & Elder Archie parody.
This was before A.I.D.S.
ORIGINALS HUMOR
35¢
BB
HUMOR IN A
The MAD READER
Y'know the one, where the elderly prisoner "Starchie" ponders "Salonica" & "Biddy".
HER! DEEPLY ONLY
AND IS..
WAK WAK
JUST THINK! I GOT RID OF HER! SHE THREW HERSELF! JERK! FOOL! IDIOT!

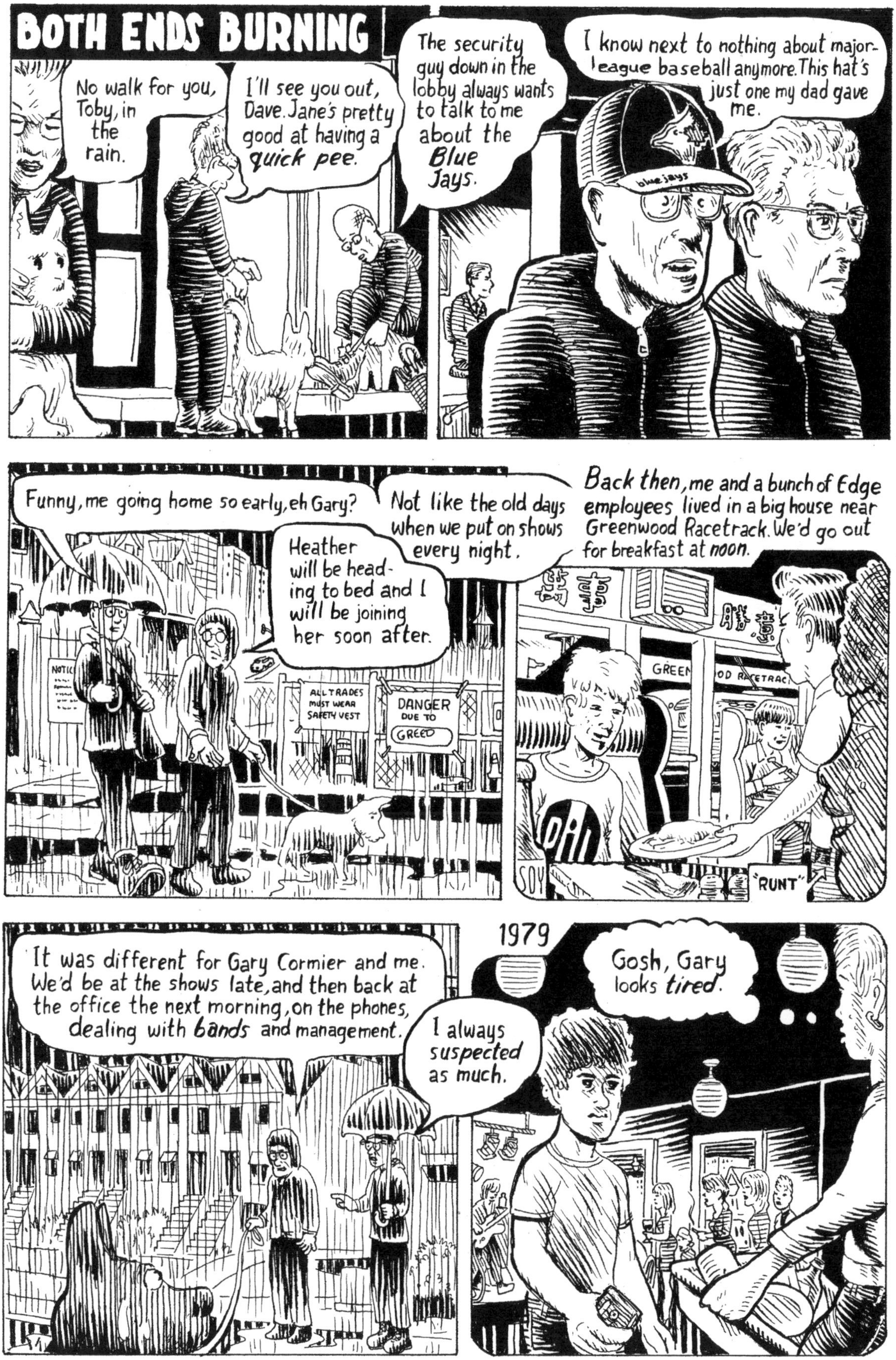

BOTH ENDS BURNING
No walk for you, Toby, in the rain.
I'll see you out, Dave. Jane's pretty good at having a quick pee.
The security guy down in the lobby always wants to talk to me about the Blue Jays.
I know next to nothing about major-league baseball anymore. This hat's just one my dad gave me.
blue jays
Funny, me going home so early, eh Gary?
Heather will be heading to bed and I will be joining her soon after.
Not like the old days when we put on shows every night.
ALL TRADES MUST WEAR SAFETY VEST
DANGER DUE TO GREED
Back then, me and a bunch of Edge employees lived in a big house near Greenwood Racetrack. We'd go out for breakfast at noon.
DAN
SOY
"RUNT"
It was different for Gary Cormier and me. We'd be at the shows late, and then back at the office the next morning, on the phones, dealing with bands and management.
I always suspected as much.
1979
Gosh, Gary looks tired.

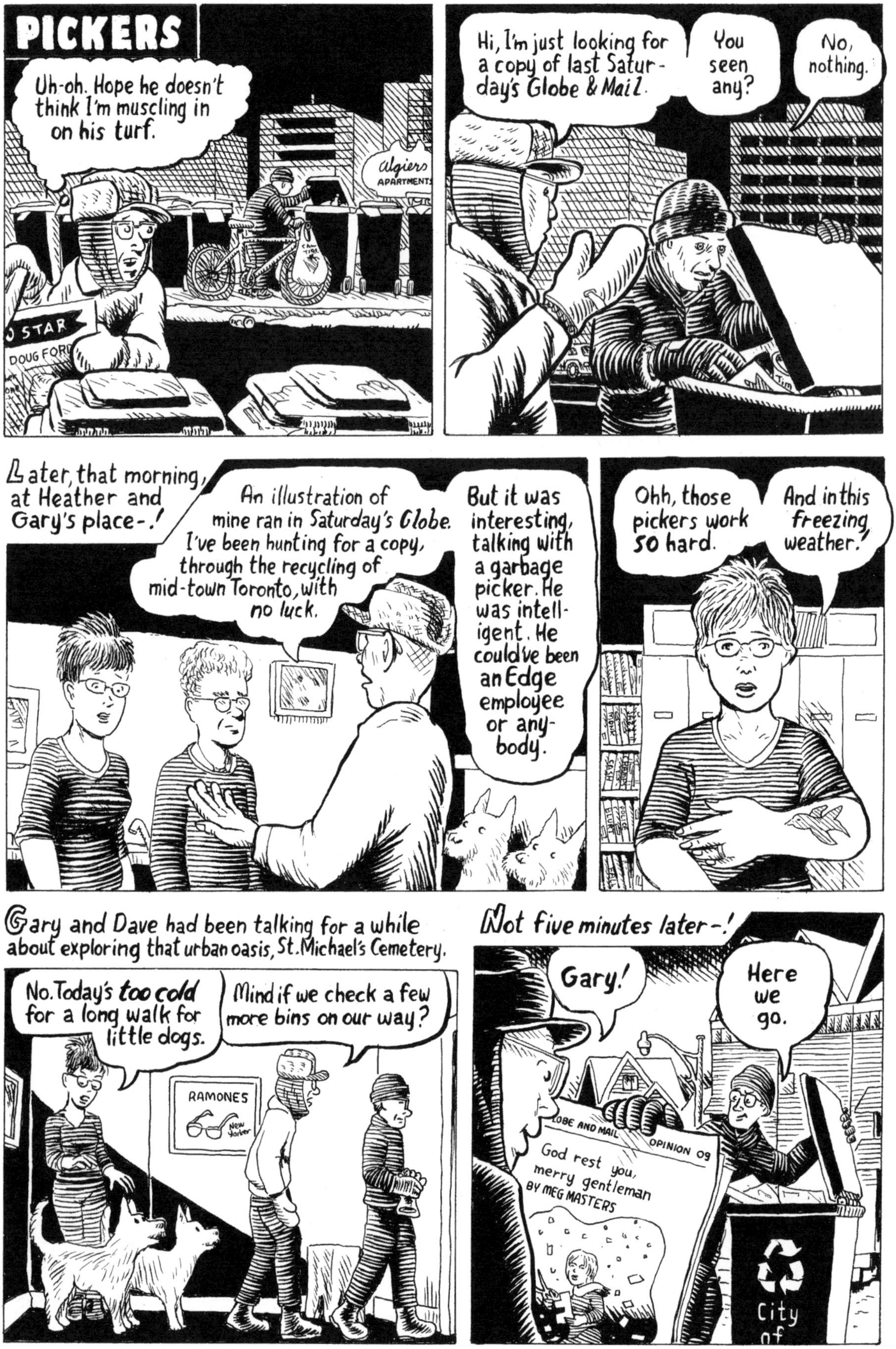
PICKERS
Uh-oh. Hope he doesn't think I'm muscling in on his turf.
STAR
DOUG FORD
Algiers APARTMENTS
Hi, I'm just looking for a copy of last Saturday's Globe & Mail.
You seen any?
No, nothing.
Later, that morning, at Heather and Gary's place-!
An illustration of mine ran in Saturday's Globe. I've been hunting for a copy, through the recycling of mid-town Toronto, with no luck.
But it was interesting, talking with a garbage picker. He was intelligent. He could've been an Edge employee or anybody.
Ohh, those pickers work SO hard.
And in this freezing weather.
Gary and Dave had been talking for a while about exploring that urban oasis, St. Michael's Cemetery.
No. Today's too cold for a long walk for little dogs.
Mind if we check a few more bins on our way?
RAMONES
New Yorker
Not five minutes later-!
Gary!
Here we go.
LOBE AND MAIL
OPINION 09
God rest you, merry gentleman
BY MEG MASTERS
City of

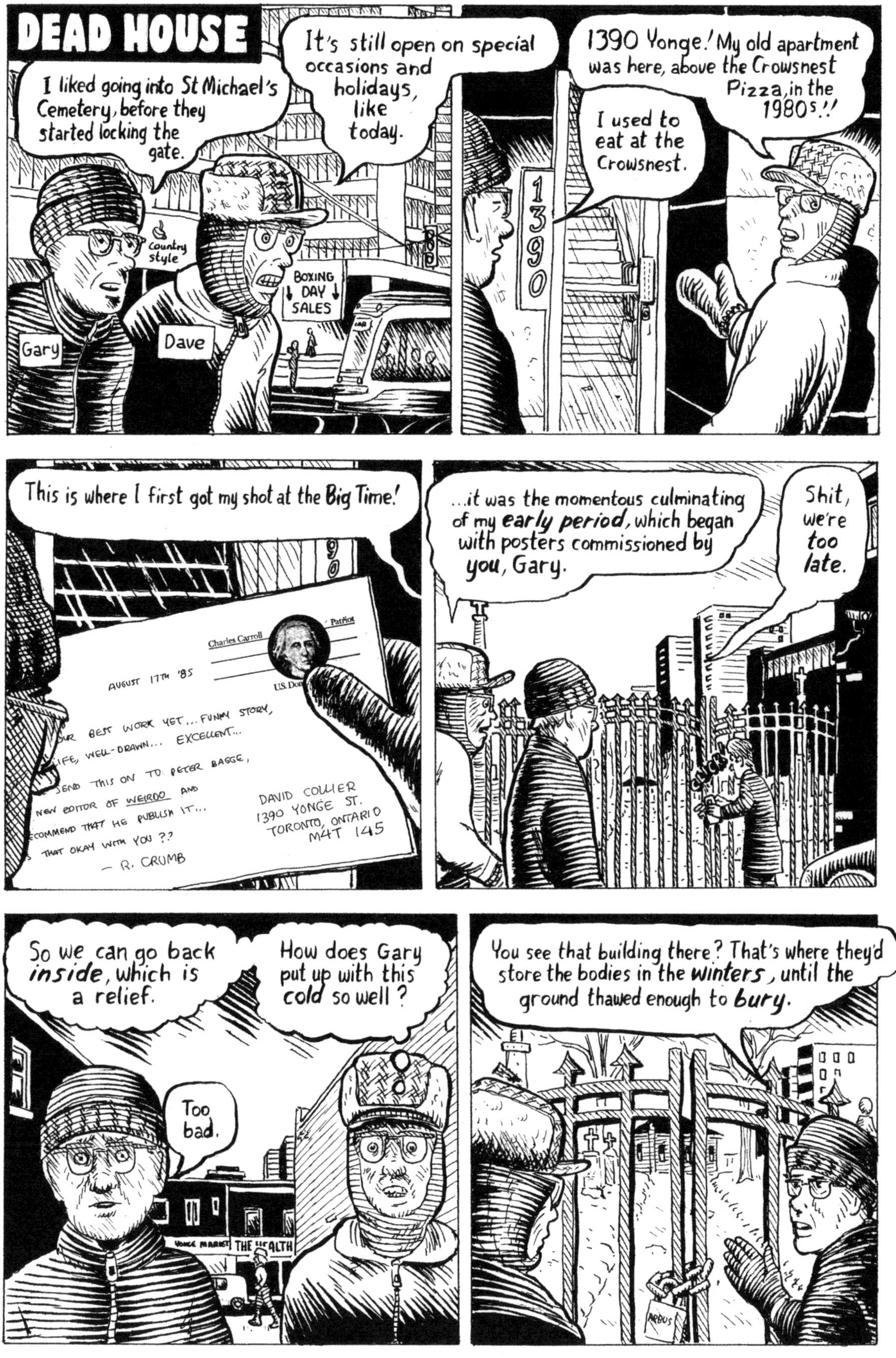
DEAD HOUSE
I liked going into St Michael's Cemetery, before they started locking the gate.
It's still open on special occasions and holidays, like today.
Country style
BOXING DAY SALES
Gary
Dave
1390 Yonge! My old apartment was here, above the Crowsnest Pizza, in the 1980s!!
I used to eat at the Crowsnest.
1390
This is where I first got my shot at the Big Time!
Charles Carroll
Patriot
U.S. Do
AUGUST 17TH '85
UR BEST WORK YET... FUNNY STORY,
LIFE, WELL-DRAWN... EXCELLENT...
SEND THIS ON TO PETER BAGGE,
NEW EDITOR OF WEIRDO AND
ECOMMEND THAT HE PUBLISH IT...
THAT OKAY WITH YOU ??
— R. CRUMB
DAVID COLLIER
1390 YONGE ST.
TORONTO, ONTARIO
M4T 145
...it was the momentous culminating of my early period, which began with posters commissioned by you, Gary.
Shit, we're too late.
So we can go back inside, which is a relief.
How does Gary put up with this cold so well?
Too bad.
YONGE MARKET
THE HEALTH
You see that building there? That's where they'd store the bodies in the winters, until the ground thawed enough to bury.
ARBUS

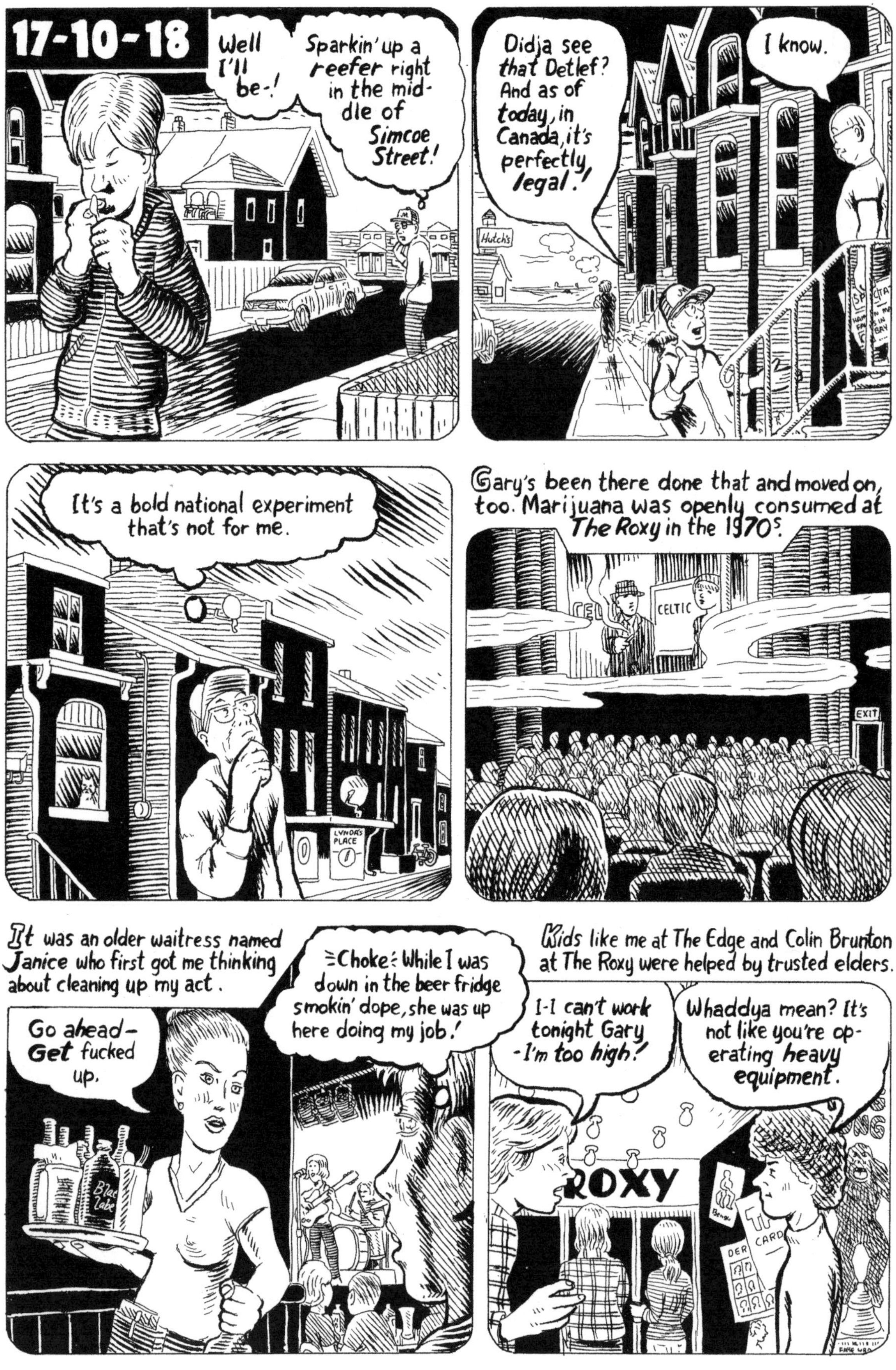
17-10-18
Well I'll be-!
Sparkin' up a reefer right in the middle of Simcoe Street!
Didja see that Detlef? And as of today, in Canada, it's perfectly legal.!
I know.
Hutch's
It's a bold national experiment that's not for me.
LYNDA'S PLACE
Gary's been there done that and moved on, too. Marijuana was openly consumed at The Roxy in the 1970s.
CELTIC
EXIT
It was an older waitress named Janice who first got me thinking about cleaning up my act.
Go ahead- Get fucked up.
≈Choke≈ While I was down in the beer fridge smokin' dope, she was up here doing my job.!
Kids like me at The Edge and Colin Brunton at The Roxy were helped by trusted elders.
I-I can't work tonight Gary -I'm too high!
Whaddya mean? It's not like you're operating heavy equipment.
ROXY

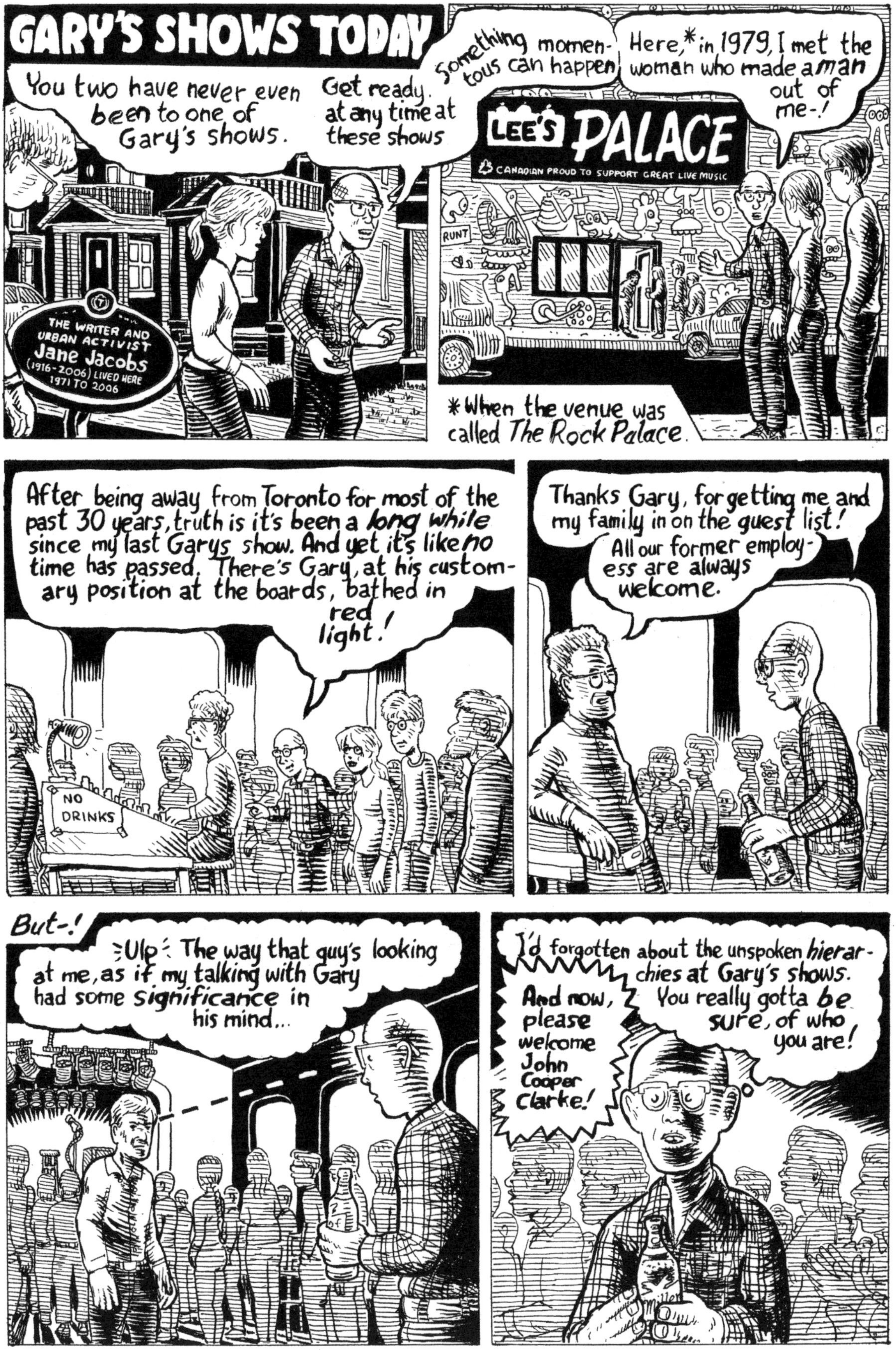
GARY'S SHOWS TODAY
You two have never even been to one of Gary's shows.
Get ready. at any time at these shows
Something momentous can happen!
THE WRITER AND URBAN ACTIVIST Jane Jacobs (1916-2006) LIVED HERE 1971 TO 2006
Here,* in 1979, I met the woman who made a man out of me-!
LEE'S PALACE
CANADIAN PROUD TO SUPPORT GREAT LIVE MUSIC
RUNT
*When the venue was called The Rock Palace.
After being away from Toronto for most of the past 30 years, truth is it's been a long while since my last Garys show. And yet it's like no time has passed. There's Gary, at his customary position at the boards, bathed in red light!
NO DRINKS
Thanks Gary, for getting me and my family in on the guest list!
All our former employess are always welcome.
But-!
Ulp The way that guy's looking at me, as if my talking with Gary had some significance in his mind...
I'd forgotten about the unspoken hierarchies at Gary's shows. You really gotta be sure, of who you are!
And now, please welcome John Cooper Clarke!

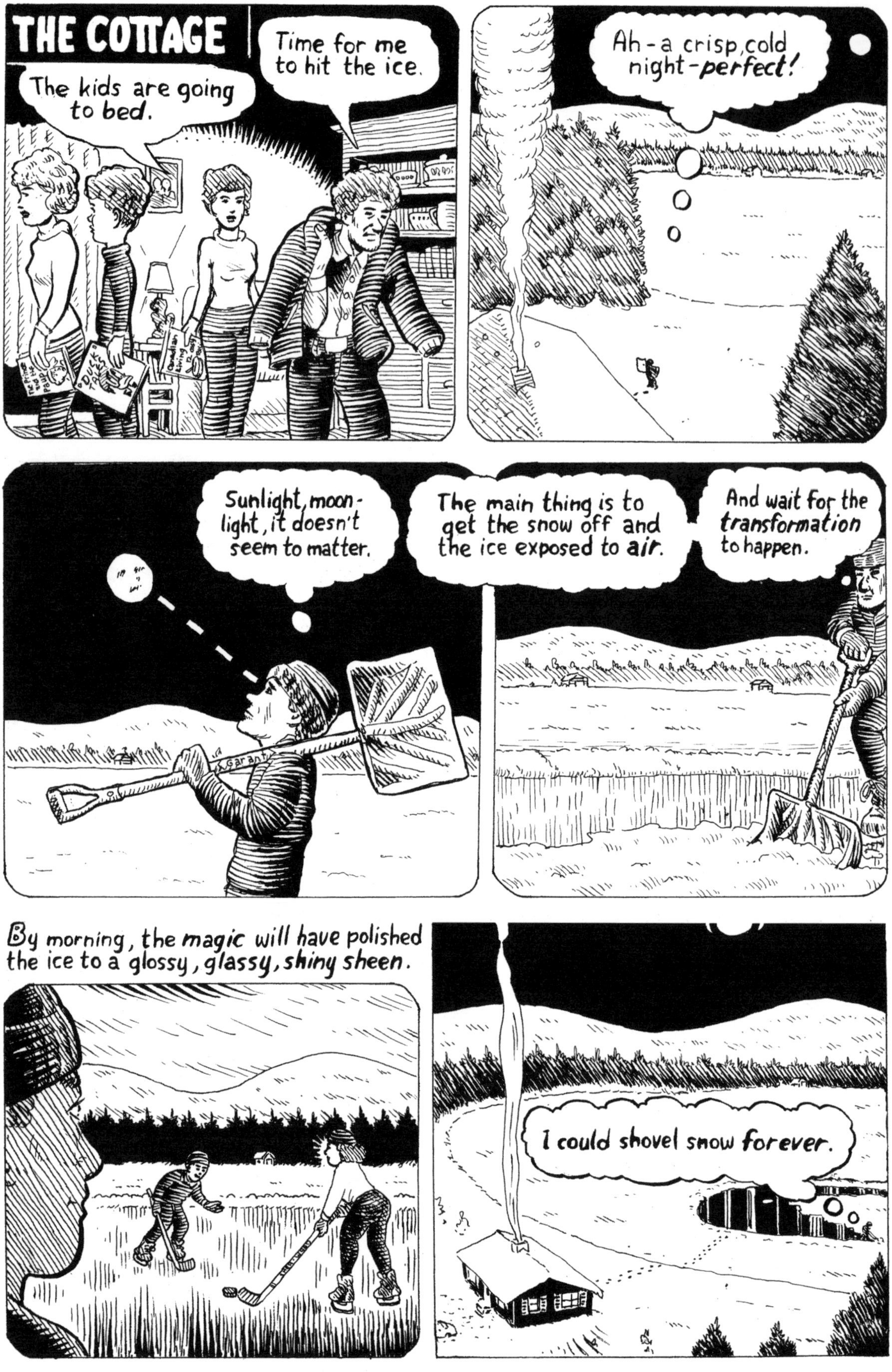
THE COTTAGE
The kids are going to bed.
Time for me to hit the ice.
Ah-a crisp, cold night-perfect!
Sunlight, moon-light, it doesn't seem to matter.
Garant
The main thing is to get the snow off and the ice exposed to air.
And wait for the transformation to happen.
By morning, the magic will have polished the ice to a glossy, glassy, shiny sheen.
I could shovel snow forever.

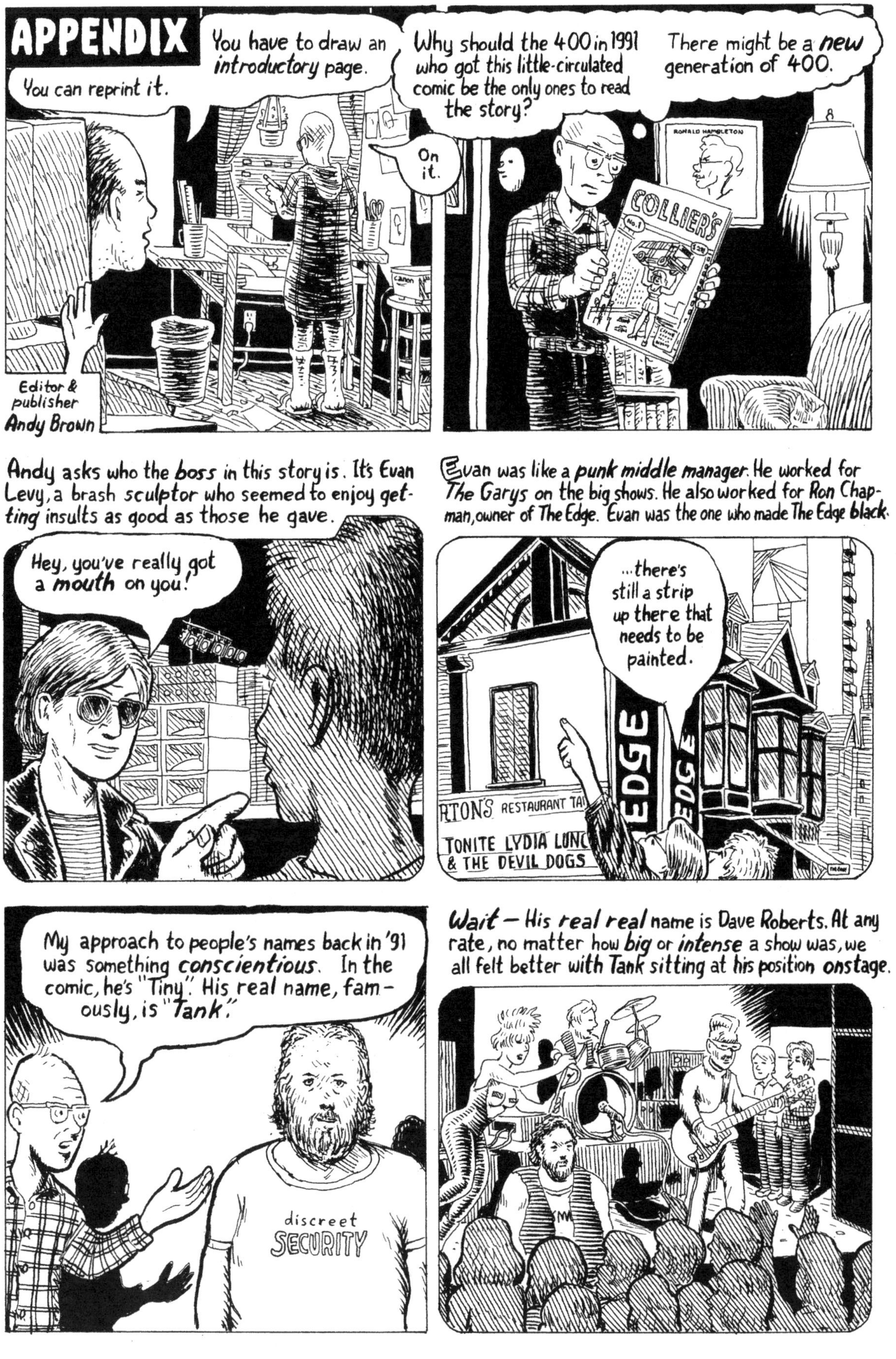
APPENDIX
You have to draw an introductory page.
You can reprint it.
Why should the 400 in 1991 who got this little-circulated comic be the only ones to read the story?
There might be a new generation of 400.
On it.
RONALD HAMBLETON
COLLIER'S
No. 1
Editor & publisher Andy Brown
Andy asks who the boss in this story is. It's Evan Levy, a brash sculptor who seemed to enjoy getting insults as good as those he gave.
Hey, you've really got a mouth on you!
Evan was like a punk middle manager. He worked for The Garys on the big shows. He also worked for Ron Chapman, owner of The Edge. Evan was the one who made The Edge black.
...there's still a strip up there that needs to be painted.
EDGE
EDGE
RTON'S RESTAURANT TA
TONITE LYDIA LUNC
& THE DEVIL DOGS
My approach to people's names back in '91 was something conscientious. In the comic, he's "Tiny". His real name, famously, is "Tank".
discreet
SECURITY
Wait — His real real name is Dave Roberts. At any rate, no matter how big or intense a show was, we all felt better with Tank sitting at his position onstage.

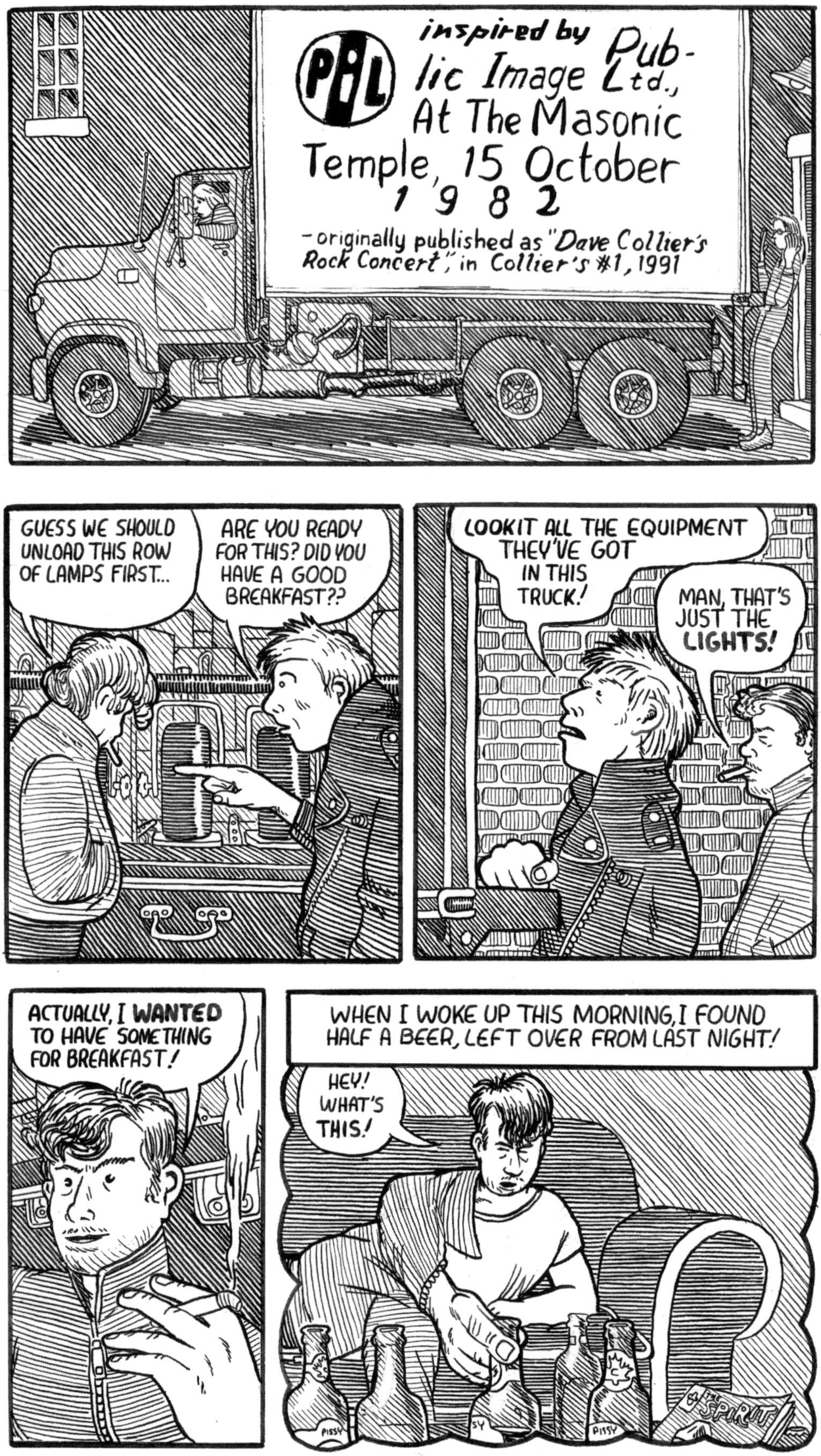
PiL
inspired by Public Image Ltd., At The Masonic Temple, 15 October 1982
–originally published as "Dave Collier's Rock Concert", in Collier's #1, 1991
GUESS WE SHOULD UNLOAD THIS ROW OF LAMPS FIRST...
ARE YOU READY FOR THIS? DID YOU HAVE A GOOD BREAKFAST??
LOOKIT ALL THE EQUIPMENT THEY'VE GOT IN THIS TRUCK!
MAN, THAT'S JUST THE **LIGHTS**!
ACTUALLY, I **WANTED** TO HAVE SOMETHING FOR BREAKFAST!
WHEN I WOKE UP THIS MORNING, I FOUND HALF A BEER, LEFT OVER FROM LAST NIGHT!
HEY! WHAT'S **THIS**!
PISSY
PISSY

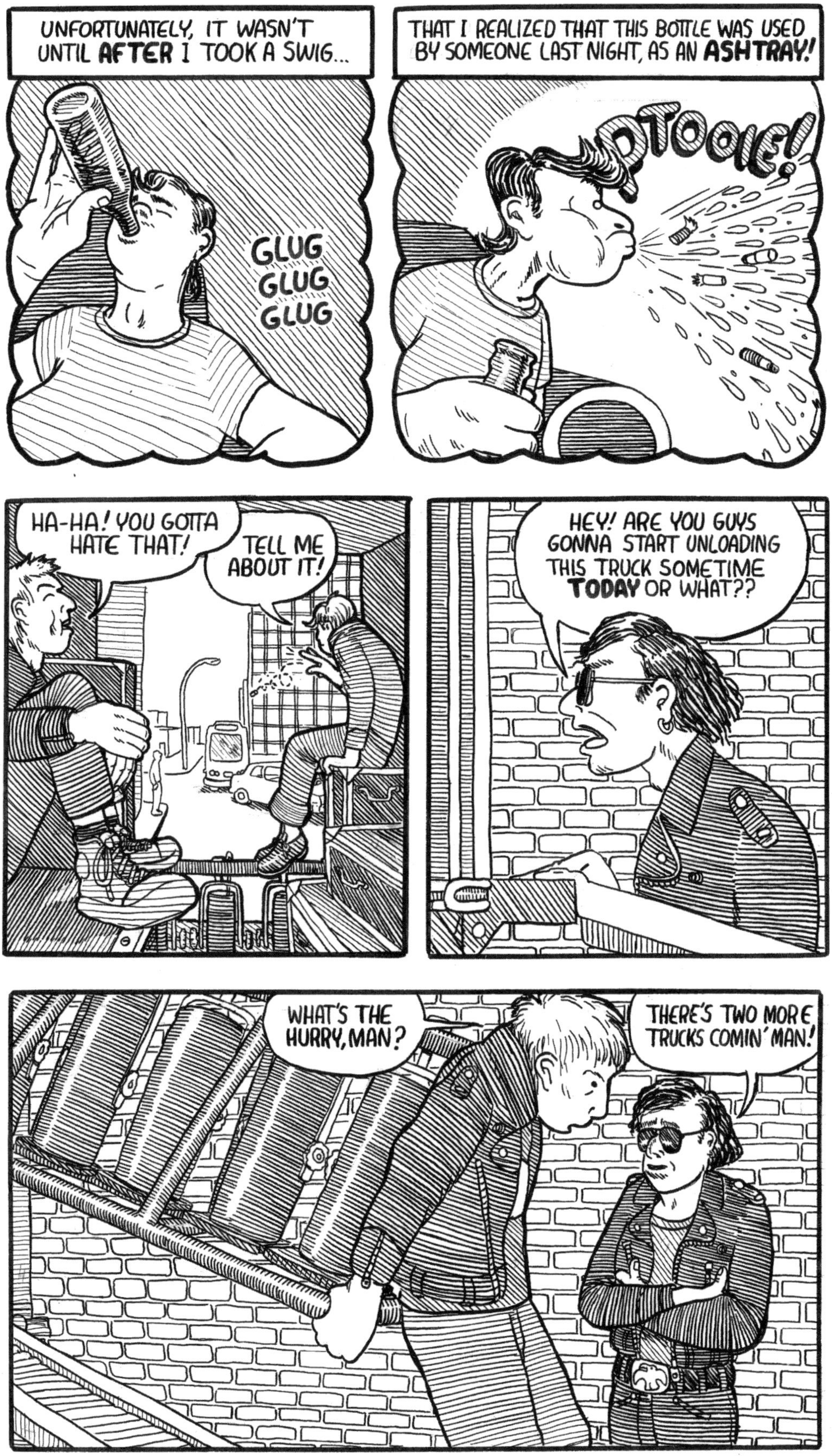
UNFORTUNATELY, IT WASN'T UNTIL **AFTER** I TOOK A SWIG...
GLUG GLUG GLUG
THAT I REALIZED THAT THIS BOTTLE WAS USED BY SOMEONE LAST NIGHT, AS AN **ASHTRAY!**
PTOOIE!
HA-HA! YOU GOTTA HATE THAT!
TELL ME ABOUT IT!
HEY! ARE YOU GUYS GONNA START UNLOADING THIS TRUCK SOMETIME **TODAY** OR WHAT??
WHAT'S THE HURRY, MAN?
THERE'S TWO MORE TRUCKS COMIN' MAN!

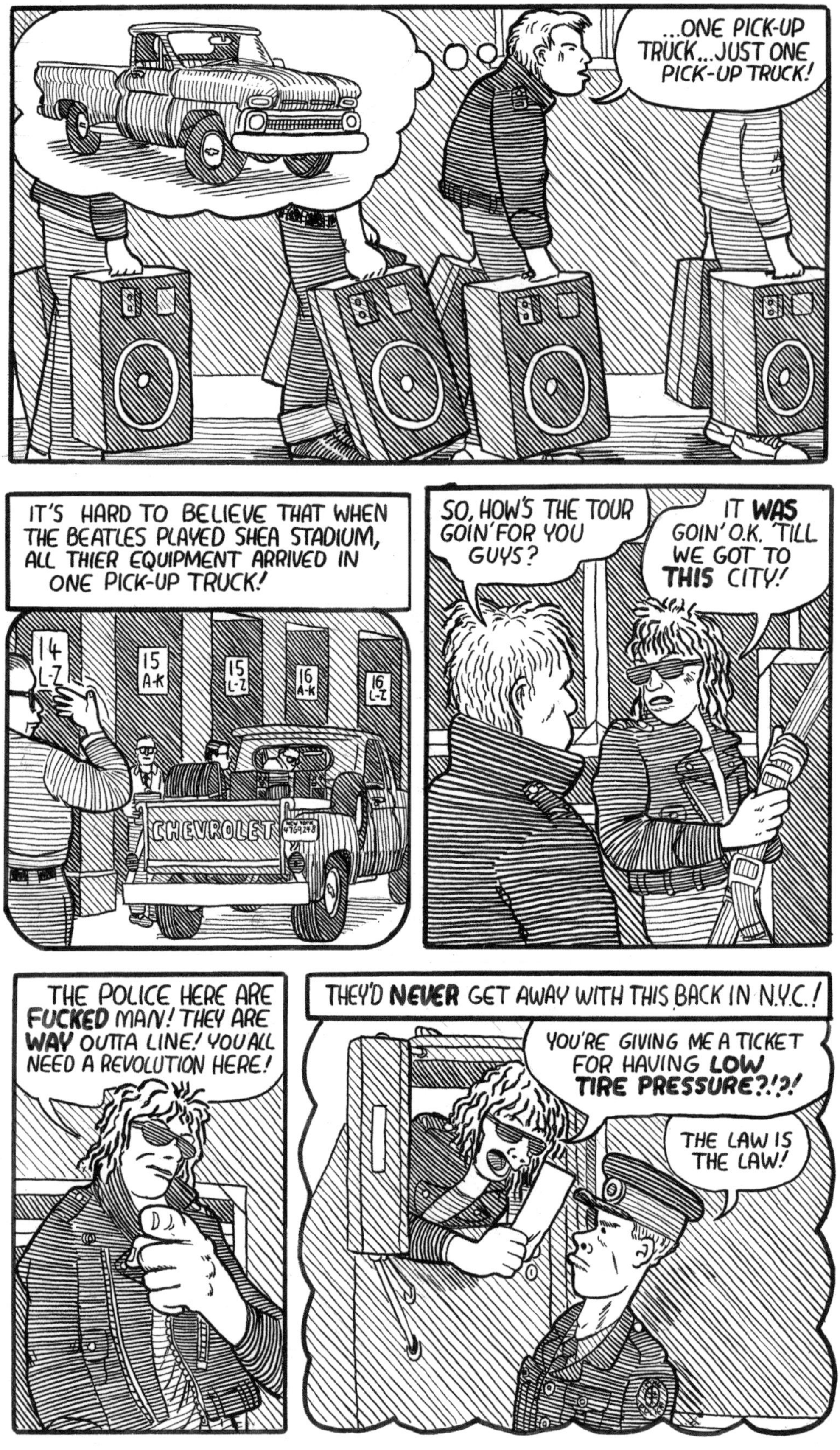
...ONE PICK-UP TRUCK...JUST ONE PICK-UP TRUCK!
IT'S HARD TO BELIEVE THAT WHEN THE BEATLES PLAYED SHEA STADIUM, ALL THIER EQUIPMENT ARRIVED IN ONE PICK-UP TRUCK!
14 L-Z
15 A-K
15 L-Z
16 A-K
16 L-Z
CHEVROLET
SO, HOW'S THE TOUR GOIN' FOR YOU GUYS?
IT WAS GOIN' O.K. 'TILL WE GOT TO THIS CITY!
THE POLICE HERE ARE FUCKED MAN! THEY ARE WAY OUTTA LINE! YOU ALL NEED A REVOLUTION HERE!
THEY'D NEVER GET AWAY WITH THIS BACK IN N.Y.C.!
YOU'RE GIVING ME A TICKET FOR HAVING LOW TIRE PRESSURE?!?!
THE LAW IS THE LAW!

'S TRUE! ABOUT THE ONLY REALLY POSITIVE THING YOU CAN SAY ABOUT THE POLICE IN THIS CITY, IS THAT THEY CONSISTENTLY WIN THE AWARD FOR THE "BEST-DRESSED FORCE" IN THE NATION!

I SURE HOPE YOU DON'T EXPECT US TO UNLOAD THIS WHOLE TRUCK BY OURSELVES!

WHAT ABOUT THOSE GUYS?

YOU'RE RIGHT... **HEY YOU GUYS! GET TO WORK!!**

SHIT!

WHAT A BLADE!

THE LITTLE FINK!

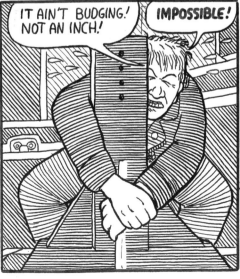

IT AIN'T BUDGING! NOT AN INCH!

IMPOSSIBLE!

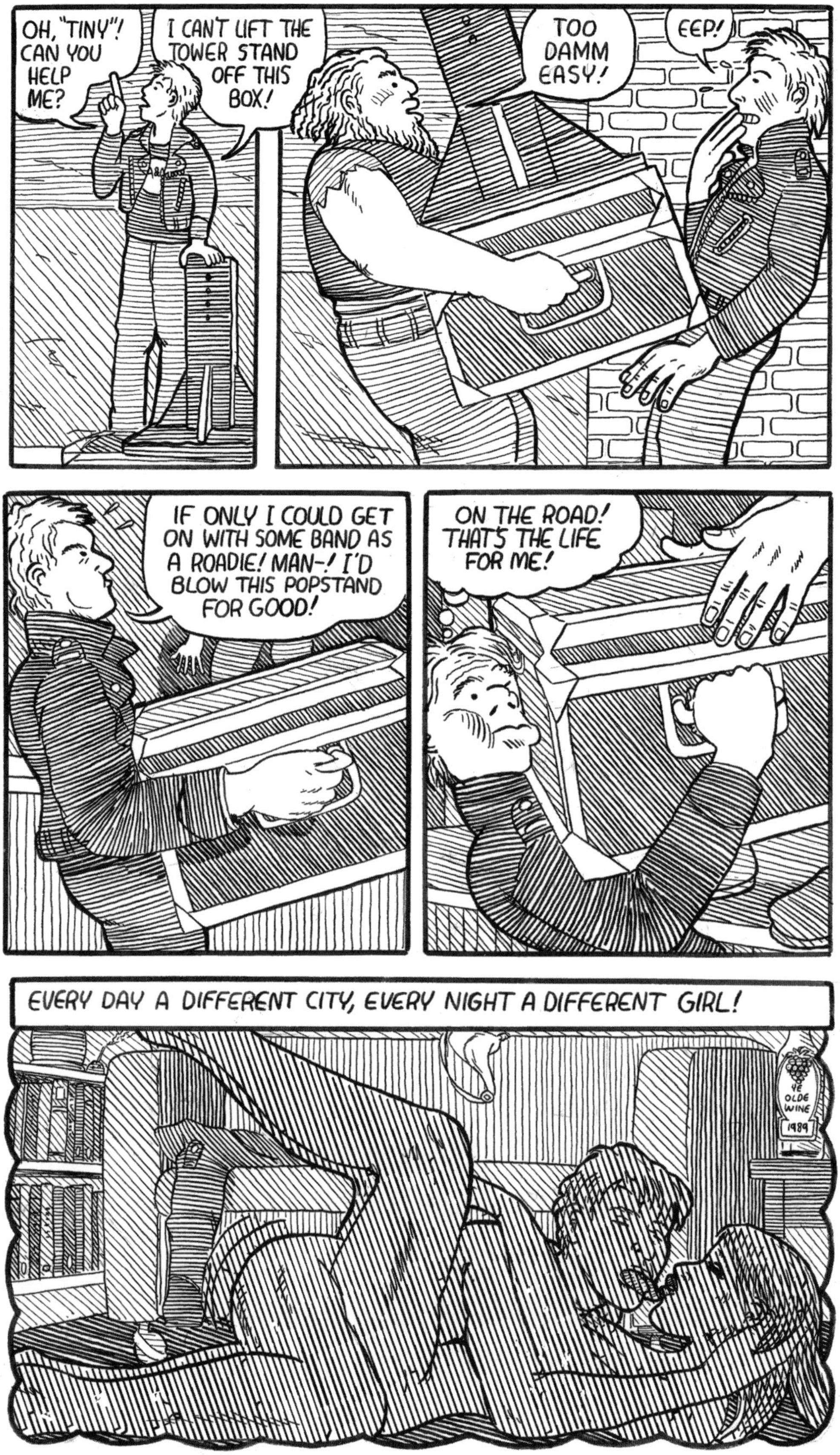

OH, "TINY"! CAN YOU HELP ME?
I CAN'T LIFT THE TOWER STAND OFF THIS BOX!
TOO DAMM EASY!
EEP!
IF ONLY I COULD GET ON WITH SOME BAND AS A ROADIE! MAN-! I'D BLOW THIS POPSTAND FOR GOOD!
ON THE ROAD! THAT'S THE LIFE FOR ME!
EVERY DAY A DIFFERENT CITY, EVERY NIGHT A DIFFERENT GIRL!
YE OLDE WINE 1989

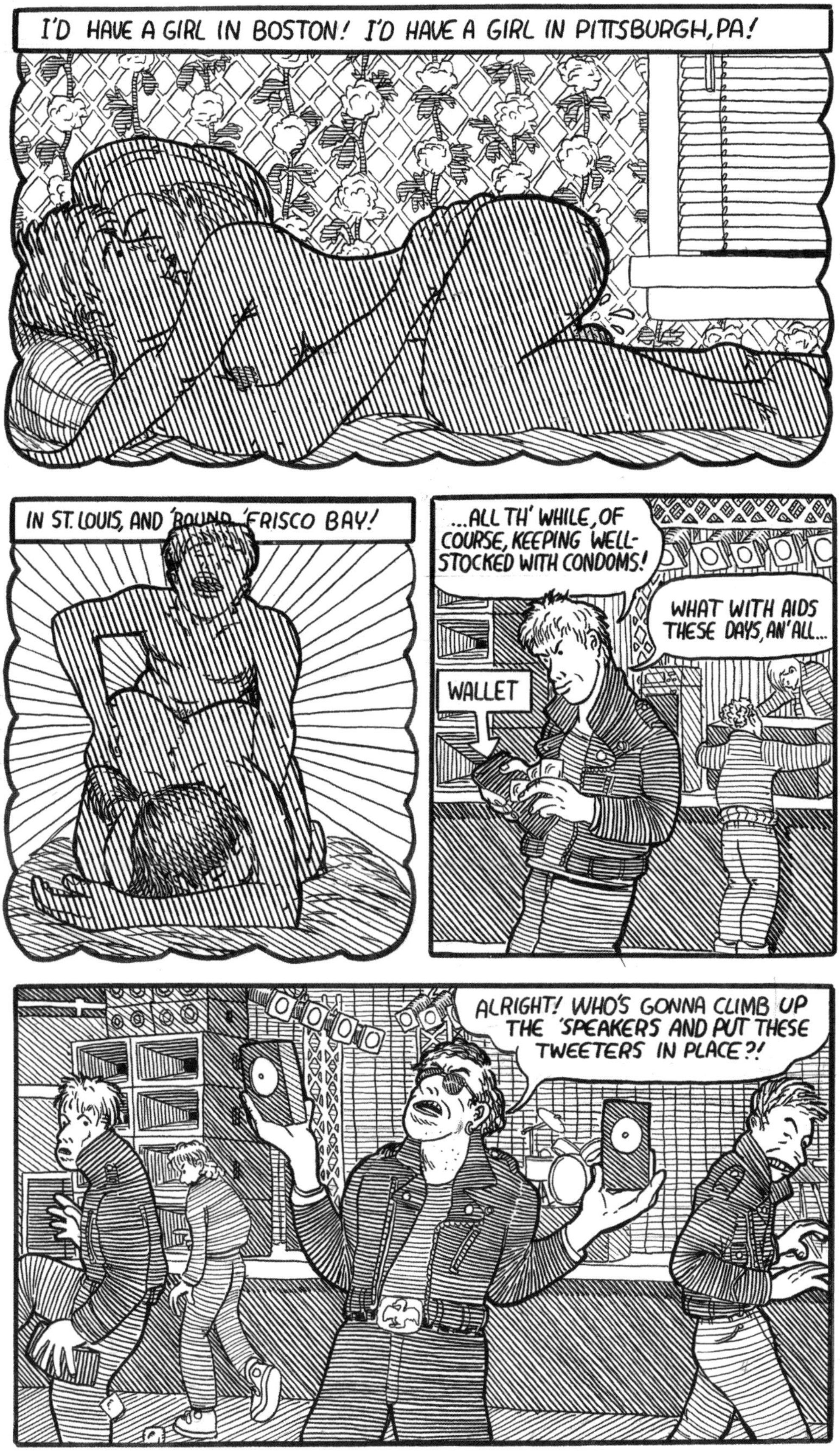

I'D HAVE A GIRL IN BOSTON! I'D HAVE A GIRL IN PITTSBURGH, PA!
IN ST. LOUIS, AND 'ROUND 'FRISCO BAY!
...ALL TH' WHILE, OF COURSE, KEEPING WELL-STOCKED WITH CONDOMS!
WHAT WITH AIDS THESE DAYS, AN' ALL...
WALLET
ALRIGHT! WHO'S GONNA CLIMB UP THE 'SPEAKERS AND PUT THESE TWEETERS IN PLACE?!

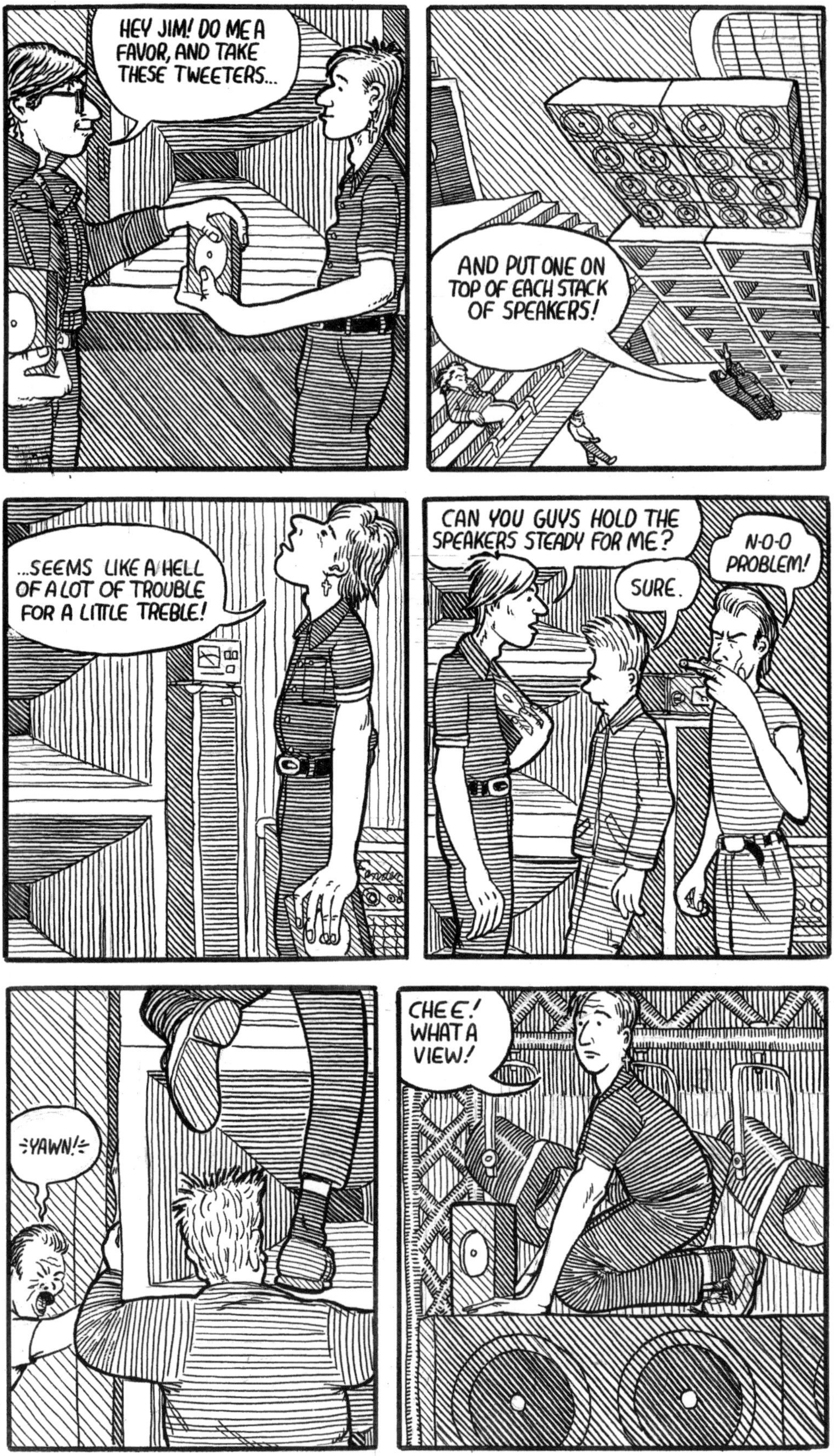
HEY JIM! DO ME A FAVOR, AND TAKE THESE TWEETERS...
AND PUT ONE ON TOP OF EACH STACK OF SPEAKERS!
...SEEMS LIKE A HELL OF A LOT OF TROUBLE FOR A LITTLE TREBLE!
CAN YOU GUYS HOLD THE SPEAKERS STEADY FOR ME?
SURE.
N-O-O PROBLEM!
=YAWN!=
CHEE! WHAT A VIEW!

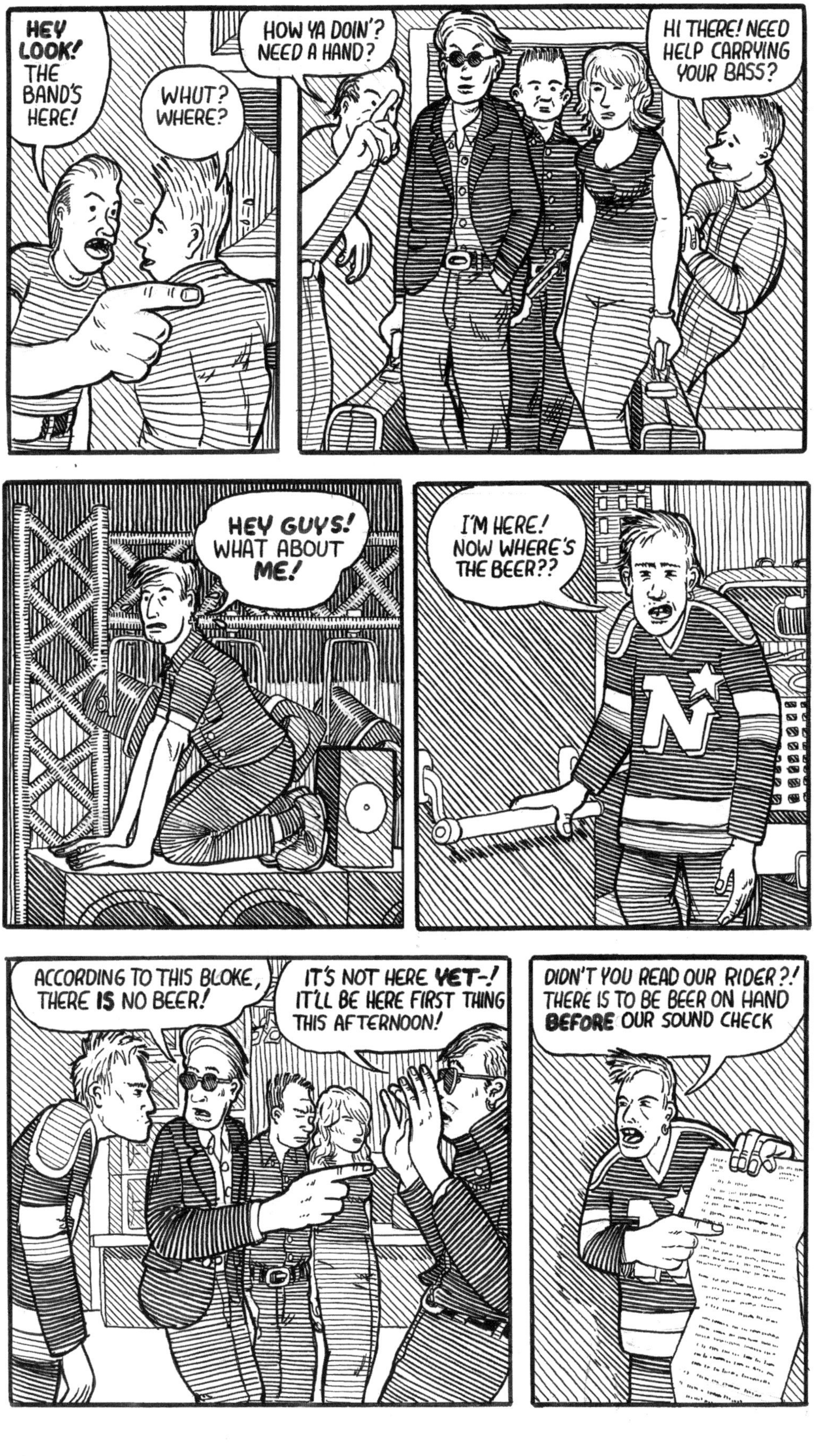
HEY LOOK! THE BAND'S HERE!
WHUT? WHERE?
HOW YA DOIN'? NEED A HAND?
HI THERE! NEED HELP CARRYING YOUR BASS?
HEY GUYS! WHAT ABOUT ME!
I'M HERE! NOW WHERE'S THE BEER??
ACCORDING TO THIS BLOKE, THERE IS NO BEER!
IT'S NOT HERE YET-! IT'LL BE HERE FIRST THING THIS AFTERNOON!
DIDN'T YOU READ OUR RIDER?! THERE IS TO BE BEER ON HAND BEFORE OUR SOUND CHECK

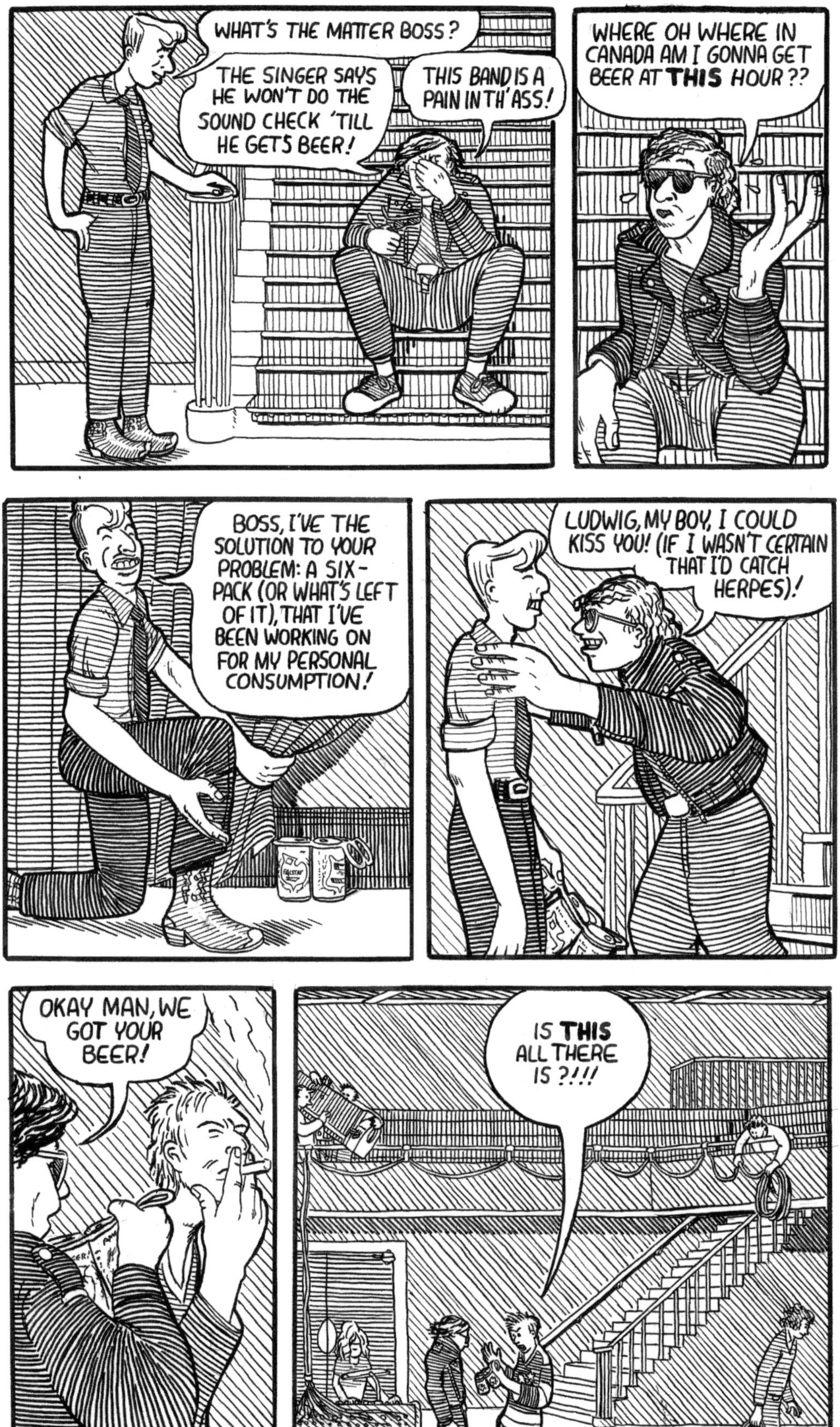
WHAT'S THE MATTER BOSS?
THE SINGER SAYS HE WON'T DO THE SOUND CHECK 'TILL HE GET'S BEER!
THIS BAND IS A PAIN IN TH' ASS!
WHERE OH WHERE IN CANADA AM I GONNA GET BEER AT **THIS** HOUR??
BOSS, I'VE THE SOLUTION TO YOUR PROBLEM: A SIX-PACK (OR WHAT'S LEFT OF IT), THAT I'VE BEEN WORKING ON FOR MY PERSONAL CONSUMPTION!
LUDWIG, MY BOY, I COULD KISS YOU! (IF I WASN'T CERTAIN THAT I'D CATCH HERPES)!
OKAY MAN, WE GOT YOUR BEER!
IS **THIS** ALL THERE IS?!!!

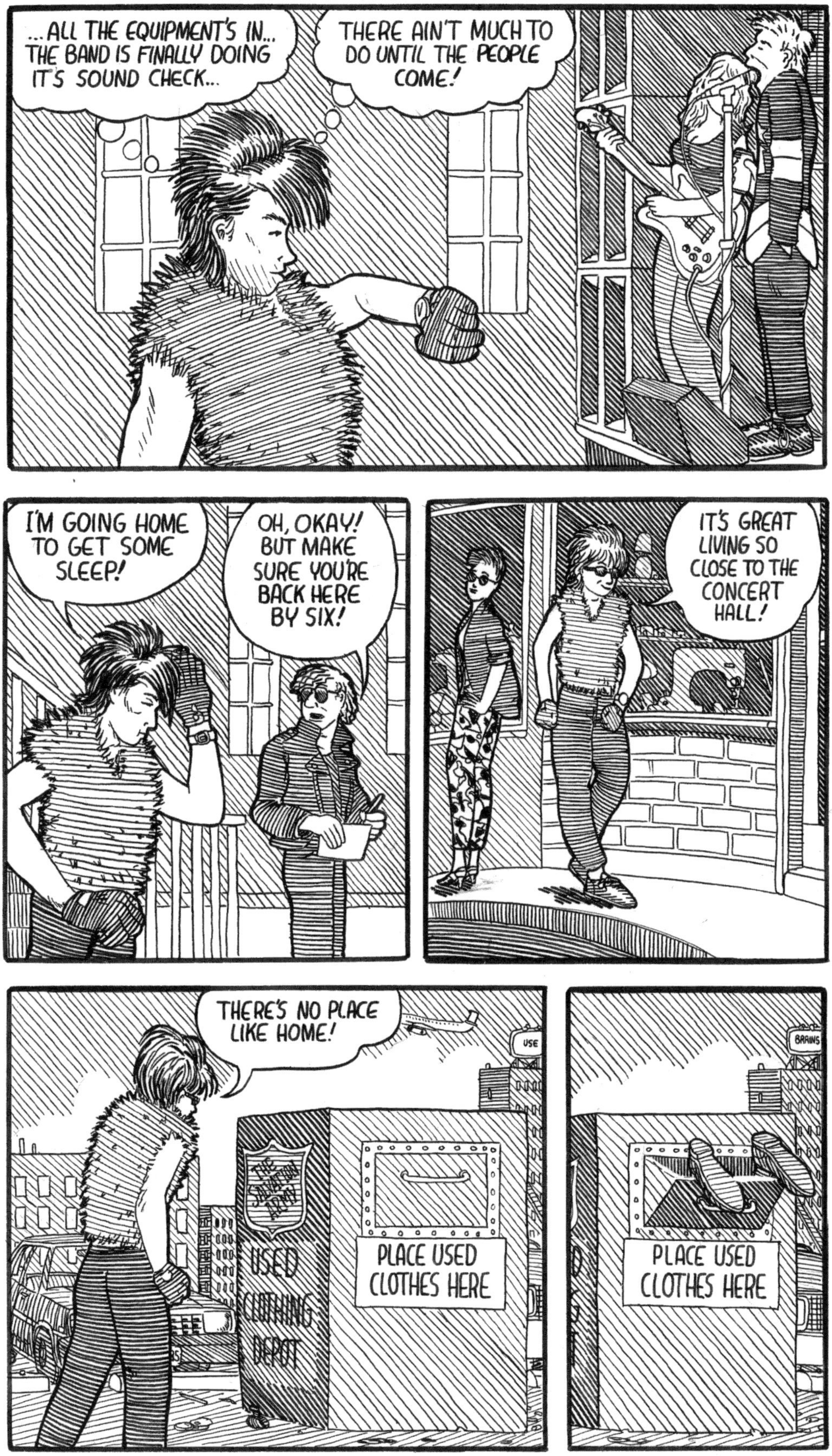
...ALL THE EQUIPMENT'S IN... THE BAND IS FINALLY DOING IT'S SOUND CHECK...
THERE AIN'T MUCH TO DO UNTIL THE PEOPLE COME!
I'M GOING HOME TO GET SOME SLEEP!
OH, OKAY! BUT MAKE SURE YOU'RE BACK HERE BY SIX!
IT'S GREAT LIVING SO CLOSE TO THE CONCERT HALL!
THERE'S NO PLACE LIKE HOME!
USE
THE SALVATION ARMY
USED CLOTHING DEPOT
PLACE USED CLOTHES HERE
BRAINS
PLACE USED CLOTHES HERE

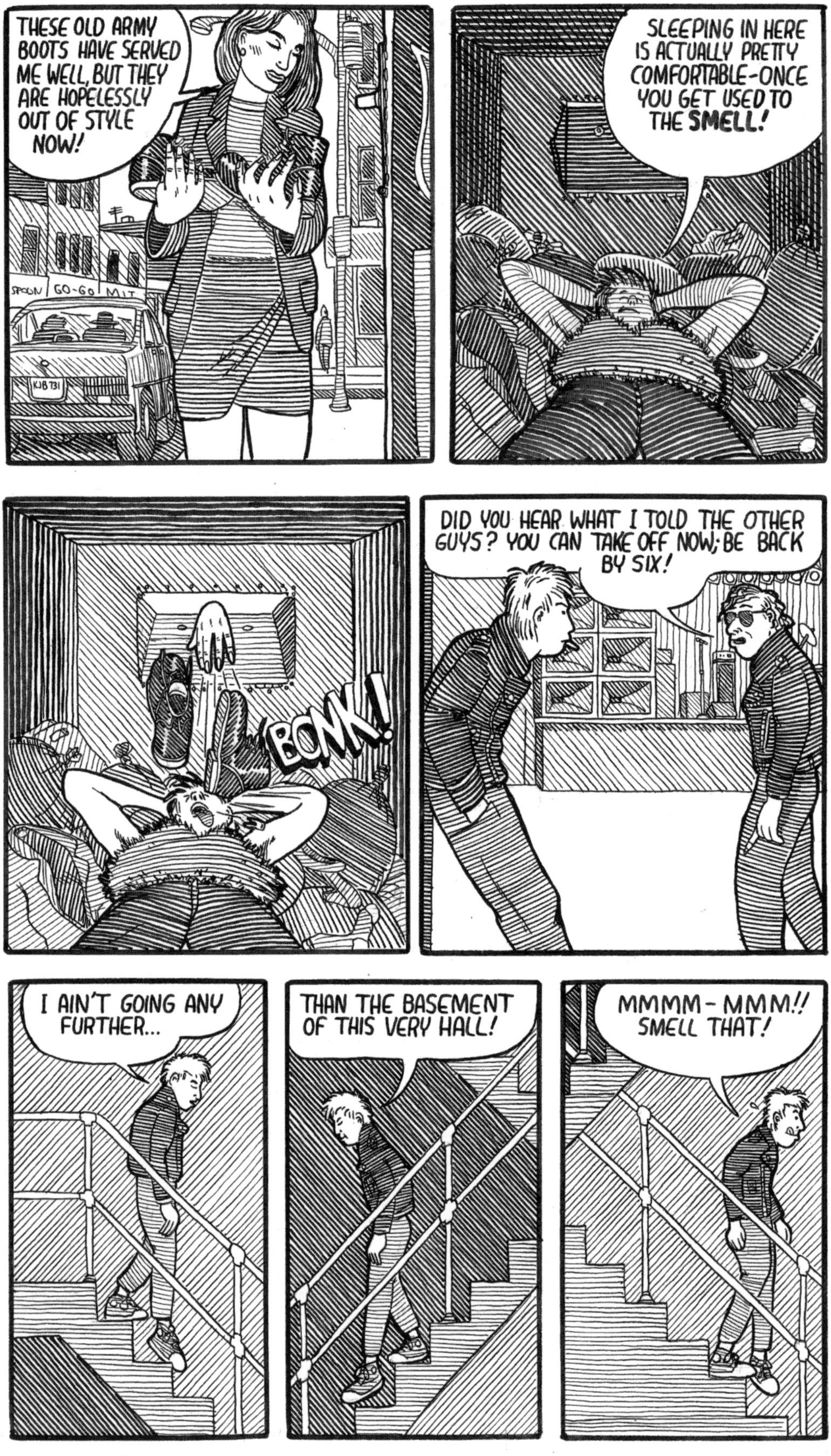

THESE OLD ARMY BOOTS HAVE SERVED ME WELL, BUT THEY ARE HOPELESSLY OUT OF STYLE NOW!
SPOON
GO-GO
KJB 731
SLEEPING IN HERE IS ACTUALLY PRETTY COMFORTABLE-ONCE YOU GET USED TO THE **SMELL**!
BONK!
DID YOU HEAR WHAT I TOLD THE OTHER GUYS? YOU CAN TAKE OFF NOW; BE BACK BY SIX!
I AIN'T GOING ANY FURTHER...
THAN THE BASEMENT OF THIS VERY HALL!
MMMM-MMM!! SMELL THAT!

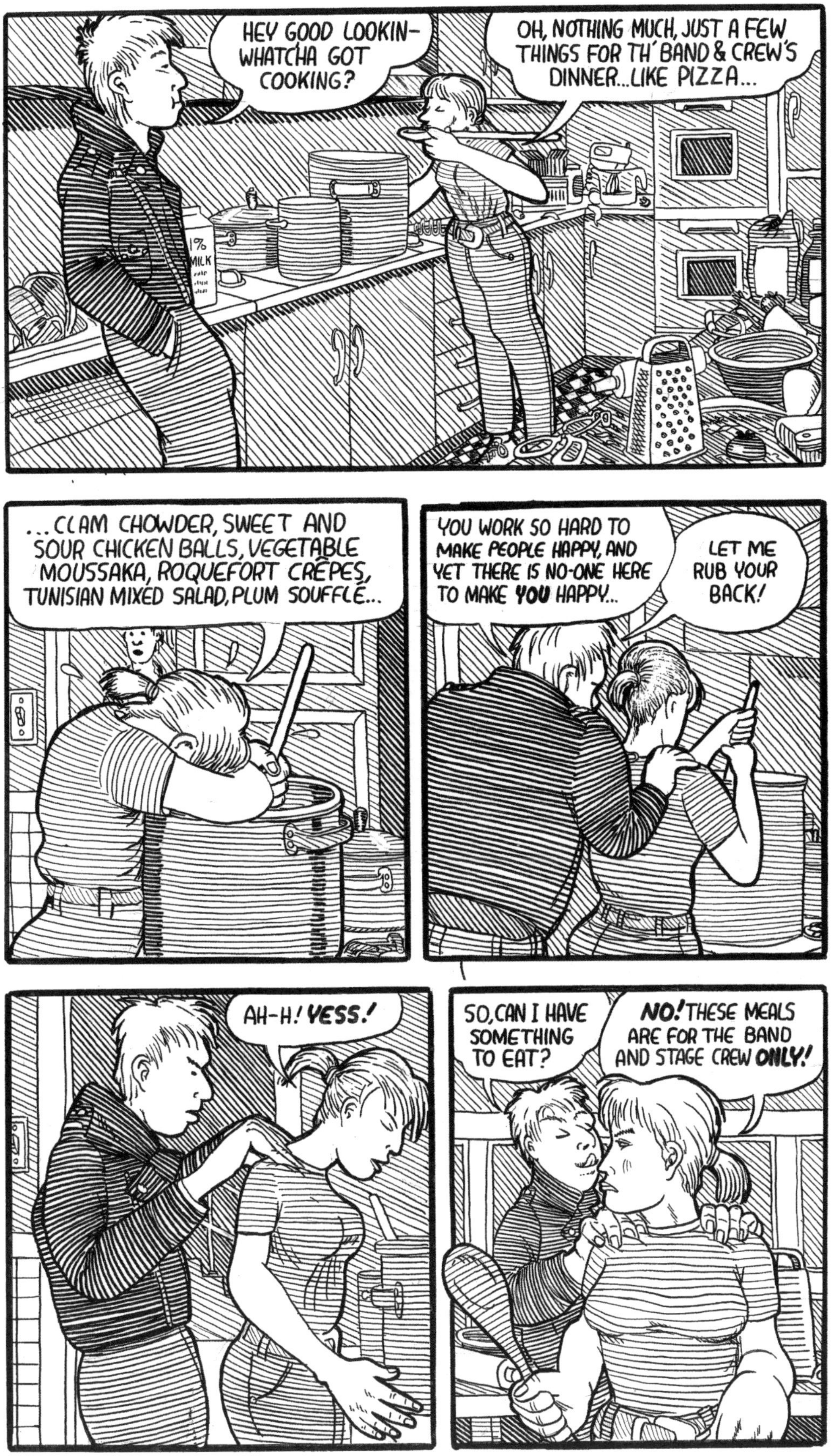
HEY GOOD LOOKIN-
WHATCHA GOT COOKING?
OH, NOTHING MUCH, JUST A FEW THINGS FOR TH' BAND & CREW'S DINNER...LIKE PIZZA...
...CLAM CHOWDER, SWEET AND SOUR CHICKEN BALLS, VEGETABLE MOUSSAKA, ROQUEFORT CRÊPES, TUNISIAN MIXED SALAD, PLUM SOUFFLÉ...
YOU WORK SO HARD TO MAKE PEOPLE HAPPY, AND YET THERE IS NO-ONE HERE TO MAKE YOU HAPPY...
LET ME RUB YOUR BACK!
AH-H! YESS!
SO, CAN I HAVE SOMETHING TO EAT?
NO! THESE MEALS ARE FOR THE BAND AND STAGE CREW ONLY!
1% MILK

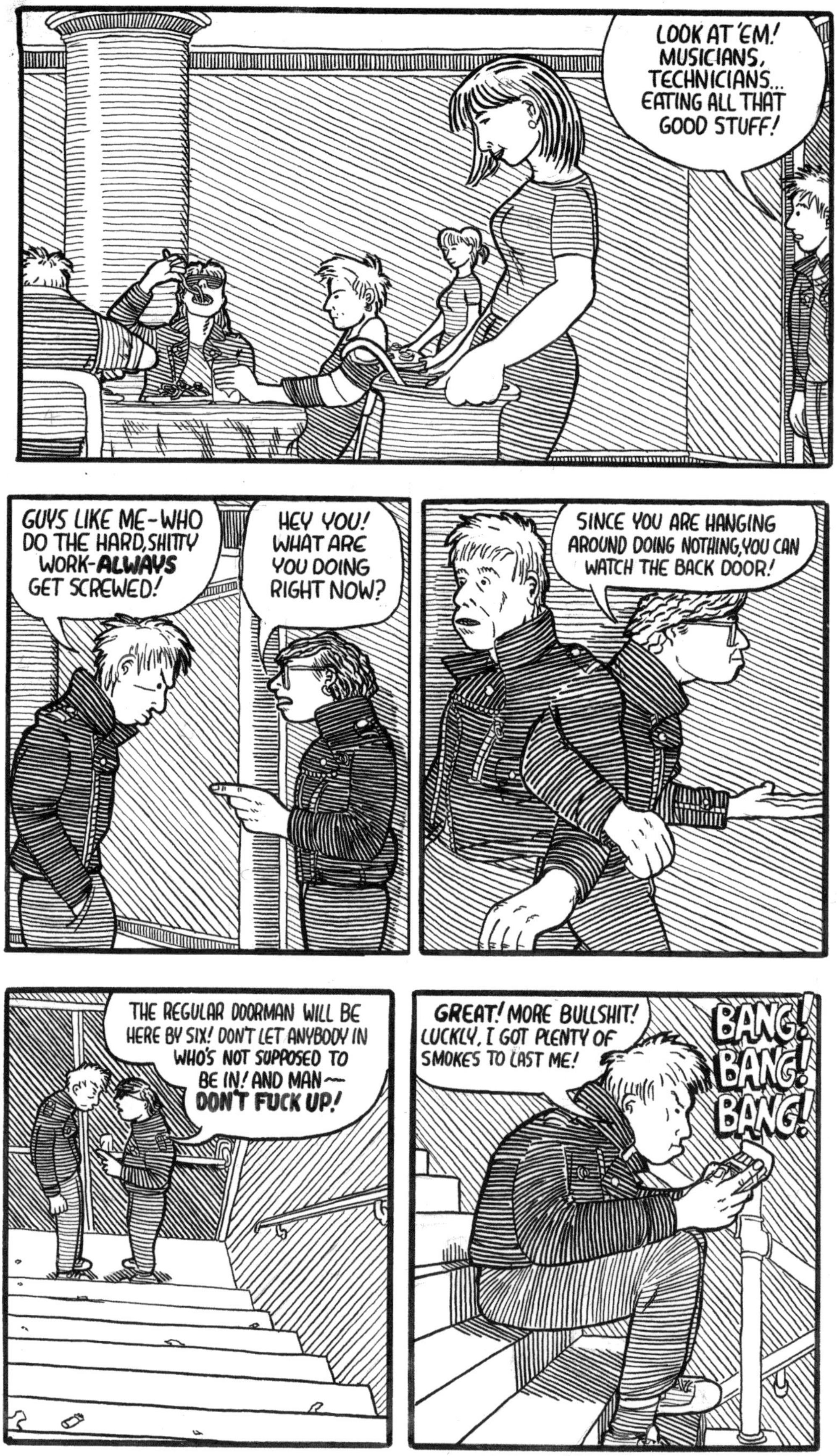
LOOK AT 'EM! MUSICIANS, TECHNICIANS... EATING ALL THAT GOOD STUFF!
GUYS LIKE ME-WHO DO THE HARD, SHITTY WORK-ALWAYS GET SCREWED!
HEY YOU! WHAT ARE YOU DOING RIGHT NOW?
SINCE YOU ARE HANGING AROUND DOING NOTHING, YOU CAN WATCH THE BACK DOOR!
THE REGULAR DOORMAN WILL BE HERE BY SIX! DON'T LET ANYBODY IN WHO'S NOT SUPPOSED TO BE IN! AND MAN~ DON'T FUCK UP!
GREAT! MORE BULLSHIT! LUCKLY, I GOT PLENTY OF SMOKES TO LAST ME!
BANG! BANG! BANG!

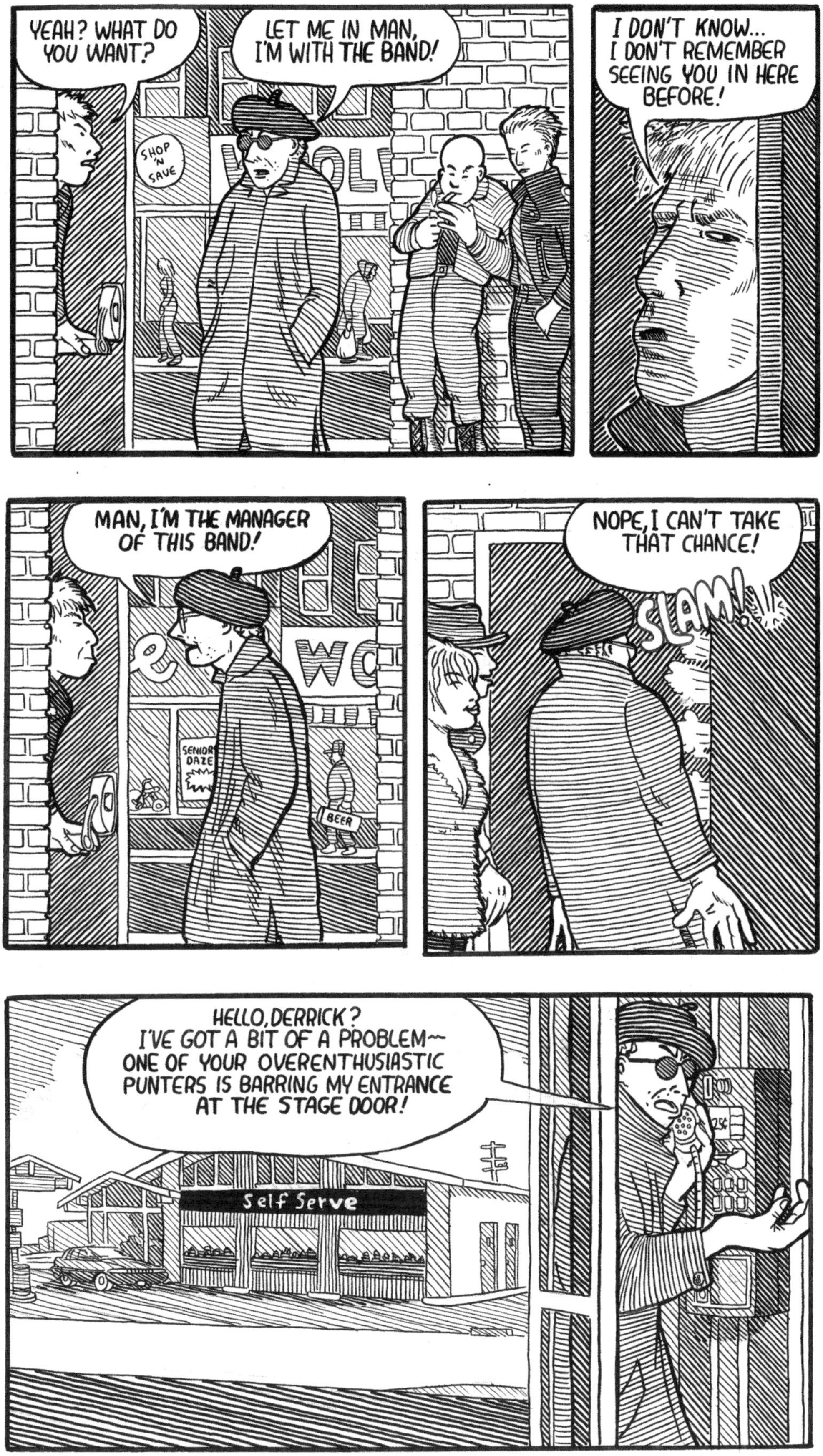
YEAH? WHAT DO YOU WANT?
LET ME IN MAN, I'M WITH THE BAND!
SHOP 'N SAVE
I DON'T KNOW... I DON'T REMEMBER SEEING YOU IN HERE BEFORE!
MAN, I'M THE MANAGER OF THIS BAND!
SENIOR DAZE
BEER
NOPE, I CAN'T TAKE THAT CHANCE!
SLAM!
HELLO, DERRICK? I'VE GOT A BIT OF A PROBLEM~ ONE OF YOUR OVERENTHUSIASTIC PUNTERS IS BARRING MY ENTRANCE AT THE STAGE DOOR!
Self Serve
25¢

PERHAPS NEXT TIME I SHOULD BOOK WITH ANOTHER PROMOTER, SINCE YOU SEEM UNABLE TO PROVIDE PEOPLE CAPABLE OF FORMING INTELLIGENT THOUGHTS!
NO, NO, DON'T WORRY— THIS WON'T HAPPEN AGAIN!
YAWN
GUESS IT'S ABOUT TIME TO BE HEADIN' BACK!
PLACE USED
OK, LOOK—I'M GOING TO MAKE IT **EASY** FOR YOU: ① EVERYBODY THAT YOU **DO NOT** KNOW; IF THEY LOOK PLAUSIBLE, LET 'EM IN. ② EVERYBODY THAT YOU **DO** KNOW; IF THEY ARE SCUM, KEEP 'EM OUT!
CONCERT HALL
LOOKS LIKE A PRETTY FAIR-SIZED CROWD FORMING UP!

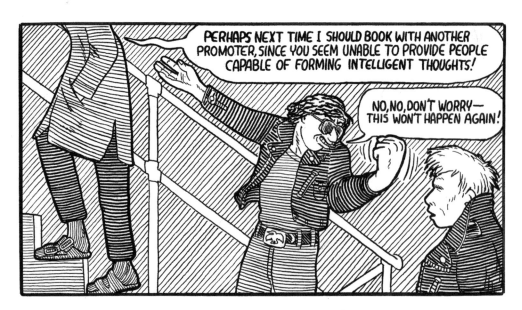

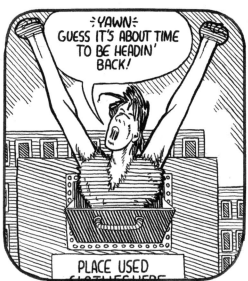

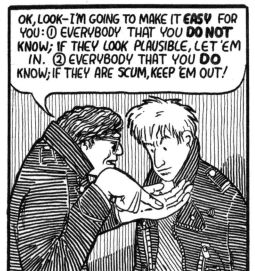

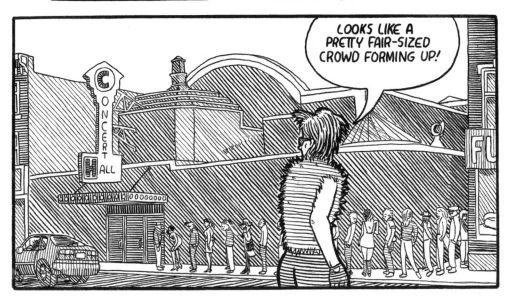

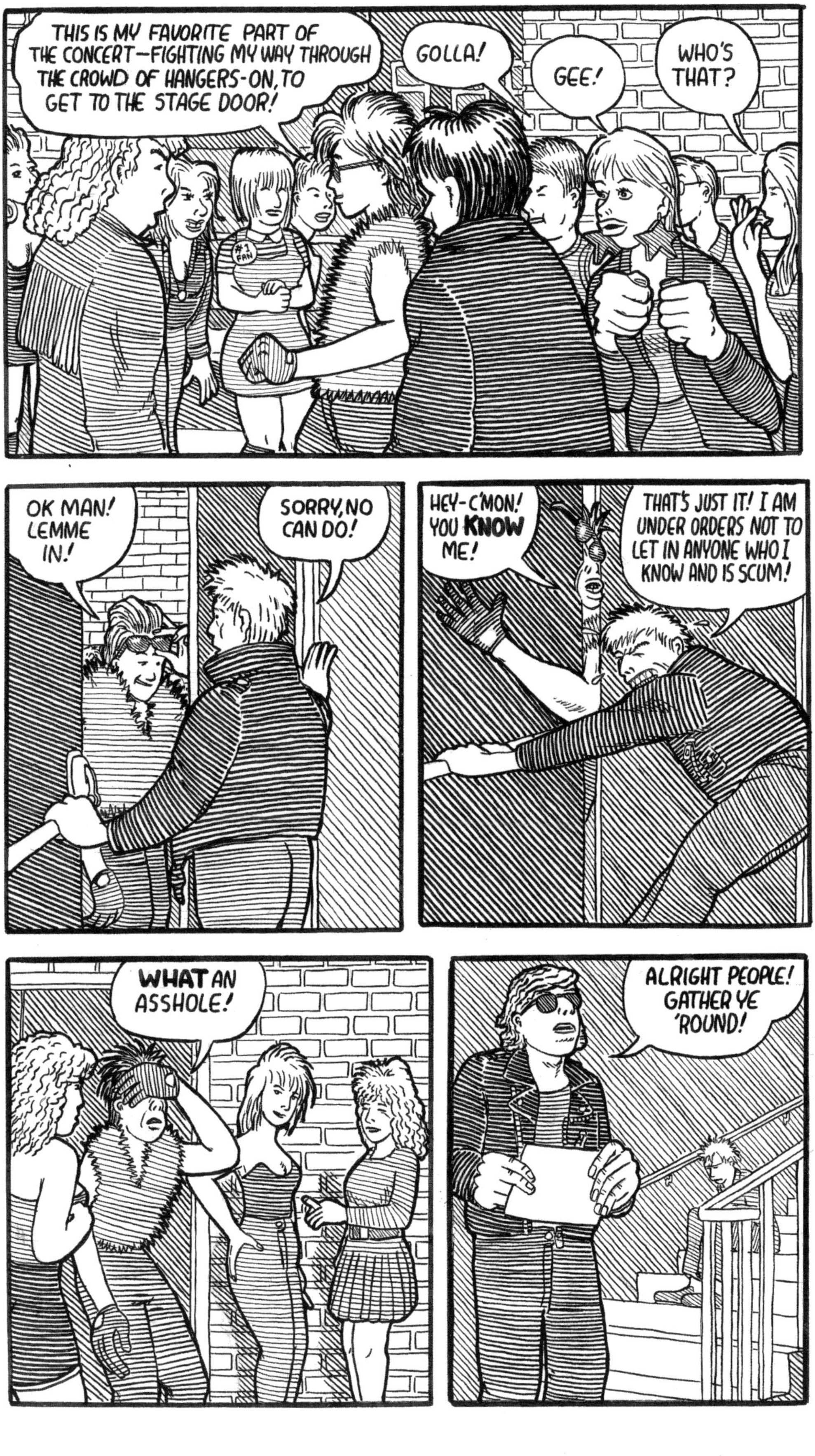
THIS IS MY FAVORITE PART OF THE CONCERT—FIGHTING MY WAY THROUGH THE CROWD OF HANGERS-ON, TO GET TO THE STAGE DOOR!
GOLLA!
GEE!
WHO'S THAT?
OK MAN! LEMME IN!
SORRY, NO CAN DO!
HEY-C'MON! YOU KNOW ME!
THAT'S JUST IT! I AM UNDER ORDERS NOT TO LET IN ANYONE WHO I KNOW AND IS SCUM!
WHAT AN ASSHOLE!
ALRIGHT PEOPLE! GATHER YE 'ROUND!

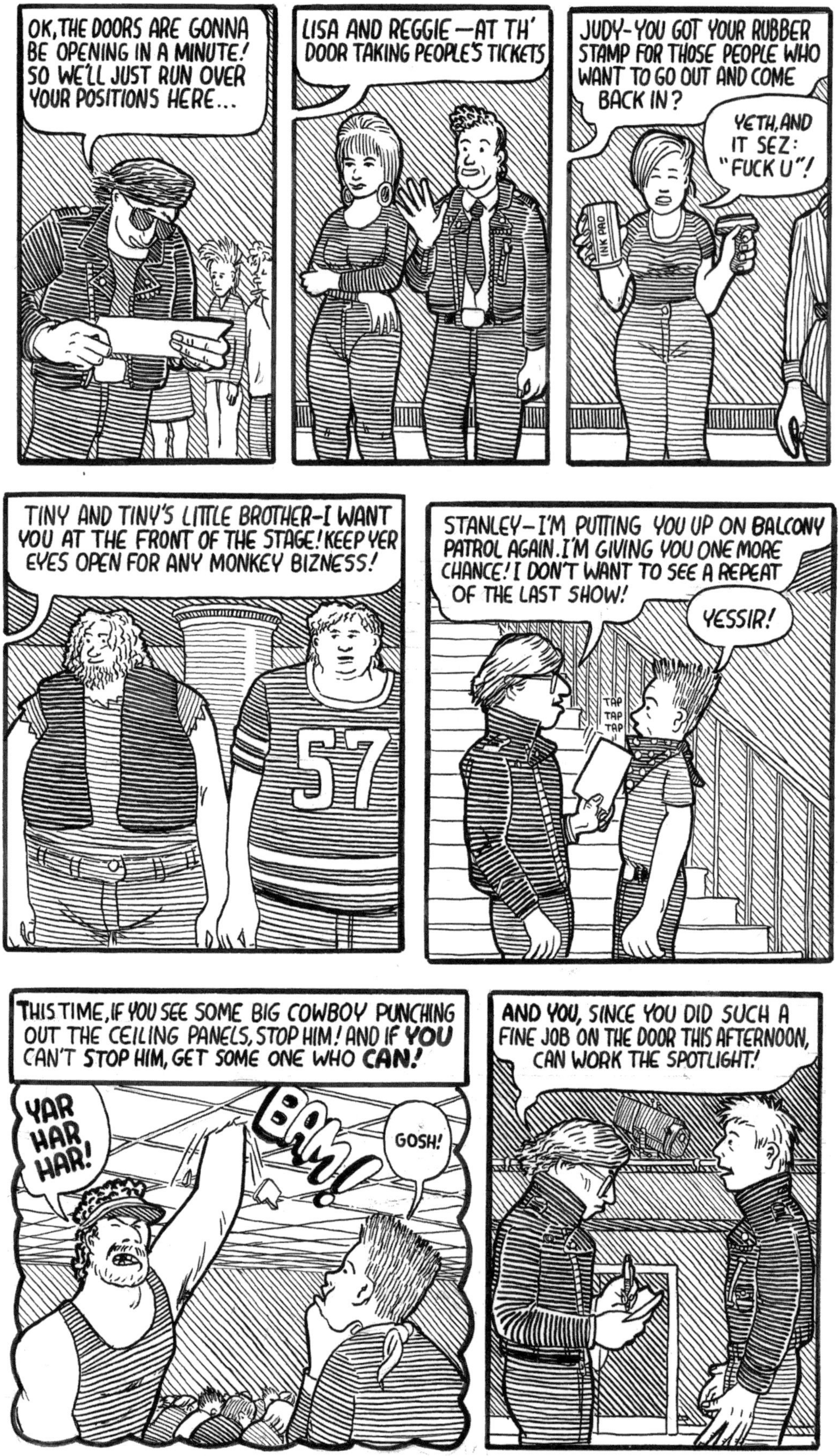
OK, THE DOORS ARE GONNA BE OPENING IN A MINUTE! SO WE'LL JUST RUN OVER YOUR POSITIONS HERE...
LISA AND REGGIE — AT TH' DOOR TAKING PEOPLE'S TICKETS
JUDY- YOU GOT YOUR RUBBER STAMP FOR THOSE PEOPLE WHO WANT TO GO OUT AND COME BACK IN?
YETH, AND IT SEZ: "FUCK U"!
INK PAD
TINY AND TINY'S LITTLE BROTHER-I WANT YOU AT THE FRONT OF THE STAGE! KEEP YER EYES OPEN FOR ANY MONKEY BIZNESS!
57
STANLEY-I'M PUTTING YOU UP ON BALCONY PATROL AGAIN. I'M GIVING YOU ONE MORE CHANCE! I DON'T WANT TO SEE A REPEAT OF THE LAST SHOW!
TAP TAP TAP
YESSIR!
THIS TIME, IF YOU SEE SOME BIG COWBOY PUNCHING OUT THE CEILING PANELS, STOP HIM! AND IF YOU CAN'T STOP HIM, GET SOME ONE WHO CAN!
YAR HAR HAR!
BAM!
GOSH!
AND YOU, SINCE YOU DID SUCH A FINE JOB ON THE DOOR THIS AFTERNOON, CAN WORK THE SPOTLIGHT!

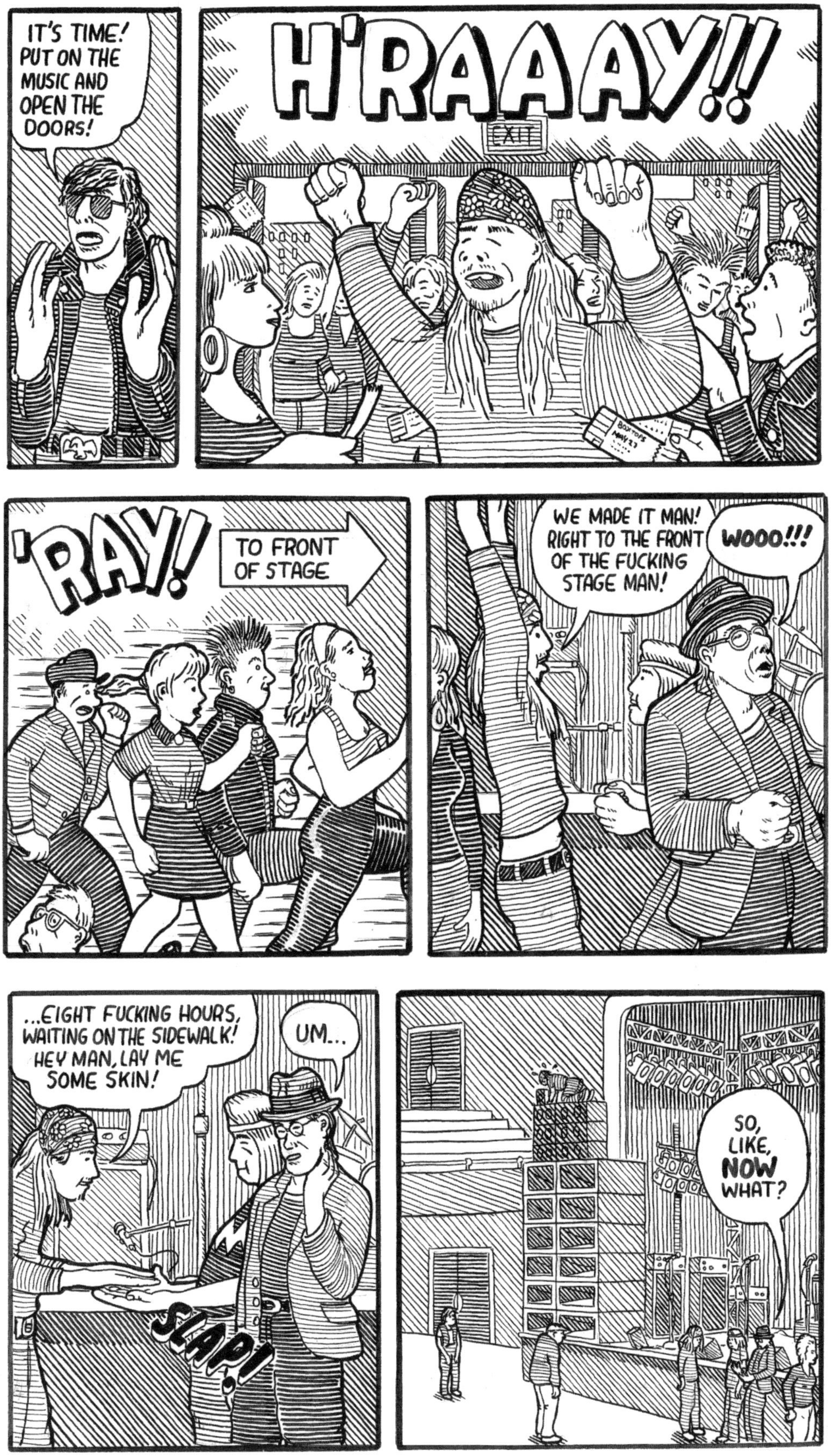
IT'S TIME! PUT ON THE MUSIC AND OPEN THE DOORS!
H'RAAAY!!
EXIT
'RAY!
TO FRONT OF STAGE
WE MADE IT MAN! RIGHT TO THE FRONT OF THE FUCKING STAGE MAN!
WOOO!!!
...EIGHT FUCKING HOURS, WAITING ON THE SIDEWALK! HEY MAN, LAY ME SOME SKIN!
UM...
SLAP!
SO, LIKE, NOW WHAT?

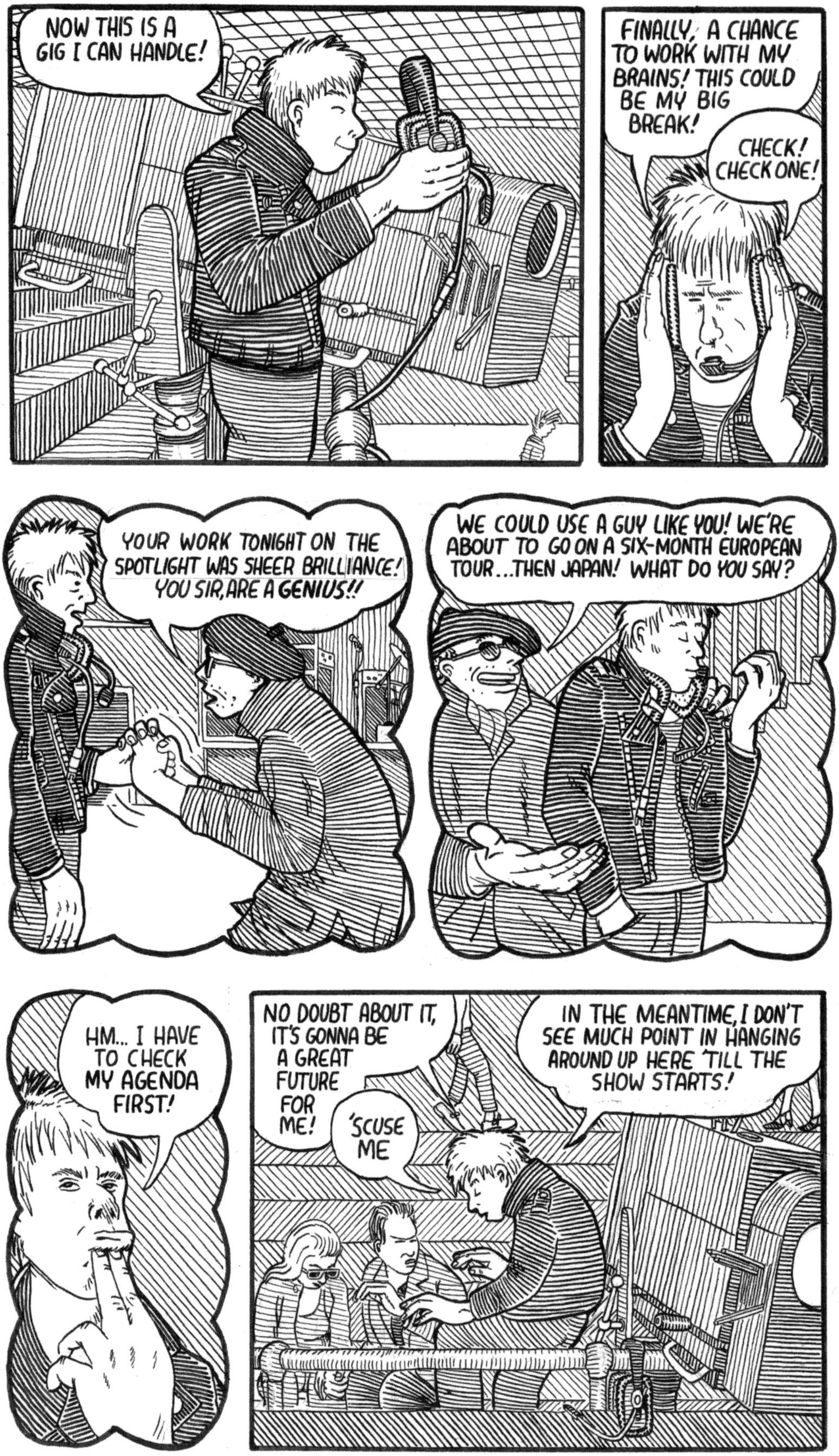
NOW THIS IS A GIG I CAN HANDLE!
FINALLY, A CHANCE TO WORK WITH MY BRAINS! THIS COULD BE MY BIG BREAK!
CHECK! CHECK ONE!
YOUR WORK TONIGHT ON THE SPOTLIGHT WAS SHEER BRILLIANCE! YOU SIR, ARE A **GENIUS**!!
WE COULD USE A GUY LIKE YOU! WE'RE ABOUT TO GO ON A SIX-MONTH EUROPEAN TOUR...THEN JAPAN! WHAT DO YOU SAY?
HM... I HAVE TO CHECK MY AGENDA FIRST!
NO DOUBT ABOUT IT, IT'S GONNA BE A GREAT FUTURE FOR ME!
'SCUSE ME
IN THE MEANTIME, I DON'T SEE MUCH POINT IN HANGING AROUND UP HERE 'TILL THE SHOW STARTS!

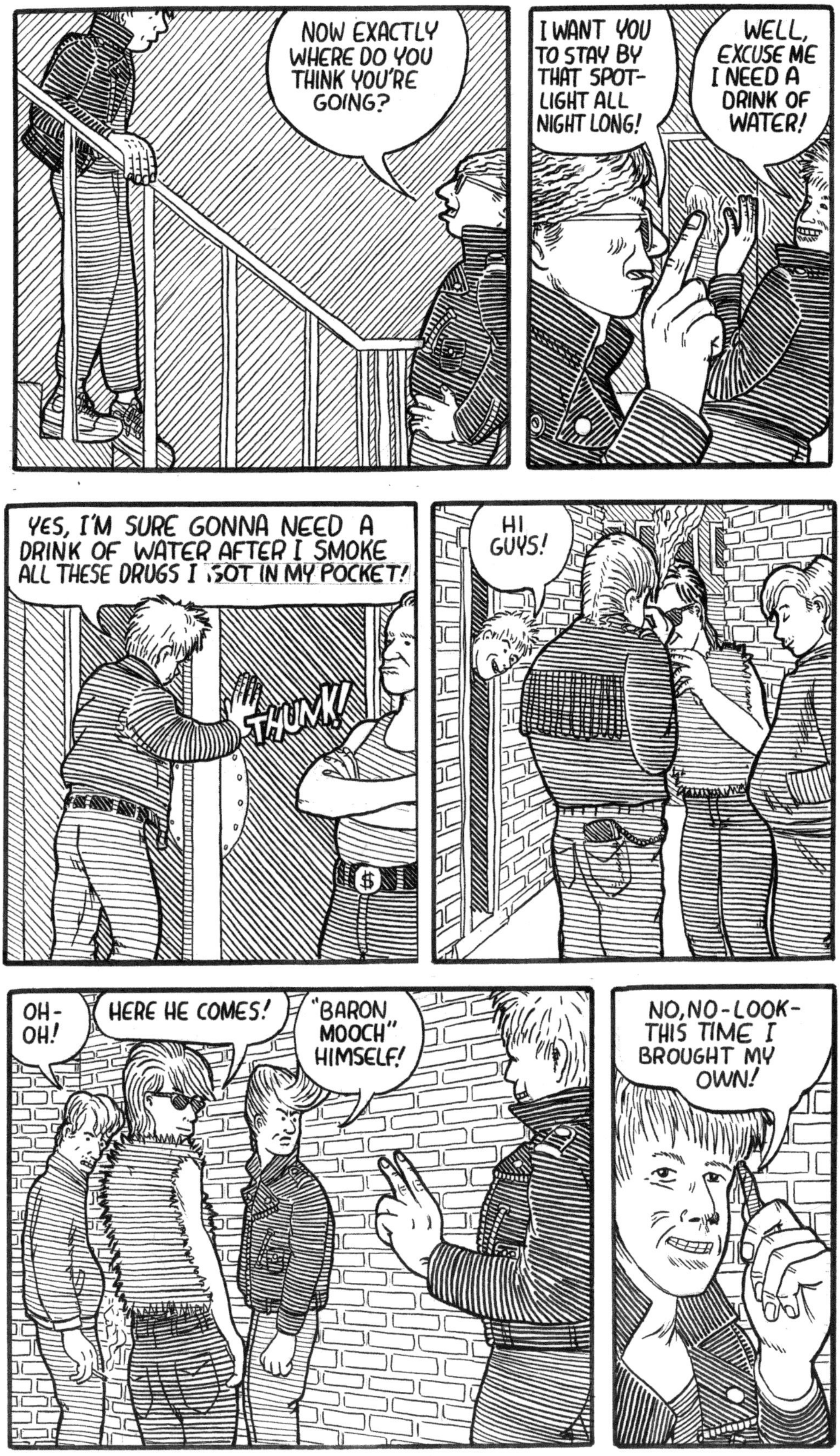
NOW EXACTLY WHERE DO YOU THINK YOU'RE GOING?
I WANT YOU TO STAY BY THAT SPOT-LIGHT ALL NIGHT LONG!
WELL, EXCUSE ME I NEED A DRINK OF WATER!
YES, I'M SURE GONNA NEED A DRINK OF WATER AFTER I SMOKE ALL THESE DRUGS I GOT IN MY POCKET!
THUNK!
HI GUYS!
OH-OH!
HERE HE COMES!
"BARON MOOCH" HIMSELF!
NO, NO-LOOK-THIS TIME I BROUGHT MY OWN!

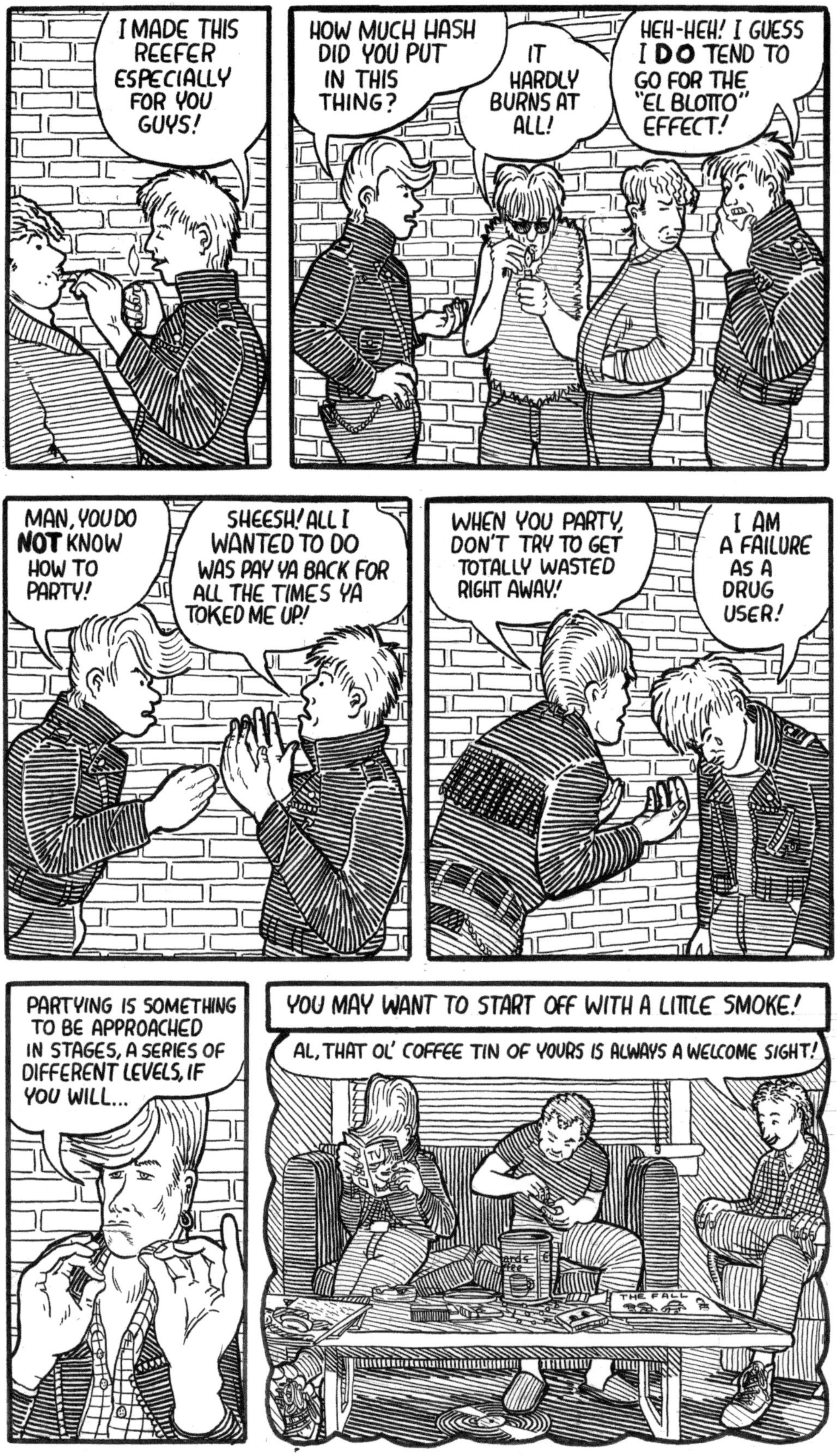
I MADE THIS REEFER ESPECIALLY FOR YOU GUYS!
HOW MUCH HASH DID YOU PUT IN THIS THING?
IT HARDLY BURNS AT ALL!
HEH-HEH! I GUESS I DO TEND TO GO FOR THE "EL BLOTTO" EFFECT!
MAN, YOU DO NOT KNOW HOW TO PARTY!
SHEESH! ALL I WANTED TO DO WAS PAY YA BACK FOR ALL THE TIMES YA TOKED ME UP!
WHEN YOU PARTY, DON'T TRY TO GET TOTALLY WASTED RIGHT AWAY!
I AM A FAILURE AS A DRUG USER!
PARTYING IS SOMETHING TO BE APPROACHED IN STAGES, A SERIES OF DIFFERENT LEVELS, IF YOU WILL...
YOU MAY WANT TO START OFF WITH A LITTLE SMOKE!
AL, THAT OL' COFFEE TIN OF YOURS IS ALWAYS A WELCOME SIGHT!
THE FALL

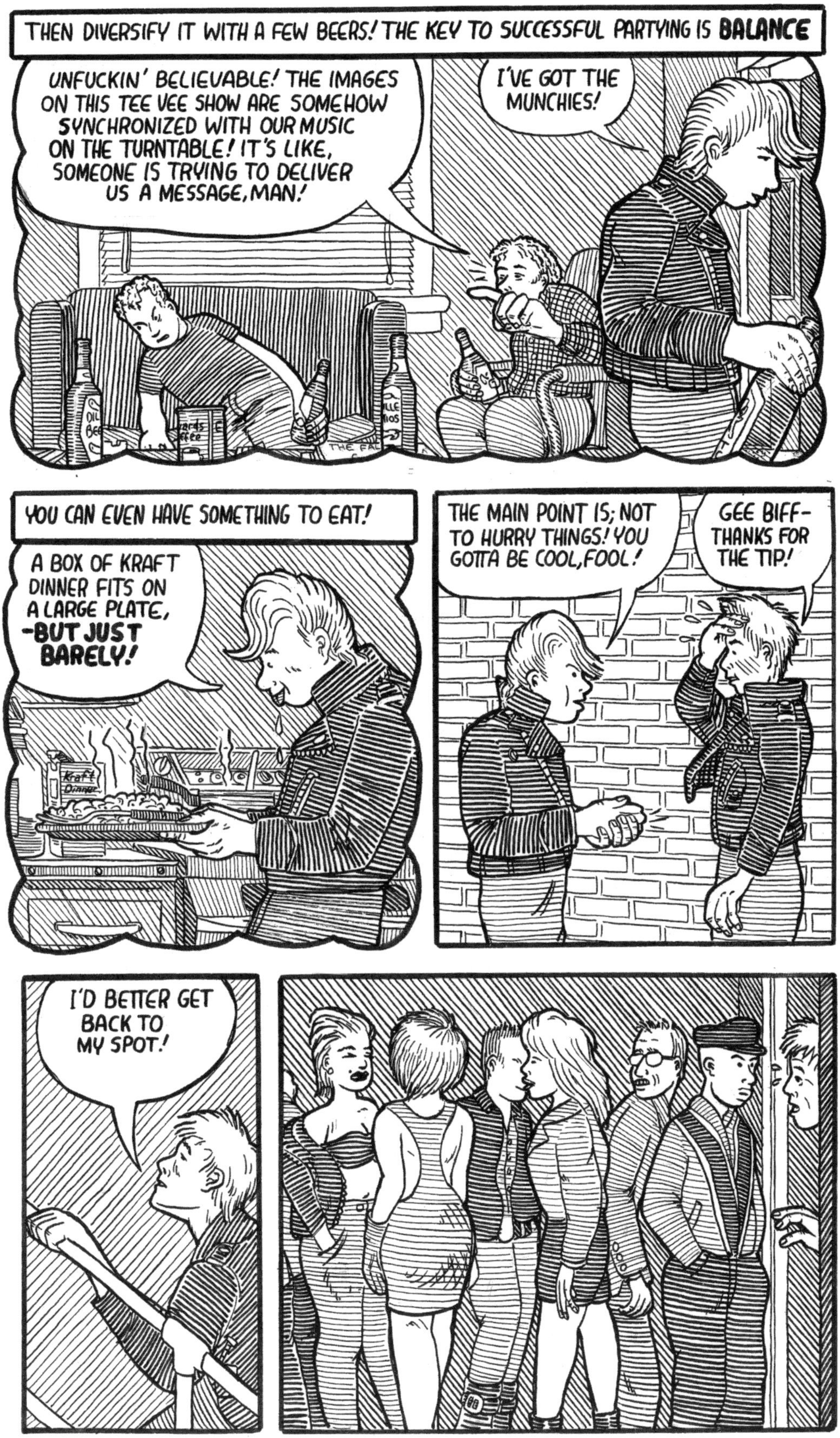
THEN DIVERSIFY IT WITH A FEW BEERS! THE KEY TO SUCCESSFUL PARTYING IS **BALANCE**
UNFUCKIN' BELIEVABLE! THE IMAGES ON THIS TEE VEE SHOW ARE SOMEHOW SYNCHRONIZED WITH OUR MUSIC ON THE TURNTABLE! IT'S LIKE, SOMEONE IS TRYING TO DELIVER US A MESSAGE, MAN!
I'VE GOT THE MUNCHIES!
YOU CAN EVEN HAVE SOMETHING TO EAT!
A BOX OF KRAFT DINNER FITS ON A LARGE PLATE, **-BUT JUST BARELY!**
Kraft Dinner
THE MAIN POINT IS; NOT TO HURRY THINGS! YOU GOTTA BE COOL, FOOL!
GEE BIFF- THANKS FOR THE TIP!
I'D BETTER GET BACK TO MY SPOT!

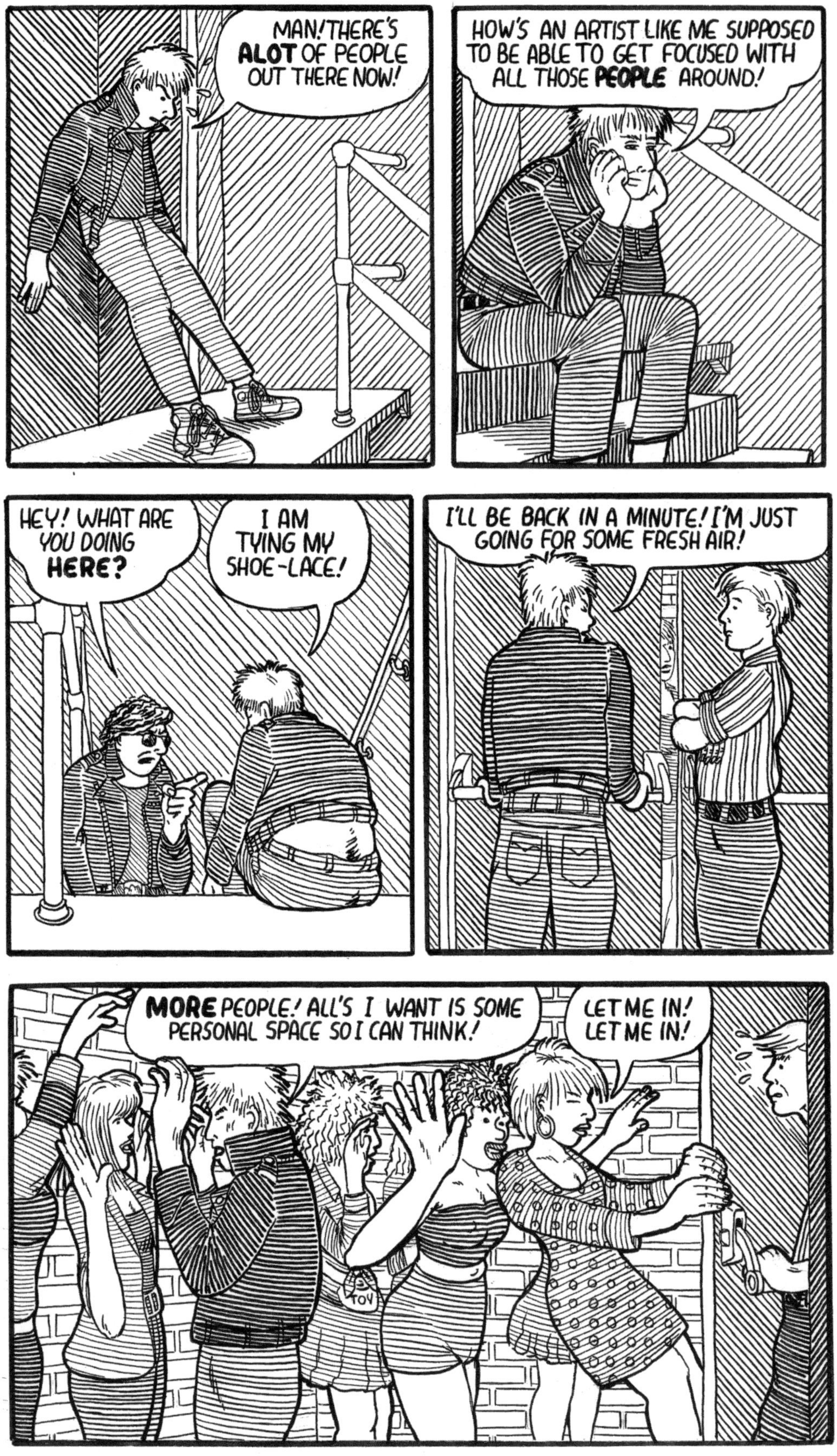
MAN! THERE'S ALOT OF PEOPLE OUT THERE NOW!
HOW'S AN ARTIST LIKE ME SUPPOSED TO BE ABLE TO GET FOCUSED WITH ALL THOSE PEOPLE AROUND!
HEY! WHAT ARE YOU DOING HERE?
I AM TYING MY SHOE-LACE!
I'LL BE BACK IN A MINUTE! I'M JUST GOING FOR SOME FRESH AIR!
MORE PEOPLE! ALL'S I WANT IS SOME PERSONAL SPACE SO I CAN THINK!
LET ME IN! LET ME IN!
TOY

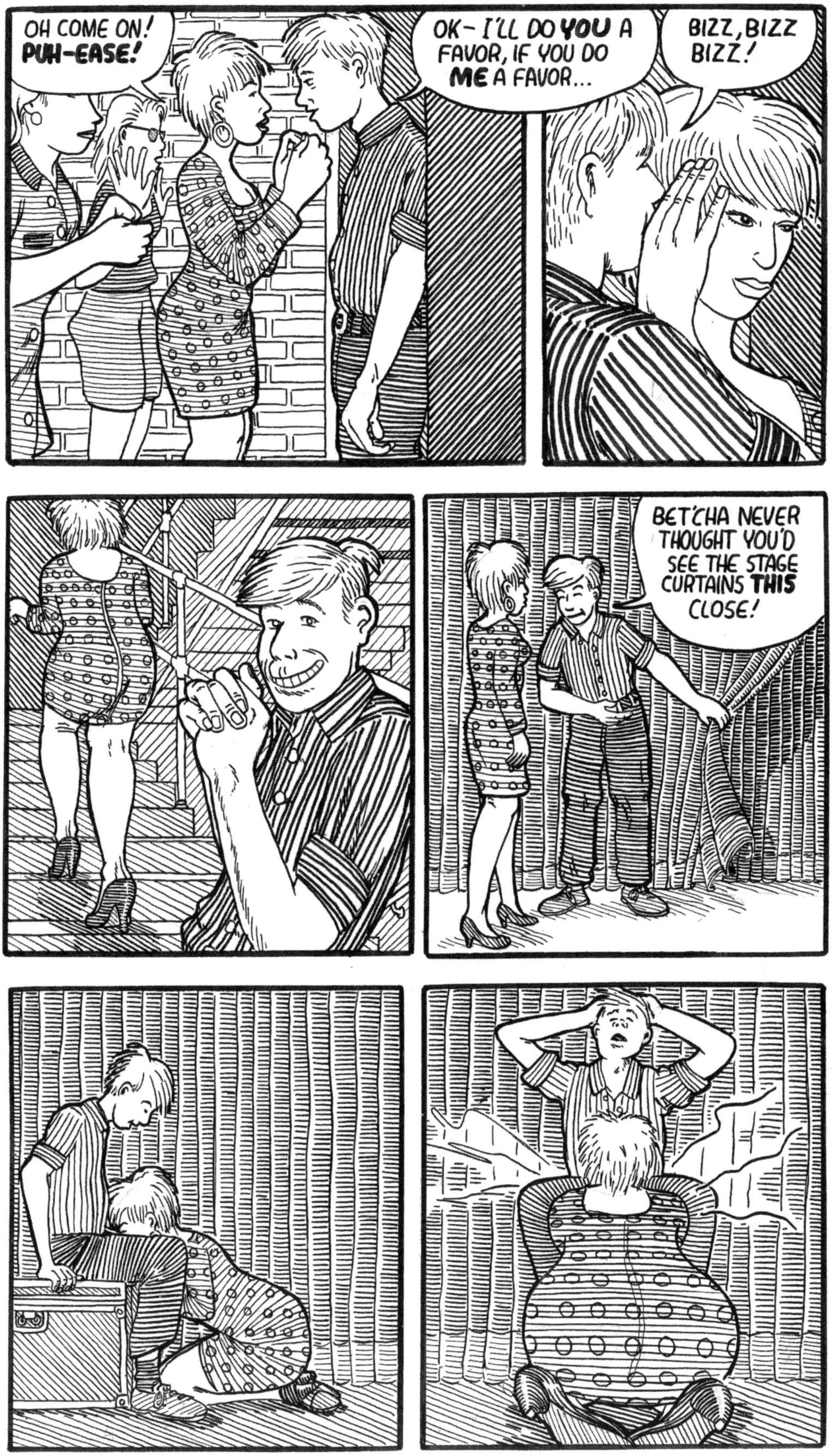
OH COME ON! **PUH-EASE!**
OK– I'LL DO **YOU** A FAVOR, IF YOU DO **ME** A FAVOR...
BIZZ, BIZZ BIZZ!
BET'CHA NEVER THOUGHT YOU'D SEE THE STAGE CURTAINS **THIS** CLOSE!

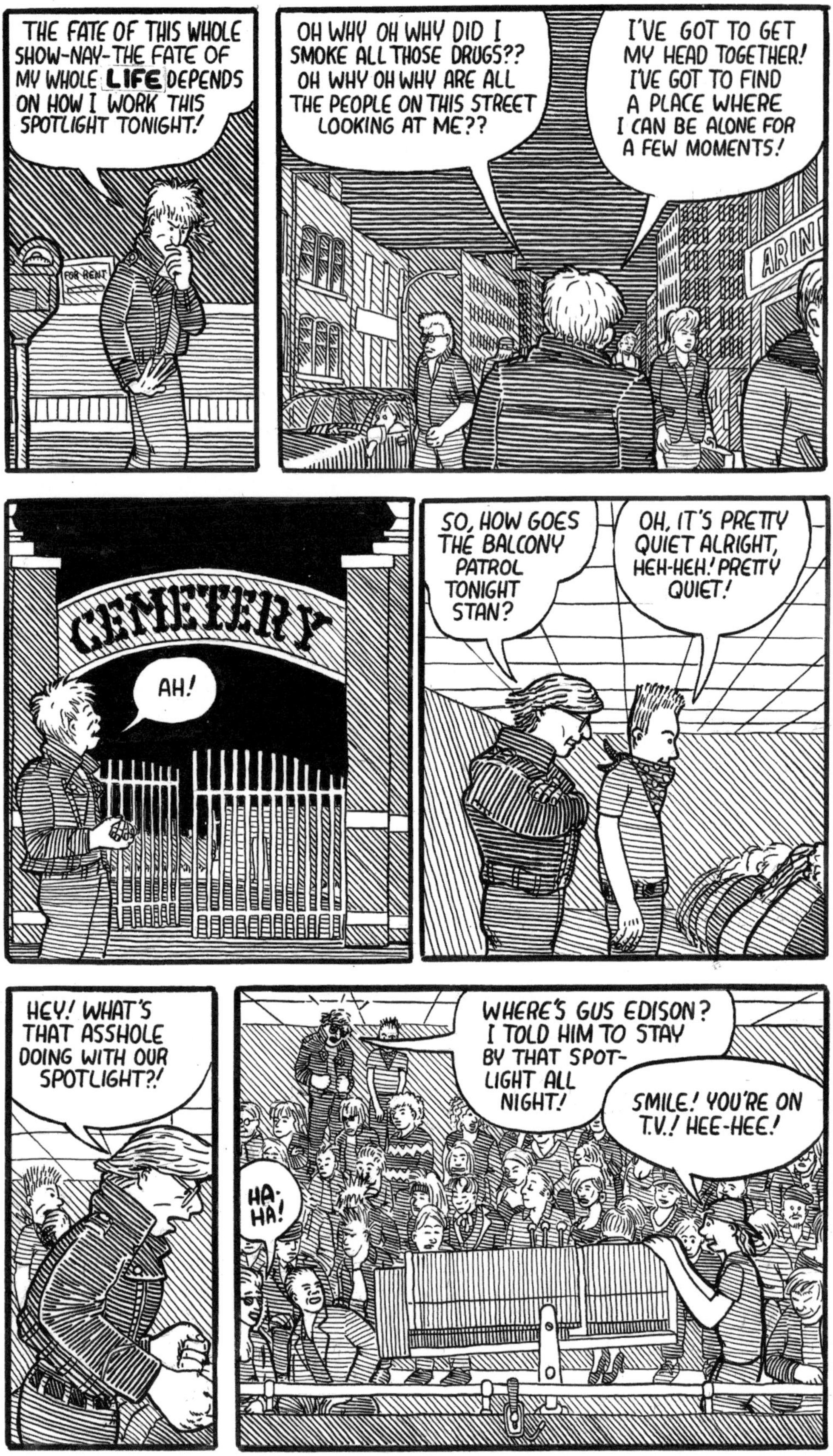
THE FATE OF THIS WHOLE SHOW-NAY-THE FATE OF MY WHOLE **LIFE** DEPENDS ON HOW I WORK THIS SPOTLIGHT TONIGHT!
FOR RENT
OH WHY OH WHY DID I SMOKE ALL THOSE DRUGS?? OH WHY OH WHY ARE ALL THE PEOPLE ON THIS STREET LOOKING AT ME??
I'VE GOT TO GET MY HEAD TOGETHER! I'VE GOT TO FIND A PLACE WHERE I CAN BE ALONE FOR A FEW MOMENTS!
CEMETERY
AH!
SO, HOW GOES THE BALCONY PATROL TONIGHT STAN?
OH, IT'S PRETTY QUIET ALRIGHT, HEH-HEH! PRETTY QUIET!
HEY! WHAT'S THAT ASSHOLE DOING WITH OUR SPOTLIGHT?!
WHERE'S GUS EDISON? I TOLD HIM TO STAY BY THAT SPOT-LIGHT ALL NIGHT!
HA-HA!
SMILE! YOU'RE ON T.V.! HEE-HEE!

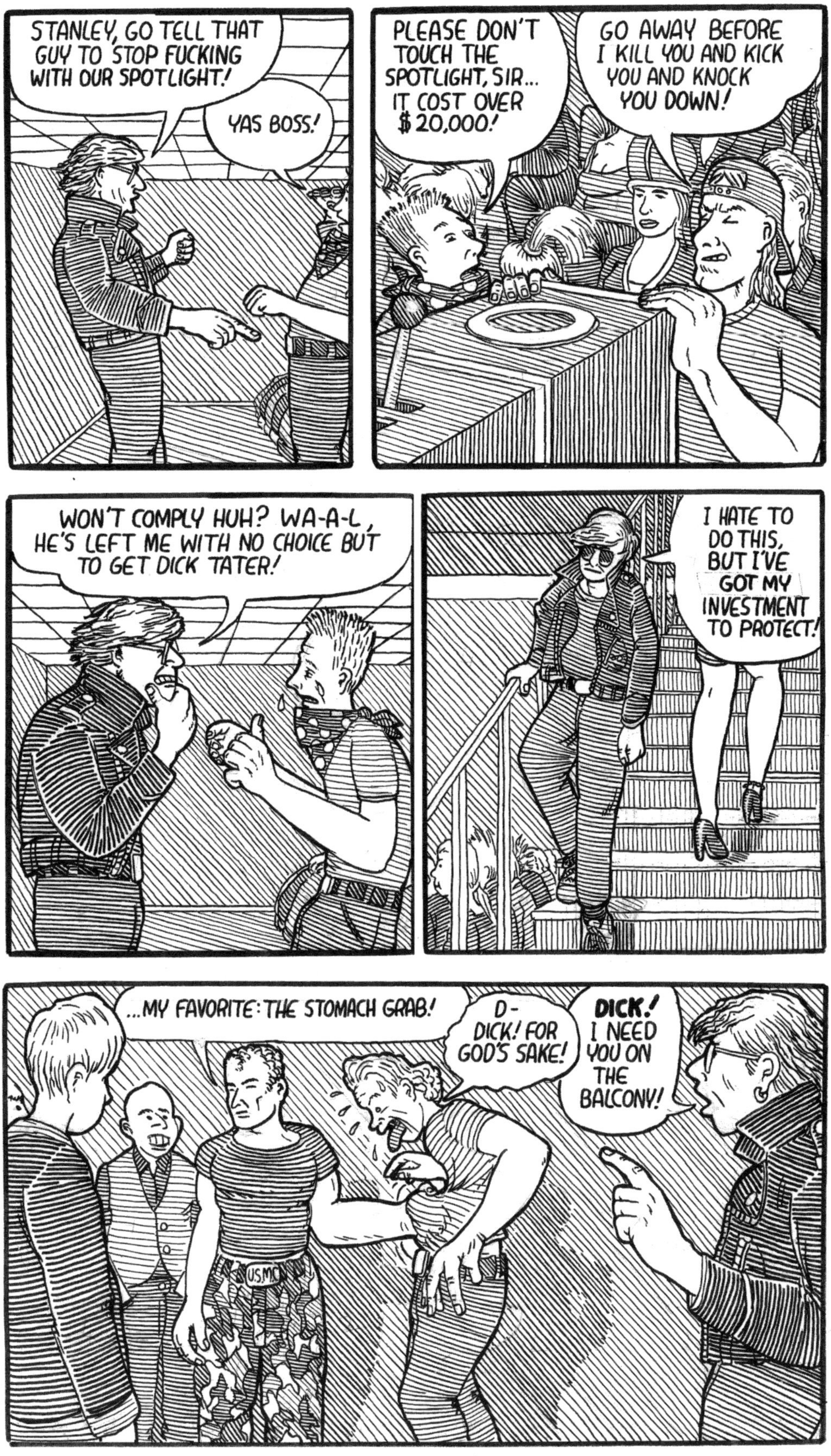
STANLEY, GO TELL THAT GUY TO STOP FUCKING WITH OUR SPOTLIGHT!
YAS BOSS!
PLEASE DON'T TOUCH THE SPOTLIGHT, SIR... IT COST OVER $20,000!
GO AWAY BEFORE I KILL YOU AND KICK YOU AND KNOCK YOU DOWN!
WON'T COMPLY HUH? WA-A-L, HE'S LEFT ME WITH NO CHOICE BUT TO GET DICK TATER!
I HATE TO DO THIS, BUT I'VE GOT MY INVESTMENT TO PROTECT!
...MY FAVORITE: THE STOMACH GRAB!
D-DICK! FOR GOD'S SAKE!
DICK! I NEED YOU ON THE BALCONY!
U.S.M.C.

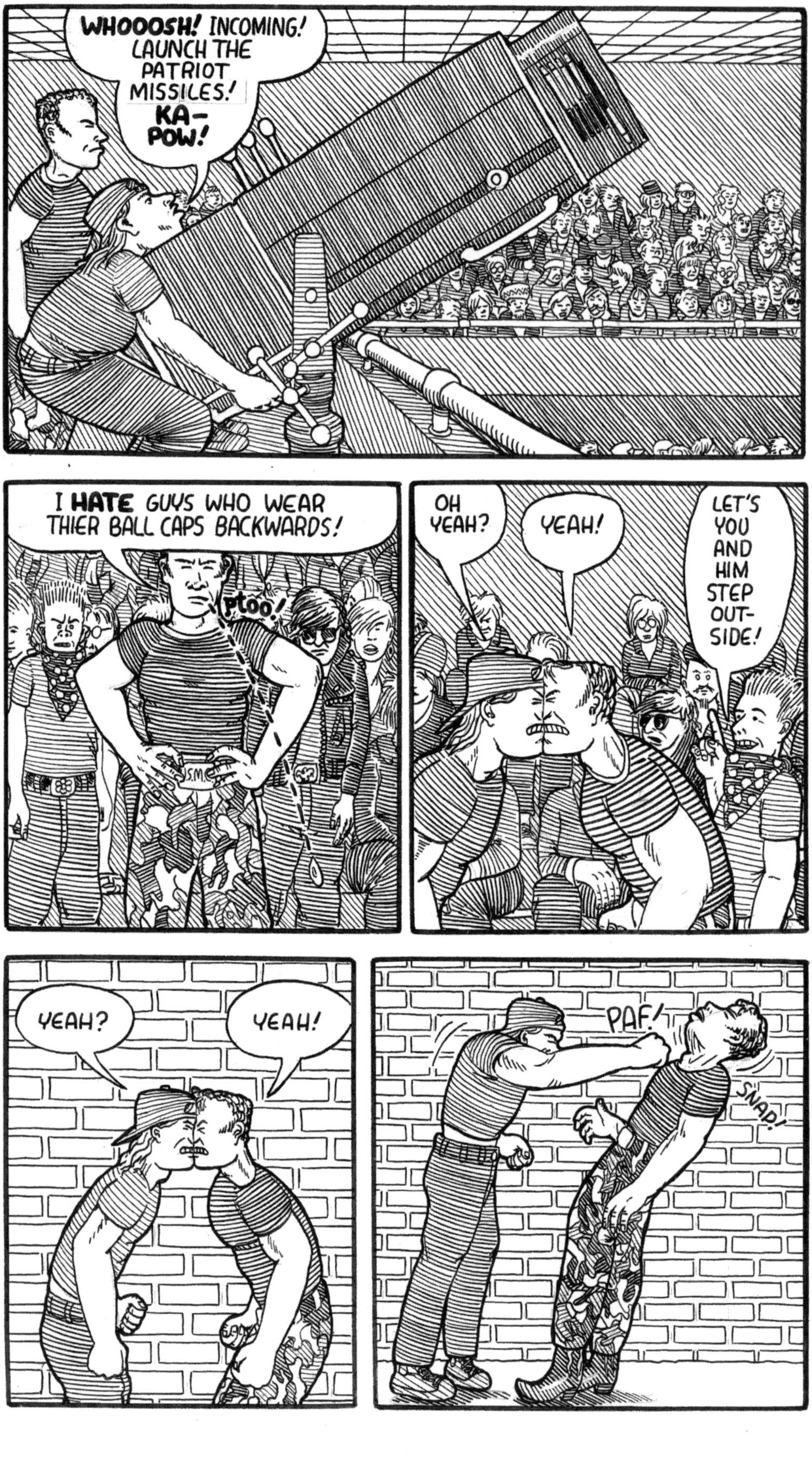
WHOOOSH! INCOMING! LAUNCH THE PATRIOT MISSILES! KA-POW!
I HATE GUYS WHO WEAR THIER BALL CAPS BACKWARDS!
PTOO!
OH YEAH?
YEAH!
LET'S YOU AND HIM STEP OUT-SIDE!
YEAH?
YEAH!
PAF!
SNAP!

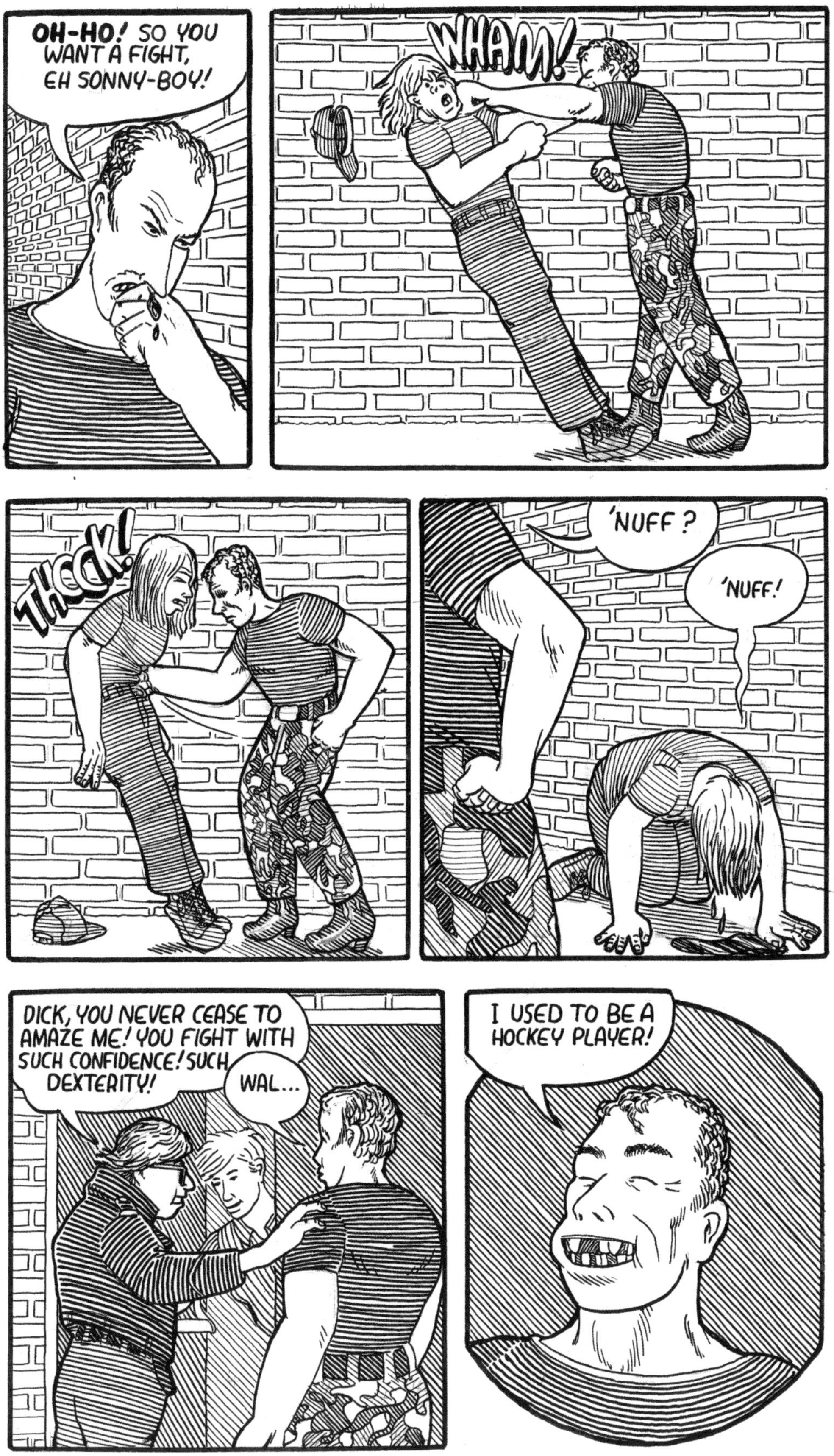
OH-HO! SO YOU WANT A FIGHT, EH SONNY-BOY!
WHAM!
THOCK!
'NUFF?
'NUFF!
DICK, YOU NEVER CEASE TO AMAZE ME! YOU FIGHT WITH SUCH CONFIDENCE! SUCH DEXTERITY!
WAL...
I USED TO BE A HOCKEY PLAYER!

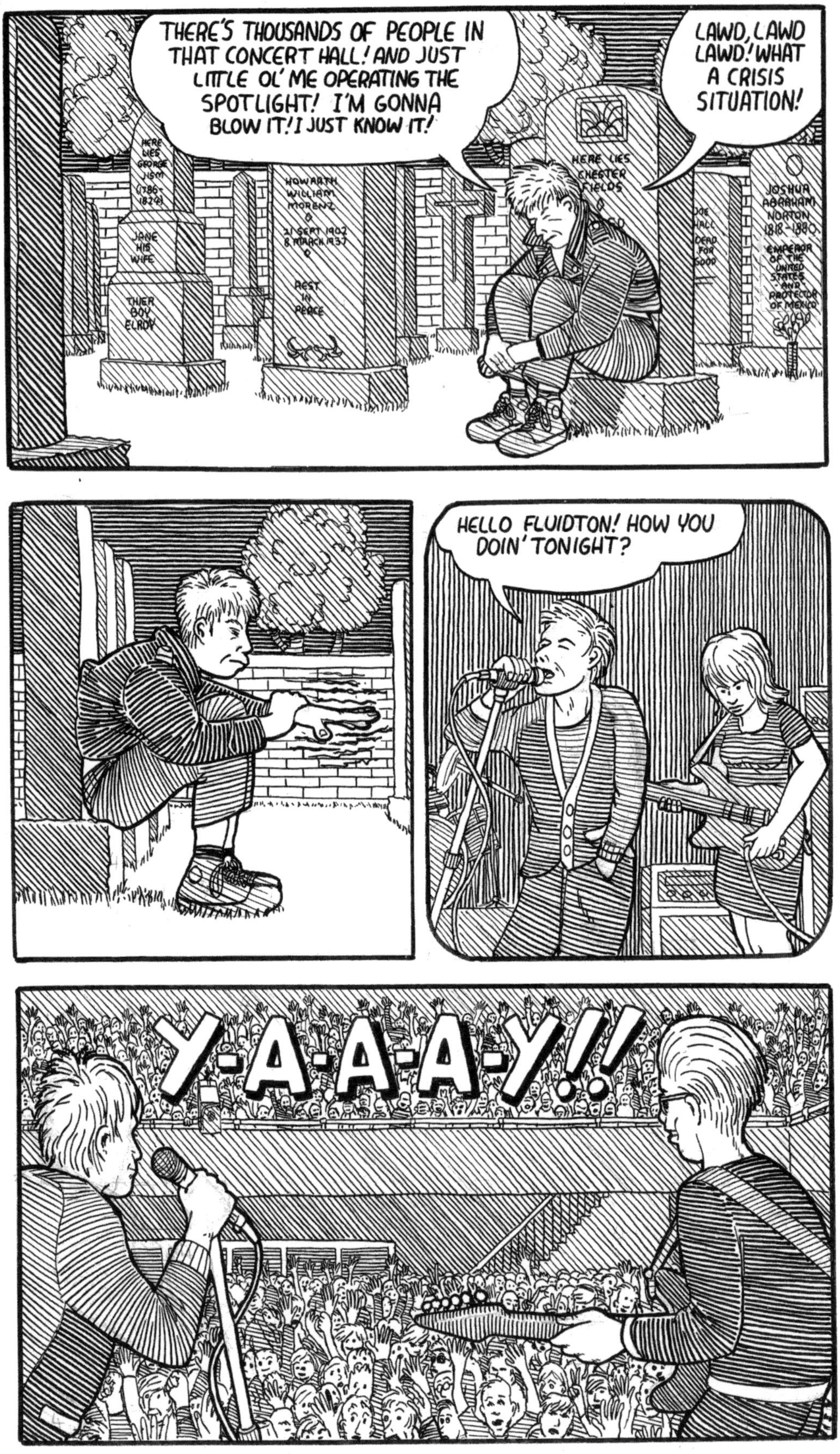
THERE'S THOUSANDS OF PEOPLE IN THAT CONCERT HALL! AND JUST LITTLE OL' ME OPERATING THE SPOTLIGHT! I'M GONNA BLOW IT! I JUST KNOW IT!
LAWD, LAWD LAWD! WHAT A CRISIS SITUATION!
HERE LIES GEORGE JISM (1786-1824)
JANE HIS WIFE
THIER BOY ELROY
HOWARTH WILLIAM MORENZ 21 SEPT 1902 8 MARCH 1937
REST IN PEACE
HERE LIES CHESTER FIELDS
JOE HALL DEAD FOR GOOD
JOSHUA ABRAHAM NORTON 1818-1880
EMPEROR OF THE UNITED STATES AND PROTECTOR OF MEXICO
HELLO FLUIDTON! HOW YOU DOIN' TONIGHT?
Y-A-A-A-Y!!

GUESS I BETTER START HEADING BACK NOW... GIVE MYSELF PLENTY OF TIME TO GET SET UP BEFORE THE BAND GOES ON!

JIM DANDY 1880-1940

FINIAND DANDY 1892-1966

CANDY DANDY 1958-

MEMORY OF JOHN ERE 1954 WIFE LEN

HERE LIES JOE JONES 1846-1923 ALSO KNOWN AS "YEASTCAKE" BECAUSE HE WORKED SO HARD TO RAISE THE DOUGH

WOW! THE OL' JOINT IS REALLY ROCKIN'!

THE GUY AT THE SOUND BOARD MUST HAVE THE TAPE PUMPED UP ALL THE WAY!

HOLY SHIT! THAT'S NO TAPE! IT'S THE BAND! *LIVE!*

I'LL COME IN AT THE START OF THE NEXT NUMBER!

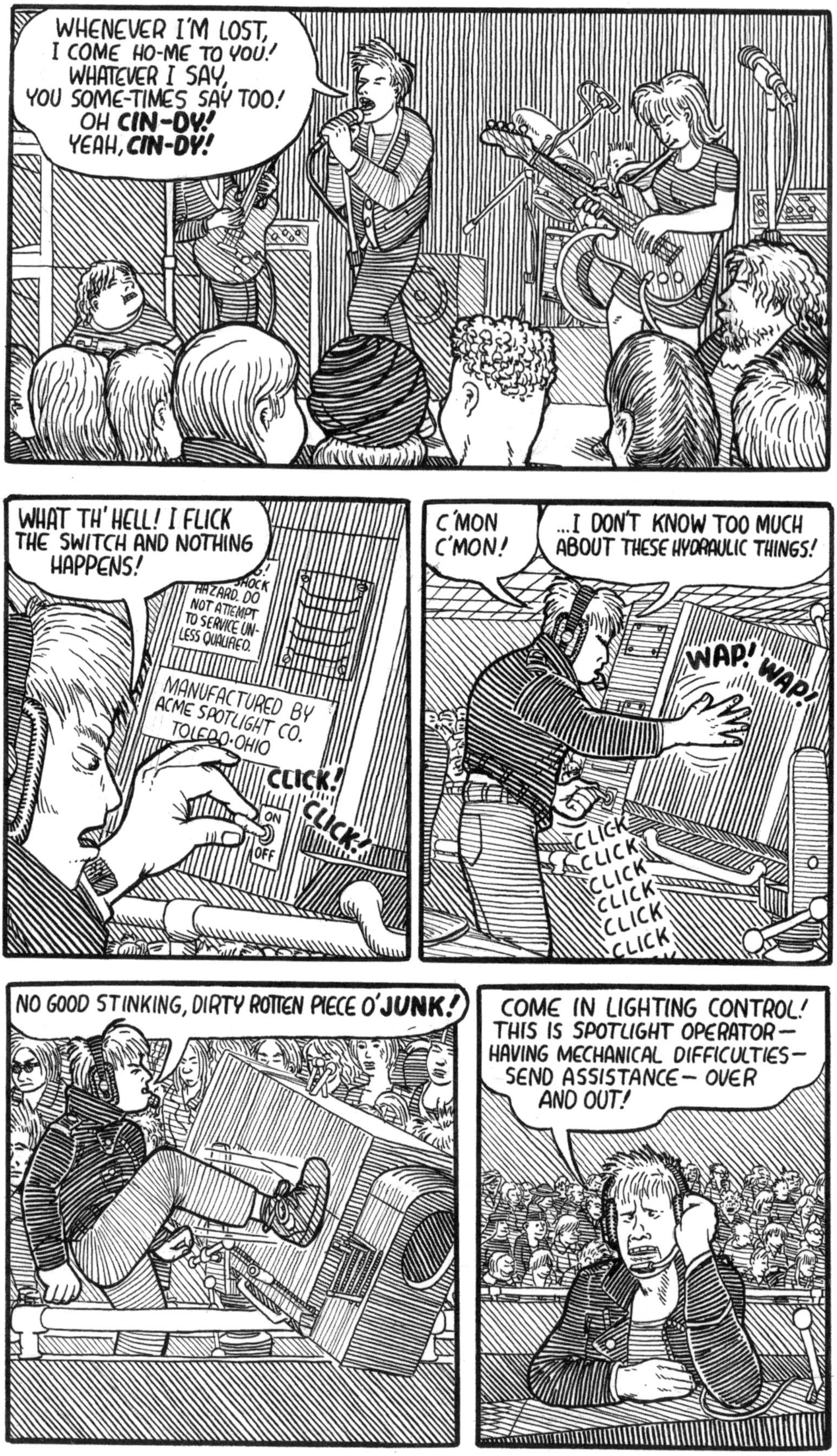
WHENEVER I'M LOST, I COME HO-ME TO YOU! WHATEVER I SAY, YOU SOME-TIMES SAY TOO! OH CIN-DY! YEAH, CIN-DY!
WHAT TH' HELL! I FLICK THE SWITCH AND NOTHING HAPPENS!
SHOCK HAZARD. DO NOT ATTEMPT TO SERVICE UN-LESS QUALIFIED.
MANUFACTURED BY ACME SPOTLIGHT CO. TOLEDO-OHIO
ON
OFF
CLICK! CLICK!
C'MON C'MON!
...I DON'T KNOW TOO MUCH ABOUT THESE HYDRAULIC THINGS!
WAP! WAP!
CLICK CLICK CLICK CLICK CLICK CLICK
NO GOOD STINKING, DIRTY ROTTEN PIECE O' JUNK!
COME IN LIGHTING CONTROL! THIS IS SPOTLIGHT OPERATOR— HAVING MECHANICAL DIFFICULTIES— SEND ASSISTANCE— OVER AND OUT!

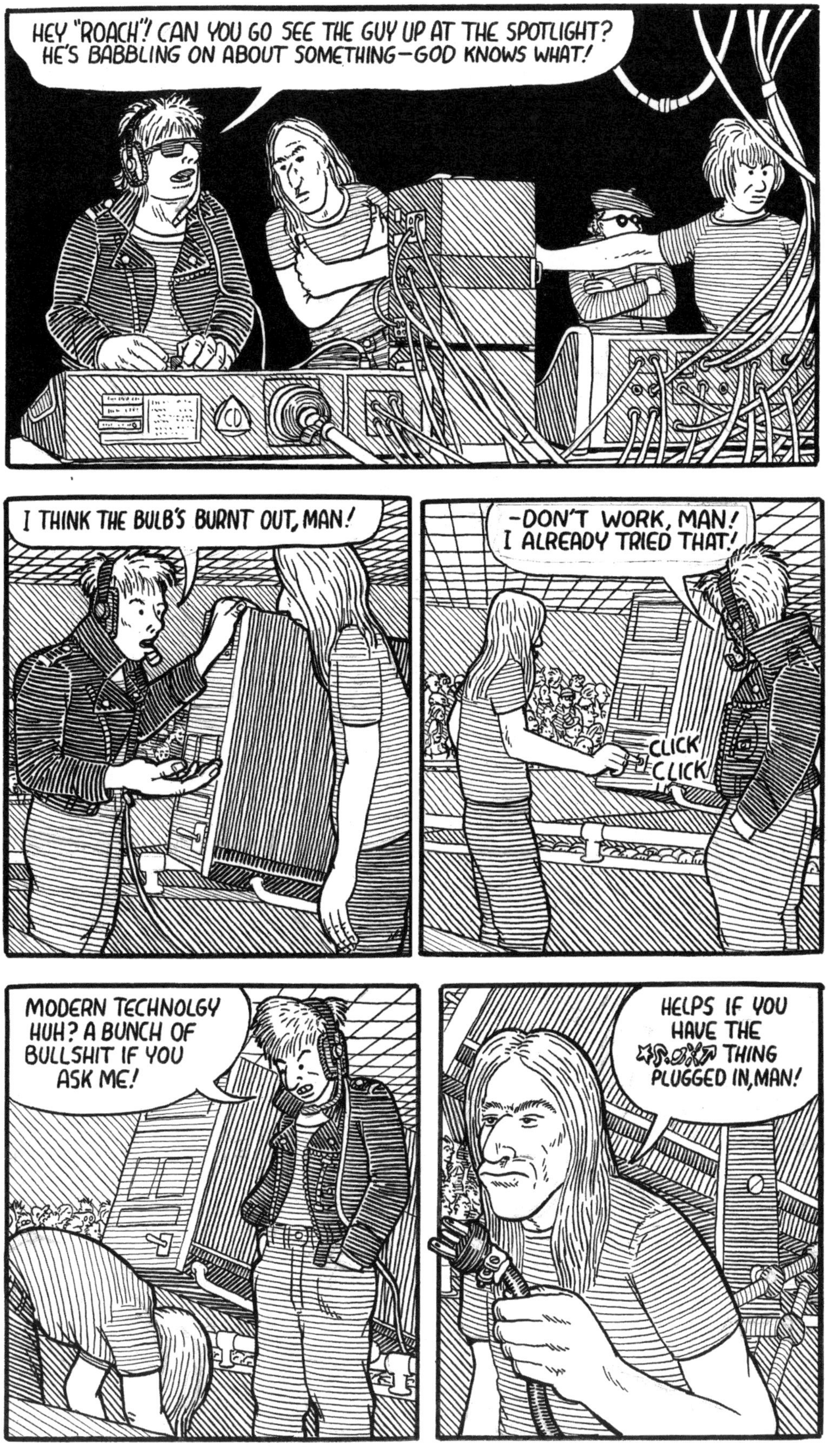

HEY "ROACH"! CAN YOU GO SEE THE GUY UP AT THE SPOTLIGHT? HE'S BABBLING ON ABOUT SOMETHING—GOD KNOWS WHAT!
I THINK THE BULB'S BURNT OUT, MAN!
-DON'T WORK, MAN! I ALREADY TRIED THAT!
CLICK CLICK
MODERN TECHNOLGY HUH? A BUNCH OF BULLSHIT IF YOU ASK ME!
HELPS IF YOU HAVE THE THING PLUGGED IN, MAN!

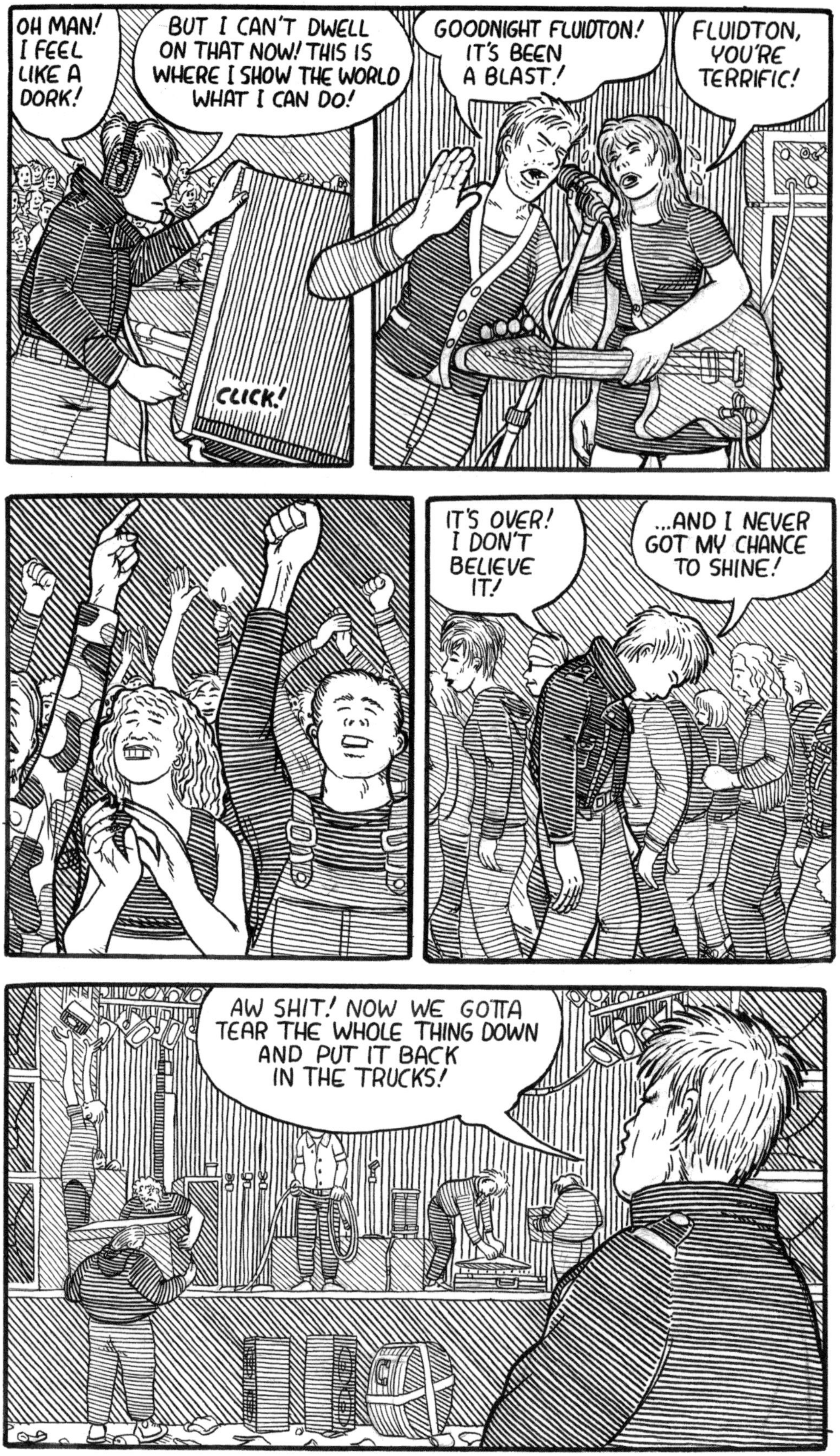
OH MAN! I FEEL LIKE A DORK!
BUT I CAN'T DWELL ON THAT NOW! THIS IS WHERE I SHOW THE WORLD WHAT I CAN DO!
CLICK!
GOODNIGHT FLUIDTON! IT'S BEEN A BLAST!
FLUIDTON, YOU'RE TERRIFIC!
IT'S OVER! I DON'T BELIEVE IT!
...AND I NEVER GOT MY CHANCE TO SHINE!
AW SHIT! NOW WE GOTTA TEAR THE WHOLE THING DOWN AND PUT IT BACK IN THE TRUCKS!

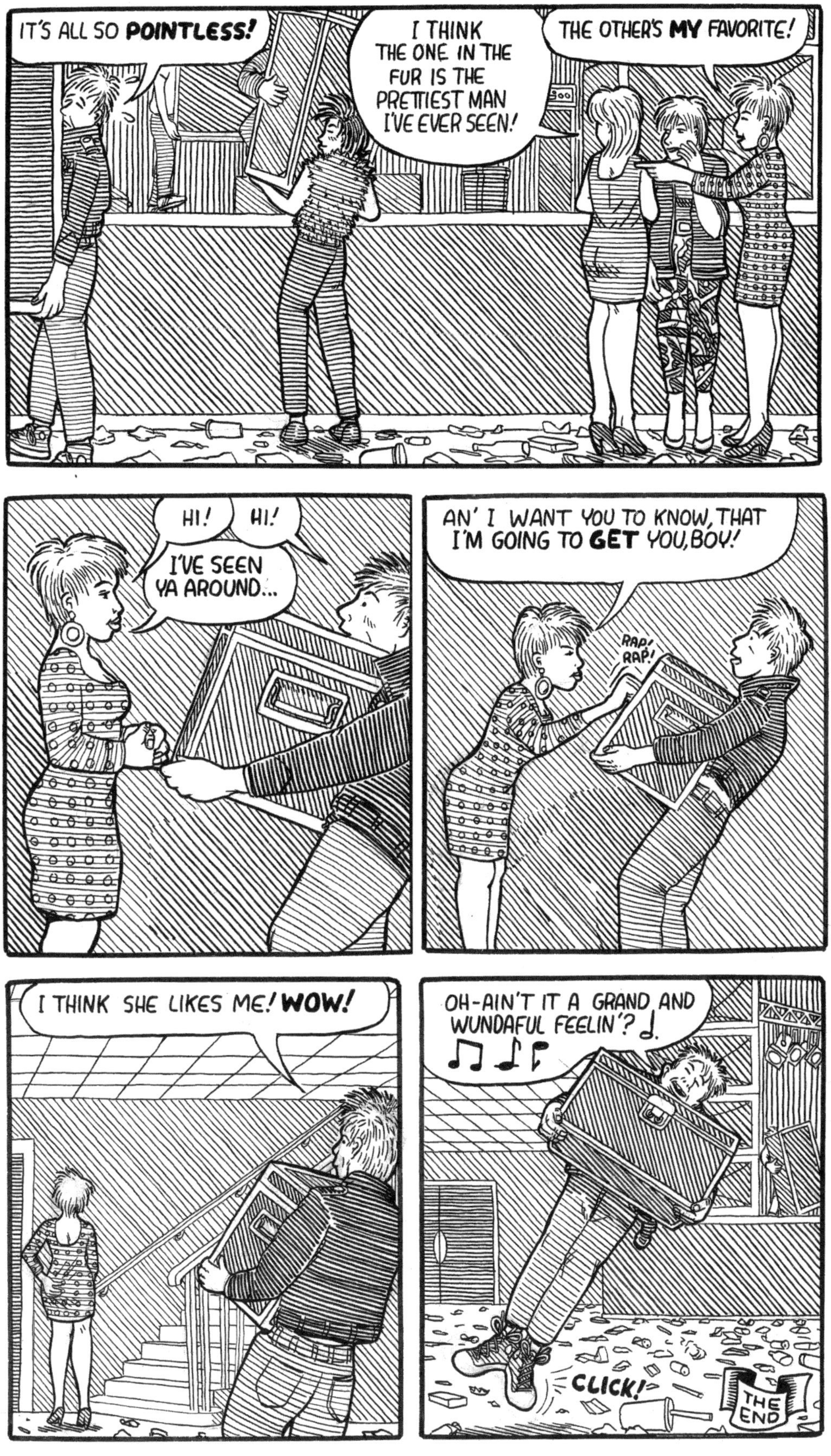
IT'S ALL SO **POINTLESS!**
I THINK THE ONE IN THE FUR IS THE PRETTIEST MAN I'VE EVER SEEN!
THE OTHER'S **MY** FAVORITE!
HI!
HI!
I'VE SEEN YA AROUND...
AN' I WANT YOU TO KNOW, THAT I'M GOING TO **GET** YOU, BOY!
RAP! RAP!
I THINK SHE LIKES ME! **WOW!**
OH-AIN'T IT A GRAND AND WUNDAFUL FEELIN'?
CLICK!
THE END

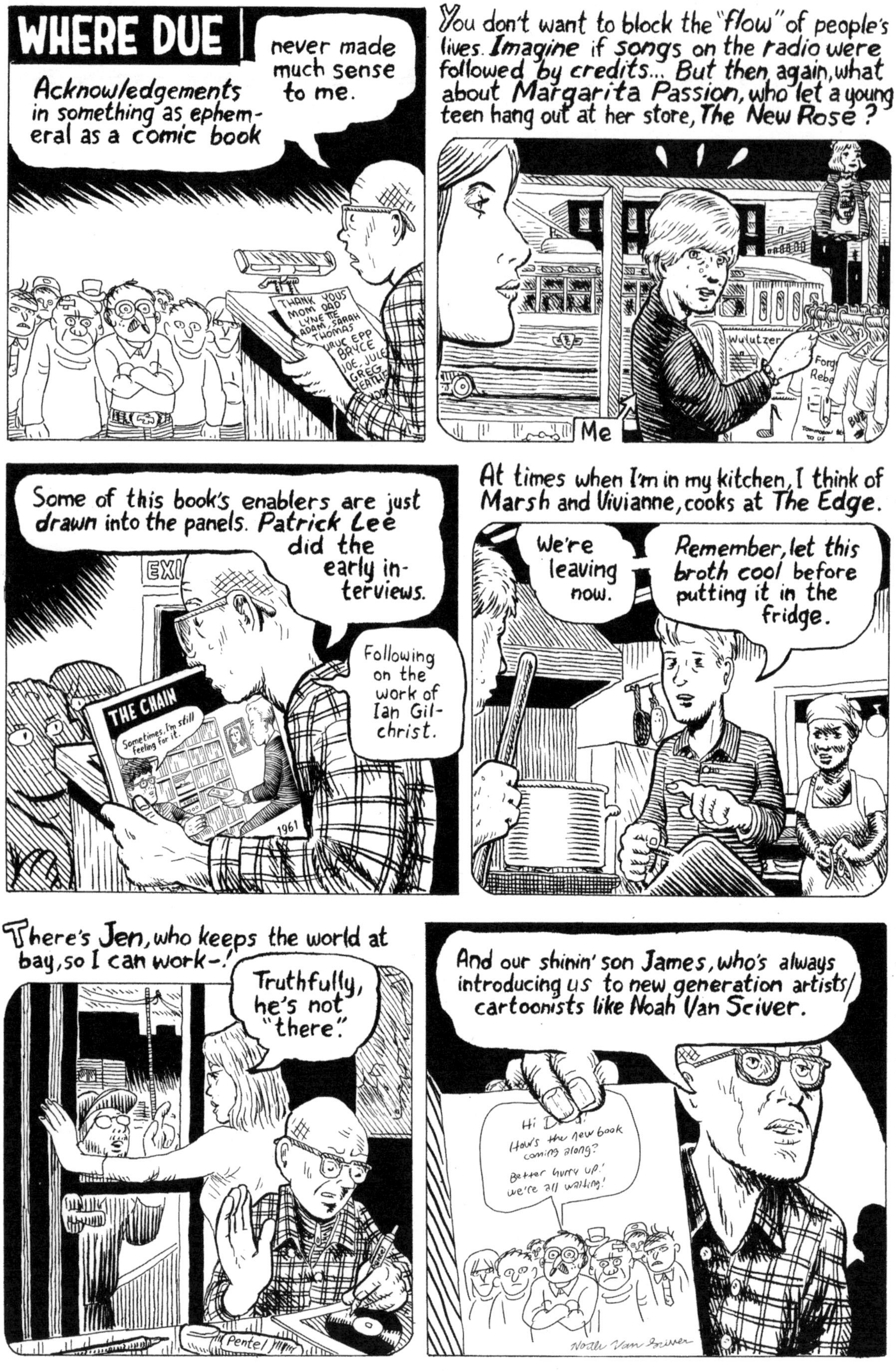
WHERE DUE
Acknowledgements in something as ephemeral as a comic book
never made much sense to me.
THANK YOUS
MOM DAD
LYNETTE
ADAM, SARAH
THOMAS
BRUCE
You don't want to block the "flow" of people's lives. Imagine if songs on the radio were followed by credits... But then again, what about Margarita Passion, who let a young teen hang out at her store, The New Rose?
Me
Some of this book's enablers are just drawn into the panels. Patrick Lee did the early interviews.
Following on the work of Ian Gilchrist.
THE CHAIN
Sometimes, I'm still feeling for it.
1961
At times when I'm in my kitchen, I think of Marsh and Vivianne, cooks at The Edge.
We're leaving now.
Remember, let this broth cool before putting it in the fridge.
There's Jen, who keeps the world at bay, so I can work–!
Truthfully, he's not "there."
Pentel
And our shinin' son James, who's always introducing us to new generation artists/cartoonists like Noah Van Sciver.
How's the new book coming along?
Better hurry up! we're all waiting!
Noah Van Sciver

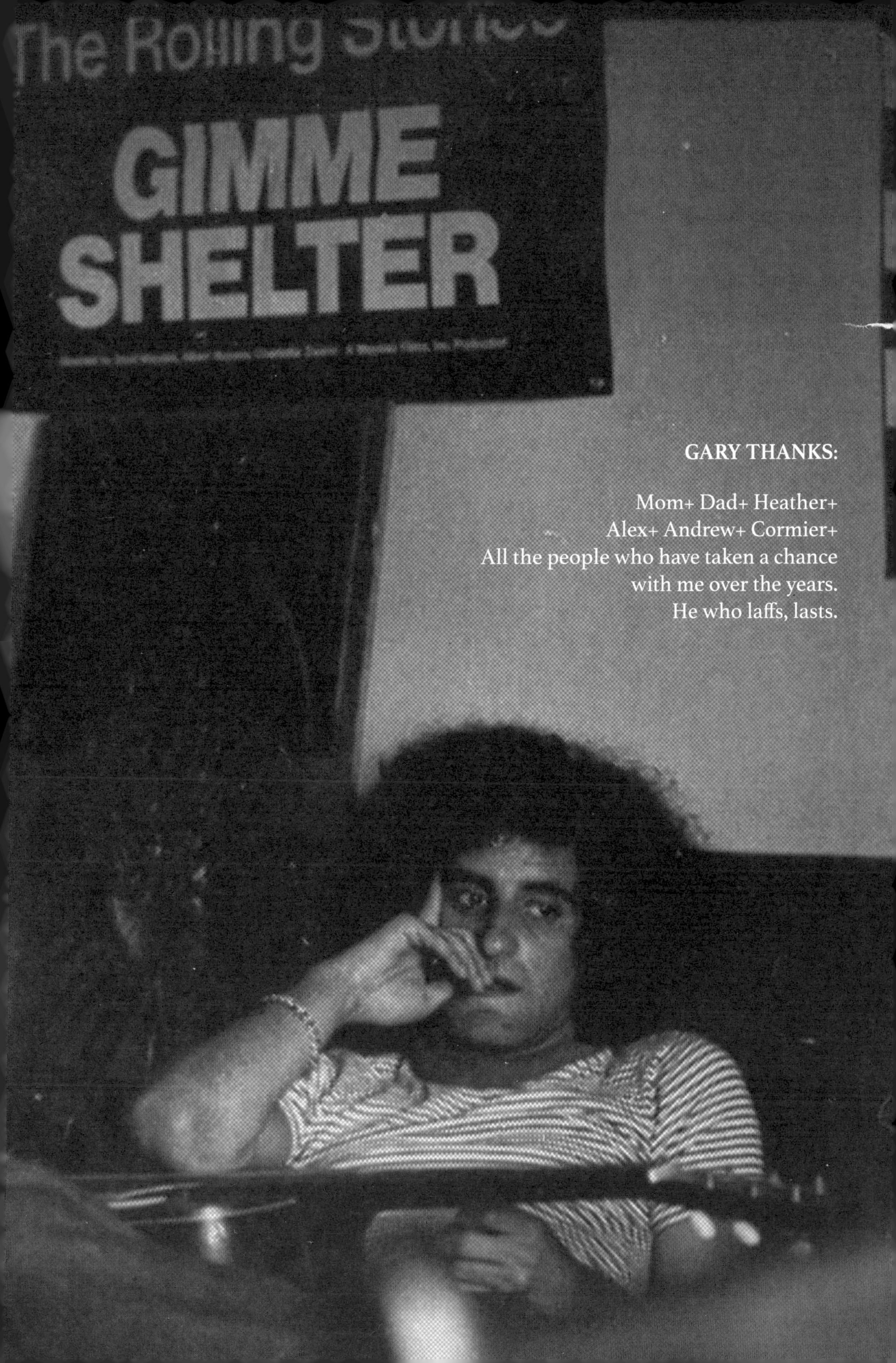
The Rolling Stones
GIMME SHELTER

GARY THANKS:

Mom+ Dad+ Heather+
Alex+ Andrew+ Cormier+
All the people who have taken a chance
with me over the years.
He who laffs, lasts.

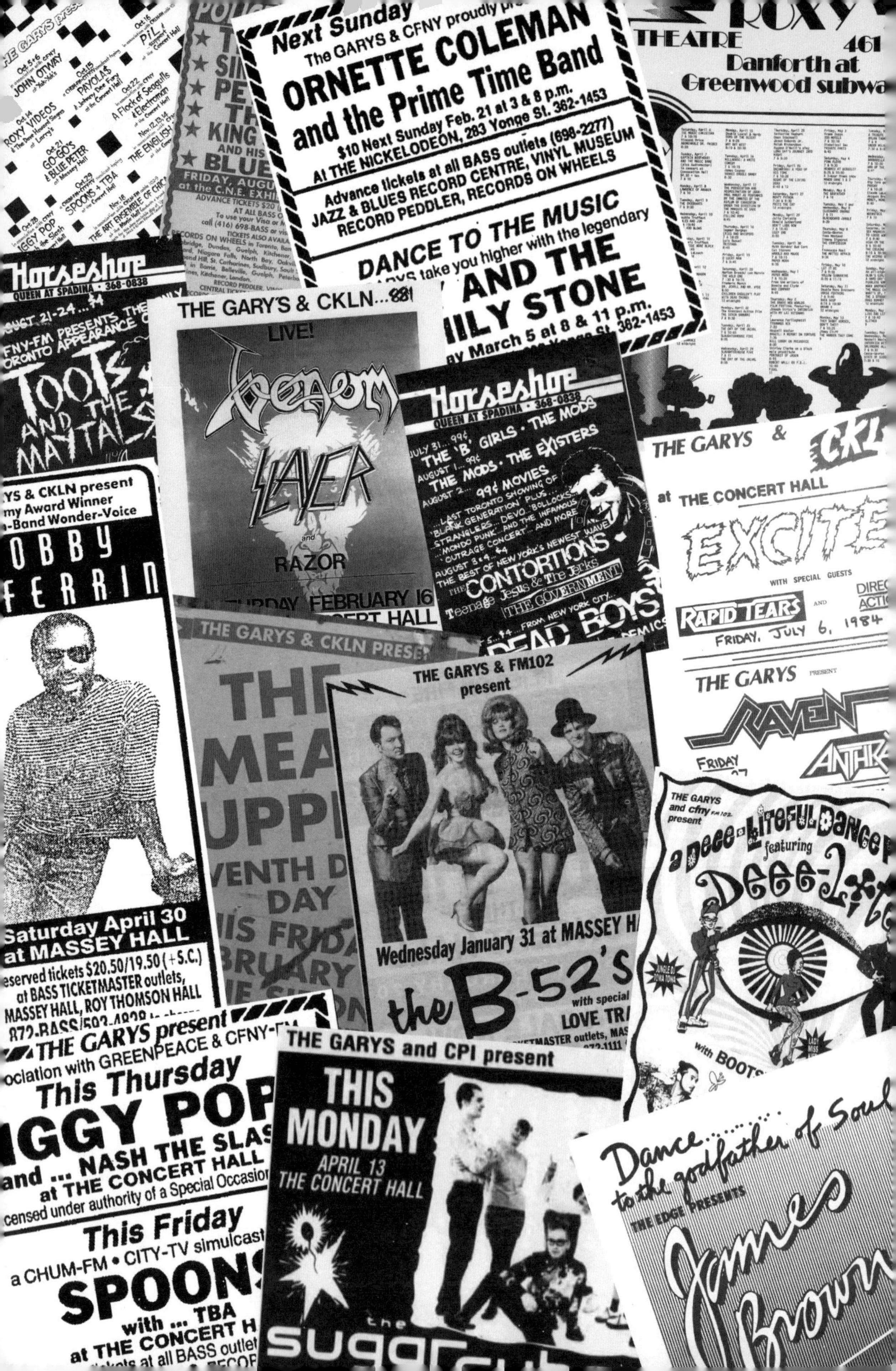

Next Sunday
The GARYS & CFNY proudly pre
ORNETTE COLEMAN
and the Prime Time Band
$10 Next Sunday Feb. 21 at 3 & 8 p.m.
At THE NICKELODEON, 283 Yonge St. 362-1453
Advance tickets at all BASS outlets (698-2277)
JAZZ & BLUES RECORD CENTRE, VINYL MUSEUM
RECORD PEDDLER, RECORDS ON WHEELS
DANCE TO THE MUSIC
take you higher with the legendary
AND THE
ILY STONE
March 5 at 8 & 11 p.m.
ROXY
THEATRE
461
Danforth at
Greenwood subwa
JOHN OTWAY
PAYOLA$
PiL
ROXY VIDEOS
A Flock of Seagulls
GO-GO'S
& BLUE PETER
SPOONS + TBA
THE ART ENSEMBLE OF CHIC
IGGY POP
Horseshoe
QUEEN AT SPADINA • 368-0838
TOOTS AND THE MAYTALS
THE GARY'S & CKLN...88.1
LIVE!
VENOM
SLAYER
and
RAZOR
FEBRUARY 16
CERT HALL
Horseshoe
QUEEN AT SPADINA • 368-0838
THE 'B' GIRLS • THE MODS
THE MODS • THE EXISTERS
99¢ MOVIES
CONTORTIONS
Teenage Jesus & The Jerks
THE GOVERNMENT
DEAD BOYS
THE GARYS &
at THE CONCERT HALL
EXCITER
WITH SPECIAL GUESTS
RAPID TEARS
AND
FRIDAY, JULY 6, 1984
THE GARYS PRESENT
RAVEN
ANTHRAX
Award Winner
Band Wonder-Voice
Saturday April 30
at MASSEY HALL
THE GARYS & CKLN PRESE
THE GARYS & FM102
present
Wednesday January 31 at MASSEY HA
the B-52'S
with special
THE GARYS
and cfny
present
a DEEE-LITEFUL DANCE P
featuring
with BOOTS
THE GARYS present
ociation with GREENPEACE & CFNY-FM
This Thursday
IGGY POP
and ... NASH THE SLAS
at THE CONCERT HALL
This Friday
a CHUM-FM • CITY-TV simulcast
SPOONS
with ... TBA
at THE CONCERT H
THE GARYS and CPI present
THIS MONDAY
APRIL 13
THE CONCERT HALL
the
sugarcubes
Dance to the godfather of Soul
THE EDGE PRESENTS
James Brown